GROWTH, FUNCTION AND REGULATION IN BACTERIAL CELLS

GROWTH, FUNCTION
AND REGULATION IN
BACTERIAL CELLS

BY

A. C. R. DEAN

AND

SIR CYRIL HINSHELWOOD

OXFORD
AT THE CLARENDON PRESS
1966

Oxford University Press, Ely House, London W. 1

GLASGOW NEW YORK TORONTO MELBOURNE WELLINGTON
CAPE TOWN SALISBURY IBADAN NAIROBI LUSAKA ADDIS ABABA
BOMBAY CALCUTTA MADRAS KARACHI LAHORE DACCA
KUALA LUMPUR HONG KONG TOKYO

PRINTED IN GREAT BRITAIN

PREFACE

In certain respects this book is a successor to *The Chemical Kinetics of the Bacterial Cell* first published by one of the present authors in 1946. The Preface of this earlier book contained the passage: 'Chemical reactions have long been studied in isolation: in a cell these reactions occur in a coordinated manner, and in particular the auto-synthetic process assumes a dominant role. The question whether any of the modes of thought and work to which the chemist is accustomed in dealing with inanimate systems helps in understanding the behaviour of the living cell is one which must be asked unless the traditional method of proceeding from the known to the unknown is abandoned.'

The question of what the general laws of chemistry and physics have to say about the properties of living matter stands out today in greater emphasis than ever in the light of the many important discoveries which have been made in recent years.

In place of what would be formally a second edition of *The Chemical Kinetics of the Bacterial Cell*, the present authors decided to join forces to produce a new book which should contain the essentials of the first as they have developed in the intervening period, together with enough critical review of modern developments in biophysics to provide a proper background for general physicochemical theses about living cells.

Some of these theses have not always been well received, for various reasons no doubt, but, probably for the most part, because they have been interpreted as constituting in some way a challenge to the validity of other widely held ideas. This they do not in essence do, and we have tried to show in true perspective the relation of the kinetic ideas to what now goes by the name of molecular biology. We have done our best to give brief but objective accounts of the most important results in this field and to fit them into a coherent pattern. We believe that this can be done only by careful consideration of the cell as a complete, functioning entity. In this respect we feel that some parts of modern work, despite their great value, have remained uncoordinated, and that this aspect reflects not so much the lack of more complete and detailed factual information, as the need for unifying principles, which physico-chemical laws are already in a position in a significant measure to supply.

A.C.R.D.
C.N.H.

St. Cross College, Oxford
Imperial College, London
1966

CONTENTS

VII QUANTITATIVE RELATION OF DRUG CONCENTRA-TION TO LAG AND GROWTH RATE IN ADAPTATION

VIII THE RESPONSE OF BACTERIAL CELLS TO NEW SOURCES OF CARBON AND NITROGEN

LIST OF PLATES

I

INTRODUCTION

1. Living cells

AMONG the most puzzling of all natural phenomena is that manifestation which constitutes life. At the level of scientific description life itself is a matter of physics and chemistry, but of physics and chemistry operating within the framework of a very special set of relationships. What these are is a major question.

Animate matter is the seat of continuous chemical changes, and of chemical changes coordinated according to elaborate patterns. Physical chemistry has in a large measure revealed the mechanism of chemical reactions in inanimate systems where the transformations occur either in isolation or combined in sequences which are relatively simple compared with the complex interlocking processes occurring in living cells. In the simplest of cells innumerable enzyme reactions of the most varied kind occur, and the end result is an exact or almost exact replication of what was present originally. Various compounds of considerable thermodynamic instability are built up, often from quite simple materials, and, according to well-known principles, this can only occur if the synthetic reactions are linked with others in which free energy runs down. All this means that highly complex reaction patterns must exist in living cells.

The capacity of self-replication is not the only remarkable property of living cells. Animate matter possesses an amazing degree of plasticity. When cells are exposed to new conditions they show a pronounced ability for adaptation. They may be able to develop resistance to high concentrations of drugs which initially would have proved lethal. Presented with different sources of growth material they may exhibit phenomena which appear not only like choice of the more favourable but of actual rejection of the less favourable. Clearly the explanation of all these phenomena of growth and adaptation offers a stimulating challenge to the principles of chemical kinetics.

All living matter is endowed with the capacity for multiplication and for coming to terms with its environment, and these fundamental properties are exhibited even by the simplest type of organism, the single cell, of which the bacterium is the commonest example. Primitive though its existence may be, the bacterium does in its fashion show most of the essential characteristics of life.

A convenient experimental approach to the central problem would seem thus to be the study of growth, multiplication, adaptation, and general chemical behaviour in these, the simplest living things capable of autonomous self-replication. Bacteria are unicellular, and though by no means internally homogeneous, possess no grossly differentiated structures of the kind appearing in the individual organs of plants and animals. In appropriate conditions they will grow and multiply in the simplest of media consisting of inorganic salts, ammonia, and a carbon source no more elaborate than acetic acid or glycerol.

The first doubt which might be cast on the possibility of a science of bacterial kinetics is in effect a vitalistic one. Since living matter is potentially the seat of consciousness, the adequacy of any description which fails to include the possible interventions of this might be questioned. The second doubt is whether any progress can be made before an almost hopeless tangle of complex biochemical reactions has to be unravelled in detail.

As to consciousness, it does not seem to be much in evidence in simple organisms such as bacteria: and even with man it appears that a large proportion of his bodily activities for a large part of the time are automatic. Thus even with the physiology of the higher animals one can probably go a long way without meeting the problem of conscious control, and with unicellular organisms one can almost certainly go, in effect, the whole way. This does not in the least imply an ultimately materialist view of existence. It means rather that the objective set is limited—though by no means unambitious—in somewhat the same way as one might study musical theory, the structure of music, and the rules of composition, without finding it expedient to enter into the nature of the aesthetic or mystical qualities of great music. To study the vehicle, whether of conscious life or of musical aesthetics, independently of what the vehicle may in proper circumstances convey, is not, as has sometimes been suggested of men of science, to ignore other values but merely to show a due sense of measuring means to ends.

However this may be, one method of approach to which no valid objection can be raised is to find out whether by the operation of known physical and chemical principles any phenomena analogous to those shown by the living cell can be accounted for. If these prove numerous and striking enough, working hypotheses about cells and about living matter in general can be established.

The question of the complexity of the total reaction pattern is of a quite different kind. Multiplicity and complication arise, as often as not, from repetitions and permutations of a few simple elements, and the principles of combination are often discernible even though the results are complex, as the kaleidoscope and the theory of spectra bear witness. Nor need all the details invariably be known in order to arrive at important general conclusions about phenomena, as, for example, the kinetic theory of matter bears witness.

Nevertheless, it may have been easy enough to take the view that the only valid approach to the study of cell mechanisms lay in the isolation of individual enzymes and the detailed study of their mode of action. As a means of obtaining valuable knowledge this procedure is unexceptionable. But it may be questioned whether by itself this method can ever lead to the solution of the central problem posed above, how, namely, a living cell is organized to display those highly characteristic properties by which it is recognized as living. The best way, it would seem, or perhaps the only way of understanding a machine is to observe it in action. The study of its dismembered parts may be valuable, but is unlikely to be sufficient.

Many striking facts have been ascertained about the biochemistry of cell reactions, about the molecular structure of the major types of cell components, about the genetic relations of bacterial properties. They form an array of immense complexity which is clearly very difficult to understand in every detail.

Nevertheless the kinetics of chemical reactions in general consists of variations on a few relatively simple themes. The cell depends upon a pattern of coordinated reactions. They involve in their sequences an organization in time. The cell, moreover, presents a texture of macromolecular substances in which some degree of spatial organization certainly exists. May not the laws according to which the spatio-temporal organization is possible at all have some sort of general character? And may not these general rules themselves be responsible for some of the typical properties of animate matter?

In their biochemistry many known types of cell and tissue follow patterns with a basic similarity. This fact might suggest that life somehow depends upon a unique set of chemical reactions. Seymour Cohen[1] has, however, pointed out that a wider search reveals many departures from the orthodox schemes of reaction. We may therefore question whether the properties of living matter are after all uniquely associated with one particular biochemical system.[2] Rather they may depend on more general conditions. In later sections of this book we shall see that some very characteristic properties of cells do indeed follow from relatively simple propositions about the nature of their organization.

The exploration of this problem, in close conjunction with the experimental observation of the behaviour of bacteria and a few related organisms, is the object of this book.

2. Chemical kinetics

Before we discuss cell phenomena further it will be useful to deal with a few of the salient properties of individual chemical reactions themselves. No attempt will be made here to expound the principles of chemical kinetics, for which reference may be made to the books cited at the end of the chapter.[3, 4] But the following may be said. Atoms and free radicals are very ready to react, and require to be supplied with little or no energy to enable them to do so (except that certain radicals have to be supplied with the energy needed for a reorganization of their bonds, e.g. in CH_3— from a planar form to a tetrahedral form on entry into combination). Molecules in general have to be supplied with activation energy (by suitable collisions or by absorption of light quanta) before they are able to react. Free radicals attack saturated molecules with an intermediate, but usually rather small, activation energy. The magnitude of the activation energy, E, is determined from the influence of temperature on the reaction velocity constant, k, by application of the Arrhenius equation: $d \ln k/dT = E/RT^2$. E is the principal factor determining the range of temperature in which a reaction occurs with appreciable velocity. For reactions to occur in the range characteristic of biological phenomena, E will usually be comparatively small. At such temperatures, resolution of most molecules into free radicals plays an appreciable role only when an initial small supply is maintained by a chain process.

Chain processes are quite common, especially, but by no means exclusively, in gas reactions at higher temperatures. They occur typically in such reactions as the oxidation of hydrocarbons. With hexane, for example, the chain process is appreciable at a temperature as low as 200° C. Certain types of molecular structure specially favour the production of free radicals,[5] and in appropriate circumstances these intervene even in liquid-phase reactions at low temperatures.

One of the problems of chemical kinetics is to relate the rate of reaction to the concentrations of the reacting substances. Usually this is quite a complicated problem. For reactions which take place homogeneously in one single stage, an elementary application of the law of mass action suffices, and changes of the first, second, and third order can be distinguished. These, however, are the exception, most chemical reactions being resolved into a series of elementary processes to each of which the law of mass action must be separately applied.

One of the most important classifications of reactions is into the two groups of homogeneous and heterogeneous processes. In the latter the rate is determined, not by the concentration of a reacting substance in a single phase, but by the density of molecules at an interface, such as the surface of a solid catalyst. The equation which relates, for a given temperature, the amount of a substance on a surface to its concentration in a gas phase or solution is therefore of great importance. It is called the adsorption isotherm. The form of such equations is of significance in connexion with enzyme reactions.

Although a detailed discussion of most aspects of kinetics is unnecessary for the present purpose, there are certain matters which will find very direct application in the discussions of cell reactions. It is proposed, therefore, to deal with these specifically in the way which will be most convenient for future reference.

3. Adsorption isotherms. Langmuir isotherm

Let a substance, S, at concentration c in a gas or solution be adsorbed at the surface of another phase (such as a solid catalyst). Consider unit area of the surface and suppose that a fraction σ is occupied by adsorbed molecules of S, $(1-\sigma)$ being left free. There is a dynamic equilibrium between free and adsorbed molecules, and this is expressed by the equation

$$k'c(1-\sigma) = k''\sigma, \tag{1}$$

where k' and k'' are constants. The left-hand side expresses the fact that the rate of deposition of S-molecules on to the surface is proportional to the amount of free surface and to the concentration of the molecules in the gas or solution: the right-hand side, the fact that the inverse process is proportional to the density of molecules on the surface. Rearrangement of (1) gives

$$\sigma = \frac{bc}{1+bc}, \tag{2}$$

where $b = k'/k''$.

If the adsorbed molecules undergo a chemical transformation at a rate proportional to their density on the surface, then

$$\text{rate} = \frac{kc}{1+bc},\qquad(3)$$

where k is a constant.

Equation (2) is known as the Langmuir isotherm. It has the following properties. For small values of c, the amount adsorbed is linearly proportional to c, while for large values the amount adsorbed becomes independent of c. This relation is shown in Fig. 1. From (2) also follows the result that for large values of c the value of $(1-\sigma)$, that is, the free surface, is inversely proportional to c.

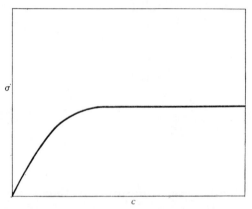

Fig. 1. Langmuir adsorption isotherm.

The Langmuir isotherm describes the simplest possible case. It is in fact often a very good approximation for the description of the behaviour of real adsorption systems. But it is based upon several assumptions, and these are not always justifiable. The kinds of deviation which occur are of importance.

4. Deviations from the Langmuir isotherm[6]

In (1) the assumption is made that deposition on the surface is determined only by the free area and by the concentration in the gas or solution, and, correspondingly, that the escape of molecules from the surface into the continuous phase depends only on the number. These postulates are equivalent to the condition that the adsorption or desorption of any given molecule is uninfluenced by the presence of other molecules on neighbouring sites. But in real cases of adsorption molecules exert mutual influences and these are of two general kinds. First, there may appear what is known as a *co-operative effect*, the presence of adsorbed molecules on given sites facilitating the adsorption of molecules on neighbouring sites. This effect depends upon mutual attractions, and plays an all-important part in the phenomena of liquefaction and solidification. It will be particularly in evidence in adsorption when the surface film can assume a configuration resembling a liquid or solid layer of the adsorbed substance. The form of the adsorption isotherm will be

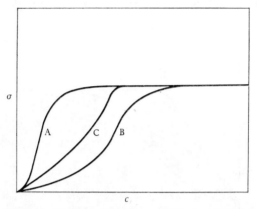

FIG. 2. Isotherms showing co-operative effects.

rather complicated, since the energy of adsorption of a new molecule will be different according to whether it goes into a site with one, two, three, or more neighbours. And the variation of the energy with the number of neighbours will itself be a function of the individual molecular structure. The co-operative effect can lead to isotherms of the various forms shown in Fig. 2. The expression of these by theoretical equations is no easy matter, and empirical or semi-empirical equations are often employed with advantage. Curve C in Fig. 2, for example, might arise if the co-operative effect operated in such a way that nearly complete surface films showed a great tendency to perfect themselves, that is, that the adsorption energy increased very steeply with the number of neighbours.

Secondly, there is an effect which acts in opposition to the above, and which consists in an interference by molecules already present with the adsorption of other molecules on neighbouring sites. This effect may in part be referred to repulsive forces between molecules, but another factor also enters (and is of special interest in connexion with the phenomena of the poisoning of catalysts). The basis of adsorption is an attractive force between atoms in the surface of the adsorbent and atoms in the molecules which are adsorbed. Thus we have a whole array of adsorptive sites spaced, in the case of a solid adsorbent, in a regular geometrical pattern, and these may engage either one or several centres of attraction in the molecules of the adsorbable substance. Now if molecules are held by multipoint adsorption and occupy several sites, the possibilities of mutual interference are more serious than if they occupy single ones only. If adsorption occurs on single sites, then, when only one of these remains free, that one is still available for use. But if

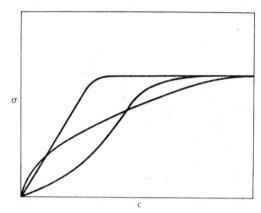

FIG. 3. Isotherms showing opposing effects.

adsorption occurs in such a way that, say, six sites are used for each molecule, then very large numbers of free sites may remain, but be quite unavailable, being grouped in unfavourable configurations which do not leave six properly related ones clear.[7] In such cases as this there will be departures from the Langmuir isotherm opposite in sense to those caused by the co-operative effect.

With the two major effects above described acting in competition, very varied shapes of adsorption isotherm can arise, as illustrated in Fig. 3. By a compensation of opposing effects it is not uncommon to have a curve which is nearly linear almost up to the saturation point.

In studying the inhibitory or anticatalytic actions of adsorbed substances on a surface reaction we are not so much interested in σ as in $(1-\sigma)$. The general course of this function is of course quite obvious from that of σ, but it will be useful for future reference to call attention to one or two specific cases. When the isotherm is linear nearly up to saturation point, then the rate of the inhibited reaction, being proportional to the free surface, will decrease linearly almost to zero with increase in the concentration of the inhibitor. We shall encounter this case in connexion with certain drug actions. A second kind of case is illustrated by Fig. 4. The dots represent adsorption sites on a surface. A is a molecule occupying six, B a molecule occupying one only. Suppose A is the inhibitor of a reaction which occurs to some other molecule in the adsorbed condition. The two molecules of A shown in the diagram leave no space for the adsorption of further A molecules. The inhibitory action of A must therefore have reached its limit. If the reacting molecule were comparable with A in size and configuration, its adsorption

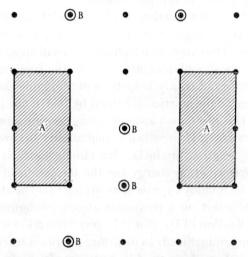

Fig. 4. Blocking of adsorption sites by molecules.

would also be prevented and the reaction rate would have been reduced to zero. If, however, the reacting molecule occupied a much smaller space, as B in the diagram, then there would still be plenty of room for it in the interstices. Thus the very quality of A which gives it a powerful inhibiting action in small concentrations presently brings its action to a limit while there is still a finite reaction velocity.

5. Adsorption isotherms and cell phenomena

Reactions in cells must partake to a considerable extent of the nature of heterogeneous reactions. Some of them will occur with adsorbed substances on the surface of enzymes: and even where it is hardly legitimate to think of a definite surface, the seat of reaction will consist of sheets or networks of macromolecular substances. Such a system, even when permeable in three dimensions, will present arrays of active centres which can be regarded as equivalent to those considered in the derivation of the Langmuir isotherm or its elaborations. Soluble and diffusible substrates, before they can react with, or under the influence of, the cell substance, must enter into a relation with it which is mathematically similar to adsorption.

One of the outstanding characteristics of adsorption systems is their saturability, and accordingly we should expect to find reaction rates proportional to substrate concentrations for very low values of the latter and independent of them for higher values. Such relations are in fact very much in evidence in cell phenomena.

The manifold inhibitory actions of antibacterial substances and drugs we should expect to be governed, in part, by the considerations of the previous section. The extent to which this is so will appear in due course.

At this stage we should draw attention to the frequency with which in the relatively simple catalytic systems of inorganic chemistry inhibition of a heterogeneous reaction is caused by one of the products.[8] The explanation of this rests upon a simple and general consideration about the activation energy. If there is a strong affinity between the catalyst and one of the reaction products, this circumstance is reflected in a lowering of the activation energy for the formation of that product. The effect may be roughly expressed by saying that the attraction which the catalyst can exert on a particular atomic configuration naturally favours the realization of it. But this very attraction which helps the formation of the product leads to its firmer retention when formed. Too firm a retention of product now blocks the access of further reactant. This principle is reflected in the commonly observed phenomenon called 'end-product inhibition' in enzyme reactions.[9]

6. The separation of complex reactions into stages

Chemical reactions are always resolved into a series of relatively simple stages. The reaction $2H_2+O_2 = 2H_2O$, for example, does not take place in the manner suggested by the equation, but in a series of steps, such as $H_2 = 2H$, $H+O_2 = OH+O$, $OH+H_2 = H_2O+H$. In these nothing more elaborate occurs than the breaking of one bond, the removal of one atom at a time, or an exchange of the type

$$XY+AB = XA+BY.^{[10]}$$

In polymerization and polycondensation reactions macromolecules of enormous size are built up, but always in a series of steps. The polymerization of ethylene, for example, is initiated by a free radical which reacts as follows:

$$R{-}+C_2H_4 = RCH_2CH_2{-}.$$

The new radical reacts with ethylene,

$$RCH_2CH_2\text{—}+C_2H_4 = RCH_2CH_2CH_2CH_2\text{—},$$

and there ensues a series of additions which, according to circumstances, may stop at two or three or proceed to hundreds or thousands.

For the purpose of subsequent discussions it is convenient here to emphasize certain consequences of this resolution of chemical reactions into stages.

(a) The fact that the individual steps are usually very simple, but may be combined in different ways and independently influenced by conditions such as temperature and concentration, leads to the result that the *same basic mechanism may yield a considerable diversity of products and in very varied proportions*. This gives the appearance of a greater complexity than is really inherent in the nature of the system.

(b) The existence of transitory intermediates *renders possible the energetic coupling of reactions which, according to the stoicheiometric equations, appear to be independent*. We may have the two reactions

1. $B+A_2 = BA_2$ with diminution of free energy;
2. $XY = X+Y$ with increase of free energy.

If the diminution of free energy in the former exceeds the increase in the latter, there is no thermodynamic reason why the two reactions should not be so coupled as to allow one to provide the free energy for the other. But the mechanism by which the requisite coupling can occur is at first sight obscure. It becomes quite clear, however, when the resolution into steps is considered. The series of changes:

$$A_2 = A+A$$
$$A+XY = AX+Y$$
$$AX+B = AB+X$$
$$AB+A = BA_2$$

is equivalent in final result to the two individual reactions 1 and 2.

(c) *The individual elementary steps of a complex mechanism are sometimes spatially separated*. One of the commonest examples of this is provided by a type of gaseous chain reaction, where certain radicals are generated initially at the wall of the vessel, undergo a series of intermediate transformations in the gas phase, and meet their final fate by diffusion once more to the wall. In some such reactions there will be established at a given moment not only definite concentrations of various intermediates at each given point of space, but definite concentration *gradients*.

Some of the intermediates in oxidations, decompositions, and so on are free radicals or molecules of very short life, and the overall course of the change depends upon the space-time relations in a variety of ways. Only one simple example need be quoted here. When a stream of radicals is produced by the pyrolysis of, say, ether at a high tempera-ture and is pumped at low pressure along a tube with a thin metallic mirror of tellurium deposited on its wall, then, if the distance from the source of the radicals to the mirror is small, methyl radicals combine with the tellurium and remove it. If, however, the distance is increased, there is no removal, because the radicals suffer alternative fates before having time to reach the metal.

The minute size of bacterial cells makes it possible in principle that highly unstable intermediates formed in one region of the cell would be able to diffuse to another region and there enter into further reactions without necessarily suffering destruction on the way.

7. Stationary states

When certain intermediates in a complex reaction series are labile and short-lived, then there is rapidly established a stationary state (quite distinct from an equilibrium), the nature of which is best illustrated by an example. Suppose a chain reaction occurs according to the following scheme (which is a rather rough over-simplification of what happens in the union of hydrogen and chlorine in presence of oxygen):

$$1. \qquad Cl_2 = 2Cl$$

$$2. \quad Cl + H_2 = HCl + H$$

$$3. \quad H + Cl_2 = HCl + Cl$$

$$4. \quad Cl + O_2 = ClO_2$$

Chlorine atoms and hydrogen atoms are transitory intermediates, the concentrations of which adjust themselves very rapidly to satisfy the equations

$$d[Cl]/dt = 0 \quad \text{and} \quad d[H]/dt = 0; \qquad (4) \text{ and } (5)$$

that is to say

$$F_1 - k_2[Cl][H_2] + k_3[H][Cl_2] - k_4[Cl][O_2] = 0 \qquad (6)$$

and

$$k_2[Cl][H_2] - k_3[H][Cl_2] = 0, \qquad (7)$$

where F_1 is the rate of process 1 and k_2, k_3, and k_4 are constants.

The actual rate of formation of hydrogen chloride is obtained by writing down the expression for $d[HCl]/dt$, which, of course, is not equated to zero. Elimination of [H] and [Cl] gives the required result.

The concentrations of chlorine and hydrogen change progressively, and difficulty is sometimes felt about the equating to zero of the net rates of formation of the atomic species. The justification is that the steady state to which this equation corresponds is established so rapidly that no appreciable change in the concentrations of the molecular species occurs in a comparable time, and that the solution of (6) and (7) gives the concentrations of atoms corresponding to these particular constant values of $[H_2]$ and $[Cl_2]$. In so far as the latter slowly change, then the atomic concentrations change with them, but always in accordance with (6) and (7). In relation to the rapid processes envisaged in the establishment of the conditions (4) and (5) changes in the molecular concentrations have the character of secular variations of constants.

These general principles will find application in the kinetics of cell processes. Such processes will necessarily involve labile intermediate substances produced and consumed at rates which, referred to unit concentration, are great compared with the changes in concentration of the primary sources of growth material.

8. Enzyme reactions[11, 12]

From cells and living tissues can be isolated, by methods generally classifiable as those appropriate to the fractionation of proteins, enzymes which are specific catalysts for one particular reaction or group of related reactions. Catalase, for example, decomposes hydrogen peroxide, β-galactosidase splits lactose into glucose and galactose, and ribonuclease brings about the breakdown of ribonucleic acids. Some enzymes can be obtained in a crystalline form and thus appear to be well defined individual substances.[13] They consist essentially of protein, often combined with other groups, and may require for their effective action the presence of specific substances of lower molecular weight known as co-enzymes.

Enzyme reactions are difficult to classify as homogeneous or heterogeneous. They may occur in solutions which are homogeneous to the eye, but since the enzymes themselves are of very great molecular weight, and since their interaction with their substrates evidently depends upon niceties of atomic spacing, the association partakes of the nature of an adsorption process. They may, however, be classified in a fairly simple way into groups, oxidation-reduction processes, transfer reactions of the type $AX + BH \rightleftharpoons AH + BX$, hydrolysis, additions to double bonds, and so on.

Normally the relation between the rate of an enzyme reaction and the concentration of the substrate is given by the Michaelis–Menten equation[14]

$$\text{rate} = \frac{kc}{1+bc}$$

where c is the concentration and k and b are constants. This, it will be observed, is of exactly the same form as a Langmuir adsorption isotherm, and one can think of the rate dependence as governed by whether or not the surface of an enzyme is sparsely or densely covered with substrate molecules. Apart from this the general considerations of chemical kinetics apply without serious modification to enzyme reactions.

Being essentially proteins enzymes are very much dependent on the hydrogen ion concentration of the medium. The activity has a maximum value at a pH, characteristic of any given enzyme, on either side of which the rate of reaction falls off sharply, and at very high or very low pH values irreversible changes leading to the destruction of enzyme often set in. Within a certain range of pH, however, the variation in the activity, which depends on the ionization of groups in the enzyme protein, is reversible. When the substrate can also exist in more than one state of ionization the kinetic treatment becomes very complicated.[11] Suitable analysis in appropriate examples will give information about the relevant dissociation constants of active groups on the enzyme or substrate or of enzyme-substrate complexes.

Many enzymes are greatly influenced in their action by the presence of the ions of particular metals. The precise nature of the action may vary. Catalase and the cytochromes appear to be definite compounds of iron. In other examples the metal may act as a coordination centre whose interaction with attached groups brings the enzyme macro-molecule into a steric relation favouring its specific activity. Magnesium ions stimulate the action of alkaline phosphatase, hexokinase, and possibly other enzymes. Amino-acid acylases are activated or inhibited by Co^{++}, according to the substrate, the activity of arginase is reported to be increased by the presence of Mn^{++}, Co^{++}, or Ni^{++}, and that of deoxy-ribonuclease by Mg^{++}, Mn^{++}, Co^{++}, or Fe^{++}.[15]

Much work has been done on the isolation and characterization of individual enzymes, and upon the identification of probable sequences of enzyme reactions by which the synthesis or breakdown of biochemically important compounds occurs. If the complete exploration of this field were the only way in which the functioning of cells could become understandable, then the immense variety and the complexity of biochemical reactions suggest that the solution of the problem would be

rather long deferred. But important as the detailed biochemical study
of enzyme reactions may be, there are other possibilities for investigating
the working of cells. To understand the general strategy of Napoleon's
campaigns it is not necessary to know the biographies of all his generals.
In chemistry surprisingly definite conclusions may follow simply from
the laws of thermodynamics, in spite of the fact that at first sight these
laws are devoid of much detailed content. We shall see that arguments
based on very general kinetic principles may throw much light upon
the working of cells and on the nature of animate matter.

As to enzymes themselves it should be said that their multifarious
catalytic actions are by the standards of *in vitro* chemistry profoundly
mysterious, a theme to which we shall have occasion to return.

9. The scale effect

The *scale effect* depends upon the simple fact that if we change the
linear dimensions of an object in a given ratio, then the ratios in which
we change its area and its volume respectively are different from that
and from one another. This means that a smaller scale model or an
enlarged version of any system can seldom give a true representation
of it in more than a limited degree. If a painter represents a building
by scaling down its linear dimensions 500 times, this may satisfy the
eye of an observer who is concerned with linear ratios such as relative
heights and widths of windows. But areas are scaled down in a different
ratio, namely $(500)^2$ and in some ways, for example, in connexion with
effects of light and colour, this changes the impression made by the
original. To correct this the painter may resort to what by the simple
linear standard of comparison would be called distortion.

In physical chemistry the scale effect is profoundly important, and
chiefly for the following reasons. The amount of a homogeneous chemical
change occurring in a system, or the amount of heat generated or absorbed is proportional to the volume: the rate at which matter or heat
can enter or leave the system is proportional to the area of its bounding
surface. There is, for a given geometrical form, only a single value of the
volume for which the ratio of volume to area has an assigned magnitude.
Suppose, for example, that an exothermic chemical reaction occurs in a
spherical vessel of radius r, and that the heat generated is removed by
conduction through the surface. A temperature distribution is established such that the rate of generation of heat by reaction equals the loss
by conduction. Now suppose the same reaction to occur in a vessel of
radius $10r$. The amount of heat generated is now 1000 times as great,

but the area through which conduction can occur is only 100 times as great. The original thermal state cannot be reproduced, but the temperature must rise. This kind of consideration gives rise to great difficulties in translating laboratory experiments to the technical scale. In some cases actual discontinuities may arise as the size of the system increases. A good example is found in the various branching-chain reactions which exhibit explosion limits. Here branching of reaction chains (dependent upon the volume) is opposed by deactivation processes (occurring at the wall and dependent upon the area). At a certain critical size the latter factor can no longer balance the former and explosion occurs.[4, 16] The various examples of this discovered among oxidation reactions of phosphorus, hydrogen, and other combustible substances were the chemical prototypes of the even more spectacular branching-chain disintegrations of uranium and plutonium.

In a cell there occur synthetic and other chemical processes which must be more or less proportional in amount to its volume. The raw materials for these reactions must arrive from the external medium through the cell wall and waste products must diffuse out by the same route, and all at rates which are more or less proportional to the surface area. As the cell grows the scale effect comes into operation. If the cell remained spherical the ratio surface/volume would be inversely proportional to the radius. It is true that this ratio would remain nearly constant during the elongation of a cylinder already long enough for the area of the ends to be negligible in comparison with the rest of its surface. Bacteria, however, when cylindrical, normally form rods so short that this last condition is not even approximately applicable and the ratio does fall. Substances formed by the cell must increase internally in concentration, while those derived from outside must tend to drop. More subtle local changes in concentration and in concentration gradients will also occur as the scale of the internal fine structure increases. At a given size of cell, certain concentrations will rise above or fall below what may be a critical value. In a quite general way we see that factors of this kind may well be responsible for those internal changes which lead to the onset of cell division.

10. The building up of ordered structures

Living matter reproduces itself, and, complex though its structure may be, it possesses some of the characteristics of crystallinity. Various proteins, enzymes, and viruses can in fact be obtained in definitely crystalline forms. It is therefore relevant, while remaining on one's

guard against facile analogies, to keep in mind some of the main principles governing the growth of crystals, which are themselves capable
of an indefinite reproduction of their own forms.

Atoms and molecules in crystals are arranged in space lattices, geometrical configurations possessing definite elements of symmetry.[17] In
virtue of this symmetry the lattice arrangement represents a state of
minimum potential energy and is stable with respect to less ordered
configurations obtained by disturbing it. It is relatively difficult for the
first few molecules of a substance to aggregate themselves with the
correct orientations to form a minute crystal, because thermal agitation
always tends to disperse them. But as the aggregate becomes larger it
offers greater atttraction to fresh molecules because it contains a number
of attracting centres reinforcing one another. For this reason crystals
grow most easily on existing nuclei, that is to say, they tend to increase
by the reproduction of an existing pattern.

This principle is not infrequently included under the general heading
of template action.

Template action, however, is more general than the addition of units
identical with those already present: the units may conform in other
energetically favourable ways, as with moulds and casts and as in the
well-known chemical examples of stereo-specific polymerization.[18] Complementarity as well as similarity may be an important factor. In some
respects the processes of living cells can with reasonable justification be
described as unique, but this does not mean to say that they are of a
wholly different order from those met with in non-living systems. In
the field of the organic chemistry of polymers, for example, metal alkyls
and titanium chlorides cause the formation of olefine polymers of high
molecular weight and regular orientation. Here, then, an initiating
molecular pattern causes the indefinitely prolonged repetition of exactly
placed new structures. When liquid acetaldehyde, which is fairly stable
at ordinary temperatures, is cooled to its freezing-point ($-123 \cdot 5°$ C) the
orientation of the solid state initiates a profound irreversible polymerization to long polyoxymethylene chains.

Two substances which are isomorphous can form mixed crystals, one
type of molecule replacing the other more or less indiscriminately in the
lattice. But there is a half-way house between this complete compatibility and the total lack of it. If there is a general similarity in the type
and spacing of the atoms between one crystal face of one substance and
another crystal face of a second, then one crystal may be able to
grow in a parallel orientation on the other.[17] Such orientated over-

C

growths occur with sodium nitrate on calcite and urea on ammonium chloride.

What suggests itself here is that the patterns of biological macromolecules may be able to guide the formation of further lines or sheets of molecules compatible with but not identical with themselves.

11. Formation of macromolecules

Bacterial cells contain macromolecules such as proteins, nucleic acids, and polysaccharides, and these are built up from the very simplest of materials like ammonia and compounds containing not more than three carbon atoms. The condition that small molecules shall participate in the formation of macromolecules is that they should be polyfunctional.[19] A dibasic acid, for example, forms a semi-ester with a dihydric alcohol: there remain a carboxyl group and a hydroxyl group which can react with further molecules of alcohol and acid respectively. The process can be repeated until a polyester of enormous molecular weight is formed. In proteins, of course, the essential polyfunctional molecules are amino-acids, which can give repeated —NHCO— linkages. Bifunctional molecules such as hydroxy-acids, amino-acids, and olefines give macromolecules consisting essentially of chains. If further groups capable of condensation reactions are present, sheets and three-dimensional arrays can be formed by the cross linking of chains. If the cross linking is frequent, the resulting structures will be insoluble and impermeable: if it is infrequent, easily permeable networks may be produced.

Many macromolecules are capable of crystallization, and not infrequently there occur mixtures of crystalline and amorphous material in which the same long-chain molecules traverse both.[20]

In principle, we can envisage regions possessing quite different kinds of crystalline order, spatially separated and yet held in definite relation by tie-molecules. This can come about if we have a long chain of condensed A, B units followed by a chain of B, C units. For example, the same giant molecule could be polyester at one end and polyamide at the other. In such an event the two regions could be of quite different character. This would look something like the very first beginnings of an organized and differentiated structure, though separated by a vast distance from the organized structures of biology.

12. Macromolecular constituents of bacterial cells

The most important high molecular weight constituents of bacterial and other cells are nucleic acids, proteins, and polysaccharides, together with compounds of mixed categories such as mucopeptides and lipopoly-saccharides. All these are polycondensation products, proteins from some twenty-odd amino-acids, nucleic acids from (usually) four nucleotide types, and polysaccharides from a selection of about twenty mono-saccharides. In contrast with protein which usually contains a large number of different amino-acid residues, a relatively small number of monosaccharide components usually occur in any given type of cell.[21]

The order and arrangement of the monomeric units is susceptible of an almost indefinitely large number of permutations, a circum-stance which lies at the basis of the limitless variability of living things.

Cells reproduce themselves and all these sequences reappear in the progeny. Those parts of any macromolecular sequences which can be deemed to determine in some way the course of events ultimately leading to their own replication are commonly said to be repositories of genetic 'information' or to constitute a genetic 'code'. The most widely held view now assigns a special significance to the order of the bases in the deoxyribonucleic acid.[22]

The molecular weights vary over a wide range, those of the major structural components running to hundreds of thousands, while other cell components, especially labile components of cells actively growing or metabolizing, may be relatively small.

The various kinds of linkage by which polysaccharides are built up facilitate the formation of extended two-dimensional sheets, and render these molecules specially appropriate for the formation of walls and membranes, and models show that patterned arrays with regularly spaced gaps and holes are produced, which may be of importance in connexion with phenomena of selective permeability.[21]

Proteins consist essentially of long polypeptide chains, but the chemical affinities, as with other compounds, are not completely satisfied in the formation of the primary structure. Hydrogen bonds, intramolecular or intermolecular, are abundant and highly complex interactions with the environment occur. In particular, proteins assume highly charac-teristic foldings, the pattern of which is frequently (though the term is not universally approved) referred to as the 'tertiary structure'.[23] This folding, which will have a decisive influence on the spatial location of various reactive or structurally specific groupings, is clearly of funda-mental importance for the whole biochemical operation of the cell. It has been argued that the method of folding of the protein chain will be predetermined by its primary structure. This principle may be true enough if applied to the most stable configuration of a protein chain in free space, but it seems hard to believe that the folding is not a function of the whole cellular environment for proteins built up *in vivo*. Subtle differences in folding can be brought about by small changes in the environment, and these variations in turn, by affecting the distances between chemically active groups, can probably lead to gradations in properties such as enzyme activities.

In a protein crystal the structure is conditioned by a minimum potential energy consistent with interatomic distances and bond angles. The natural conformation of proteins in solution may not be the same as in the crystal, nor need the protein in solution have a unique conformation. Physical studies of serum proteins in solution suggest that we may be dealing with an equilibrium pattern of a number of conformational isomers.[24]

Two kinds of nucleic acids, deoxyribonucleic acid (DNA) and ribonucleic acid (RNA) can be isolated from cells. They are macromolecules built up from nucleotides, which are formed by the condensation of a purine or pyrimidine base with a sugar, the latter being itself linked to phosphoric acid. In RNA the sugar is ribose and the bases, in general, are adenine, guanine, cytosine, and uracil, while in DNA thymine (methyl uracil) replaces uracil and the sugar is deoxyribose. The structure of DNA has been more amenable to X-ray analysis than that of RNA and indeed as early as 1947 Astbury[25] suggested that the bases in DNA were stacked one on top of the other. From electro-titrimetric studies Gulland and Jordan[26] obtained evidence of hydrogen bonding between the bases. More recently an intensive attack by refined X-ray techniques (Wilkins, Crick, and Watson[27]) has resulted in the now generally accepted view that the DNA molecule is helical in structure and may exist in a double-stranded form consisting of two polynucleotide chains joined together by base pairing, the adenine and guanine in one strand being linked by hydrogen bonding to the thymine and cytosine respectively of the other. In other words the two chains are complementary and if, as Watson and Crick[27] suggest, one acts as a template for the other during replication, continuity of the sequence of bases is assured.

The idea of complementary base pairing (adenine–thymine, guanine–cytosine) has been tested with synthetic polynucleotides. Polythymidylic acid, for example, is stated to complex with polyadenylic acid. The polycondensation reaction of uridine phosphate is stated, moreover, to take place, in the absence of enzymes, much more readily if polyadenylic acid is present.[28] The pairing is believed to have been demonstrated with nucleic acids and with synthetic polynucleotides with various combinations of all the bases.[29]

Nucleic acids which form hybrid molecules with one another are commonly assumed to have a substantial degree of complementarity in the base sequences.[30] RNA/DNA hybrids are prepared and characterized by rather elaborate methods, which have to be very carefully controlled[31] and it is open to a good deal of doubt how far conclusions based upon hybrid formation are absolute.

Nucleic acids are very often associated with protein in the form of nucleoproteins and in this connexion Astbury long ago suggested that the spacing of the nucleic acids controlled the structure of the protein. In plant and animal cells containing visible chromosomes these bodies are specially rich in DNA, a fact which first led to the idea that this substance has a special function in bearing the genetic code. Studies of the interaction of bacteria and phages (see next section), most of which consist essentially of DNA together with some protein, have been thought to support the idea. Bacteria do not reveal obvious chromosomes but by converse argument the DNA which they contain is sometimes regarded as being the equivalent of the chromosome.

Proteins are the main constituents of enzymes, which are essential for practically all cell reactions, and if in their turn they are in some way influenced in their own formation by nucleic acids then an important mutual dependence begins to appear. A further mutual dependence would exist between the carbohydrate of a cell wall which was specifically permeable to the substrates of enzymes, and the enzymes which build up the polysaccharides of the wall itself.

In the immense experiment by trial and error which natural selection has represented these three types of macromolecule can hardly have remained associated together without good reason.

13. Phages[32]

Of some considerable importance in the study of bacteria, and of great interest in their own right, are the bacteriophages, or, as they are often called, simply phages. They are particulate entities consisting almost wholly of nucleic acid, usually but not universally of deoxyribonucleic acid. Opinions differ about the significance of the small amounts of protein commonly detectable in phage though the 1 per cent of protein transferred alongside the DNA when bacteriophage T2 infects a cell is equal in weight to a fragment of the tobacco mosaic virus that is fully infective.[33] Phages do not multiply by themselves. They can invade

bacterial cells, the relation of phage to host cell being highly
specific, and there multiply with subsequent lysis of the cell whereby
the phage particles are released. Sometimes an organized symbiotic
relation is established whereby phage and bacterium multiply in step
and no lysis occurs. The balance may, however, be unstable, and if a
disturbance such as exposure to ultraviolet light occurs, the latent or
'lysogenic' phage may become 'virulent' and the lysis of the bacteria
set in.

14. The structure of bacteria

Bacteria possess nothing in the way of a grossly differentiated structure but the internal composition is not uniform, physically or chemically.
A cell wall can be distinguished, and it is claimed by some writers that
a nuclear apparatus can be demonstrated by appropriate staining
methods.[34] The inhomogeneities observed are of a fine-grained and
subtle kind.

Bacteria contain particulate structures known as ribosomes.[35] Some
possess what are called flagella.[36] These are minute processes protruding
from the surface. They cannot, however, be regarded as separate organs.

The pneumococcus can surround itself with a so-called capsule. This
is associated with a polysaccharide material, specific to the particular
type of pneumococcus. It is stated that with careful technique the
capsule can be revealed in electron microscope pictures as a definite
structure surrounding the cell wall which, in turn, is demonstrable as a
distinct structure bounding the inner protoplasm.[37]

In the cells of higher plants and animals a well-defined, more or less
central nucleus can be observed while in bacteria it is less defined and
the DNA (a major compact of nuclei) is not separated from the cytoplasm
by a nuclear membrane.[38] Genetic material is segregated in distinct
chromosomes in such cells. With most cells of plants and animals
division occurs after a splitting of the nucleus and an elaborate rearrangement and division of the chromosomes themselves.[39] The question
arises whether the at first sight greater simplicity of the reproduction
process with bacteria is apparent or real. This will be considered later.

15. Some cell mechanisms

The study of living matter has naturally been approached from many
directions and certain general principles have gradually emerged.
Classical biochemistry identified biologically significant compounds

essentially by the methods of organic chemistry, and physical chemistry was applied in the analysis of enzyme reactions. X-ray analysis added more detailed information about structures and configurations, and led to the picture of the DNA helix. The permutations of the base sequences in nucleic acids, and of amino-acids in proteins long ago suggested the idea of a code of information or genetic code, now, as we have said, believed to reside essentially in the DNA.

Important advances followed the use of techniques for the fractionation and microanalysis of cell materials and revealed the localization of nuclear matter, ribosomes,[35] and so on. Autoradiography of intact cells made it possible to follow in some detail the fate of radioactively labelled compounds taken up by them.

In cells possessing well-defined nuclei it became clear that DNA is almost exclusively and RNA largely synthesized in the nuclear regions, a conclusion strengthened by experiments on cells from which the nucleus had been removed. RNA synthesized in the nucleus migrates into the cytoplasm of the cell.[40, 41]

There are numerous varieties of it. Roberts[42], for example, lists ribosomal, soluble, transfer, complementary, informational, DNA-like, template, pulse, nascent, and messenger RNA's.

Enucleated cells can still elaborate enzyme proteins. If the genetic information is in the nucleus, then there must be an intermediary to convey this information to the centres where protein is made. This has given rise to the idea of a 'messenger RNA' formed in contact with nuclear material and migrating into the other parts of the cell.[40]

Less direct evidence has led to similar conclusions about cells like bacteria in which the nuclear type material is diffusely scattered rather than concentrated in a well-defined central body. The use of isotopically labelled medium constituents for short bursts enabled the fate of the various RNA fractions to be followed and it was found that a major part of the RNA in the cell was associated with protein and could be separated in the ultracentrifuge into particulate fractions with different molecular weights. These particles or ribosomes are said to contain about two-thirds RNA and one-third protein, and, since they can coalesce or dissociate, the number of classes depends on the precise experimental conditions, and in particular on the concentration of divalent cations (usually Mg^{++}) in the medium in which the cells are broken up.[43] In an actively growing bacterial cell there are said to be two predominating classes (referred to as 70s and 85s)[44] and these, it is claimed, can form aggregates which have been called 'polysomes' or 'ergosomes'.[42, 45] The remainder of the RNA in the cell has a much lower molecular weight and part of it is labile.[42]

Very gentle methods of cell rupture are supposed to yield polysomes. These have also been obtained by lysing the protoplasts produced from *Escherichia coli* by treatment with penicillin, when it has been calculated that between 70 and 80 per cent of the ribosomes were present as polysomes. A similar result has also been reported for *Bacillus megaterium* where most of the polysomes were said to occur in a membrane fraction from which they could not be washed off with buffer. If the concentration of magnesium ions was reduced, however, they could be removed.[42]

Some workers believe that the polysomes are the site of protein synthesis. It has been stated that the ribosomes are held together by messenger RNA and that the different sizes of polysomes arise from different lengths of messenger RNA associated with different proteins. Cells which are manufacturing a large variety of proteins are stated to have a broad distribution of sizes of polysomes.[46]

Protoplasts from *Bacillus megaterium* can be separated into a nuclear fraction containing all the DNA of the cell, a membrane fraction and a supernatant cytoplasmic fraction.[47]

Various developments in amino-acid and nucleotide chemistry led to the conclusion that before incorporation into protein the amino-acids are first activated and attached to a specific RNA molecule, and this led to the view that the low-molecular-weight RNA fraction contains a specific 'transfer RNA' and a specific activating enzyme for each amino-acid. A mechanism was then postulated by which the amino-acids are not only transferred to the site of protein synthesis but are also aligned in the correct order on a pre-existing template which at one time was assumed to be contained in the RNA of the ribosome, though it is now believed that 'messenger RNA' is the active agent.[48] Activating enzymes have been isolated by chromatographic procedures and although the degree of specificity is considerable it is not, so far, absolute. More than forty different amino-acid transfer RNA's in yeast or *Escherichia coli* have been reported.[49]

It had been known for some time that when the bacteriophage T2 invades a cell its DNA and a small amount of its protein enter.[32, 50] The use of isotopically labelled medium constituents showed that a rapid turnover of some of the low-molecular-weight RNA in the cell then ensues. The RNA, it is claimed, has a base composition similar to that of the DNA of the invading bacteriophage but quite different from that of the total RNA extracted from the ribosomes of the cell. The proteins synthesized by the cell after infection are, in general, typical of the phage rather than of the host cell. If, according to Watson and Crick, the information for the synthesis of these proteins is contained in the sequence of the bases in the DNA of the bacteriophage, and if the assembly of the appropriate parts takes place on the ribosomes of the cell,[42] a transfer of information from the DNA to the ribosomes is necessary. Current theory assumes that part of the labile RNA (the above mentioned 'messenger RNA') performs this function, and it is argued that a similar mechanism operates when normal (uninfected) cells are transferred from one environment to another.[51]

Another important development was the isolation from *Azotobacter vinelandii* of the enzyme polynucleotide phosphorylase (which catalyses the reaction nX—R—P—P $\rightleftharpoons$ $(X$—R—P$)_n + nP_i$, where R = ribose, X = adenine, hypoxanthine, guanine, uracil, or cytosine, P = phosphate, and P_i = orthophosphate). By the action of this enzyme synthetic polynucleotides could be prepared. When one of these substances, polyuridylic acid, was added in small amount to a cell-free *Escherichia coli* system it stimulated the incorporation of ^{14}C-phenylalanine into protein one thousandfold and the protein had the properties characteristic of authentic polyphenylalanine. This phenomenon is described by the statement that polyuridylic acid 'codes for' phenylalanine.

The activity of the polymer depended on various factors since single-stranded polyuridylic acid was more active than double- or triple-stranded polyuridylic acid and longer chains were better than shorter chains, very great activity being associated with a molecular weight of between 50 000 and 100 000. Randomly ordered polynucleotides containing different bases have also been examined and a marked specificity claimed. (Leucine was 'coded for' by two different mixed polynucleotides, the interpretation being that the code for leucine is 'degenerate'.)[52]

Experiments of this kind with synthetic polymers have been interpreted as confirmation of the view that the specificity for the synthesis of protein resides entirely in that part of the labile low molecular weight RNA referred to as 'messenger RNA' and hence in the DNA whose base sequence is assumed to have guided its formation.

Similar enzymes have been found and no doubt the total number is considerable.†

† Enzymes have been isolated which catalyse the formation of polydeoxyribonucleotides. The isolation of an enzyme which catalyses the synthesis of a hybrid ordered polymer composed of homopolymeric chains of deoxyribonucleotides and ribonucleotides has also been reported.[53]

DNA polymerase can synthesize DNA *in vitro*[54] from the four bases, in the form of nucleoside triphosphates, and a suitable DNA primer. According to the base pairing in the Watson–Crick model for the replication of DNA (section 12) the ratios of adenine to thymine and of guanine to cytosine should be unity. It is found, however, that those of adenine+ thymine/guanine+cytosine vary from 0·5 to 2·5 according to the source of the DNA, and if the synthetic DNA produced in the above reaction is an exact copy of the primer the appropriate ratio should be reproduced. This has been claimed and would seem to indicate again that all the specificity resides in the primer DNA molecule.[55] In some circumstances, however, if the primer is omitted from the reaction mixture, a long lag ensues and then an adenine-thymine copolymer with a regular alternating order of nucleotides ...ATAT... is produced.[56]

Caution, however, has to be exercised. Friedman and Weinstein,[57] for example, raise the question of how accurately *in vitro* experiments of this kind reflect the *in vivo* situation. They say that when cell-free preparations from *Bacillus stearothermophilus* are used in conjunction with synthetic polynucleotides the polypeptide produced is a function of the temperature at which the experiment is carried out and of the cationic environment. Other workers have reported that besides coding for phenylalanine polyuridylic acid also codes for leucine, and this ambiguity was enhanced in the experiments of Friedman and Weinstein at low temperature and high concentrations of magnesium ions. Moreover, in the presence of spermine, spermidine, or dihydro-streptomycin polyuridylic acid also coded for isoleucine, serine, valine, and tyrosine, and conditions which led to ambiguity with polyuridylic acid also changed the coding properties of co-polymers formed from uridylic acid and cytidylic acid or uridylic acid and guanylic acid (see also Davies, Gorini, and Davis[58]).

Thus we have examples both of the same code corresponding to more than one amino-acid and of one amino-acid being coded for by different sequences.[59]

Whatever criticisms in detail may be made of all the above and similar experiments and interpretations, the overall picture which emerges is that of a complex system of interacting cell components of varying degrees of stability. An important role has been assigned to labile RNA fractions which are rapidly labelled in isotope experiments and which can be split into 30 to 40 per cent DNA-like RNA and 60 to 70 per cent ribosome-like RNA.[60] The underlying theme is the transfer of information between macromolecular species and in this process the structure of one component guides that of another. One point of view insists on a unidirectional flow of the information coded in the sequence of the bases in the DNA to the protein (enzyme) mediated by labile RNA fractions,[61] and it is an open question whether information can ever flow in the opposite direction. The precise picture will undoubtedly change (and indeed may be said to be changing all the time) yet it illustrates the kind of systems operating in the cell. In later chapters we shall be concerned with the general laws which any such systems must follow.

Contrary to a widespread impression, the general laws we shall discuss are in no way in conflict with, though they are in considerable measure independent of, detailed hypotheses about the mechanism of information transfer or the particular agents concerned in it at any given stage.

One important general consideration is that in the last resort the reproduction of structure depends upon the stability attainable when fresh elements fit into their place in an existing structure. To this extent early analogies between self-replication and crystallization had some validity.

It may also be said that, however complex the individual details of cell biochemistry may be, every part of the cell is reproduced, and if a steady supply of material is available and no toxic products are allowed to accumulate, this reproduction continues indefinitely according to an exponential law. If m_0 is the initial mass of any kind of cell substance and m the amount at time t, then $dm/dt = km$, or $m = m_0 e^{kt}$. This exponential law is a straightforward expression of experimental fact. Every component of a cell gives the appearance of being autocatalytically formed. This is something which must be allowed for in any attempts to combine the above-mentioned facts about the mutual dependences into a coherent dynamical theory of growth.

Different regions of the cell possess different functions, probably determined by the molecular pattern and by the specific active groups prevailing locally. These various departments of the cell, according to one quite possible picture, would not so much resemble the separate rooms of a house as the counters in a large multiple store. They must be held in a kind of spatial organization, and this could be imagined to occur through the intervention of polyfunctional tie-molecules linking the various regions.

The great variety of chemical reactions which can be brought about is most easily understood if the enzymatic processes are thought of as resolved into sequences of rather simple steps (for example, removal of hydrogen atoms, addition of oxygen atoms, and so on), which can be combined and permuted in all sorts of ways, so that the initial raw materials are operated on by a whole succession of enzymes. Intermediate products, many of which must be very active and labile, must diffuse from one region of enzymatic activity to another. They may be of high or low molecular weight. The concentrations in which the intermediates reach the next enzyme of a sequence or a nucleic acid molecule depend upon the spatial distribution of matter in the cell—and this applies whether or not they are labile substances. On their way from one processing department to the next they may either suffer partial decay, if unstable, or, if stable, be exposed to alternative fates such as loss by diffusion.

According to this general picture, the activity of the cell consists in a sequence of reactions with relative speeds determined by the spatial relations as well as by the specific chemical properties of the substances involved. In a steady state, definite concentration gradients will be established between one enzyme region and the next, a fact which gives us a glimpse of how a spatio-temporal organization could arise. The fundamental geometry of the macromolecular systems will determine the spatial relations of the enzyme or nucleic acid regions, the chemical character of those regions determines the reactions which occur there, and the different concentration gradients help to control the sequence and relative rates. In the general context of cell organization we must not forget the possible part played by the stereochemistry of the complexes formed by the various metal atoms (e.g. iron) which have considerable importance in all life.

Whatever may be said of the reactions mentioned earlier in this section, there remain some crucial questions: those, namely, of how the autosynthetic reactions are initiated, how they are propagated with such ease while the cell remains alive, how they may be interrupted for considerable periods during the non-proliferating periods of the cell's existence and yet renewed again with the appropriate change of conditions, and finally what happens when the cell dies. Free radical mechanisms provide one suggestive possibility. If a free radical reacts with a saturated molecule a new free radical is produced. In the ordinary chemical processes of the laboratory such free radicals must continue to be kept in play or they are lost by various recombination processes unhelpful to the main reaction. With the elaborate structural organization of the cell one can imagine their preservation for long periods: they do not combine since they are fixed in space, being simply unfinished ends of a more or less rigid structure. In such a way they could remain mobilized for use for considerable periods. If the structure decays or the radicals are used up by foreign bodies not utilizable in growth, the cell dies. From this point of view the macromolecular structure of the living cell might be regarded as an extremely elaborate and finely adjusted support for active radicals, and the death of the cell would represent on a higher plane what on a lower plane occurs in the sintering of a catalyst, in the disappearance of the free radicals after the light is turned off in a photochemical reaction, or in the various manifestations connected with what are now actually sometimes called 'living polymers' in the field of plastics.[62] This whole question is discussed in more detail in Chapters XIV and XVI.

On the whole it would seem that the possibility of an autosynthetic structure is—given the right initial conditions—conceivable in not wholly unfamiliar terms. As such a structure expands by utilizing raw materials supplied from outside, the scale effect must come into play. No steady expansion according to the exponential autosynthetic growth law will be possible unless in some way an approximately constant set of conditions can be maintained, and this involves a preservation of an approximately constant surface-volume relation. The required relation is in fact preserved by the division of the cell at more or less regular intervals, and we have to inquire whether any analogies exist which help in the understanding of this. The two most obvious do not seem at first sight to take us very far. One is the fact that crystals which have grown to a large size, although having the appearance of a single geometrical figure, are nearly always found on inspection to consist of a mosaic of very many small crystals. But here there is no question of a two-way diffusion process in the system. The second analogy is that of a column of liquid breaking up into small drops under the influence of surface tension. This is helpful only in a limited degree as will be seen in a later chapter. It will appear rather that cell division arises from a subtle interplay of chemical and mechanical factors.

16. Transfer of information between cells[63]

In organisms with sexual reproduction elements from two separate sets of genetic information codes are combined. This does not normally occur with bacteria but in special circumstances information-bearing material does pass from cell to cell. Three main mechanisms by which information may be transferred from one cell to another are called transformation, transduction, and conjugation.

In transformation the DNA extracted from one strain of bacteria by the experimenter is added to a culture of another closely related strain. The phenomenon was first demonstrated in pneumococci and involved the production of a capsule when cells without one were treated with preparations made from cells which had one.[64] It has since been demonstrated with some other strains of bacteria[65, 66] and it is stated that different characters can be transferred, usually one at a time. Under the most favourable conditions an efficiency of about 17 per cent has been reported, and since it is thought that the process works best just after the cells have divided, cultures are often artificially induced to divide in step (synchronized).[65]

A bacterial virus (bacteriophage) is the agent by which information is transferred in transduction. Bacteriophages only reproduce within a living cell, and in this situation there are the two main patterns of behaviour already described, one leading to the destruction and lysis of the cell, the other to a continuing symbiotic relationship. For transduction both these processes are applied in turn. A culture of bacteria is first of all infected with a virus under conditions where the host cells are destroyed and the liberated phage particles, after separation from the bacterial debris, are then used to infect another culture in which the bacteria are likely to survive. It is assumed that during the first process the virus particles may assimilate into their own codes information from the cells they destroy and that this can then be transmitted in some way to the cells in the second process. Experimentally it is found that a small proportion of the progeny of the recipient cells (about 1 in 10^6) show new characters.

Conjugation is a quasi-sexual process in which, when two suitable cells come into contact, information passes from a donor to an acceptor. It is a rare event whose frequency depends on the type of donor. With a so-called F+ donor it rarely exceeds 10^{-5} while with an Hfr (high frequency of recombination) donor it may be 1000 times as high for some of the characters. Acceptor (F−) cells are assumed to lack a sex factor which, it is claimed, is present in F+ cells in the form of one or more cytoplasmic particles. The F+ character is readily transferred to F− cells on contact and may be eliminated by growth in the presence of acridine dyes. Since Hfr cells do not transmit the sex factor to F− cells and since the factor is not eliminated from them by the action of acridine dyes it is assumed that it is attached to what has been called a bacterial chromosome. Usually less than one-half of the donor characters are transferred, and this has been interpreted in terms of a breakage of the hypothetical donor chromosome during conjugation. It is important to realize that the acceptor cell contributes not only its entire genetic complement but also its cytoplasm, with the result that the genetic type of the recipient bacteria tends to predominate among the recombinants.

The term episome has been given to particles which behave like the sex factor, such as the resistance transfer factors (RTF) by which multiple drug resistance may on occasion be transferred from cell to cell and indeed from the cells of one species to those of another (see p. 133).

Hypothetical chromosome 'maps', that is diagrams showing the order on the chromosome of the genes supposed to control the various characters and the distance between them, have been constructed from a statistical analysis of recombinant types, supplemented by information from the so-called 'time' and radioactive experiments. The latter two methods are based upon a crudely mechanical picture of a chromosome from the donor cell boring its way into the acceptor cell. This penetration is supposed to be interrupted by shaking, which can be done at chosen intervals. On the other hand, the chromosome is supposed capable of being broken before mating starts by the decay of ^{32}P previously incorporated into it. Analysis of the characters in the progeny obtained after a series of variations on these procedures can, it is claimed, supply information about the chromosome map.

A current theory proposes that the greater part of the fertility of F^+ cultures is due to the presence of Hfr mutants arising in them. It has been stated that in F^+ bacteria the chromosome is circular[67] and that the change from F^+ to Hfr involves its opening by the insertion of the sex factor at one of many possible sites, an assumption which had to be made to explain some otherwise disconcertingly erratic results.† (Another conceivable explanation of such results is that some of the basic assumptions are not really valid.)

Experimental and theoretical treatment of the problems involved in the transfer of information between bacterial cells, and in particular on the crossing of two different strains comes under the heading of what is now called *bacterial genetics*. The phrase 'under genetic control' is not infrequently used of particular properties. In so far as living cells, whatever their evolutionary origin may have been, come into being only by the replication of others of the same kind, everything living is genetically

---

† Visual evidence for circular chromosomes has been claimed.[68] If the DNA molecules from bacteriophage T2 are denatured by treatment with alkali and then renatured at a neutral pH they assume a circular form. This is said to confirm the hypothesis that native linear DNA molecules of bacteriophage T2 have nucleotide sequences which are various circular permutations of a common sequence. If the molecules are broken before treatment the circular form does not appear.[69]

controlled, and the phrase is somewhat otiose. If, moreover, two living cells of different type can somehow jointly contribute the information on which a new cell is built, then this transaction, too, must always be genetic from the nature of living matter itself and its dependence on templates of some sort. The only point of distinguishing any special sense in which a character is under genetic control is where discrete changes in properties can be, if only hypothetically, associated with particular discrete structural elements in the information-bearing material. The formulation of chromosome maps is an attempt to do this. The difficulty, however, lies in the definition of discrete characters. Some critical observations on this matter will be made later (pp. 332 et seq.). The essential point, however, will be exemplified now. Bacterial cells can often be made drug-resistant. Let us call the resistant type R and the sensitive S. Now two different strains can give the possibilities R_1, R_2, S_1, S_2. R_1 can be crossed with R_2 or S_2 and S_1 with R_2 or S_2 and the properties of the recombinants noted. This sounds like a simple Mendelian kind of experiment. But there is really no simple character R or S. The degree of resistance can usually vary in a quantitative way over a very wide continuous range so that the schedule of combinations just given would be a wholly artificial idealization. As we shall see, it is only too easy to impose artificially appearances of discreteness where they do not exist. Strains of *Escherichia coli* K 12, sensitive or resistant in various degrees to chloramphenicol, proflavine, or brilliant green were crossed, for example, and the drug resistances of the recombinant strains were measured on a quantitative scale. In general, the recombinants showed a continuous spectrum of resistance in the range between the values for the two parent strains, with a greater likelihood of values in the middle of the range.[70]

It is formally possible to preserve a correspondence between discrete units of information and discrete characters by postulating that a property such as drug resistance is governed by a very large number of hereditary units, 'polygenes'. But the number for each type of drug resistance would have to be very large indeed (and the postulate would accord ill with another hypothesis, at one time favoured, of 'one gene one enzyme'). This hypothesis itself runs into the difficulty that different types of cell may show the same kind of enzyme activity in continuously variable degree.

On the whole, there is no escape from the conclusion that, although all properties of a cell are ultimately dependent upon information, and although this information may be added to or shared, none the less the use made of it depends upon conditions of organization which demand study in their own right. This simple thesis, strange to say, has evoked much prejudice, but it will recur throughout this book.

17. Matters to be dealt with in subsequent chapters

The classical biochemistry of bacteria is a study of great importance but by itself will hardly yield the secret of cell function. Structural investigation of biologically significant substances is an indispensable basis for theories of replication, and of codes of genetic information. Bacterial genetics has much to reveal about these codes themselves. But there still remains the key question of the relation between the structure and the function. To come to terms with this it is necessary to observe the cell in action, study its growth and behaviour, and to try to formulate general propositions about the operation of physico-chemical laws in the kind of system which the cell is. This task will be attempted in the following chapters. One of the outstanding characteristics of living matter will be seen to be its plasticity and adaptability, properties which, it may be repeated, do not release it from its ultimate dependence upon hereditary endowment.

REFERENCES

1. S. S. Cohen, *Science* **139,** 1017 (1963).
2. A. I. Oparin, *Chemical Origin of Life,* C. C. Thomas, Springfield, Illinois, U.S.A. (1964).
3. V. N. Kondrat'ev, *Chemical Kinetics of Gas Reactions,* Pergamon Press, Oxford (1964).
4. C. N. Hinshelwood, *Kinetics of Chemical Change,* Clarendon Press, Oxford (1945).
5. Cf. A. Kossiakoff and F. O. Rice, *J. Am. chem. Soc.* **65,** 590 (1943).
6. See S. Brunauer, *The Adsorption of Gases and Vapours, Volume* 1, *Physical Adsorption,* Oxford University Press, London (1944).
7. Cf. E. F. G. Herington and E. K. Rideal, *Trans. Faraday Soc.* **40,** 505 (1944).
8. G. M. Schwab, H. Noller, and J. Block, *Handbuch der Katalyse,* p. 160, Springer-Verlag, Wien (1957).
9. See A. B. Pardee in Ciba Found. Symp. *Regulation of Cell Metabolism,* edited by G. E. W. Wolstenholme and Cecilia M. O'Connor, p. 295, Churchill, London (1959); and H. E. Umbarger and H. J. Vogel in *Control Mechanisms in Cellular Processes,* edited by D. M. Bonner, Ronald Press Co., New York (1961).
10. See A. H. Willbourn and C. N. Hinshelwood, *Proc. R. Soc.* A **185,** 353 (1946).
11. K. J. Laidler, *Chemical Kinetics of Enzyme Action,* Clarendon Press, Oxford (1958).
12. M. Dixon and E. C. Webb, *Enzymes,* Longmans Green & Co., London (1958).

13. J. H. Northrop, M. Kunitz, and R. M. Herriott, *Crystalline Enzymes*, 2nd ed., Columbia University Press, New York (1948).
14. L. Michaelis and M. L. Menten, *Biochem. Z.* **49**, 333 (1913).
15. *Data for Biochemical Research*, edited by R. M. C. Dawson, Daphne C. Elliott, W. H. Elliott, and K. M. Jones, p. 178, Clarendon Press, Oxford (1959).
16. N. Semenoff, *Chemical Kinetics and Chain Reactions*, Clarendon Press, Oxford (1935).
17. For an account of this and all related matters see C. W. Bunn, *Chemical Crystallography*, Clarendon Press, Oxford (1945).
18. See C. E. H. Bawn and A. Ledwith, *Q. Rev. chem. Soc.* **16**, 361 (1962).
19. W. H. Carothers, Collected Papers in *High Polymers*, vol. 1, Interscience, New York (1940).
20. Cf. C. W. Bunn, *Proc. R. Soc.* A **180**, 82 (1942); C. W. Bunn and T. C. Alcock, *Trans. Faraday Soc.* **41**, 317 (1945); E. Hunter and W. G. Oakes, ibid. **41**, 49 (1945); H. C. Raine, R. B. Richards, and H. Ryder, ibid. **41**, 56 (1945).
21. M. Stacey and S. A. Barker, *Polysaccharides of Micro-organisms*, Clarendon Press, Oxford (1960).
22. F. H. C. Crick, L. Barnett, S. Brenner, and R. J. Watts-Tobin, *Nature, Lond.* **192**, 1227 (1961); S. Ochoa, *Fed. Proc.* **22**, 62 (1963).
23. J. G. Kendrew in *Les Prix Nobel en 1962*, p. 103, Imprimerie Royale, P. A. Norstedt und Söner, Stockholm (1963); M. Perutz, *Proteins and Nucleic Acids*, Elsevier, Amsterdam (1962).
24. N. H. Martin, *Biochem. J.* **88**, 3p (1963).
25. W. T. Astbury, *Symp. Soc. exp. Biol.* **1**, 66 (1947).
26. J. M. Gulland and D. O. Jordan, *Symp. Soc. exp. Biol.* **1**, 56 (1947).
27. See M. H. F. Wilkins, F. H. C. Crick, and J. D. Watson in *Les Prix Nobel en 1962*, Imprimerie Royale, P. A. Norstedt und Söner, Stockholm (1963).
28. G. Schramm, H. Groetsch, and W. Pollman, *Angew. Chem.* **74**, 53 (1962).
29. A. Kornberg, *Science*, **131**, 1503 (1960).
30. C. L. Schildkraut, J. Marmur, and P. Doty, *J. molec. Biol.* **3**, 595 (1961).
31. G. Turncock and D. G. Wild, *Biochem. J.* **95**, 597 (1965).
32. See A. D. Hershey, *Adv. Virus Res.* **4**, 25 (1957); A. Lwoff, *Proc. R. Soc.* B **154**, 1 (1961).
33. B. Dixon, *Sch. Sci. Rev.* **44**, 341 (1963).
34. C. F. Robinow, *Proc. R. Soc.* B**130**, 299 (1942); *Symp. Soc. gen. Microbiol.* **6**, 181 (1956).
35. See references under 43.
36. B. A. D. Stocker, *Symp. Soc. gen. Microbiol.* **6**, 19 (1956).
37. S. Mudd, F. Heinmets, and T. F. Anderson, *J. Bact.* **46**, 205 (1943).
38. R. Byrne, J. G. Levin, H. A. Bladen, and M. W. Nirenberg, *Proc. natn. Acad. Sci. U.S.A.* **52**, 140 (1964).
39. W. D'Arcy Thompson, *On Growth and Form*, Cambridge University Press chapter 4 (1942).
40. See J. Brachet, *Nova Acta Leopoldina*, **26**, 17 (1963).
41. H. Harris, *Endeavour*, **24**, 50 (1965).
42. Cited by K. McQuillen, *Symp. Soc. gen. Microbiol.* **15**, 134 (1965).
43. T. J. Bowen, S. Dagley, J. Sykes, and D. G. Wild, *Nature, Lond.* **189**, 638 (1961); E. T. Bolton, R. J. Britten, D. B. Cowie, B. J. McCarthy, J. E. Midgley, and R. B. Roberts, *Carnegie Inst. Wash. Year Book*, **61**, 244 (1961–2);

Mary L. Petermann, *The Physical and Chemical Properties of Ribosomes* Elsevier, Amsterdam (1964); K. A. Camnack and H. E. Wade, *Biochem. J.* **96**, 671 (1965).

44. See, however, J. Sykes, *Nature, Lond.* **206**, 434 (1965).

45. R. W. Risebrough, A. Tissières, and J. D. Watson, *Proc. natn. Acad. Sci. U.S.A.* **48**, 430 (1962); J. R. Warner, A. Rich, and C. E. Hall, *Science*, **138**, 1399 (1962); A. Gierer, *J. molec. Biol.* **6**, 148 (1963); T. Staehelin, F. O. Wettstein, H. Oura, and H. Noll, *Nature, Lond.* **201**, 264 (1964).

46. Y. Kiho and A. Rich, *Proc. natn. Acad. Sci. U.S.A.* **51**, 111 (1964); for a full review on protein biosynthesis see H. R. V. Arnstein, *Br. med. Bull.* **21**, 217 (1965).

47. G. C. Barr and J. A. V. Butler, *Biochem. J.* **87**, 36P (1963).

48. Elizabeth B. Keller and P. C. Zamecnik, *J. biol. Chem.* **221**, 45 (1956); P. Berg, ibid. **222**, 1025 (1956); J. A. De Moss and G. D. Novelli, *Biochim. Biophys. Acta*, **22**, 49 (1956); P. Berg, F. H. Bergmann, E. J. Ofengand, and M. Diekman, *J. biol. Chem.* **236**, 1726 (1961).

49. Jean Apgar, R. W. Holley, and Susan H. Merrill, *J. biol. Chem.* **237**, 796 (1962); J. Goldstein, T. P. Bennett, and L. C. Craig, *Proc. natn. Acad. Sci. U.S.A.* **51**, 119 (1964); see also G. L. Brown and Sheila Lee, *Br. med. Bull.* **21**, 236 (1965).

50. A. D. Hershey and Martha Chase, *J. gen. Physiol.* **36**, 39 (1952); E. Volkin and L. Astrachan, *Virology*, **2**, 149 (1956).

51. S. Brenner, F. Jacob, and M. Meselson, *Nature, Lond.* **190**, 576 (1961); F. Gros, H. Hiatt, W. Gilbert, C. G. Kurland, R. W. Risebrough, and J. D· Watson, *Nature, Lond.* **190**, 581 (1961).

52. Marianne Grunberg-Manago and S. Ochoa, *J. Am. chem. Soc.* **77**, 3165 (1955); M. W. Nirenberg and J. H. Matthaei, *Proc. natn. Acad. Sci. U.S.A.* **47**, 1588 (1961); P. Lengyel, J. F. Speyer, and S. Ochoa, ibid. **47**, 1936 (1961); M. W. Nirenberg, J. H. Matthaei, O. W. Jones, R. G. Martin, and S. H. Barondes, *Fed. Proc.* **22**, 55 (1963).

53. Sylvia Lee-Huang and L. F. Cavalieri, *Proc. natn. Acad. Sci. U.S.A.* **51**, 1022 (1964).

54. A. Kornberg, *Enzymatic Synthesis of DNA*, Wiley, New York (1961).

55. I. R. Lehman, S. B. Zimmerman, J. Adler, M. J. Bessman, E. S. Sims, and A. Kornberg, *Proc. natn. Acad. Sci. U.S.A.* **44**, 1191 (1958).

56. H. K. Schachman, J. Adler, C. M. Radding, I. R. Lehman, and A. Kornberg, *J. biol. Chem.* **235**, 3242 (1960); J. Josse, A. D. Kaiser, and A. Kornberg, ibid. **236**, 864 (1961).

57. S. M. Friedman and I. B. Weinstein, *Proc. natn. Acad. Sci. U.S.A.* **52**, 988 (1964).

58. L. Davies, L. Gorini, and B. D. Davis, *Molec. Pharmac.* **1**, 93 (1965).

59. B. Weisblum, F. Gonano, G. von Ehrenstein, and S. Benzer, *Proc. natn. Acad. Sci. U.S.A.* **53**, 328 (1965); J. S. Trupin, F. M. Rottman, R. L. C. Brimacombe, P. Leder, M. R. Bernfield, and M. W. Nirenberg, ibid. **53**, 807 (1965).

60. See Bolton et al., reference 43.

61. F. H. C. Crick, *Symp. Soc. exp. Biol.* **12**, 138 (1958).

62. M. Szwarc, *Proc. R. Soc.* A**279**, 260 (1964).

63. For details and references see F. Jacob and E. L. Wollman, *Sexuality and*

the Genetics of Bacteria, Academic Press, New York, 1961; W. Hayes, *The Genetics of Bacteria and their Viruses*, Blackwell, Oxford, 1964; J. D. Gross, *Br. med. Bull.* **21**, 206 (1965).

64. O. T. Avery, C. M. MacLeod, and M. McCarty, *J. exp. Med.* **79**, 137 (1944)·

65. R. D. Hotchkiss and Esther Weiss, *Scient. Am.* **195**, 48 (1956).

66. Harriett Ephrussi-Taylor, *Symp. Soc. gen. Microbiol.* **10**, 132 (1960).

67. See M. Hayashi, M. N. Hayashi, and S. Spiegelman, *Proc. natn. Acad. Sci. U.S.A.* **51**, 351 (1964) for references.

68. J. Cairns, *J. molec. Biol.* **6**, 208 (1963); *Cold Spring Harbor Symp. quant· Biol.* **28**, 43 (1963); see also W. Hayes, *Symp. Soc. gen. Microbiol.* **15**, 294 (1965).

69. C. A. Thomas and L. A. MacHattie, *Proc. natn. Acad. Sci. U.S.A.* **52**, 1297 (1964).

70. G. W. Bartlett and Sir Cyril Hinshelwood, *Proc. R. Soc.* B **150**, 318 (1959).

II

THE GROWTH CYCLE OF BACTERIA

1. Introductory

BACTERIA are unicellular organisms and this relative simplicity makes them specially suitable for study in the attempt to understand what light the principles of chemical kinetics can throw on the nature of the processes characteristic of living matter. In their small way bacteria exemplify, as we have indicated, many of the major phenomena of life: they increase and multiply and, as we shall see, they show remarkable powers of adaptation which simulate, though of course do not depend on choice and purpose. Bacteriology was once virtually a branch of medicine, but in fact a minute proportion only of bacteria are pathogenic, and, scientifically at least, they are more important as examples of self-contained biochemical systems than as infective agents.

Most of the cells which will be discussed in what follows will be bacteria, but occasional references will be made to yeasts and other micro-organisms.

Since bacteria are unicellular they naturally do not give much direct help in the understanding of the properties of the tissues and especially the differentiated tissues of which so called higher or more complex organisms are formed. Nevertheless the self-contained character of bacterial cells is far from absolute. The members of a population do exert an influence on one another, even in dilute suspension, by means of substances diffusing through the medium, and in some respects, which will be considered later, a culture of bacteria has distinct aspects of a community. This is specially true of the dense congregations or colonies which can form on solid media, and which themselves possess a character which could be not altogether inappropriately likened to a morphology.

The facts which will be given in this section about general bacteriology will be those only which will be needed by readers primarily interested in chemistry and physics who have not previously acquainted themselves with micro-organisms.[1]

Bacteria multiply by elongation and binary fission. They are isolated from air, from the soil, from animal tissues and fluids both in health and disease, and from other varied and sometimes improbable sounding locations. Their many activities include fixation of nitrogen, formation of methane, and even the consumption of elementary sulphur to form sulphuric acid. Nowadays collections of pure and more or less standard strains exist, in various collections, from which the starting material for investigations can conveniently be obtained.

The sizes and shapes of different bacteria vary between fairly wide limits. Generally speaking there are two main divisions, *cocci*, which are spheroidal in shape and have diameters in the region of 1 μ, and rod-shaped cells, the length of which is usually between 1 and 10 μ, and the breadth from 0·2 to 1 μ. Under special conditions much longer filaments may be formed, and occasionally Y-shaped cells are produced (which can divide in such a way as to produce new cells at each arm of the Y).[2] The rods are characteristic of the genera *Bacterium*, *Bacillus*, and others. The bacteria of individual strains are themselves variable as will appear.

There has been a more or less generally accepted system of classification of bacteria, which, however, is not of special interest for the present purpose, being based, from practical necessity, upon somewhat mixed categories. In one group the species are distinguished by their specific fermentation reactions with sugars, in another by the action upon blood, and so on. All that will be necessary here will be to mention for practical purposes, some of the important genera and species. Among cocci, the two main classes are *Staphylococcus* and *Streptococcus*. In the former the spheroidal cells tend to remain bunched together in grape-like clusters, whereas in the latter they tend to remain adhering to one another in long chains. Both groups are often associated with febrile and pus-producing infections, and the subdivisions on the whole are based upon criteria which are principally of concern to pathology. The genus *Bacterium* is an important one containing several common species. *Escherichia coli* is the common inhabitant of the intestine, *Aerobacter aerogenes* (*Bacterium lactis aerogenes*) is a closely related species obtainable from soil, *Salmonella typhi*, *Salmonella paratyphi A*, and *Salmonella paratyphi B* are respectively responsible for typhoid and the two commoner forms of paratyphoid. There are also various forms of *Shigella*. All these constitute a rather well-defined group, the subdivisions of which rest upon biochemical reactions such as the specific fermentations of sugars and on antigenic reactions.

Another large genus of rod-like organisms is that of *Bacillus*, which includes many species pathogenic and non-pathogenic. Typical members are *Bacillus anthracis* and *Bacillus subtilis*, the latter frequent in atmospheric dust. The outstanding characteristic of the group is their ability to assume an alternative morphological modification, considerably more resistant to heat and chemical agencies and known as a spore. Spores are normally more nearly spherical than the bacilli from which they are derived, and more refractile. They also have different staining properties. They represent a resting form of the cell and when placed in suitable nutrient media are re-transformed into bacilli, a process referred to as germination.[3] Germination must precede division. The conditions for the formation of spores are very specific and they are sometimes formed in a more or less constant proportion as growth proceeds.

Two other genera only will be mentioned here: *Corynebacterium* of which *Corynebacterium diphtheriae* is a typical member and which is characterized by having a rod-like form with slightly swollen, or 'club-like' ends: and *Mycobacterium* characterized by the presence of a waxy constituent and known from certain consequent staining properties as 'acid-fast'. The bacteria of tuberculosis belong to this class.

Bacteria have long been divided into two classes known as Gram-positive and Gram-negative respectively, according to their behaviour in the Gram staining test. The cells are treated with methyl violet and then with dilute iodine solution. After this they are washed with alcohol or acetone for a standard time. With the one class the stain is retained and with the other it is lost. The test depends upon some characteristic of the surface of the cell. The chemical nature of the staining is highly complex and no single component appears adequately to explain the reaction.[4] Although the behaviour of some bacteria is rather indefinite, the Gram test on the whole separates the genera into two main groups. Of the genera which were (somewhat arbitrarily) selected for mention above, *Streptococcus*, *Staphylococcus*, *Mycobacterium*, *Corynebacterium*, and *Bacillus* are Gram-positive while *Bacterium* is Gram-negative. Plenty of other Gram-negative genera are, however, known.

Vast differences exist between the composition of the walls of Gram-positive and Gram-negative cells.[5-10] A recurring type of basal unit containing the hexosamines, glucosamine, and muramic acid and three amino-acids bound in peptide linkage has been found in the former. A given bacterial species often has a characteristic pattern of amino-acids, amino-sugars, and sugars superimposed on the basal mucopeptide unit. The walls of Gram-negative organisms are much more complex in composition and contain lipids, proteins, and polysaccharides as well as a relatively smaller amount of the mucopeptide components found in Gram-positive organisms. Much work has been carried out on the composition of the cell walls and much remains to be done. A group of polymers containing ribitol or glycerol phosphates, the teichoic acids, have also been found in Gram-positive cell walls.[11]

Mucopeptide is thought to be the major component responsible for the mechanical support which preserves the shape of the bacterial cell and in Gram-positive organisms may amount to well over half the total material, though in Gram-negative organisms it may be as low as about 5 per cent. Rogers[6] pictures the elongation of the polymer chains in the formation of these mucopeptides as determining the shape of the organism.

Stable 'L-forms' of bacteria are known in which the cell wall is almost entirely absent[12] and a similar situation is found in pleuropneumonia-like (PPLO) organisms.[13] A somewhat analogous state can be achieved by the action of benzyl penicillin on *Escherichia coli* although a total loss of wall components does not appear to take place. The resulting structures called protoplasts are only stable, however, in a medium of high osmotic pressure and on removal of the drug are said to revert to the normal rod-like forms.[14]

Bacteria are very variable, and although the main species characteristics usually remain fixed, a great deal of doubt and controversy may surround the question of detailed subdivisions. This variability will be discussed in detail in connexion with adaptation and mutation.

Attempts continue to be made to improve the classification of bacteria.[15] The potentialities of a cell are laid down in its genetic code and the interesting question now arises as to how far a classification based on a complete knowledge of this code (assuming that all the practical difficulties in unravelling it could be overcome) would agree with one based on the sort of tests just described.

Complex or 'hybrid' formation takes place under suitable conditions between DNA molecules containing similar base sequences, and using this criterion Hoyer et al.[16] have shown that homologies exist between the DNA extracted from various animals, e.g. salmon and chickens. There are, however, many practical difficulties to be overcome and it is not known how similar two sequences of nucleotides must be to form duplex structures under specified experimental conditions. In gauging hybrid formation conditions may be chosen which have been called 'lax' or 'stringent'. Stringent conditions (i.e. involving structures which can withstand incubation at $60°$ C in 0.3 M NaCl overnight) are thought to minimize adventitious associations of smaller significance.[16]

Bacteria, of course, assume the temperature of their surroundings. They survive cooling to very low temperatures, but are usually killed by heating to about 55–65°. Some species, called thermophilic, not only survive, but flourish at higher temperatures than these. Spores usually survive even prolonged heating at 100°. For many bacterial species the temperature of optimum growth is between 30° and 40°.

Yeasts are unicellular organisms like bacteria, but usually a good deal larger. They appear in nature in fermenting fluids, and are cultivated as more or less standard strains, brewer's yeasts and baker's yeasts. *Saccharomyces cerevisiae* is perhaps the best-known type. Biochemically they resemble bacteria fairly closely, but there are some important differences in other ways. They multiply by budding rather than by elongation. Characteristically yeasts form spores, sporulation demanding nicely adjusted conditions, and many strains appear to have lost the power to achieve it.

Much more commonly than bacteria yeast cells conjugate, two 'haploid' cells fusing to give a 'diploid'. Diploids may sporulate to give a structure, called an ascus, containing four spores. Each spore (isolable by microdissection methods) can give rise to a new haploid strain. Properties of the original haploid strains involved in the conjugation may appear in these derived strains in simple Mendelian ratios.

2. Cultivation

Bacteria may be cultivated on solid or in liquid media. The former consist usually of a jelly (such as agar-agar or gelatine) to which appropriate nutrient substances have been added. A suspension containing the bacteria at a suitable dilution is smeared over the surface (or sometimes inserted by puncture, or mixed before the setting of the jelly) and the preparation, usually in a shallow covered glass dish, is incubated for a day or more at a suitable temperature. *Colonies* of bacteria grow, each from a single cell. If the original dilution was suitably judged, these colonies are well separated from one another. They are more or less circular in shape, and quite often about 1 mm in diameter (though the size varies a good deal from case to case). According to their actual appearance and texture colonies have sometimes been classified as *rough* (R) and *smooth* (S), the former having wavy edges and a crinkly surface, the latter being even and glossy.[1] Many bacteria are capable of giving either type according to conditions.

The cultivation of colonies is the normal means of isolating pure strains of bacteria. Since each colony grows from one cell, a mixture of bacteria can be separated by selecting individual colonies. Another technique consists in the direct manipulation of single cells under the microscope. This is more difficult but obviates the risk that a given colony may have originated from two cells adventitiously adhering together.

Many liquid media are available for growing bacteria. A common one is bouillon or broth, prepared from meat, but, for the kind of experimental work with which we shall be chiefly concerned, defined media consisting of sugars, amino-acids, certain salts, and, on occasion, specific growth factors are more satisfactory.

A small quantity of a parent culture, the *inoculum*, is transferred to the culture medium. As fresh growth proceeds the medium becomes turbid, and the course of the proliferation can be followed either by turbidimetric measurements, or by the direct counting of samples under the microscope. For the latter purpose a small chamber of accurately known depth and provided with fine rulings of known spacing is needed. The haemocytometer used for counting blood-cells is very convenient. Turbidity is perceptible with about ten million cells per ml and with some strains of bacteria the growth goes on till the number per ml exceeds a thousand million.

For many purposes it is expedient to maintain the strain by *serial subculture*. When fully grown, a given fraction (say 1/100, 1/1000, or 1/10 000) of a culture is used as inoculum for a fresh supply of the original medium.

It is advantageous to bubble a gentle stream of air through many cultures during growth. When a culture is growing rapidly very vigorous aeration may be required if there is to be no lack of oxygen. A class of bacteria known as anaerobes, on the other hand, must be grown in almost complete absence of oxygen.

Bacterial enzymes do not operate only when cells are growing. The culture may be centrifuged and the cells separated from the growth medium. They may then be suspended in appropriate solutions in which chemical reactions, such as reduction, deamination, hydrogen peroxide decomposition, and so on, are caused to take place by the bacterial enzymes, the activity and amounts of which can be thus characterized.[17]

For some purposes, as when large quantities of cells are wanted, a process known as continuous culture is conveniently used (see p. 79). In it medium is siphoned off from a growing culture while fresh medium is added at such a rate as to maintain a steady cell population.

3. Raw materials required for bacterial growth

Supplies of carbon and nitrogen are obviously needed. Phosphorus and sulphur must be provided, and inorganic phosphate and sulphate are usually quite satisfactory sources. Some bacteria require gaseous oxygen and most, if not all, require a small concentration of carbon dioxide. Traces of iron and magnesium are usually required as well as potassium, and sometimes calcium.

The sequence of cell reactions can begin with very simple chemical substances, since some bacteria will grow readily in media which contain ammonium ion or nitrate ion as the sole source of nitrogen, and a comparatively simple compound such as glycerol or acetate as the sole source of carbon. From such raw materials all the complex and varied products can be built up by what must be a very versatile and adaptable system of transformations involving a vast number of stages.

With many bacteria, however, more elaborate molecules must be supplied ready-made, or growth is impossible. The demands in this respect are continuously graded between the so-called 'exacting' and the 'non-exacting' strains.[18]

Certain bacteria refuse to grow except in quite specialized environments: *Mycobacterium leprae*, for example, is particularly exigent. Most of the pathogenic streptococci need ready-made glutamine.[19] In the absence of air *Staphylococcus aureus* in an artificial medium was found to need uracil and according to Richardson[20] none of twenty-one somewhat similar compounds would serve instead. *Staphylococcus aureus* has also to be provided with a potential source of the —SH group,[21] provided in an organic compound. Many examples of this sort of demand are known. In addition to glutamine and uracil, one might mention nicotinic acid, thiamin,[18] tryptophan,[22] and various amino-acids or combinations of amino-acids.[18] Non-exacting strains may become exacting after irradiation with X-rays or ultraviolet light. Different substrains isolated as colonies after irradiation may show requirements for one or other or several of the amino-acids which normally occur in proteins.

A natural hypothesis is that compounds similar to these various growth requirements are intermediates in the chain of processes occurring in cells which can start with simpler materials. This view receives support from the fact that many bacteria as originally isolated (for example, from animal tissues in which they have been parasitic) require definite organic compounds for growth, but can be 'trained' to dispense with them. The training is effected by serial subculture, with gradual reduction to zero of the supply of the compound in question. For example, *Salmonella typhi* normally requires tryptophan, which is an essential constituent of protein, but can be induced to build it up, first from indole and then from ammonia.[23]

We shall not discuss here the question whether training modifies all the members of the population or simply selects from a spectrum of different types. This matter will be gone into fully in later chapters. Quite independently of this problem the training sequence in the example just quoted suggests strongly that bacteria which utilize ammonia to form the tryptophan units of their substance do so by way of indole.

In the light of such observations on the gradations in the series of growth requisites passed through during training, it would seem that the essential difference between the exacting and the non-exacting types of bacteria is merely the precise point in the series of reactions at which operations begin. In the exacting species the necessary enzymes for the earlier stages of the sequence are either absent or are inactive until they have been developed by an adaptive process. When cultivated in a highly specific environment where complex organic substances important to cell life are freely provided, the enzymes necessary for the simpler initial stages of synthesis pass out of use. In this way pathogenic (i.e. parasitic) bacteria usually become exacting (see also enzyme repression, p. 278).

The intermediates added as ready-made growth factors are not necessarily used in the form in which they are supplied: they may rather be the source of intermediates common to more than one possible reaction. When *Staphylococcus aureus* has become adapted to grow without added alanine, it becomes able to dispense also with valine, leucine, and histidine, which it normally demands.[24] This suggests that the mechanisms which are mobilized deal not specifically with the individual amino-acids but with something common to them all.

The overall picture is that of a sequence of linked reactions which begins with the utilization of such simple compounds as carbon dioxide and ammonia, and builds up successively more complex molecules. Some of these are diffusible and pass from one region of enzymatic activity to the next, there to be used in the further stages of the sequence. At each stage macromolecular polycondensation reactions must occur since in growth the actual substance of each part of the cell is reproduced.

The chemical functions of the various regions of enzymatic activity may well be relatively simple and the changes occurring at some of them may well yield fragments of great reactiveness such as free radicals. If there are a large number of such regions, then the permutations and combinations possible are very great and the synthetic and transformative power of the cell will be as varied as it is intense. It is helpful to think of the chemical operation of the cell less as the piecing together of a jigsaw cut into large fragments which will fit together in one way only, than as the formation of a mosaic from simple units which can be combined in innumerable ways. There will be occasion later to return to this analogy, and to express it in a somewhat different form.

4. Alkali metal ions

Whether simple or complex, the sources of carbon, nitrogen, phosphorus, and sulphur, as well naturally as of hydrogen and oxygen have to provide the basis of the actual cell substance. The function of metal ions is somewhat different, and though possibly some may, like iron and magnesium, be incorporated in the structure of enzymes, they may be said to be functional rather than structural. As an example we will consider the position of the alkali metals. Although bacteria vary somewhat in their alkali metal ion needs, the example of *Aerobacter* may be taken as typical. The necessity for potassium is shown by the following experiments.[25] In the simple medium in which *Aerobacter aerogenes* is commonly grown a sodium phosphate–potassium phosphate buffer (see p. 56) is used and thus sodium and potassium ions are present in abundance. If, however, the medium is buffered entirely by sodium phosphates and the concentration of potassium ions is reduced, the total population of cells which can be supported becomes almost linearly dependent on the potassium ion concentration in the range 10^{-6} to 10^{-4} g ion/l. Moreover, when the concentration is reduced below 2×10^{-5} g ion/l. the growth rate becomes progressively slower. On the other hand, in a medium buffered by a mixture of potassium phosphates the concentration of sodium ions has no effect on either the total population or the growth rate. The ionic radii of the unhydrated alkali metal ions are:

$$Li^+ \quad Na^+ \quad K^+ \quad Rb^+ \quad Cs^+$$
$$0{\cdot}78 \quad 0{\cdot}98 \quad 1{\cdot}33 \quad 1{\cdot}49 \quad 1{\cdot}65 \text{ Ångström units}$$

and these figures throw light on the reason why potassium ions can be replaced by rubidium ions, though, with about one-quarter of the efficiency, but not at all by the smaller lithium or sodium ions or the larger caesium ions.

During the early stages of growth or during the oxidation of carbon substrates in the absence of a nitrogen source, potassium (or rubidium) ions enter the cell and the positive stream they create is balanced by the simultaneous entry of negatively charged phosphate ions. These positive ions appear to become bound in some structure involving an enzyme surface where phosphorylated intermediates arising from the metabolism of the carbon source in the medium are dealt with, and for this binding to be effective it seems that the size of the ion must be specifically correct and not merely small enough for entry. The phosphate is used for the synthesis of cell material (e.g. nucleic acids) and the potassium or rubidium ions are set free to deal with more phosphate.

Experiments with radioactive tracers have shown that when the pH of cells actively metabolizing glucose is lowered, alkali ions are displaced by the direct competition of hydrion. This state of affairs is only temporary and is followed by an increased uptake of alkali ion once certain readjustments in the cells have taken place. During growth or fermentation, however, a stage is eventually reached when the increase in hydrion concentration is too great for such adjustments, and the enzyme reactions by which phosphate is incorporated into cell material are slowed down. The alkali metal ions which in other circumstances would be released now remain bound and the total amount in the cell increases. In this sense these ions protect the cell against the effect of the adverse pH. When growth or fermentation ceases the alkali metal ions leave the cell. They are not essential structural components of the cell, at any rate in considerable amounts, but serve as enzyme activators and cellular regulators.

Results somewhat similar to the above were obtained with *Escherichia coli*[26] but here, in contrast with the example of *Aerobacter*, caesium could replace potassium. *Staphylococci* have also been shown to need potassium but not sodium ions.[27]

5. Phases of growth

According to what has already been said, a growing cell constitutes a manufactory with numerous departments, the conveyor belt leading from one to another being represented by the appropriate concentration gradients. Raw materials are broken down and built up into fresh forms in a series of stages. Moreover, since the material of the cell is constantly increasing in amount, and since new cells continually formed by division are nearly identical with the original ones, every single part of the machinery must in effect devote some of its effort to making more of the same kind. If all the raw materials are supplied from a constant environment, a steady state will be established in which all parts of the cell material expand at rates such that their relative proportions remain unchanged. As has been explained (p. 15), the scale effect would interfere with the maintenance of a steady state were it not for the phenomenon of cell division, which enables it to be preserved. With regular division, and a constant environment each cell can go on growing at the same rate as its parent. Hence the total number increases with time in geometrical progression according to the law

$$n = n_0 e^{kt},$$

where n_0 is the original number and n the number at time t, k being a constant. This law is in fact rather closely followed (with understandable deviations which will be discussed later) over quite wide ranges of growth. The steady state during which the above law is followed is known as the *logarithmic phase* of growth. If in its own individual generation time the cell always grows from one standard size to just double and then divides, then for a large number of cells in random phases of their individual generation periods the total mass will be strictly proportional to the total number. In fact, however, as the medium changes the mean size of the cells varies somewhat as will be considered on p. 86. Except in extreme cases this variation is not very marked and a straight line plot against time is shown over a considerable range both by the logarithm of the cell mass and that of cell number.

A peculiar phenomenon known as *synchronization* can sometimes be induced in a culture by certain kinds of shock treatment such as exposure to sudden changes of temperature.[28] Growth is interrupted and when it is allowed to begin again it sometimes happens that all the cells are, as it were, in phase and the next division occurs in all of them more or less simultaneously. The result is that the curve of the logarithm of cell number against time shows a series of steps which the corresponding mass curve does not. The action of the shock is complicated and a little obscure but a more obvious way of achieving the same end is to separate from an actively growing culture by a suitable filtration process cells in a narrow size range.[28] Synchronous cultures, it should be said, never preserve this character for many generations but soon revert to a state in which the phases of the individual cells in their cycles are random. In the synchronous cultures prepared by shock treatment the DNA has been stated to increase only in one short fraction of the cell generation time whereas the RNA and the protein are synthesized steadily throughout. But results obtained with cells far removed from any steady state are of very uncertain meaning (see p. 108) and it is significant that with synchronized cells obtained by the gentler method of size fractionation by filtration this finding is not repeated.[29, 30]

Cells are seldom grown in a constant environment except when the method of continuous culture (p. 79) is employed. In more usual practice they are inoculated into a given volume of medium and allowed to grow, either until an essential raw material has been exhausted, or until the

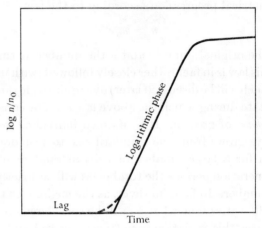

FIG. 5. Bacterial growth cycle: total numbers.

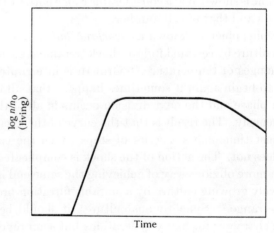

FIG. 6. Bacterial growth cycle: numbers of living cells.

metabolic products which they themselves form inhibit further multiplication. The total number of cells then remains constant. The culture is now in the *stationary phase*. The total *stationary population* is to be distinguished from the number of living cells (viable population), which begins after a time to diminish.

During the stationary phase certain changes must occur in the living cells themselves. In the first place, the activities of the various enzymes decline.[31, 32] This can be shown by direct experiments on washed cells. In the second place, various intermediates of low molecular weight will be lost from the cell by diffusion. The first effect changes the nature of the actual sites of reaction, while the second completely alters the

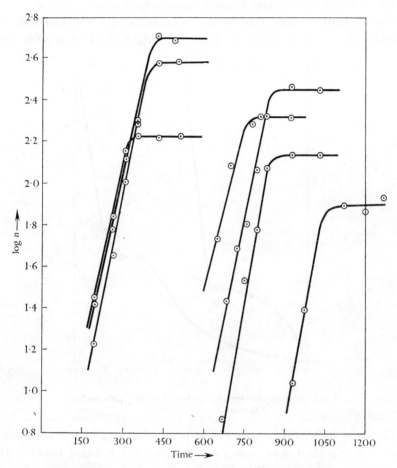

Fig. 7. Experimental growth curves for *Aerobacter aerogenes*.

concentrations and concentration gradients which had been established in the steady state. Both combine to prevent the story from being taken up just where it was left off, even when the cells are transferred to fresh medium. The result is that, before steady growth can be re-established, there is in general a time interval known as the *lag phase*. During this the various intermediates are accumulated once more in the requisite concentrations, and the activities of the enzymes are restored. The latter process may involve a certain amount of reconstruction of material, in the likely event that some denaturation of the protein occurred during the stationary phase. This seems quite probable, since there is a continuous decline in the various functions ending with the actual death of the cell if the stationary phase is unduly prolonged.

The expected sequence of events is indeed observed when cells are inoculated into fresh medium. A lag, the length of which is a function

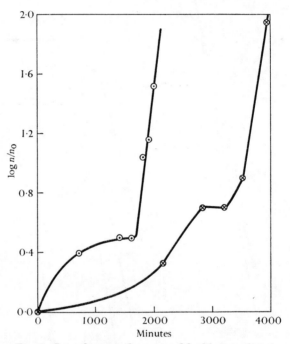

FIG. 8. Irregular growth curves of freshly transferred
Escherichia coli mutabile.

of the previous history, is followed by a period of logarithmic multiplication. Growth then slows down and ceases. The relation between the total number of cells and the time from inoculation is shown by Fig. 5.

The relation between the number actually living and the time is somewhat different and is shown by Fig. 6. Fig. 7 gives some actual growth curves for a strain of *Aerobacter aerogenes* grown in an artificial medium at various concentrations which support correspondingly different values of the stationary population.

If cells have been repeatedly cultured in a given medium and are transferred to one of a different composition, the proportions of the enzymes which they contain may be far removed from that corresponding to optimum growth. The various reactions of the sequence involved in reproduction may be completely out of balance and a steadily maintained logarithmic increase may not occur until several subcultures have been made. Fig. 8 shows some irregular growth curves obtained with *Escherichia coli mutabile* just transferred to an artificial medium after

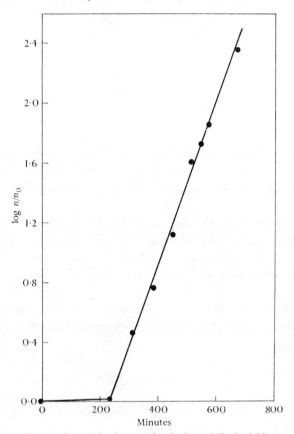

Fig. 9. Logarithmic growth of adapted *Escherichia coli mutabile*.

cultivation in broth. Fig. 9, on the other hand, shows the almost ideally logarithmic form of curve attained after a considerable number of subcultures in this same artificial medium (consisting of ammonium sulphate, lactose, and salts).

6. Experimental measurement of lag and growth rate

The law of growth is $dn/dt = kn$,

where n is the number of cells present at time t, and k is a constant.

The limitations of the law, and the corrections which should be applied in certain circumstances, will be discussed later.

Integration gives: $\ln(n/n_0) = k(t-L)$,

where n_0 is the original number of cells and L is the time from the beginning of the observations (usually the moment of inoculation) at which growth according to logarithmic law begins. L is the lag.

k determines the growth rate. A convenient quantity by which to characterize the growth is the *mean generation time*, that is, the time required for the number of cells to double during the logarithmic phase. Representing it by T we have the equation

$$\ln 2 = k(t_1 - t_2) = kT,$$

whence $$T = \ln 2/k = 0 \cdot 693/k.$$

The mean generation time is best found from a plot of $\ln n$ against time.

From such a plot by extrapolation to $n = n_0$, the value of L may be read off. (Alternatively one plots $\ln(n/n_0)$ against time and extrapolates to zero.)

The transition from the lag phase to the logarithmic phase is not always sharp: it may be gradual as shown by the dotted line in Fig. 5. In such a case it is still convenient to define the lag as the intercept of the truly logarithmic part of the curve on the time axis.

To characterize the behaviour of a bacterial culture it is desirable to determine L, k, and the total population reached by the time growth ceases. Instead of k it is equally convenient to record the mean generation time.

REFERENCES

1. For further information see, for example, W. Burrows, *Textbook of Microbiology*, 18th ed., W. B. Saunders & Co., Philadelphia (1963); *Medical Microbiology*, edited by R. Cruickshank, J. P. Duguid, and R. H. A .Swain, Livingstone, Edinburgh (1965); Topley and Wilson's *Principles of Bacteriology and Immunity*, 5th ed., Sir G. S. Wilson and A. A. Miles, Arnold, London (1964).
2. A. D. Gardner, *J. Path. Bact.* **28**, 189 (1925).
3. See W. G. Murrell, *Symp. Soc. gen. Microbiol.* **11**, 100 (1961).
4. J. W. Bartholomew, F. L. Tucker, and H. Finkelstein, *J. gen. Microbiol.* **36**, 257 (1964).
5. Elizabeth Work, *J. gen. Microbiol.* **25**, 167 (1961); *Nature, Lond.* **179**, 841 (1957).
6. H. J. Rogers, *Symp. Soc. gen. Microbiol.* **15**, 186 (1965).
7. C. S. Cummins, *Int. Rev. Cytol.* **5**, 25 (1956).
8. H. R. Perkins, *Bact. Rev.* **27**, 18 (1963).

9. M. R. J. Salton, *The Bacterial Cell Wall*, Elsevier, Amsterdam (1964).

10. J. T. Park, *Symp. Soc. gen. Microbiol.* **8**, 49 (1958).

11. J. J. Armstrong, J. Baddiley, J. G. Buchanan, B. Carss, and G. R. Greenberg, *J. chem. Soc.*, p. 4344 (1958).

12. O. E. Landman and H. S. Ginoza, *J. Bact.* **81**, 875 (1961).

13. Emmy Klieneberger-Nobel, *Pleuropneumoniae-like Organisms (PPLO)* Mycoplasmataceae, Academic Press, London (1962).

14. J. Lederberg, *Proc. natn. Acad. Sci. U.S.A.* **42**, 574 (1956); R. G. E. Murray, *Symp. Soc. gen. Microbiol.* **12**, 119 (1962); K. McQuillen, *The Bacteria*, edited by I. C. Gunsalus and R. Y. Stanier, Academic Press, New York, **1**, 249 (1960).

15. See *Symp. Soc. gen. Microbiol.* **12** (1962), *passim*.

16. B. H. Hoyer, B. J. McCarthy, and E. T. Bolton, *Science*, **144**, 959 (1964).

17. See J. H. Quastel, *J. Hyg., Camb.* **28**, 139 (1928); B. J. McCarthy and Sir Cyril Hinshelwood, *Proc. R. Soc.* B **150**, 13, 474 (1959).

18. See especially B. C. J. G. Knight, *Bacterial Nutrition*, H.M. Stationery Office (1936).

19. H. McIlwain, P. Fildes, G. P. Gladstone, and B. C. J. G. Knight, *Biochem. J.* **33**, 223 (1939).

20. G. M. Richardson, *Biochem. J.* **30**, 2184 (1936).

21. P. Fildes and G. M. Richardson, *Br. J. exp. Path.* **18**, 292 (1937).

22. P. Fildes, G. P. Gladstone, and B. C. J. G. Knight, *Br. J. exp. Path.* **14**, 189 (1933).

23. P. Fildes and B. C. J. G. Knight, *Br. J. exp. Path.* **14**, 343 (1933); P. Fildes, ibid. **21**, 67 (1940).

24. G. P. Gladstone, *Br. J. exp. Path.* **18**, 322 (1937).

25. A. A. Eddy and Sir Cyril Hinshelwood, *Proc. R. Soc.* B **136**, 544 (1950); **138**, 228, 237 (1951); A. A. Eddy, T. C. N. Carroll, C. J. Danby, and Sir Cyril Hinshelwood, *Proc. R. Soc.* B **138**, 219 (1951).

26. R. B. Roberts, D. B. Cowie, P. H. Abelson, E. T. Bolton, and R. J. Britten, *Studies of Biosynthesis in* Escherichia coli, p. 76, Carnegie Inst. of Washington Publication 607, Washington, D.C. (1955).

27. R. A. Shooter and H. V. Wyatt, *Br. J. exp. Path.* **37**, 311 (1956); **38**, 473 (1957); J. H. B. Christian and Judith A. Waltho, *J. gen. Microbiol.* **35**, 205 (1964).

28. See for details and references *Synchrony in Cell Division and Growth*, edited by E. Zeuthen, Interscience, New York (1964).

29. D. Herbert, *Symp. Soc. gen. Microbiol.* **11**, 391 (1961).

30. F. E. Abbo and A. B. Pardee, *Biochim. Biophys. Acta*, **39**, 478 (1960).

31. E. F. Gale, *Biochem. J.* **34**, 392, 486 (1940).

32. B. J. McCarthy and Sir Cyril Hinshelwood, *Proc. R. Soc.* B **150**, 410 (1959).

III

PHASES OF THE GROWTH CYCLE

1. General

THE functioning of the cell depends upon highly elaborate sequences of reactions involving many stages, and combined in a great variety of ways. Intermediates must diffuse from one region of enzyme activity to another: genetic information is transferred continuously by chemical messengers, and the whole complex organization must come into a state of balance before it is working smoothly.

Even the relatively simple reactions of the inanimate world frequently show *induction periods* during which, for example, the concentrations of various active radicals or free atoms build up from zero to the steady values which they presently assume. With the much more complicated processes of the living cell one must expect in general an analogous period of induction, or as it is usually called a *lag*, which precedes the establishment of the logarithmic phase. During the earlier stages of the lag phase there is no apparent increase in cell substance. As the end of it approaches there is an increase in cell volume and this is usually heralded by an increased production of metabolites such as carbon dioxide,[1] and sometimes an excretion of amino-acids into the medium.[2] It is as though sections of the cell factory were now working and turning out components which are rejected because other parts are not yet ready to process them.

The lag is shorter in media which contain a varied supply of ready-made compounds such as amino-acids, than in the simpler artificial media the use of which demands more preliminary stages to be gone through.

Lag, growth rate, and stationary population may vary in complete independence. A long delay may be followed by rapid growth, slow growth may set in with very little lag. Some adverse conditions may lower the total population while having little effect on the rate or the lag. This fact emphasizes the extremely misleading character of the information which may be inferred from records that growth in a culture is + or − after some arbitrary period of time such as 48 hours. Occasionally the presence or absence of genetic characters has been judged on this basis. The method creates a wholly artificial kind of discreteness or discontinuity. The contrast of plus and minus suggests sharply differing characters, in a way which a lag of 40 hours compared with one of 50 hours does not.

2. Lag and concentration of medium constituents

When artificial media are thoroughly freed from carbon dioxide by a stream of purified air, the growth of several typical species of bacteria is delayed indefinitely.[3] In broth, the cells may cause an active enough

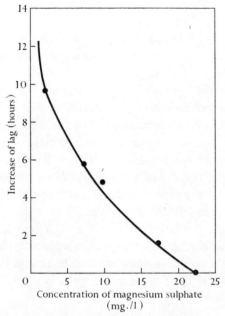

Fig. 10. Lag increase on reduction of magnesium concentration.

fermentation to produce carbon dioxide more rapidly than it can be carried away by the air-stream. The carbon dioxide affects not only the lag, but also the growth rate, as has been found for *Aerobacter aerogenes*[4] and for *pneumococcus*.[5] With the former the optimum amount of carbon dioxide corresponded to about 0·15 per cent in the gas phase, which, under the conditions of working, corresponded to about 4×10^{-8} g mole/ ml.[4] Carbonate and bicarbonate ions will not replace carbon dioxide itself.[3]

In an artificial medium containing glucose and a phosphate buffer the lag of *Aerobacter aerogenes* is indefinitely prolonged as the concentration of magnesium ions is reduced towards zero.[6] Biochemical evidence shows that magnesium is a phosphatase activator (see Chapter I, section 8), so that the undue slowing down of a phosphorylation reaction can evidently cause the observed prolongation of the lag. Fig. 10 shows the manner in which the lag increases as the magnesium concentration falls.

With some strains of *Aerobacter aerogenes* the lag increases somewhat with increase in the glucose concentration (of an ammonium sulphate, glucose, phosphate buffer medium) from 4 to 40 g/l., but with others it remains almost constant over this range. Change in the ammonium sulphate concentration of the same medium from 0·2 to 5 g/l. has little effect. This is shown in Fig. 14c.

These results are hardly surprising, since the concentrations are large, even at the lower ends of their respective ranges. Experiments with very low concentrations are not easy, since, in the range where a significant effect on the lag might be expected, there would be too little total carbon or nitrogen in the medium to support appreciable growth. From the numbers quoted above in connexion with the carbon dioxide requirements it can be seen how small are the concentrations at which optimum effects are reached in respect of lags or growth rates. But the matter is quite different in respect of total population, the support of which demands quite large supplies of material even though the concentration at which it is furnished is not important.

More surprisingly the influence of pH on the lag phase of *Aerobacter aerogenes* in an artificial phosphate-glucose medium is small over a range in which numerous enzymes show very wide changes in activity. The contrast is illustrated by Fig. 11 and Fig. 12 (with which also Fig. 14d may be compared).

The lag is largely and specifically influenced by various drugs, and this influence is markedly subject to adaptive changes. This subject will be considered at length in a subsequent chapter.

3. Lag and age of cells

Lag depends upon the age of cells.[7] The quantitative study of the lag phase fully confirms the idea that bacteria which can utilize the simplest sources of carbon and nitrogen build up their substance by way of intermediates which can sometimes diffuse from the cell into the medium, and which, therefore, must certainly be able to pass from one internal department of the cell to another in the manner suggested by the conveyor-belt analogy.

We shall begin with the consideration of some quantitative work on *Aerobacter aerogenes*.[8] This bacterium grows well in a medium consisting

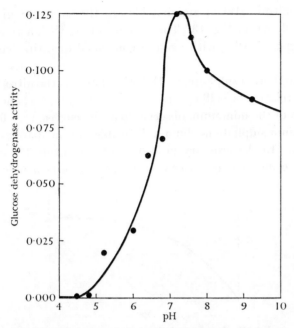

FIG. 11. Variation of glucose-dehydrogenase activity of
Aerobacter aerogenes with pH.

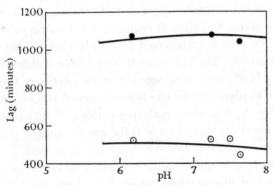

FIG. 12. Variation of lag with pH.

of a phosphate buffer of pH 7·1, glucose, a small amount of magnesium, and, as source of nitrogen, either ammonium sulphate or an amino-acid type of compound such as asparagine. Cells may be transferred from a growing culture to a fresh supply of the same medium and the length of the lag may be determined. It proves to be a definite and characteristic function of the age of the parent cells. By age is meant the time between the start of growth of the parent culture and the transfer of the inoculum in the subculture. When amino-acids are the source of nitrogen the result is as shown in Fig. 13. The absence of lag with a young culture and the increase in lag with age are confirmed quantitatively by this figure.

When ammonium sulphate, on the other hand, is the nitrogen source, the lag-age relation is as illustrated in Figs. 14a, 14b, 14c, and 14d. The explanation of the minimum, observable in the curves, is as follows. In the ammonium sulphate medium a diffusible intermediate escapes into the solution. In the ordinary procedure of subculture the cells transferred to the new medium carry with them a certain volume of the

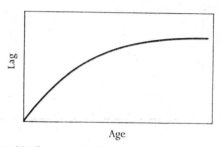

FIG. 13. Lag–age relation in amino-acid medium.

original solution. When the inoculum consists of very young cells, there is not enough of the diffusible intermediate transferred to satisfy needs in the new medium, and time is required for it to be produced. With older inocula, enough is transferred to supply these needs, and the lag falls to a minimum. The subsequent rise in the value of the lag on further ageing is of course analogous to what occurs in the amino-acid medium. The explanation of the falling part of the curve in Fig. 14a is confirmed by the fact that small quantities of solution separated (by filtration or centrifuging) from a fully grown culture and added to young cultures completely remove the delay in growth.

There is an obvious relationship between this influence of filtrate on the lag phase and observations which have been made in other connexions upon diffusible co-enzymes. Sahyun, Beard, Schultz, Snow, and Cross[9] described a 'growth activator' for *Escherichia coli*. Diffusible co-enzymes have been postulated in connexion with the deaminases of *Escherichia coli* by Gale and Stephenson[10] and in connexion with the lactic acid dehydrogenase of the same organism by Yudkin.[11] With the deaminases of *Clostridium Welchii* there is a variation of activity with dilution which also strongly suggests a diffusible substance capable of escaping from the cells in the earlier stages of growth.[12]

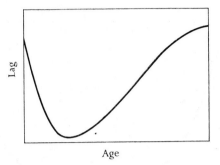

FIG. 14a. General form of lag–age relation
in ammonium sulphate medium.

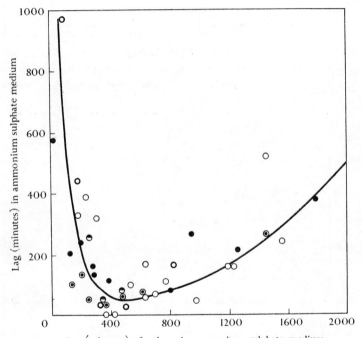

FIG. 14b. Experimental lag–age curves for various parent cultures.

The lag of the young cultures is clearly interpretable in terms of a
diffusible intermediate involved in the utilization of the simpler nitrogen
sources. The increased lag which accompanies ageing beyond the point
of minimal lag may be explained by all or any of the following factors:
(a) chemical decay of active intermediates in the cells or the surrounding
medium; (b) loss of intermediates by diffusion from the cell; (c) inactivation of cell enzymes by processes such as denaturing of proteins;

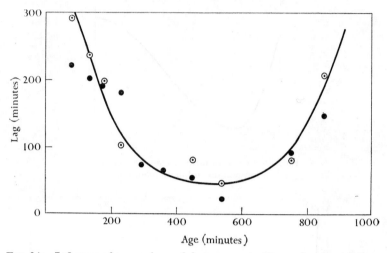

Fig. 14c. Influence of ammonium sulphate concentration on lag–age relation.
⊙ 0·2 g/l. $(NH_4)_2SO_4$　　　　　● 5·0 g/l. $(NH_4)_2SO_4$

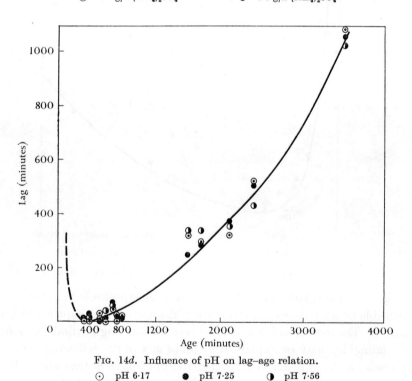

Fig. 14d. Influence of pH on lag–age relation.
⊙ pH 6·17　　　● pH 7·25　　　◑ pH 7·56

(*d*) chemical saturation of free radical ends of macromolecules so that they become incapable of further expansion. The relative importance of these is uncertain: (*b*) undoubtedly does occur and (*a*) may very well do; (*c*) and (*d*) stand possibly in a fairly close relation. The activities of individual enzymes, as shown by tests on washed cells, undoubtedly decline as ageing progresses, and the time scale of this process is in fact

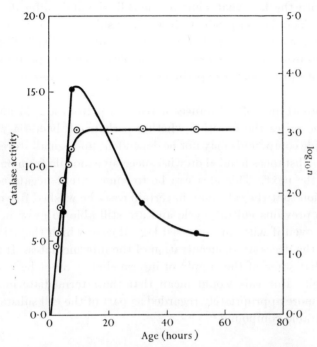

Fig. 15. Variation in catalase activity of *Aerobacter aerogenes* with age of cells.

● catalase activity   ⊙ growth curve

comparable with that of the lag development. An example is given in Fig. 15 which shows the variation of the catalase activity of *Aerobacter aerogenes*[13] and may be compared with Fig. 13. One observation which suggests, though it does not prove, the dispersal of supplies of intermediate during the first stages of the development of the lag of ageing cultures is that the value of the latter often rises fairly rapidly at first and then settles down to a more or less steady value. This does not suggest a progressive decay of cell substance so much as a fairly rapid loss of intermediates. On the other hand, at still greater ages the lag eventually increases rapidly and the cells die, so that the inactivation of actual cell material does in the end occur. The rate of 'ageing' of the cells as represented by the increase of lag is a function of the medium and seems to be increased by acidity. For example, *Aerobacter aerogenes* develops lag less rapidly in a glycerol medium than in a glucose medium.[14] In the former little acid is formed, in the latter considerable amounts. It may be mentioned here that the lag over a space of many days may in some cases actually show slight rises and falls. This is probably connected with the fact that some of the cells die and suffer destruction, and that degradation products from their substance become available to permit a small renewal of growth in some of the others. The effect is sometimes termed cannibalization.[15] Sometimes it is important to know for the interpretation of experiments whether it is present or not (see p. 223).

The importance of substances carried over from an old medium to a new one raises the question whether perhaps all bacteria which use very simple compounds may not be dependent upon small stores of more complex substances handed on with successive inocula from one growth cycle to the next. This idea can be to some extent negatived by the observation that the cells may in certain cases be washed free of filtrate from the previous culture cycle and are still able to grow in the new medium, even if with an increased lag—during which they themselves build up the necessary concentration of the intermediates. It might be argued that some of the supply of intermediate cannot be washed out of the cell. But this would mean that the intermediate in question could be more appropriately regarded as part of the cell substance than as a separable compound.

4. Lag in relation to the number of cells transferred in the inoculum

Numerous qualitative references to the influence of inoculum size on lag occur in the earlier literature.[16] The phenomenon is best understood in relation to the lag of young cultures discussed in the last section. If the termination of the lag demands a certain minimum concentration of a diffusible intermediate, and if insufficient of this is transferred with the actual medium accompanying the inoculum, then the cells must build it up in the new environment for themselves. Since they all form the intermediate and pour it out into the medium to make a common store, the more of them there are to contribute their quota the sooner is the critical concentration built up.

Aerobacter aerogenes shows a very marked dependence of lag upon number of cells in the inoculum when growth takes place in the ammonium sulphate medium referred to above. When amino-acids are used instead of ammonium sulphate the young inocula do not lag, a fact which shows growth to be much less dependent upon diffusible intermediates in the solution: and accordingly there is little or no influence of inoculum size on the lag. The contrast is illustrated by the following numbers.

TABLE 1

Growth in ammonium sulphate medium

Inoculum size (millions per ml)	Lag (min) observed	Lag (min) calculated— see next section
3·18	136	136
0·42	804	640
0·18	1000	950
0·069	1220	1220

Growth in asparagine medium

Inoculum size (millions per ml)	Lag (min)
37·0	350
18·5	490
7·4	350
2·2	338
0·75	345

5. Quantitative theory of the lag of young inocula and the influence of inoculum size

It will be assumed that the lag ends when the concentration, c, of some active substance reaches in each cell a critical value c'. We write

$$c = \alpha v + \beta n_0 t + \gamma t,$$

where v is the volume of the old medium transferred with the inoculum, and αv is the concentration of the active substance thereby set up. α will be a function of the count n_1 of the parent medium (so long as the bacteria have not been separated from their medium by centrifuging or otherwise), and n_0 is the number of cells per unit volume of the new medium, so that $\beta n_0 t$ is the contribution to c which they will have made in time t by generating active substance in the medium. The cells will retain some of the active substance which they individually build up, so that a term γt is added to represent what is built up in a given cell without the contribution of the others. The simple summation of the last two terms can only be regarded as an approximation, but it will probably not be far from the truth.

When $c = c'$, $t = L$, where L is the lag, whence

$$L = (c'/\beta - \alpha v/\beta)/(n_0 + \gamma/\beta).$$

From this equation may be deduced the following:

(a) When n_0 is constant but v varies, as when filtrate from grown cultures is added with the inoculum, the lag should decrease linearly with increase of v.

(b) When v is constant and n_0 varies, L assumes the form

$$L = \text{const}/(n_0 + \text{const}),$$

which is in fact used to express the numbers in the last column of Table 1 (previous section). (The independent variation of n_0 is effected by centrifuging cells from their medium and then employing cells and medium in any required amounts.)

(c) In the normal subculture experiment variation either of v or n_0 will have an effect.

The requirement (a) is, at any rate qualitatively, satisfied, as illustrated by the following numbers:

n_0 constant:

Added filtrate (v)	0	0·1	0·25	0·5	1·0
Lag	182	106	46	70	12

The form (b) is shown to be approximately correct by the table referred to.

Some measurements illustrating (c) are shown in Fig. 16. Two separate parent cultures of different total count, indicated on the diagram by n_1 (in arbitrary units) were used as inocula for the two series plotted. n_0 is the actual inoculum size (arbitrary units), v varying in proportion to it, since no adjustment by use of washed cells or of filtrate was made. From a set of measurements similar to those given in Table 1 of the last section (constant v) the value of γ/β is calculated. The upper curve in Fig. 16 is then expressible by the equation

$$L = (448 - 2350v)/(n_0 + 0·258).$$

For the lower curve, to obtain the correct value of the lag at the smallest value of n_0, α/β must be taken as 2950. With these various constants the experimental results can be expressed as well as can be expected having regard to the inherent experimental difficulties.

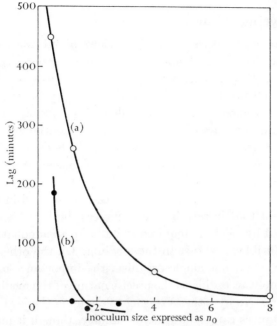

Fig. 16. Dependence of lag upon number of cells in inoculum.
(a) $n_1 = 960$ (b) $n_1 = 132$

	$n_1 = 132$				$n_1 = 960$		
v	n_0	lag (obs.)	lag (calc.)	v	n_0	lag (obs.)	lag (calc.)
0·1	0·57	185	185	0·01	0·40	450	645
0·2	1·13	0	0	0·03	1·20	260	260
0·3	1·70	0	0	0·10	4·0	50	50
0·5	2·83	0	0	0·20	8·0	10	0

Since β should be a constant, the values of α/β will vary as α. To the above values is added one for a very young parent culture and the set is tabulated below:

n_1	25	132	960
α/β	660	2950	2350

This indicates that the amount of active substance in the medium of the parent culture rises at first and then slowly declines as might be expected.

The general outlines of the above theory seem to be in good accord with experiment. The assumption that the lag ends when a definite critical concentration of an active intermediate is built up should not be taken in too literal a way. It is simply an approximation which is nearly enough satisfied in practice.

6. Lag of ageing cultures

In the earlier literature[16, 17] various views about the nature of the lag phase are expressed. Penfold's is the most general and the most satisfactory in that it places the primary emphasis on the step-like character of cell processes, and upon the necessity for the building up of the right intermediates. The so-called 'Bios' hypothesis postulated the need for an adequate concentration of an essential growth factor in the medium. Chesney's hypothesis regarded the lag as the time required for recovery from the toxic effects of the previous environment. In the light of the foregoing discussion it would seem that all these hypotheses contain elements of truth. The facts already described in this chapter leave no doubt that in certain circumstances the lag of a culture may be determined by the time required to build up an adequate concentration of a diffusible substance in the medium. On the other hand, they show that even for one single organism the importance of this factor may vary widely according to the precise nature of the medium in which growth occurs. No hypothesis resting solely upon the idea of diffusible growth substances can claim general validity, though it may perfectly correctly describe what does often happen. It correlates the facts about the influence of inoculum size, for those examples where such facts are met. But they are not met universally.

There is perhaps no real incompatibility between what has been described as Penfold's hypothesis and that of Chesney. The former lays more stress upon the disturbance of the balance of the intermediate substances, the latter upon the deleterious action of toxins. The main observations are consistent with the general idea expressed by Penfold, but leave plenty of room also for the factors upon which Chesney laid stress. During the stationary phase the steady concentrations of the intermediates established in the logarithmic phase will be disturbed and, at the same time, there will be a gradual decay of the enzyme activities, possibly attended with an actual denaturation or destruction of the enzyme substance. The question is not so much which hypothesis is correct, as what is the relative importance of the two factors in each given instance. This is a matter for detailed experiment with various organisms, which are allowed to age under different conditions in different media. One might well imagine that in a medium such as a carefully chosen buffer solution loss of intermediates, at least for a time, would constitute the more serious cause of ageing, while in a very acid medium actual enzyme decay would soon become the dominant factor.

Theories which involve terms such as 'inertia', or 'rejuvenescence' may possibly have some descriptive value in appropriate contexts, but they do not come within the scope of the present considerations.

When we come to consider the question of the integration of cell processes (Chapter V) we shall see that for cultures not already in a steady relation to their environment a lag phase is a general and a necessary consequence of quite general kinetic laws.

One further hypothesis must, however, in the meantime be considered. It is that which has been referred to as the selection hypothesis. According to this, there is a wide range of variation in the power of individual cells to grow. During the lag, although the total number of organisms may show only a negligibly or immeasurably small increase, there is a great multiplication of certain more rapidly growing variants initially present in very minute proportion. If the initial strain is indeed mixed, then such a selection of the more rapidly multiplying types will in fact occur. But it is quite gratuitous to assume without evidence that in all cultures during the lag phase the bulk of the population constitute mere passive spectators of events in which only a favoured few participate. The extent to which such a phenomenon occurs in any given kind of example is, however, determinable by experiment with the help of appropriate methods, one of which will be described.

When a culture is allowed to age considerably, many of the cells die. Quite evidently, then, if an inoculum is taken from such a mixture of living and dead cells an extreme form of selection must take place. Suppose the total number of cells, living and non-living, is initially n_0', of which n_0 are living, and suppose n_0 is small compared with n_0'. Then if the lag is determined by extrapolation to n_0' of the logarithmic part of a growth curve, the time taken for the living cells to increase in number from n_0 to a number comparable with n_0' will be reckoned as part of the lag phase. The value so found may be termed the *apparent lag* in contrast with the *true lag* which is the time between inoculation and the onset of growth among the living cells themselves. In an analogous way, even if the bulk of the population consists not of dead cells but merely of slow-growing ones, the apparent lag of the whole culture will be quite different from the true lags of the individuals which contribute most to the observed growth. Now it can be shown that in certain cultures exhibiting lag, the true lag and the apparent lag are nearly equal. This means that the apparent lag, in these examples, is not in fact the time required for a small minority of the population to grow up to the threshold of measurability: most of the organisms are therefore alive and endowed with at least approximately equal powers of multiplication (although a certain statistical variation about the mean is not excluded). In other examples it appears equally clearly that the apparent lag is due to the presence of a majority of dead cells in the inoculum. It is, therefore, evident that the intermediate case of cultures containing many cells of low reproductive power is in principle very probable. But it is quite incorrect to suppose that this constitutes in any sense a general explanation of lag phenomena.

It will be convenient to consider the means of distinguishing true and apparent lag in a separate section.

7. True and apparent lag[8]

Let n_0 be the initial number of living cells, x_0 the number of dead cells, n the total number at time t, and L the true lag of the living cells. The death of organisms during the period of observation will be neglected, so that we have

$$n = x_0 + n_0 e^{k(t-L)};$$

whence

$$\frac{d \ln n}{dt} = \frac{1}{n} \frac{dn}{dt} = \frac{k n_0 e^{k(t-L)}}{n} = \frac{k(n - x_0)}{n}.$$

If all the cells had been living and had grown at the same rate, $d \ln n/dt$ would have been equal to k: so that we shall in the actual case call it k_{app}. From the above equation then

$$x_0/n = (1 - k_{\mathrm{app}}/k).$$

The true and apparent mean generation times are in the inverse ratios of the corresponding values of k.

In the experimental determination of a growth curve it is usual to employ a small inoculum, in which case the values of n in the range of the actual measurements are very much greater than either n_0 or x_0. When this applies the last equation shows that $(1 - k_{\mathrm{app}}/k)$ approaches zero; in other words that the true and apparent values of the growth rate are indistinguishable. If, however, the normal method of procedure is modified so that a very large inoculum is employed, and if x_0/n_0 is appreciable, then k_{app} will differ significantly from k, and, moreover, the value will vary with n, so that the logarithmic law of growth will not be even approximately followed. The form of the deviation allows the calculation of x_0/n_0. The following is an example of the application of the method.

A culture of *Aerobacter aerogenes* showing considerable lag was inoculated into broth. In one experiment a very small inoculum was employed and the true value of the mean generation time was measured when the logarithmic phase was established: the value was 22·2 minutes. In a second experiment a heavy inoculum, about a hundred times greater than before, was used so that $n_0 + x_0$ remained comparable with n over most of the range of observation. The growth was, however, still logarithmic, with a mean generation time of 22·7 minutes, measured at the point where $n = 90$. From the last equation, therefore,

$$x_0/n = 1 - \frac{22\cdot2}{22\cdot7},$$

whence it follows that x_0 does not exceed about 2 in the arbitrary units employed. n_0 in those same units being 48, it appears that about 96 per cent of the original inoculum was living.

The same method applied in a slightly different way is exemplified by the following. A culture of the same bacterium with a lag of 300 minutes was transferred to an asparagine-glucose medium in a series of experiments with different inoculum sizes. Growth curves were determined and, from their slope at a given value of n, the apparent mean generation times were measured. These were compared with the values calculated from the equation for k_{app} (a) on the assumption that all the cells were alive and that the true lag and the apparent lag were identical, and (b) on the assumption that there was no true lag and that the whole of the observed lag was due to the presence of non-growing cells. The table of typical numbers quoted below shows that for the culture in question (a) comes very much nearer to the truth than (b).

Inoculum size	Mean generation times at value of $n = 220$		
	Calc. (a)	Calc. (b)	Observed
6·5	29·3	30	28
18	29·3	32	29
54	29·3	39	31·5
171	29·3	130	33

Under unfavourable conditions cells do in fact die and as a result the apparent lag increases with time. It sometimes happens that the whole increase can be attributed to this cause, as the following consideration shows. If we *assume* that under rather markedly adverse conditions the increasing apparent lag is due to the drop in n_0, then we can follow the course of n_0 as ageing of the culture proceeds. It is then easy to predict the time at which n_0 will have fallen to less than one cell per culture tube.

At this point, of course, the statistical laws of growth or death no longer apply: nevertheless, we can see that some of the culture tubes, if not most, are likely to contain no living cell at all, and that further ageing should result, not in further prolongation of the apparent lag, but in complete sterility. This is in fact precisely what can sometimes be observed.

All varieties of behaviour thus seem to be represented. But it is as well to restrict the term lag to what we have termed true lag, and to regard non-viability not as a cause of lag, but as a source of error in the measurement of the true lag. In conclusion we may say that the lag is a real period of adjustment.

The attitude which tries to attribute all phenomena of bacterial response and adjustment to selective shifts in populations of discretely different types ignores a basic property of living matter.

8. The stationary phase; maximum bacterial population

Before we treat the logarithmic growth phase, it will be convenient to discuss those factors which lead to the ultimate termination of growth, and which determine the maximum population which the medium can support.

Various suggestions are made in the older literature[16] about the reasons for the cessation of growth at the end of the logarithmic phase. One obvious possibility is exhaustion of necessary nutrient materials in the medium. Some investigators have, however, observed that the organisms can be separated from the fully grown culture and the filtrate used, after various treatments such as boiling, to support further growth on reinoculation. Thus exhaustion cannot invariably be the controlling factor. According to Bail, the cells have filled all the available 'biological space', and other authors assume that the cells have consumed all the available oxygen, or that accumulated toxic products, or unfavourable pH, are responsible for the inhibition of further growth.

The matter becomes clearer in the light of quantitative experiments on the dependence of the maximum population, which will be designated n_s, on various factors, such as the foodstuff concentration and pH. These observations show that according to circumstances either exhaustion of food supplies, on the one hand, or the accumulation of toxic products on the other, may become the limiting factor, even with one and the same organism in the same type of medium.

It will be convenient first to consider what effect dilution of the medium should have upon n_s (1) when cessation of growth is governed by exhaustion, and (2) when it is governed by the accumulation of products antagonistic to further multiplication.

First suppose growth continues until the concentration, g, of a given nutrient falls to zero. In fact the growth rate does not drop until the exhaustion is almost complete (see p. 80). Hence the equation

$$dn/dt = kn$$

describes the growth rate over practically the whole course. If the average rate of consumption is f per organism, then $-dg/dt = fn$, and

$$g = g_0 - f \int_0^t n \, dt.$$

When $g = 0$, $n = n_s$, and neglecting n_0 the initial count, compared with n_s, we have $n_s = g_0 k/f$. In other words the maximum population should be directly proportional to the initial concentration of the foodstuff.

If, on the other hand, toxic products play an important part, their influence on the rate of growth must be expressed. It will be shown later (p. 145) that the reduction in growth rate is often linearly proportional to the concentration of the inhibitor. Thus

$$dn/dt = kn(1-ac),$$

where c is the inhibitor concentration and a is a constant. If, on the average, the toxic material is formed at a rate r per organism, then $dc/dt = nr$. Therefore

$$c = r \int_0^t n \, dt$$

and

$$dn/dt = kn\left(1 - ar \int_0^t n \, dt\right).$$

$\int n \, dt$ is the area under the curve of number against time. Dilution of the medium does not by its effect on nutrient concentrations seriously affect the growth rate, and at the end of a given time the concentration of toxic products formed will at least not be greater than in a more concentrated medium. Thus on dilution the value of n_s will not be decreased.

In the light of these considerations we may examine some observations on *Aerobacter aerogenes*, which has formed the subject of a fairly detailed study.[18, 19, 20]

In a lactose-ammonium tartrate medium the variation of n_s with concentration of lactose and of tartrate respectively is shown in Fig. 17. The relation is evidently nearly linear over most of the range, a result showing that exhaustion is the principal factor. But the slight curvature of the line representing the results with the tartrate, and the pronounced bend corresponding to the higher lactose concentrations, show that toxic products are exerting an influence which begins to be important at the higher concentrations. Similarly in a medium containing glucose and ammonium sulphate n_s varies linearly with the glucose concentration over a fairly wide range, and finally tends to become independent of it.

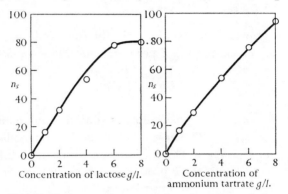

FIG. 17. Influence of concentration on total population.

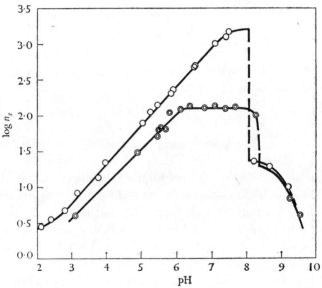

FIG. 18. Influence of pH on total population in two glucose-phosphate media.

That the development of acidity in the medium (for example, by fermentation of carbohydrate) is in itself capable of causing a cessation of growth is shown by the influence of initial pH on the value of n_s. In Fig. 18 it is evident that the value of n_s drops rapidly towards zero if the initial pH is outside a certain range.

The comparison of the two curves in the figure is itself of some interest. The higher curve, which has no horizontal plateau, refers to a medium with a high glucose concentration. The stationary population is seen to vary with the pH over the whole range, indicating that pH is always a limiting factor. The lower curve refers to a dilute glucose solution. It possesses a horizontal plateau, showing that, over a certain range, the pH ceases to be the limiting factor, and that cessation of growth is determined in this region by the exhaustion of glucose. The converse case is illustrated by the following results. In a phosphate-glucose medium of favourable pH the value of n_s is strongly dependent on the glucose concentration. In a similar medium of unfavourable pH exhaustion of glucose ceases to be the limiting factor and the value of n_s becomes independent of glucose concentration.

Relative values of n_s

	Glucose 24·6 g/l.	Glucose 0·99 g/l.
pH 7·11	1000	172
pH 5·20	95	95

When *Aerobacter aerogenes* is grown in glucose–amino-acid media, n_s in general is much increased by aeration of the medium, but to an extent which varies with the particular nitrogen source employed.[20] One effect of the aeration seems to be to aid the removal of an inhibitor, formed during growth, which, if it remains in the medium, can become the limiting factor and bring the logarithmic phase to an end. In a glucose-salts medium the inhibitor blown off during growth is acidic in nature and on neutralization does not have any effect on the growth of a fresh culture.

Monod[21] found that the total population of *Escherichia coli* and of *Bacillus subtilis*, in different media varied according to an accurately linear relation with the concentration of the foodstuff. The following are typical: for *Bacillus subtilis* growing on a medium containing saccharose he finds:

Concentration, c mg/l.	Relative n_s	n_s/c
300	82·5	27·5
250	68·0	27·2
200	56·5	28·3
150	38·3	25·5
100	26·2	26·2
50	15·5	31·0
25	8·0	32·0

Under the conditions of these experiments exhaustion is evidently the limiting factor.

But the maximum concentrations used by Monod are small in comparison with those in which bacteria will still grow readily. For example, the concentration of lactose corresponding to the sharp bend in the curve in Fig. 17 is of about tenfold the highest employed by Monod. While, therefore, his results show the exactness with which concentration in

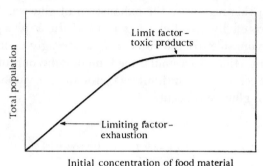

Initial concentration of food material

FIG. 19. Total population and concentration.
General form of relation.

appropriate circumstances determines n_s, they do not give the whole picture, which remains: that exhaustion on the one hand, or adverse changes in the medium on the other, each according to circumstances, is capable of becoming the limiting factor. The general relation is summarized in Fig. 19.

9. The logarithmic phase of growth

In the logarithmic phase the autosynthetic activity of the cell material achieves its full expression.

With a bacterial culture growth may be represented either in terms of total bacterial mass, m, or alternatively, in terms of the *number* of cells, n. Under ideal conditions, when division occurs at a perfectly standard cell size, these two methods are identical. Within a given cell, there must be a small alternation of conditions as it increases from the size of a newly formed cell to that of one just about to divide, but this effect, even though it is itself responsible for the occurrence of division, is, from the point of view of growth rate, averaged out over the whole assemblage of cells making up the culture. Thus, with a constant environment, the two laws,

$$n = n_0 e^{kt} \quad \text{and} \quad m = m_0 e^{kt},$$

express the same thing.

In practice the logarithmic law is found to be a very good approximation over quite a wide range of conditions, both when growth is measured by microscopic counts of cell numbers, and when it is determined by methods such as turbidimetric observations which depend essentially upon total mass.[21]

Turbidimeters may be calibrated in terms of the equivalent number of cells of a standard size, or the calibration may be referred to the dry weight or the nitrogen content of the culture. That turbidity is proportional to total mass has been shown by dry-weight determinations. It also follows from the finding that when bacteria are grown in media containing different carbon sources but with growth limited by the same concentration of ammonium sulphate the turbidimeter counts are identical although the actual number of cells may vary several-fold.[22]

The reasons why, on the one hand, the logarithmic law lacks an absolute character, and, on the other hand, why it is such a good approximation are interesting. It lacks absolute character for the following reasons: first, the concentration of foodstuff in the medium must change as the cells grow. Secondly, products formed by the cells pass into the medium and exert effects, sometimes inhibitory effects, as they accumulate. Thirdly, not every cell formed by the division of a parent survives to divide itself; thus although the logarithmic law might be followed by the number of living cells, it may not be followed by the total number. Fourthly, the conditions for cell division vary somewhat according to the state of the medium and, therefore, according to the stage of the growth: thus the actual size of the cells varies during the period of active multiplication, and the logarithmic law may describe either the total number or the total mass, but not both simultaneously. Fifthly, the logarithmic form can only be expected to apply in a truly steady state, when all the cell enzymes have settled down to constant proportions: that is to say, when the cells are fully adapted to the medium in which they are growing. When transferred to new media, cultures tend to exhibit growth curves of non-logarithmic and sometimes erratic form.

Over quite wide ranges of experimentally realizable conditions, however, these factors are often unimportant, so that the law usually works well enough in practice. First, as will appear in the next section, growth rate is usually very nearly independent of foodstuff concentration over wide ranges, so that the medium can become almost completely exhausted before a slowing down of growth sets in. Secondly, there is usually a range of concentration within which toxic substances exert little effect, but outside which their action increases steeply.

Thirdly, the mortality under favourable conditions may be very low. According to Wilson,[23] with some organisms, even during the logarithmic phase, the percentage of new cells which survive seldom exceeds 90 per cent of the total. Kelly and Rahn,[24] however, made direct observations on the division of individual cells of various bacterial species and found that under favourable conditions all cells continued to divide. Even with Wilson's figure of 90 per cent the departure from the logarithmic law for total numbers would not be serious.

Fourthly, although quite important variations in cell size occur during the course of a growth cycle (see Chapters IV and XIV) they do not affect the total cell mass. In logarithmic plots, moreover, moderate deviations do not show up to any marked extent even when actual numbers of cells are used.

The various factors which cause departures from the logarithmic law usually rise from negligibility to importance in the rather short period as the bacterial count passes through a certain limited range. In this region the foodstuff concentration falls, oxygen may become deficient, the toxic products accumulate, and division conditions change. The result is a rather abrupt slowing down of growth as shown in Fig. 7. The normal method of plotting emphasizes this abruptness: the ordinates represent the logarithm of the number of cells (or of the bacterial mass), and equal increments of the ordinate therefore represent rapidly increasing increments of cell substance produced, which in turn mean rapidly increasing consumption of foodstuff or oxygen or production of toxic products. If a growth curve is observed over ten mean generation times, the amount of nutrient consumed during the last of them is approximately equal to that consumed over the whole of the other nine.

Attempts have sometimes been made to represent the whole of the growth curve, including the transition to the stationary phase, by a single equation.[25] In general the problem reduces to replacing k in the logarithmic equation by a function of m or n, and determining this function. Thus instead of

$$\frac{dm}{dt} = km \tag{1}$$

we write

$$\frac{dm}{dt} = f(m)m, \tag{2}$$

or, regarding k itself as a variable, we write $k = f(m)$.

Verhulst[25] proposed a law of growth of the form

$$\frac{dm}{dt} = Am\,\frac{B-m}{B}.$$

When m is small in comparison with B this reduces to $dm/dt = Am$ and if $A = k$ this is the original simple law: when m grows to a value B the rate of increase becomes zero so that a limiting population is reached.

Equations analogous to those of autocatalytic chemical reactions attended by consumption of a finite amount of substance have been applied to growth phenomena in general, for example,

$$\frac{dm}{dt} = Km(a-m).$$

From what has been said about the reasons for the onset of the stationary phase, it follows that no single equation can be expected to give a correct analytical expression of the transition. Sometimes growth stops because foodstuff is exhausted, sometimes because toxic products have accumulated. On occasion, these two effects will be superposed. For convenience, however, the two cases will be considered separately.

When exhaustion is the controlling factor we must first know k as a function of c, the concentration of the foodstuff, and then in turn the concentration c itself must be expressed in terms of m. This case has been considered by Teissier[25] and by Monod.[21] The reasonable assumption is made that the rate of fall in c is always proportional to the rate of increase in bacterial substance. Thus

$$-\frac{dc}{dt} = A\frac{dm}{dt}. \tag{3}$$

The variation of k with c is expressed in the form

$$k = k_0\frac{c}{c_1+c}, \tag{4}$$

which, as will appear in the next section, is well satisfied by experiment. c_1 is a constant.

Integration of (3) gives

$$c_0-c = A(m-m_0),$$

where c_0 is the initial concentration and m_0 the initial amount of bacterial substance. Substituting from the last in (4) and then introducing the value of k into (1) one obtains

$$\frac{dm}{dt} = k_0\left\{\frac{c_0+Am_0-Am}{c_1+c_0+Am_0-Am}\right\}m,$$

which gives on integration

$$k_0 t = \frac{c_1+c_0+Am_0}{c_0+Am_0}\ln\frac{m}{m_0} - \frac{c_1}{c_0+Am_0}\ln\frac{c_0+Am_0-Am}{c_0}.$$

Under conditions where exhaustion is in fact the limiting factor this equation gives a correct expression of the course of growth. In practice c_1 is usually very small in comparison with c_0. Over a considerable range therefore it may be neglected: under which conditions the last equation reduces to

$$k_0 t = \ln \frac{m}{m_0},$$

that is, to the simple logarithmic law. When, however, c_0 drops to a value comparable with c_1 the law changes rapidly: at this point, however, exhaustion is nearly complete and the growth rate falls very quickly to zero.

The fall is, in experimentally measurable examples, so rapid that it does not constitute a sensitive test of the precise form of the expression (4), which, however, is quite well founded theoretically, as will appear in the next section.

Equation (3) is a reasonable assumption and probably obeyed over quite wide ranges: but will not be true in general. Cells often ferment carbohydrates without actually growing. In principle, therefore, any foodstuff may be destroyed by the bacteria in a way unrelated to growth, and the proportion which suffers this fate may change as the composition of the medium changes. This factor is often enough unimportant, but it emphasizes the lack of fundamental significance in any one simple formula which purports to describe the whole course of the growth curve.

When accumulation of toxic products is the limiting factor, rather similar equations apply. We now have

$$\frac{dm}{dt} = km,$$

$$k = k_0 - f(x), \tag{5}$$

where x is the amount of toxic product.

During the period of active growth it is a reasonable approximation to write

$$\frac{dx}{dt} = B \frac{dm}{dt}, \tag{6}$$

but this is subject to reservations analogous to those made above in connexion with the linking of foodstuff consumption and growth. Accepting (6), however, we have

$$x = B(m - m_0),$$

the value of x being zero at the beginning of growth.

The form of the function in (5) can be studied by separate experiment on the addition of inhibitors. In general it is of rather complicated form, but often enough a linear relation, with $f(x) = B'x$, will serve: in which case the equations can be easily integrated. But, once again, it is evident that in principle no simple analytical form really expresses the transition between the logarithmic and the stationary phase. Fortunately, however, the logarithmic phase is usually well enough defined over a long enough range to render possible the characterization of growth by a single value of k in the fundamental equation.

10. Continuous culture

During the course of a growth cycle the accumulation of metabolic products subjects the cells to a continually changing environment and thus balanced growth is not really provided for. It can be established, however, in a process called continuous culture in which the cell mass is maintained at any chosen value until the various properties have settled down to steady values in a constant medium. If the procedure is repeated with the cell mass kept constant at a series of selected values, a direct comparison with the corresponding parts of the growth cycle may be obtained.[26]

Continuous culture is achieved by two main methods. In the first a medium, in which all the ingredients are present in excess, is allowed to drip into a vessel from which it subsequently overflows at such a rate that the cell mass is maintained at the desired level. Under these conditions the growth rate is the optimum for the particular medium and can only be changed by altering the temperature. In the second method one of the constituents of the medium is kept in such short supply that the growth rate is a function of the rate at which the medium is added. The apparatus used for the first method is sometimes referred to as a turbidostat[27] and that for the second as a chemostat.[28]

A general expression covers both cases: if m is the mass or number of cells per unit volume then

$$\frac{dm}{dt} = \left(\frac{bkc}{1+bc}\right)m - \frac{m}{T},$$

where c is the concentration of the nutrient limiting growth (when this is not small the first term on the right-hand side becomes km) and T is the *mean* time for which any portion of the solution remains in the culture vessel.

11. Growth rate and concentration of medium constituents

Over wide ranges the growth rate is independent of the concentration of the principal medium constituents. The centres which deal with these substances are easily brought to a state of saturation. The relation between rate and concentration might be expected to follow an equation of form similar to an adsorption isotherm: in other words to be expressible by

$$\text{rate} = \frac{Ac}{1+bc},$$

where b is a constant, or by a more complex equation, describing, however, a curve of the same general shape.

If k_∞ is the limiting value of the rate constant when the concentration is large, the above may be written in the form

$$k = \frac{k_\infty c}{c_1 + c},$$

c_1 being a new constant. c_1 has the dimensions of a concentration and is in fact that concentration at which the value of k would lie half-way between zero and k_∞. The last equation is that which was introduced in the course of the discussion in a previous section.

The experimental determination of the relation between k and concentration is attended with not inconsiderable difficulty. The growth rate does not begin to diminish seriously until the medium is made very dilute indeed: and precisely at this point the stationary bacterial population becomes so small that observations have to be confined to a range too small for satisfactory accuracy. All observers seem to be agreed that the general course of the rate-concentration curve is given by an equation similar to that written above,[18, 21, 29] but none of the results really allow a choice between one of the Langmuir type, as given, and one of rather more complicated form. What is, however, perfectly clear is the early saturation of the growth centres as the concentration rises.

The rate-concentration relation may be sought directly by determination of mean generation times at different initial concentrations or indirectly. An indirect method is as follows.[18] We first select a set of conditions such that growth is limited by exhaustion of foodstuff. A curve is then determined which gives the total bacterial population, n_s, as a function of the initial concentration of the particular medium constituent, the influence of which on the growth rate is to be measured. Now a growth curve is taken in a medium with an initial concentration c_0 of the constituent in question. A series of tangents to this curve are measured at various values of the count, n, in the region where the logarithmic phase is passing into the stationary phase. When the count is n, the amount of foodstuff consumed is that which would have been required to produce a total population of n, and this corresponds to a concentration c which can be read off from the first curve. The amount still unused at the point where the tangent is taken is therefore c_0-c. From the tangent the mean generation time, or the value of k, is obtained, and this value can then be plotted against c_0-c, and the required relation found. Fig. 20 shows a curve plotted by this method from experiments on the variation of phosphate concentration in cultures of *Aerobacter aerogenes* in an artificial medium.

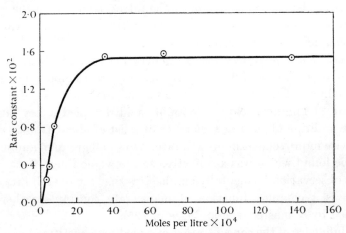

FIG. 20. Growth rate and substrate concentration.

An extensive series of measurements on the variations of carbohydrate concentration is given by Monod[21] partly for *Bacillus subtilis* but chiefly for *Escherichia coli*. The following are some typical results.

Escherichia coli *in synthetic medium*

Concentration of lactose (mg/l.)	Mean generation time (min)
2	860
9	550
29	85
43	65
90	53
114	56
137	57

The constant c_1 of the formula, representing the concentration at which the growth constant attains half its maximum value, gives a convenient measure of the scale of the phenomenon. Some values given by Monod are as follows:

Escherichia coli and glucose	4 mg/l.
Escherichia coli and mannite	2 mg/l.
Escherichia coli and lactose	20 mg/l.

The influence of different carbohydrates on the growth rate is rather diverse, but the results of measurements are of little significance unless they are made in relation with detailed studies of the state of adaptation of the bacteria to the source in question. Many coliform organisms, for example, grow considerably more slowly in glycerol or in lactose than in glucose when they are first transferred to these media. But after a period of adaptation they grow with equal facility in all three. The influence of the carbon source or of the nitrogen source on the growth rate will therefore be considered at a later stage and in connexion with the phenomenon of bacterial adaptation.

Aerobacter aerogenes has a mean generation time of about 30 to 32 minutes at 40° C when fully adapted to a glucose ammonium sulphate-salts medium. The addition of some twenty amino-acids reduced this to about 21 minutes. No single amino-acid occupied a key position, but the addition of each new member of a list of about twenty caused a stepwise improvement in growth rate. No small group of amino-acids could be found which was as effective as the whole range.[30]

This observation incidentally emphasizes that the overall rate of cell growth is a complex function of many rate constants rather than governed by a 'master-reaction' (see p. 125).

The influence of the concentration of a medium constituent of a somewhat different kind is shown in Fig. 21, which gives the growth rate of *Aerobacter aerogenes* as a function of the carbon dioxide content of the air-stream aspirated continuously through the cultures in a synthetic medium.[4] It may be mentioned that when the amount of carbon dioxide in the air is 0·15 per cent the concentration dissolved in pure water at the temperature of the experiments (40·0°) is 4×10^{-8} g mole/ml.

It is interesting to note that the bacterial mechanism can function satisfactorily over a wide range of speeds. Various species will grow continuously and well at 40° in media in which the generation time varies from 18 minutes to over 200 minutes. Much of the information about the influence of the medium is of doubtful quantitative value, since the growth rate, as explained above, depends upon the degree of adaptation. The limiting rate attained after thorough acclimatization to the new medium is certainly different for different media. The mean generation time of *Aerobacter aerogenes* in bouillon is about 18 minutes. The minimum value in a glucose-ammonium sulphate synthetic medium is about 32 minutes. If glucose is replaced by lactose, the generation time is at first very much longer, a fact which shows a new rate-determining step to have been added. After adaptation, however, the generation time falls to 32 minutes: one part of the mechanism has, therefore, improved in efficacy in such a way as no longer to constitute a bottleneck. But in each case there comes a stage at which no further adaptive improvement is possible.

Often in the literature the effects of the medium on growth rate and on stationary population are not clearly distinguished, all that is recorded being the abundance of growth after some chosen standard time. The

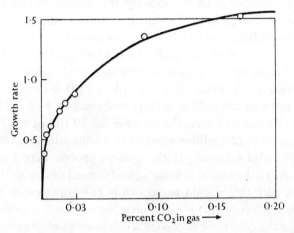

FIG. 21. Growth rate and carbon dioxide concentration.

aeration of bacterial cultures often has a marked influence on the total population, but not necessarily a corresponding one on the growth rate.[9, 20, 31] The following numbers illustrate the kind of effect observed.

Aerobacter aerogenes *in glucose-amino acid-phosphate medium*

	Total population (millions per ml)	
Amino acid	Aerated	Unaerated
Valine	1530	69
Aspartic acid	2710	790
Asparagine	6000	1250
Glutamic acid	1950	62

In the early stages of growth, at least, the aeration made little difference to the generation time. The total population seems in such examples to be controlled in part by the formation of an inhibitor removable by cellular oxidation or simple blowing off.

12. Influence of pH of medium on growth rate

The pH of the medium can hardly affect the total supply of any of the essential nutrient components, although it may cause wide changes in the availability of some of them. Its principal influence will be exerted upon the cell proteins, and enzyme activities are in fact strongly dependent on it. One might, therefore, have expected that changes of pH would have very marked effects on the growth rate and little on the final total population. Almost exactly the reverse of this is found, at least in one example, which there is no reason to suppose is not typical.

The profound influence of pH on n_s has already been considered. In the experiments referred to, an adverse pH reduced the total population drastically before any serious reduction occurred in the actual rate of the sparse residual growth. For example, at pH 6·45 a culture which ultimately grew to 190 million cells per ml reached 11·9 million in 1000 minutes, while one in which the adverse initial pH of 8·3 reduced the total population to 12·5 million reached 11·9 million in about 900 minutes.

In a medium of adverse pH the growth process may become much more sensitive to the action of toxic agents formed during the logarithmic phase. But why this should be so, while the growth rate itself is not much influenced, constitutes an interesting problem. Certainly change in pH during the growth of *Escherichia coli* causes a change in the enzyme content of the cells, as shown by the work of Gale and Epps[32] to which further reference will be made later.

REFERENCES

1. Grace Mooney and C. E. A. Winslow, *J. Bact.* **30**, 427 (1935).
2. G. A. Morrison and Sir Cyril Hinshelwood, *J. chem. Soc.*, pp. 372, 375, 380 (1949).
3. G. P. Gladstone, P. Fildes, and G. M. Richardson, *Br. J. exp. Path.* **16**, 335 (1935).
4. S. Dagley and C. N. Hinshelwood, *J. chem. Soc.*, p. 1936 (1938).
5. W. Kempner and C. Schlayer, *J. Bact.* **43**, 387 (1942).
6. R. M. Lodge and C. N. Hinshelwood, *J. chem. Soc.*, p. 1692 (1939).
7. W. J. Penfold, *J. Hyg., Camb.* **14**, 215 (1914); R. M. Stern and W. C. Frazier, *J. Bact.* **42**, 479 (1941).
8. R. M. Lodge and C. N. Hinshelwood, *J. chem. Soc.*, p. 213 (1943).
9. M. Sahyun, P. Beard, E. W. Schultz, J. Snow, and E. Cross, *J. infect. Dis.* **58**, 28 (1936).
10. E. F. Gale and Margery Stephenson, *Biochem. J.* **32**, 392 (1938).
11. J. Yudkin, *Biochem. J.* **31**, 865 (1937).
12. D. D. Woods and A. R. Trim, *Biochem. J.* **36**, 501 (1942).
13. E. H. Cole and C. N. Hinshelwood, *Trans. Faraday Soc.* **43**, 266 (1947).
14. A. H. Fogg and R. M. Lodge, unpublished observations.

15. See, for example, E. A. Steinhaus and J. M. Birkeland, *J. Bact.* **38**, 249 (1939).

16. See for details W. W. C. Topley and G. S. Wilson, *Principles of Bacteriology and Immunity*, 1st ed., 4th imp., Arnold, London (1934).

17. See for details C. E. A. Winslow and H. H. Walker, *Bact. Rev.* **3**, 147 (1939).

18. S. Dagley and C. N. Hinshelwood, *J. chem. Soc.*, p. 1930 (1938).

19. R. M. Lodge and C. N. Hinshelwood, *J. chem. Soc.*, p. 1683 (1939).

20. R. M. Lodge and C. N. Hinshelwood, *J. chem. Soc.*, p. 208 (1943).

21. J. Monod, *La Croissance des Cultures Bactériennes*, Hermann et Cie, Paris (1942).

22. A. C. Baskett and Sir Cyril Hinshelwood, *Proc. R. Soc.* B **137**, 524 (1950).

23. G. S. Wilson, *J. Bact.* **7**, 405 (1922).

24. G. D. Kelly and O. Rahn, *J. Bact.* **23**, 147 (1932).

25. See reference 21 for details.

26. See, for example, A. C. R. Dean and Sir Cyril Hinshelwood, *Proc. R. Soc.* B **151**, 348 (1960); A. C. R. Dean, *Proc. R. Soc.* B **155**, 580 (1962).

27. V. Bryson, *Science*, **116**, 48 (1952).

28. J. Monod, *Annls Inst. Pasteur, Paris*, **79**, 390 (1950); A. Novick and L. Szilard, *Science*, **112**, 715 (1950).

29. W. J. Penfold and Dorothy Norris, *J. Hyg., Camb.* **12**, 527 (1912).

30. D. Stephens and Sir Cyril Hinshelwood, *J. chem. Soc.*, p. 2516 (1949).

31. O. Rahn and G. L. Richardson, *J. Bact.* **44**, 321 (1942).

32. E. F. Gale and Helen M. R. Epps, *Biochem. J.* **36**, 600 (1942).

IV

VARIATION IN CELL COMPOSITION AND ENZYME ACTIVITY DURING THE GROWTH CYCLE

1. Variation in cell size and composition

WHEN a bacterial culture passes through its growth cycle (that is to say when a small number of cells are transferred to a fresh supply of medium and after traversing any period of lag, multiply until the exhaustion of nutrients or the accumulation of toxic products bring further increase to a halt), the cells do not remain of steady composition through all the phases. Nor do their enzyme activities stay constant, nor is the same average size maintained throughout. Although there is no doubt that essential genetic information is passed on unchanged, any idea of exact replication must be supplemented by one of a cell system adjusting itself or tending to adjust itself sensitively to the changing environmental conditions. The whole picture, so far from suggesting a mere mechanical printing off of replicas, suggests an elaborately geared process of control and response, and it is hard to resist the conclusion that the variations in composition and enzyme activity are closely linked with the regulation of the whole cell function. In this chapter we shall examine some typical kinds of composition and activity variation.

The kind of experiment on which the results to be described are based may be carried out by transferring a relatively small number of cells to fresh medium and then, at appropriate intervals, sampling the culture and carrying out analyses or enzyme activity determinations. For this purpose the inoculum itself needs to be standardized as far as possible, and, for reasons of convenience, to be in such a state that the lag in the new medium is of minimum duration. One way to ensure this is to take the inoculum from the logarithmic phase of a previous cycle, and another, more convenient, is to take it from a 24-hour culture in which increase of bacterial substance has been limited by the exhaustion of the glucose in a salts-glucose medium.

With *Aerobacter aerogenes* from an exhausted glucose culture of this latter kind the cells are small and contain about twice as much RNA as DNA. After inoculation of these cells into a medium containing an ample supply of glucose (no longer growth-limiting) the average mass of an individual cell (σ) increases and then passes through a maximum at a stage when the total mass of the culture (as estimated turbidimetrically, p. 75) has increased about tenfold (Fig. 22). The ratio RNA/DNA, which we denote by ρ, also passes through a maximum (Fig. 23) but the amount of DNA per unit mass, which will be called Δ, after a slight

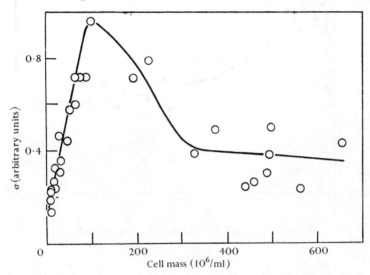

FIG. 22. σ (cell mass/cell number) during a growth cycle.

initial fall, remains nearly constant over the major part of the growth cycle (Fig. 24). Protein/RNA, π, also falls at first, then remains more or less constant until the last stages of the cycle when it rises again (Fig. 25).[1, 2] From ρ, Δ, and π we can calculate RNA/mass and protein/mass, and observe that the former passes through a maximum like cell size but earlier in the cycle, and that protein/mass does so earlier still.[1, 2] Polysaccharide/mass falls in the early part of the cycle and then rises again (Fig. 26).[3]

When the amounts of these constituents are related not to total bacterial mass but to number of cells it appears that the level of each per cell passes through a maximum, much the least pronounced with DNA, the variation in the ratio ρ being in large measure the result of change in the RNA content.[1, 2]

The height and position of the maximum in ρ is a function of the inoculum size, as shown in the family of curves in Fig. 27. There are two general possibilities about the nature of the maxima there represented. One is that the fall in ρ sets in after a certain number of cell divisions

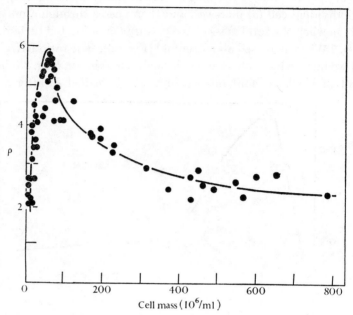

FIG. 23. ρ (RNA/DNA) during a growth cycle.

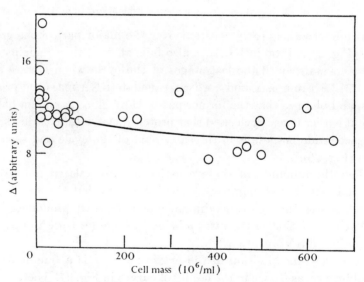

Fig. 24. Δ (DNA per unit of mass) during a growth cycle.

have taken place (case 1) while the other is that it begins when a given total increase of mass has occurred (case 2). Case 2 would apply if the fall were due to the influence of substances formed in the medium, since the integral amount of chemical change at any time is easily shown to be proportional to the total increase in mass.

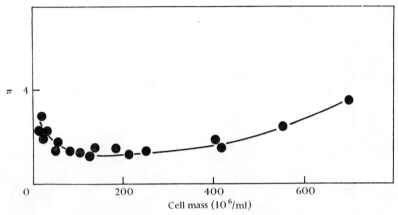

FIG. 25. π (protein/RNA) during a growth cycle.

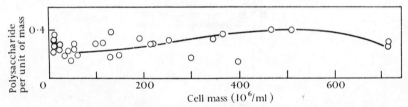

FIG. 26. Polysaccharide per unit of mass (as optical density) during a growth cycle.

A simple calculation will show the essential difference between the two cases. ρ_∞ is the value of the ratio RNA/DNA at the end of the previous cycle and so the value at the beginning of the new one, during the early stages of which let the ratio for freshly formed material be ρ_1. Let us assume for simplicity that this value is maintained, for fresh material, up to the time when the total mass has increased from the initial value m_0 to some value m_c, after which stage fresh material is characterized by the value ρ_∞. Then the value of the ratio averaged over the total mass will be given by

$$\rho = \{m_0 \rho_\infty + (m - m_0)\rho_1\}/m$$

from $m = m_0$ to $m = m_c$ and by

$$\rho = \{m_0 \rho_\infty + (m_c - m_0)\rho_1 + (m - m_c)\rho_\infty\}/m$$

from $m = m_c$ onwards, where m is the mass at the time of sampling.

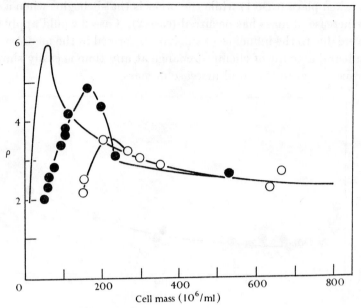

FIG. 27. Effect of inoculum size on ρ.

——— inoculum 10^7/ml
●—● inoculum 5×10^7/ml
○—○ inoculum 15×10^7/ml

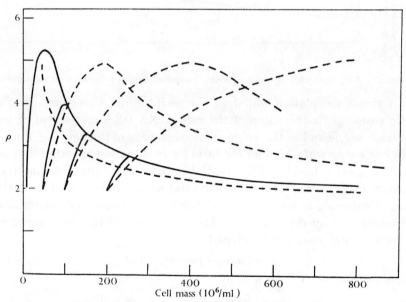

FIG. 28. Theoretical curves predicting the ratio ρ during the growth cycle.

------ case 1 ——— case 2

In case 1 the change-over occurs when $m_c = \alpha m_0$ and in case 2 when $m_c = m_0 + \mu$, where α and μ are constants. The two formulae predict quite different dependences on inoculum size, as is shown in Fig. 28, where in one set of curves $m_c = 4m_0$ and in the other set $m_c = m_0 + 50$. For the calculation ρ_∞ is taken as 2·0 and ρ_1 as 6·0, and the four curves of each set correspond to m_0 values of 10, 50, 100, and 200 respectively. The experimental curves form a family corresponding more closely to case 2 (Fig. 27) and this indicates that the state of the medium is the major factor determining the maximum. That it is not the only one is suggested by the fact that the curves do not completely merge together after the fall from the maximum.

Measurable changes in the medium do in fact occur during the growth cycle. The reducing potential increases, and towards the end the supply of oxygen may be difficult to maintain, the concentrations of certain metabolites increase, growth-antagonists accumulate and in a glucose medium the pH may eventually fall to a level where growth ceases.[1, 2] In certain other media the pH may increase.

The cell size is particularly subject to variation and the position of the maximum shows that early in the cycle increase of substance is favoured relatively to division, and at this stage the amount of DNA per unit mass is falling, though the amount per cell is increasing.

Although a critical amount of DNA per cell is a prerequisite for the transmission of the genetic information and although for a wide range of conditions the amount of DNA per cell has in fact nearly a standard value (see p. 95), this is evidently not the only factor which influences division. Some 'division factor' or set of factors appears to accumulate steadily in the medium. With *Aerobacter* next to cell size the ratio ρ varies most. It reaches its maximum earlier in the cycle than σ. Before the medium has enough division factor an excess of RNA seems to accumulate, and in this part of the cycle the reducing potential of the medium rises, a factor which, formally at least, should begin to favour DNA at the expense of RNA. By the time σ has reached its maximum the balance of RNA and DNA has already begun to move in favour of the latter. While RNA is rising rapidly π is falling, so that the increase of RNA (or its precursors) is not accompanied by any corresponding rise in protein. During the whole cycle RNA varies more than DNA or protein, as though RNA could constitute some sort of buffer or reserve.

The illustrations given have referred to *Aerobacter aerogenes* in a glucose-salts medium, but they are fairly typical of those found with other strains of bacteria growing at the optimum rate.[1, 4, 5]

2. RNA content and growth rate

When the growth rate is altered by a change in the nature of the nutrient medium there is often a general parallelism between this rate and the RNA content of the cells. This is shown in Fig. 29 which gives the RNA content of the cells of *Aerobacter aerogenes* grown at rates

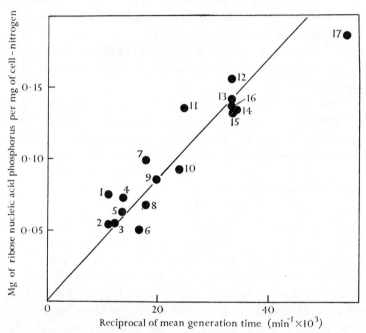

Fig. 29. Relation between the ribose nucleic acid content per cell and the growth rate.

(1) Phenol 0·09 per cent; (2) phenol 0·06 per cent; (3) *m*-cresol 0·08 per cent; (4) succinic acid as sole carbon source; (5) proflavine 120 mg/l.*; (6) proflavine 80 mg/l.*; (7) decyl alcohol (12 per cent of a saturated solution); (8) barbitone 9·23 mg/l.; (9) proflavine 40 mg/l.*; (10) glucose-salts medium, anaerobic conditions; (11) malic acid as sole carbon source; (12, 13, 14, and 15) standard glucose-salts medium; (16) colchicine 0·1%; (17) broth.

* 'trained' strains.

which were varied by fairly extensive changes of medium.[6] In this diagram the RNA content is that corresponding to the end of the growth cycle.

The relation illustrated, however, does not hold for still slower growth rates,[7] nor does it seem to apply to variations in rate brought about by change of temperature, even if the cells have been given time to become acclimatized to the new conditions. Growth of *Aerobacter* is slower at 31° C than at 37° and still slower at 25°, yet the height of the maximum in the RNA/mass curve is the same at both 25° and 31°.[8]

The particulate nature of much of the RNA in the cell has already been referred to (Chapter I, section 15) and it is stated that the changes in RNA during a growth cycle are paralleled by changes in the ribosome content. In a culture in the logarithmic phase the predominating sizes are 70s and 85s (although smaller particles are also present). In a culture taken from an exhausted glucose-limited medium (a convenient source of the inoculum for a fresh culture) the particles are observed to be almost exclusively of the 100s type[9] which is supposed to result from a dimerization of 70s particles.[10] If glucose is added the distribution of sizes characteristic of exponential growth is soon observed. It has been claimed that the anomalous relation between growth rate and RNA content is no longer found if instead of total RNA, the RNA in the ribosomes is considered.[11, 12] But the position is not wholly clear.[13,14,15]

3. Steady and non-steady states: abnormal conditions of growth

The determination of cell properties at intervals during a growth cycle amounts to the scanning of a continuous range of changing environments, the last of which is unfavourable enough to stop further increase. Thus the values for different properties so measured may not be equilibrium ones, in the sense of corresponding to a true steady state between cell and environment. If an equilibrium value is needed then the method of continuous culture (p. 79) must be employed. A comparison between samples taken from systems in continuous culture at various total populations and samples taken at the corresponding populations in a growth cycle shows that in a general way the equilibrium relations are similar to those found in the growth cycle, though with some quantitative differences.[1, 2] The departure from a steady state in the growth cycle is thus not very serious, but is enough to exaggerate the maximum in ρ and to leave π too high in the early stages (see Fig. 30). The principal difference between the curves for σ in this figure is not in the height of the maximum, but in the delay in reaching it when insufficient time is allowed for equilibrium to be established. Indeed it appears that in continuous culture the maximum may well occur at the very beginning and the value fall steadily as 'division factor' accumulates in the medium.

Marked departures from equilibrium occur when nutrients are deficient or when drugs are added to the medium. For example, the ratio protein/ RNA drops for a time when chloramphenicol[16] or terramycin[17] is added. When a constituent of the medium is deficient the cells remain smaller than usual for most of the growth cycle, as though the rate of formation of cell substance were more adversely affected than division. Deficiency of potassium, however, gives abnormally large cells at the end of the cycle, and abolishes the usual maximum in σ.[18]

When growth is stopped by the exhaustion of nitrogen or phosphorus in an otherwise complete medium, the culture as a whole is found to

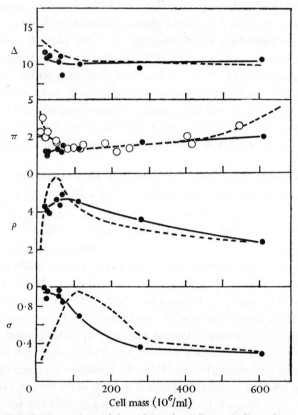

FIG. 30. Comparison of the values of σ (cell mass/cell number), ρ (RNA/DNA), π (protein/RNA) and Δ (DNA per unit of mass) in continuous culture and in a normal growth cycle.

    ●   continuous culture (each point is the mean of 4 to 5 determinations over 24 h).

    Standard curves, growth cycle σ, ρ, and Δ ---------, π ------○------

contain a very much enhanced amount of polysaccharide, some of which may be extra-cellular.[3, 19] Shortage of magnesium reduces the content of ribosomal RNA, and, if the cells are allowed to recover in a complete medium, protein is synthesized at a rate proportional to this content.[20]

4. DNA/mass and DNA/cell

The scanning of growth cycles gives a general picture of a constantly changing composition with the relative constancy of DNA/mass standing out in sharp contrast.[1, 2] Even under abnormal conditions this varies less than the proportion of other constituents.[8, 16, 18] In changes to quite different media there is also a tendency for the DNA content to remain nearly constant (Chapter XIV).

At the beginning of the cycle, however, DNA/mass is enhanced, and this reflects a corresponding enhancement at the very end of the preceding cycle from which the inoculum is derived. At the end of the cycle a process which we may call 'division without growth' often occurs. The medium is apparently rich in the division factor referred to above, and the cells continue to divide even after any increase in total substance has ceased to be possible. Thus they become smaller. At this stage several separate tendencies appear to be at work. On the one hand, in a chemical system in a truly steady state the DNA would normally be formed as a constant proportion of the total mass, and, on the other hand, it is apparently needed as a constant quota in each cell (as the analogy of printing off copies might suggest). If division is stimulated in conditions where fresh material cannot be formed, a compromise appears to be reached. The total DNA per unit mass rises, at the expense presumably of RNA broken down and reprocessed, but it is shared out as widely as possible among new cells, the amount per cell dropping to the minimum compatible with any further activity of the cell. Thus DNA/mass rises and DNA/cell falls, the increase in the former reflecting the greater number of cells, the decrease in the latter their impoverishment to the limit in DNA.[1, 2]

5. Variations in the cell enzymes

As the growth cycle progresses and the composition of the medium changes, variations in the activity of enzymes are often, indeed usually, observed. The measured activity, in some examples, is increased when the cell is broken up by mechanical means, so that it is not solely determined by the amount of enzyme present but may also be conditioned by the accessibility of the substrate and the permeability of the outer layers of the cell. According to one hypothesis, the access of the substrate is mediated by a specific enzyme called a 'permease', first postulated on the basis of investigations with the enzyme β-galactosidase which splits lactose into glucose and galactose.[21] The relation between the measured activities of intact and disintegrated cells is, however, quite a complex one and varies with the nature of the enzyme, the age of the culture, and the state of adaptation to the substrate. In some examples no increase in activity whatever is observed on disintegration.[22] Thus it appears that either the amount of enzyme present or the access of the substrate may, according to circumstances, be the limiting factor governing what is measured.

The following account is not intended to be exhaustive but is confined to a few typical examples from the enormous range of enzymes occurring in bacterial cells. In some ways the simplest picture, with *Aerobacter aerogenes* at least, is shown by the dehydrogenase systems, which bring

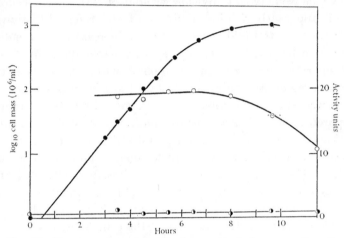

Fig. 31. Glucose and succinic dehydrogenases during a growth cycle
in glucose-salts medium.
●   Growth curve (left-hand scale)
○   Glucose dehydrogenase (right-hand scale)
◑   Succinic dehydrogenase (right-hand scale)

about oxidation of the carbon substrate by the specific removal of hydrogen. Apart from a gradual decay in the activity during the stationary phase of the culture, glucose and succinic dehydrogenases vary relatively little over the greater part of the growth cycle.[23]

The dehydrogenase activity, R, may be measured by the rate of consumption of dissolved oxygen under standard conditions and the reduction of methylene blue or 2,3,5-triphenyl tetrazolium chloride. The value of R increases with the adaptation of the cells to the particular carbon substrate used, and once they have become fully adapted, it remains more or less constant throughout the logarithmic phase (Fig. 31). During any process of adaptation to a given substrate R increases more or less in proportion to the growth rate. The limit to which it rises after adaptation to the substrate is complete varies only in a relatively narrow range, even though the possible growth rates change considerably from one carbon source to another.[24]

Various deaminases, in contrast with the dehydrogenases, show a regular variation during the bacterial growth cycle: it seems to be principally connected with the changes in the pH of the medium. With asparagine deaminase, for example, the enzyme activity per unit mass, as measured in a standard test, rises rapidly towards the end of the growth cycle as the medium becomes acid. During the early stages of

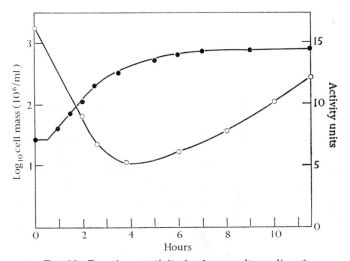

FIG. 32. Deaminase activity in glucose-salts medium.*

    ●   Growth curve (left-hand scale)
    ○   Asparagine deaminase activity (right-hand scale)
  *   Ammonium sulphate is the sole nitrogen source in this medium.

a cycle started with an inoculum of this high deaminase content the enzyme activity per unit mass falls rapidly by dilution with new material of lower content (Fig. 32).[23]

An increase in measured enzyme activity very frequently occurs when the pH of the medium moves into a region at which the enzyme operates below its optimum. Gale and Epps[25] found in quite a number of examples that with *Escherichia coli* the amount of enzyme, as measured under standard conditions of test at an optimum pH, increased in the cells as the pH of the culture became more adverse. There was sometimes a rather clear compensation whereby the increased amount formed at the adverse pH just made up for the decreased specific activity in such a way that the effective total activity in the actual growth medium (as distinct from the test medium) remained constant. The significance of this observation will become very apparent when we come to deal with the subject of adaptation in general.

A compensatory phenomenon of similar nature has been observed with the lactose-splitting enzyme β-galactosidase when a culture utilizing lactose as its source of carbon runs short of oxygen.[26] The anaerobic processes of growth are less efficient in that they have to metabolize more sugar to provide a given increase of cell mass, and, as more enzyme becomes thus needed more is formed. The appearance of enzymes in

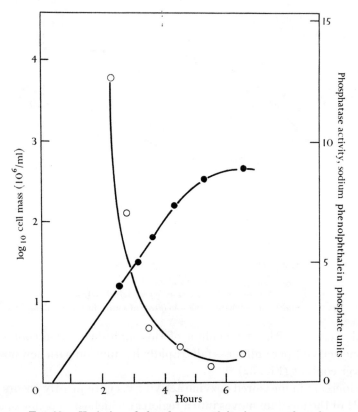

Fig. 33a. Variation of phosphatase activity in a growth cycle.

● Growth curve (left-hand scale)
○ Phosphatase activity (right-hand scale)

response to a freshly created need is a characteristic phenomenon very widely encountered.

The phosphatase enzymes which remove the phosphate group from organic phosphates (and are often classified into the two broad groups of the so-called acid and alkaline phosphatases) may show an interesting pattern of variation. As an example we may quote the enzyme in *Aerobacter aerogenes* which can be assayed by its hydrolysis of disodium phenolphthalein diphosphate in tests at pH 5·6.[27] An actual culture of cells may be grown in a glucose-salts medium with an initial pH 7·1. In the early stages of the cycle the enzyme activity rises to a high level, at about the place where RNA is increasing rapidly, and then declines, as though by progressive dilution with less active material (Figs. 33a, 33b). As was observed with the RNA/DNA ratio itself (Fig. 27) the use

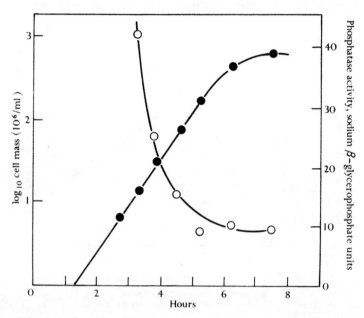

FIG. 33b. (same legend as Fig. 33a): another substrate used in enzyme assay.

of a larger inoculum leads to a lower maximum. The maintenance of the pH at a constant level does not prevent the decline: nor does dilution with fresh medium in such a way as to keep the cell count steady. The pattern of variation depends on the medium, the addition of amino-acids, for example, lowering the maximum, and deprivation of molecular oxygen depressing the activity throughout. In a medium where acetate replaces glucose the activity remains approximately constant at a high level in the logarithmic phase of the growth cycle and declines only in the stationary phase where, in this medium, the pH rises.

Catalase is the enzyme which decomposes hydrogen peroxide. It appears to be intimately connected with aerobic growth, being present universally in aerobes and absent from obligate anaerobes which, however, are still unable to grow aerobically in presence of added enzyme. During most of the logarithmic phase of *Aerobacter aerogenes* the rate of catalase formation is very small. Later on there is a steep increase (Fig. 34). The rise occurs at about the stage when the pH is falling but is much too great to be explained solely in terms of the compensation effect which has already been described. Nevertheless if the pH is kept constant at 7·1 the rise is prevented, so it would seem that the metabolism under acid conditions produces products from which the cell has to be protected by the formation of a greater amount of catalase.[28]

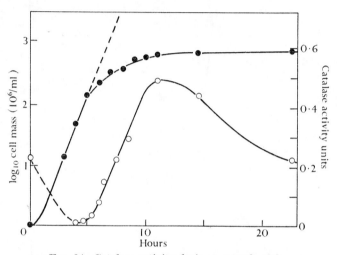

FIG. 34. Catalase activity during a growth cycle.
●   Growth curve (left-hand scale)
○   Catalase activity (right-hand scale)

6. Conclusion

The variations in the composition of the cell and in the amounts of its enzymes give a very strong impression of a regulatory response to environmental changes. This theme will be more fully developed in the following chapters, where it will appear that, according to physico-chemical principles, the cell should indeed be capable of responses of the type often called cybernetic, and should show phenomena simulating choice between alternatives and adjustment to meet needs (although there is no question of any metaphysical or anthropomorphic overtones to these phrases).

The changes which have been described illustrate one aspect of the immense plasticity of living matter. There are other aspects which will be dealt with later. There is no reason whatever to suppose that the effects which have just been illustrated involve any change at all in the essential genetic information contained in the cell, that is to say in the nature, as distinct from the amounts, of the macromolecular substances in the structure of which this information is recorded. But changes in these structures, and in the genetic code do take place. Such mutations, as they are called, are said to occur spontaneously, though the word spontaneously itself has a somewhat metaphysical ring unless it means, as it usually does here, as a result of hidden or unknown causes. Mutations can be caused by exposure to radiation, and by the action of certain kinds of drug. They are normally held to be random, in the sense that they lead to changes in the cell bearing no special relation to the agency which produces them, or in other words they are not adaptive. Whether a more purposeful kind of mutation can be induced is a controversial question. The whole subject will be discussed in Chapter XIII.

Yet another kind of change can come about by the interaction of one cell with a second cell of different type. There may then be something akin to a sexual fusion, or simply the transfer of a certain amount of genetic material. In any event one cell acquires information-bearing matter which it previously lacked (Chapter I, section 16).

REFERENCES

1. A. C. R. Dean and Sir Cyril Hinshelwood, *Proc. R. Soc.* B **151**, 348 (1960).
2. A. C. R. Dean, *Proc. R. Soc.* B **155**, 580 (1962).
3. A. C. R. Dean, *Proc. R. Soc.* B **160**, 402 (1964).
4. For a comprehensive review of the synthesis of nucleic acids and proteins see E. F. Gale, in *The Bacteria*, edited by I. C. Gunsalus and R. Y. Stanier, Academic Press, New York **3**, 471 (1962).
5. A. C. R. Dean, *Proc. R. Soc.* B **157**, 574 (1963).
6. P. C. Caldwell, E. L. Mackor, and Sir Cyril Hinshelwood, *J. chem. Soc.* p. 3151 (1950).
7. B. Magasanik, Adèle K. Magasanik, and F. C. Neidhardt, Ciba Found. Symp., *Regulation of Cell Metabolism*, edited by G. E. W. Wolstenholme and Cecilia M. O'Connor, p. 334, Churchill, London (1959).
8. A. C. R. Dean, *Proc. R. Soc.* B **160**, 396 (1964).
9. B. J. McCarthy, *Biochim. Biophys. Acta*, **39**, 563 (1960).
10. J. D. Watson, in *Les Prix Nobel en 1962*, p. 155, Imprimerie Royale P. A. Norstedt und Söner, Stockholm (1963).
11. Ø. Maaløe and C. G. Kurland, *Symp. Int. Soc. Cell Biol.* **2**, 93 (1963).
12. N. O. Kjelgaard and C. G. Kurland, *J. molec. Biol.* **6**, 341 (1963).
13. F. C. Neidhardt and D. G. Fraenkel, *Cold Spring Harbor Symp. quant. Biol.* **26**, 63 (1961).
14. F. C. Neidhardt and B. Magasanik, *Biochim. Biophys. Acta*, **42**, 99 (1960).
15. H. E. Wade and H. K. Robinson, *Biochem. J.* **96**, 753 (1965); see also D. W. Tempest and J. R. Hunter, *J. gen. Microbiol.* **41**, 267 (1965).
16. A. C. R. Dean, *Proc. R. Soc.* B**155**, 599 (1962).
17. A. C. R. Dean and B. L. Giordan, *Proc. R. Soc.* B **161**, 571 (1964).

18. A. C. R. Dean, *Proc. R. Soc.* B **155**, 589 (1962).

19. See also D. Herbert, *Symp. Soc. gen. Microbiol.* **11**, 391 (1961).

20. D. Kennell and B. Magasanik, *Biochim. Biophys. Acta*, **55**, 139 (1962).

21. See G. N. Cohen and J. Monod, *Bact. Rev.* **21**, 169 (1957).

22. D. J. W. Grant and Sir Cyril Hinshelwood, *Proc. R. Soc.* B **160**, 25 (1964).

23. B. J. McCarthy, *Proc. R. Soc.* B **150**, 410 (1959).

24. P. R. Lewis and C. N. Hinshelwood, *Proc. R. Soc.* B **135**, 301 (1948); C. N. Hinshelwood and P. R. Lewis, *Proc. R. Soc.* B **135**, 316 (1948); A. C. Baskett and Sir Cyril Hinshelwood, ibid. B **137**, 524 (1950).

25. E. F. Gale and Helen M. R. Epps, *Biochem. J.* **36**, 600, 619 (1942).

26. N. Richards and Sir Cyril Hinshelwood, *Proc. R. Soc.* B **154**, 463 (1961).

27. B. J. McCarthy and Sir Cyril Hinshelwood, *Proc. R. Soc.* B **150**, 474 (1959).

28. B. J. McCarthy and Sir Cyril Hinshelwood, *Proc. R. Soc.* B **150**, 13 (1959).

V

TOTAL INTEGRATION

1. Introduction

In this chapter we shall examine some general propositions about living cells. This proves to be quite a fruitful task, since many important and characteristic cell properties may be seen to follow from simple principles. If an observed result follows from a general proposition it cannot by itself provide unambiguous evidence for more specialized assumptions, although these may still be consistent with it. Alternative mechanisms for a chemical reaction, for example, are often consistent with the laws of thermodynamics. But such conformity is only a minimum qualification and a necessary rather than a sufficient condition.

At the present stage of development of biophysics any theory of the living cell must involve models which are in some measure oversimplified. Various abstractions are current to describe the characteristics of cells. All serve particular purposes well enough, but some of them taken in isolation appear more arbitrary than they need be. We propose to investigate where certain minimum assumptions lead.

The cell, in the first place, can be regarded as something where organic matter is replicated according to a code. Ever since Brachet, Caspersson, and others[1] emphasized the importance of nucleic acid in the nuclei of certain cells, and showed how 'messenger' RNA moved from nucleus to cytoplasm, since 'priming' of protein synthesis by RNA has been observed in broken cell preparations, and since single and double DNA helices were found by X-ray crystallography, the base sequence in DNA has played a dominant part in thought about the code. Nevertheless any polymeric molecule with several kinds of monomer unit can contain coded information, and indeed the whole of human knowledge, at the intellectual level, could be expressed in the Morse code with dots, dashes, and spaces. Proteins can express codes and so too can polysaccharides. Nor do nucleic acid spirals simply replicate, complementary base bonding to complementary base, in unorganized systems like crystals growing in a solution. What happens depends upon extremely complex and subtle chemistry. This brings us to the second aspect of the cell.

It is a chemical manufactory of enormous range and versatility.

Nucleic acids, polysaccharides, and proteins, to mention only the major cell constituents, can all be built up from very simple compounds such as ammonia, inorganic salts, and acetate. Vastly different carbon and nitrogen compounds can be processed to give the same complex end-products. The biochemical steps are often ascertainable and the total number of chemical compounds involved in cell metabolism is very large indeed. The reactions to give the highly condensed end-products must consist of a series of steps, each consisting of a relatively simple process such as dehydrogenation, hydrogenation, hydrolysis, water elimination, and so on. The most complicated of organic chemical syntheses resolves itself into a succession of unit processes conforming to a rather limited set of types. The ring closures by which elaborate mosaic-like molecules are formed usually depend themselves upon removal of water or hydrogen or the saturation of double bonds. The reason why synthetic organic chemistry in the laboratory is such a delicate and difficult art lies essentially in the difficulty of bringing and holding the potentially reactive groups into the right position at the right time. In the simpler heterogeneous catalytic reactions of inorganic chemistry chemisorption on appropriate surfaces allows reactions such as $2SO_2+O_2 = 2SO_3$ to occur much more readily than the hazards of random encounters in a gas phase would permit. In the living cell a most wonderfully coordinated set of reactions occurs. Enzymes, nucleic acids, polysaccharides all have beautifully graded varieties of spacings and these facilitate interaction with other structures when these are suitably juxtaposed. One of the potent agencies in bringing molecules into close association is the formation of hydrogen bonds. Everything depends upon the right spatial relation between the groups which bond molecules into a complex and those which are concerned in the particular unit process of a synthesis or degradation. Hence the dominance of the 'template' conception in cell biology, whether in the helical nucleic acid replication or in the specific action of enzymes or, probably, in the specific permeability of walls containing polysaccharides. The possible role of free valencies in cell reactions will be considered later (p. 413).

From a given starting-point to a given end-product there must be many alternative routes. The ammonia needed in an amination reaction can be derived from some twenty-odd amino-acids, to mention only these: hydrolysis might follow oxidation or oxidation follow hydrolysis. An almost indefinitely large variety of media permit efficient growth of many types of cell. So we imagine the whole scheme of possible reactions in the cell to resemble somewhat a town map in which progress from A

to *B* could follow many different routes. The set of reaction steps actually followed in given circumstances we shall refer to as the *reaction pattern* of the cell. This does not need always to be the same but will vary according to the nature of the raw materials supplied for growth.

We now turn to consider the more important types of cell component. DNA is sometimes thought of as a self-replicating substance with RNA closely dependent on it, and it is supposed to be the sole repository of the 'genetic code' or the 'information' which guides the life and reproduction of the cell. This cannot be too rigidly maintained. Neither DNA nor RNA replicate themselves in the way that crystals of salt will do in a solution. Phages, which consist essentially of nucleic acid, do indeed multiply but only in so far as they have invaded an intact cell and taken possession of its machinery and organization. In cell-free systems DNA formation may proceed to a limited extent and then stop, but its continuous replication demands an intact functioning cell. DNA and RNA are formed only under the influence of enzymes, essentially protein in nature, and possessing a high degree of specificity. Unless the appropriate enzymes are present no nucleic acid is formed in a cell. Zamecnik[2] has justly observed that enzymes are too easily taken for granted and the very remarkable nature of their contribution ignored. RNA, according to a widely held view, based on observations with mammalian cells, is formed in the nuclear region of a cell, and some of it, relatively unstable and of not very high molecular weight, enters the cytoplasm. Such RNA, called transfer RNA,[1] is of many different types and each one is supposed to combine specifically with a single amino-acid which eventually it somehow guides into position to be joined up in a protein chain. This process appears to involve many different enzymes, a separate one at least being probably needed for each RNA-enzyme combination.[3] If this is so the specificity of the protein structure is comparable in importance with that of the nucleic acid itself.

The cell can only maintain its character by periodic division, and for division to be possible wall material must be built up. The wall has a complex and variable structure of polysaccharide, muco- and lipoprotein,[4] and is as specific as everything else in the cell. The wall substance is synthesized by enzyme reactions and is almost certainly itself the seat of various enzyme activities, some of these being connected with the very important property of specific permeability by which the access of substances from the medium to the cell is controlled.[5]

Yet another kind of specificity exists in the cell and this resides in the foldings and spatial distributions of the various macromolecular components themselves. The equilibrium folding of proteins may be predetermined by the amino-acid sequence[6] but a state of equilibrium is not a normal characteristic of functioning biological systems.

The widely repeated 'dogma'[7] that the 'code' of living matter is enshrined solely in DNA may conceivably be true in the sense that a mutation caused in this substance would rapidly transmit effects to the other cell constituents while changes chemically induced in enzymes or polysaccharides would soon be eliminated if the DNA remained intact, though even this seems hard to believe as an absolute principle. DNA is built up by the successive addition of small molecules to a chain. If a very different chemical environment is maintained for long enough, an abnormal addition may be forced and the code slightly changed. The addition of a monomer unit to a growing chain is much more likely if it conforms to optimum spatial requirements: in the language of chemical kinetics the reaction will have a lower activation energy. But reactions of higher activation energy can compete, and do, with those of lower activation energy if the prevailing concentration relations favour them sufficiently. Enzymes which present the 'wrong' base in high enough concentration could in principle lead to abnormalities in the nucleic acid.

However this may be—and there is no need to decide the question here—the essential matter is that the working and reproduction of a cell demands the harmonious gearing of all its parts and reflects what we shall refer to as the principle of *total integration*, a principle which, as we shall see, could hardly have been missed by nature after long ages of evolution and selection, and which predicts important cell characteristics.

2. Total integration. The network theorem

The cell, then, presents a vast system of mutual dependences. Nucleic acids cannot be synthesized without enzymes, enzyme proteins are formed under the guidance of nucleic acid. They are essential to the building of the wall material which itself affects the supply of raw materials from outside and the escape of waste products. Without the enzyme-mediated synthesis of wall material the cell cannot divide and maintain its individuality.

We have seen that the reaction pattern of the cell partakes of the nature of a network, which we will now consider further.

At each stage something is dependent on something else, and in the network of dependences there will be numerous branches. All proteins containing a given amino-acid residue (Class A) depend upon the smaller number of enzymes (Class B) which manufacture this amino-acid. That is to say a greater number of things here depend upon a smaller number. The enzymes of this class B themselves contain up to about twenty amino-acid residues, so their formation depends upon the ministration of a larger number of other enzymes. Regarded from the point of view of the mutual dependences, in the first example we have a diverging relation (many depending on few) and in the second a converging relation (few depending on many). Thus the network of dependences has branchings and rejoinings.

Furthermore every mesh of the network is closed. There may be an appearance of open-endedness in so far as some of the chains of synthesis start from medium constituents. But a medium constituent is only processed by an enzyme and this is only built up under the influence of a nucleic acid which in turn demands enzymes, and so on.

This closed and meshed network of mutual dependences expresses the total integration of the cell activity. It is of great importance and we shall now examine its consequences in some detail. What we shall consider is the network not of chemical reactions, but of mutual dependences. This must be borne in mind because a scheme such as $X \!\!\begin{array}{c} \nearrow Y \\ \searrow Z \end{array}$ will mean not that X yields Y and Z but that its formation *depends* upon the activity of Y and Z. In this sense we think of matters with a reversed time sequence. Such dependences express the interplay and the coupling of the various parts of the cell, and they are fundamental to the working of the cell as a machine.

Much work has been done on broken-up cells, extracted enzymes, and similar preparations. Experiments on incomplete systems of this kind are valuable in revealing parts of the chemical sequences, since, for example, intermediates which in intact cells are rapidly further transformed now accumulate to the point of detectability owing to the destruction or removal of the enzymes which would have processed them. But informative as such indications may be, the laws of integration alone complete the description of cell function.

The first proposition we shall establish is that substances which are by no means self-replicating in their own right may nevertheless increase according to the law of autocatalysis which makes them appear auto-synthetic. The principle can be illustrated by the simplest possible example. Suppose the rate of formation of a substance X depends upon the amount of Y, while the rate of formation of Y depends upon the amount of X. This condition is expressed by the equations

$$\frac{dX}{dt} = \alpha Y \quad \text{and} \quad \frac{dY}{dt} = \beta X$$

(if we may allow ourselves to use the symbol X also to express the *amount* of X).

The solution of these equations gives

$$X = \frac{1}{2}\left(X_0 + \frac{\alpha}{k}Y_0\right)e^{kt} + \frac{1}{2}\left(X_0 - \frac{\alpha}{k}Y_0\right)e^{-kt},$$

$$Y = \frac{1}{2}\left(Y_0 + \frac{k}{\alpha}X_0\right)e^{kt} + \frac{1}{2}\left(Y_0 - \frac{k}{\alpha}X_0\right)e^{-kt},$$

where X_0 and Y_0 are the amounts at zero time and $\alpha\beta = k^2$. When growth has continued for a long time the ratio X/Y settles down to

$$\left(X_0 + \frac{\alpha}{k}Y_0\right)\bigg/\left(Y_0 + \frac{k}{\alpha}X_0\right),$$

which is α/k, a constant value. If some of the system is isolated and allowed to continue growing from this point (which becomes a new time zero), we have $X_0/Y_0 = \alpha/k$, so that the equations reduce to

$$X = X_0 e^{kt} \quad \text{and} \quad Y = Y_0 e^{kt}.$$

Both components maintain a constant ratio and obey the autosynthetic law.

It will be noted, however, that before the steady state is reached there may be any arbitrary relation between the two rates of increase. If, for example, we started with $Y_0 = 0$, the initial rate of increase of X is zero, while that of Y is finite (since it is proportional to X_0). The exact inverse could also be observed. This means that very great care and some reserve are necessary in interpreting the common kind of experiment in which the differential synthesis of various cell components is measured. Observations on the replication of DNA at different times in the cell cycle of cells not in dynamic balance with their environment, or of growth under conditions of recent deprivation of medium constituents or after recent transfer to a new medium, or after temperature shock, all may show anomalies and disturbances from which misleading conclusions could be drawn. What happens is analogous to the behaviour predicted by short term solutions of the equations with arbitrary values of X_0 and Y_0.

The simple system of two components has illustrated the principle. It can now be made more general, and we consider a more elaborate closed network of mutual dependences. For the moment we will disregard the branching of this network and consider a continuous closed cycle such that

$$dX_1/dt = \alpha_1 X_2, \quad dX_2/dt = \alpha_2 X_3, \quad ..., \quad dX_j/dt = \alpha_j X_{j+1} \quad ,...,$$

and finally, expressing the closed nature of the mutual dependence system,

$$dX_n/dt = \alpha_n X_1.$$

$X_1, X_2,..., X_j,...$ represent various structural elements of the cell, nucleic acids which govern the formation of proteins, proteins which, as enzymes, are essential for the building of other parts of the cell (including the nucleic acids) and so on. Concentrations of medium constituents and metabolites do not appear explicitly. In so far as their concentration enters it is reflected in changes of the α-coefficients. From one medium to another some of these coefficients will change, but for the present they are taken as constants.

For arbitrary initial values of $(X_1)_0$, $(X_2)_0$,... the solution of the equations is very complicated, as may be judged from the simple example of the two components given above. But for longer times when the values of X_1, X_2,... have become large compared with $(X_1)_0$, $(X_2)_0$,... growth settles down to follow the equations

$$dX_1/dt = kX_1, \quad dX_2/dt = kX_2, \quad ..., \quad dX_j/dt = kX_j.$$

Just as in the simple case first discussed k^2 was $\alpha\beta$, so in this more general one the relation

$$k^n = \alpha_1 \alpha_2 ... \alpha_n$$

may easily be established by differentiation and substitution.

In the steady state the ratios of the various components are given by a set of equations of the type $X_j/X_{j+1} = \alpha_j/k$. If a small portion of the cell substance is now transferred to a fresh supply of medium $(X_1)_0$, $(X_2)_0$,... are already in the steady ratios and growth of all constituents continues according to equations of the type

$$X_1 = (X_1)_0 e^{kt}, \quad X_2 = (X_2)_0 e^{kt}, \quad ..., \quad X_j = (X_j)_0 e^{kt}.$$

Suppose now that some of this multiplying cell substance is transferred to an entirely new kind of medium in which the values for some of the coefficients α_1, α_2,... are widely different from the original. Many of them may well be much the same as before and will refer to identical processes involving intermediates formed in the synthetic chain itself. Some, however, for example those closely related to the initial stages of nutrient utilization, may be changed. If any of them is actually zero, then growth will be impossible according to this unbranched network, since $k = (\alpha_1 \alpha_2 \ldots \alpha_n)^{1/n}$ and this vanishes if any single one of the α-terms vanishes. The interesting situation, however, is that which arises if a few of the α-terms are just very much reduced in magnitude without completely vanishing. This might occur in a medium where, for example, one of the primary sources was inefficiently metabolized. Suppose, for example, α_j fell to one-fifth of its original value. Since $dX_j/dt = \alpha_j X_{j+1}$ the initial rate of formation of X_j will be reduced to one-fifth and this constitutes a serious bottle-neck to the whole rhythm of growth. Gradually, however, the steady state is re-established and when this is achieved the ratio X_{j+1}/X_j will settle down to k/α_j as before. Since α_j is only one-fifth of its original value, this ratio will have increased fivefold. Thus the reduction in α_j in the equation dX_j/dt will have been balanced by an increase in X_{j+1}/X_j. The overall growth rate constant k will have suffered only a minor change. If, for example, n is 20, and if α_j is reduced to one-fifth the effect on k is to reduce it in the ratio $(0 \cdot 2)^{0 \cdot 05}$, that is by about 7·5 per cent.

The primitive model which has just been considered shows, therefore, some highly suggestive properties. All the mutually dependent components increase with time in a way which simulates autosynthesis once a steady state is established. Chaotic behaviour may be shown initially in a new medium where changed growth constants prevail, and the increase of some parts of the substance may now appear to be strongly inhibited. But an adjustment takes place when time is allowed for the establishment of a new steady state, and when this is complete the overall growth rate may have returned to a value not very far below its original. This is clearly an adaptive process. Its basis is a shift in the relative proportions of the different mutually dependent components.

Bacterial cells vary widely in the proportions of their components, as the precise conditions of growth are changed (Chapter IV). They also show very remarkable ability to adapt themselves so as to give gradually improving growth rates after transfer to initially unfavourable conditions. The probable connexion between these phenomena is now obvious.

At the same time the above considerations again emphasize the care which is needed in interpreting the initial disturbances in systems not yet in balance with their environment.

The very important matter of the branching of the mutual dependence cycles must now be considered.

As we have already pointed out, the formation of a given cell component may be dependent upon more than one other. Sometimes, moreover, alternative sources of the substrate it requires for its own unit process are possible. The simplest equation we can write to express this state of affairs is

$$dX_j/dt = \alpha_j X_{j+1} + \beta_j Y_1,$$

where Y_1 like X_{j+1} is itself involved in a closed chain of dependences which must ultimately be connected with one of the main metabolic routes.

The equations describing the branching relations could be of varied and complex form and we are using the simplest. But a short digression on their form will be useful. Where two dependences are essential there could be, instead of the form given, an 'either-or' relation, or a product relation. The former would reduce to a one-term expression on the right-hand side, the latter would give equations difficult to handle but in their consequences probably qualitatively similar to the additive form we have written. When alternatives occur, the state of affairs would probably be as follows. Suppose an intermediate, C, is needed at a given stage for the formation of X_j and suppose C can be provided either by X_{j+1} or by Y_1. Let the local concentration of this intermediate be c. Then we should have for a steady state

$$dc/dt = \beta X_{j+1} + \gamma Y_1 - \delta c = 0,$$

the first term on the right representing formation by X_{j+1}, the second formation by Y_1, and the third loss by diffusion away from the locality and otherwise. β, γ, δ are constants. Then $c = (\beta/\delta)X_{j+1} + (\gamma/\delta)Y_1$ and if dX_j/dt is proportional to c then $dX_j/dt = \alpha_j X_{j+1} + \beta_j Y_1$ as already postulated.

We shall in any event adopt this very simple form as expressing the essential nature of the branching. We now need to make some provision for the rejoining of the Y loop to the main cycle. We shall simply assume that it runs from X_j to X_{j+l} and that there are m members in the branch as shown schematically in the diagram

$$\text{--------}X_{j-1}\text{--}X_j \begin{array}{l} \diagup X_{j+1}\text{---}X_{j+2}\cdots\text{--}X_{j+l}\text{--}X_{j+l+1}\cdots \\ \diagdown Y_1 \text{---------} Y_2 \ldots Y_m \end{array}$$

Then we have

$$dX_1/dt = \alpha_1 X_2, \quad dX_2/dt = \alpha_2 X_3, \quad \ldots,$$

$$dX_j/dt = \alpha_j X_{j+1} + \beta_j Y_1,$$

$$dY_1/dt = b_1 Y_2, \quad dY_2/dt = b_2 Y_3, \quad \ldots,$$

$$dY_m/dt = b_m X_{j+l}.$$

In the steady-state condition all the components will increase according to the exponential law, with the same constant k. There is no need here to examine the complicated solutions applying before the steady state is reached. For the steady state, $dX_1/dt = kX_1$, ... and so on. To find the steady-state ratios we progressively differentiate the basic equations and substitute from the steady-state general solution. We find then that

$$k^n = \alpha_1 \alpha_2 \dots \alpha_{j-1}(\alpha_j \dots \alpha_{j+l-1} + \beta_j b_1 \dots b_m k^{l-m-1})\alpha_{j+l} \dots \alpha_n.$$

If there were no branch this would reduce to the simple geometrical mean previously found. With the branch there is a stretch where sums of α and β terms occur. (The presence of k also on the right-hand side arises from the unequal number of members in the two parts of the branch.) The value of k is still in effect a geometrical mean, and considerable changes in one single member or a few members of the set of coefficients would not make a very serious difference to its value.

If we simply had Y_1 spanning the gap between X_j and X_{j+2} as a by-pass of X_{j+1} the expression for k would become

$$k^n = \alpha_1 \alpha_2 \dots \alpha_{j-1}(\alpha_j \alpha_{j+1} + \beta_j b_1)\alpha_{j+2} \dots \alpha_n.$$

This simple case illustrates the essential properties of the model.

At the branch we have

$$dX_j/dt = \alpha_j X_{j+1} + \beta_j Y_1,$$

but in the steady state

$$\frac{1}{X_j}\frac{dX_j}{dt} = k,$$

so that

$$\alpha_j \frac{X_{j+1}}{X_j} + \beta_j \frac{Y_1}{X_j} = k.$$

This equation predicts behaviour which bears a remarkable resemblance to many important biological phenomena.

Suppose in the steady state that the term $\beta_j Y_1/X_j$ is quite small, the branch involving Y_1 being of rather subsidiary importance in the reaction scheme. Suppose, however, that the medium is changed, and that in the new conditions of supply α_j has become very small or even zero. It will be easier to consider the extreme case where it is zero. There would be a sudden and serious inhibition of the growth owing to the bottle-neck created by the very small value of $\beta_j Y_1/X_j$. But gradually as a new stationary state is established $\beta_j Y_1/X_j$ will rise to k', the value of the new steady state rate constant, k' being not much less than k itself as explained above. The change is associated with an increase in the ratio Y_1/X_j. Thus the increase in the amount of Y_1 has compensated for the lower inherent activity. This automatically occurring adaptation has the appearance of a direct response to a need. As will appear, living organisms very frequently show just this kind of adjustment when the conditions of their environment are altered.

When the new conditions are established and the relative proportion of Y_1 has increased in this way the system may be transferred back to its original environment where α_j is once again large, and where consequently the Y_1 route is no longer of much importance. The composition now alters again so that $\alpha_j \dfrac{X_{j+1}}{X_j} + \beta_j \dfrac{Y_1}{X_j}$ returns to the value k, in which process Y_1/X_j reverts to its original low value. Y_1 is in fact diluted out as growth goes on. If one began to study the phenomenon only from the moment of re-transfer to the original medium, one would say that this medium inhibited the synthesis of Y_1.

The phenomenon described is very reminiscent of that designated enzyme repression (see p. 278). It depends, however, not on any positive inhibiting action but simply on the competition of an alternative process permitting more efficient overall growth.

The principal result of the foregoing discussion may be summed up in what we shall refer to as the *network theorem*. It may be recapitulated as follows. The growth of living matter depends upon closed cycles of mutually dependent interactions, as a result of which, in a constant environment, a steady state is reached where the proportions of the various constituents have settled down to constant values. These correspond to an optimum rate of increase, since any lack of the perfect balance achieved in the steady state leads to bottle-necks and rate-limiting steps. In a new environment the proportions modulate to new values again consistent with optimum growth in the changed circumstances.

The reaction pattern is a branched one, with the formation of some components dependent on more than one other, and some themselves serving the needs of more than one other. There may also be alternative routes from given initial substances to the final cell components, and the relative extent to which the alternatives are used depends upon the medium in which growth occurs. Components such as enzymes on which large demands are made tend to increase in amount: others which are no longer useful diminish.

The network theorem reflects much of the plasticity and adaptability of living matter, but by itself it is incomplete in various ways.

In the first place, as we have developed it, it may well oversimplify the nature of the mutual dependences. This is, however, very unlikely to have led to the prediction of possibilities which do not exist, and, indeed, the actual behaviour of living matter is probably more and not less subtly adaptive than we have foreseen.

In the second place, we have dealt only with the total masses of the various components, and tacitly assumed the possibility of maintaining constant conditions. But in practice these can only be maintained if regular cell division occurs. A condition for cell division must be superposed on what has already been postulated, and this constitutes a problem which will be dealt with in the following chapters, especially Chapter XIV.

Thirdly, no account has so far been taken of the mechanical, geometrical, or steric relations of the nucleic acids, enzymes, and so on packed in the cell. This is a matter which will prove to be very closely connected with the stability or persistence of adaptive changes. It will be dealt with in Chapter X.

In concluding this part of the discussion we should like to make certain general observations. So far the treatment has been confined to broad outlines. This has been because the principle of the total integration of all processes seems to be absolutely central to the understanding of living matter. Many valuable and useful conceptions have grown up in the field of cell chemistry. Genetic codes are in effect chemical formulae, and genes are regions of a macromolecular structure containing enough information to lead to the appearance of given characters in a cell. For example, there is experimental evidence which can be interpreted to mean that a sequence of three specific nucleotide bases favours the incorporation of a particular amino-acid into protein in an artificially made broken cell preparation.[8] Operons and cistrons play an important part in modern genetic theory and are visualized from the results of genetic experiments (see Jacob and Wollman,[9] and Benzer[10]). Messenger and transfer RNA represent diffusible forms of nucleic acid which can be formed in one part of a cell and mediate synthesis in another (see p. 24). Ribosomes are discrete particles in the cytoplasm of the cell which appear to be major sites of protein synthesis (see p. 24). For certain limited purposes all these things can be discussed in isolation and specific hypotheses made about their functioning. But it is only when they are assembled into a machine that they make complete sense, and when the assembly and its laws are ignored, unnecessary *ad hoc* hypotheses may appear needed to explain in terms of an isolated part of the machine facts which simply reflect the essential relation of this part to others.

Isolation of particular aspects of the total function is often the basis of very valuable experimental techniques, for example, the incorporation of radioactively labelled compounds into broken cell preparations which contain various enzymes and nucleic acids but no longer have an intact function. The biochemistry of isolated enzymes or groups of enzymes can be studied, with invaluable results for the understanding of sequences of chemical steps. But all the information so obtained needs ultimately to be coordinated in the light of the principle of total integration. The influence of inhibitory substances on the differential rates of formation of cell components may be studied: for example, chloramphenicol is commonly stated specifically to inhibit the synthesis of protein. But a more correct statement would be that in certain types of experiment the ratio nucleic acid/protein continues to rise for a time during the uncoordinated happenings which follow the disturbance of normal function by the addition of this drug.

A good deal of experimental material will presently be considered, and when possible mathematical interpretations of phenomena will be given. We shall need to deal with individual parts of the cell mechanism in more detail than has been done in the foregoing paragraphs, and in order to reduce the complication to manageable proportions we shall introduce certain simplifications. In the first place, during growth and reproduction of cell material we shall, on the basis of the general proposition established in the present chapter, represent the increase of each cell component according to a simple autocatalytic law $dx/dt = kx$. This, as has been shown, does not in any sense imply that it has the power of auto-replication in its own right.

In the complete train of chemical processes there will be whole sequences of enzymes, and a great deal of importance will attach to the way in which an influence affecting one enzyme in a sequence reacts upon its neighbours in the chain.

We proceed, therefore, to discuss certain propositions about such linked processes. However much oversimplified they may be they illuminate important cell properties.

3. Elementary model of linked-cell processes

(a) Reaction sequences

Although quite similar considerations would apply to nucleic acids and other macromolecular cell components, we shall in what follows be largely concerned with enzymes. If, however, for enzyme we choose in places to read nucleic acid little difference would result.

We imagine a series of enzymes so linked that the product of the operation of each one constitutes the substrate for the next. As has been shown, each one will in effect increase according to the auto-synthetic law, with expansion of its own substance and, necessarily, the simultaneous formation of a diffusible compound which can pass to the succeeding enzyme. This clearly is the condition that a sequence is possible at all. The rate of growth of each enzyme is taken to be proportional to its own instantaneous amount and to be a function of the concentration of the substrate. This function, which we now introduce for greater generality will probably have the general form of an adsorption isotherm, giving direct proportionality to concentration for low concentrations and independence of rate and concentration for high ones. For the purposes of calculation it will be convenient to assume one or other of these limiting cases, rather than to introduce more elaborate forms of the function at this stage.

Let e_μ be the amount of the μth enzyme of the series. It will be expedient to define this, not as the amount in each cell, but as the total amount in the whole culture. e_μ, therefore, increases both when the number of cells, n, remains constant and the supply per cell increases, and also when the amount per cell is constant but the value of n becomes greater as a result of growth and division. The value of de_μ/dt thus represents the rate of expansion of bacterial substance, regardless of whether division is taking place or not.

For the expansion of the μth enzyme, then, we write

$$\frac{de_\mu}{dt} = k_\mu e_\mu c_{\mu-1} \tag{1}$$

or
$$\frac{de_\mu}{dt} = k_\mu e_\mu, \tag{1a}$$

according to the dependence on c_μ (the constants having, of course, a different meaning in the two cases). $c_{\mu-1}$ is the concentration of the substrate provided by the previous enzyme of the series.

The value of $c_{\mu-1}$ is determined by the balance of several factors: (1) the gross rate of production of the intermediate by the $(\mu-1)$th enzyme, (2) the rate of its consumption by the μth enzyme, and (3) the loss due to diffusion or to participation in irrelevant chemical reactions.

The calculations may be simplified, without effect on the essential results, by neglect of (2) in comparison with (3), i.e. the production of intermediates is supposed for simplicity to be rather prodigal, a fraction only being used in the direct reaction sequence.

For the net rate of production of the μth intermediate we write

$$n\frac{dc_\mu}{dt} = k'_\mu e_\mu c_{\mu-1} - K_\mu c_\mu n, \tag{2}$$

or the corresponding equation derived from (1 a). The terms in this equation require some comment. That on the left gives the rise in *concentration* multiplied by the number of cells: this term, therefore, represents the total *net* increase in amount of intermediate contained in all the cells. Strictly speaking, c_μ is thus expressed as the quantity per cell rather than per unit volume of substance, but, the average cell size being for the present assumed constant, the appropriate numerical factor can be taken as incorporated in k'_μ and K_μ on the other side of the equation.

This net increase is balanced by the two terms on the right, the first giving the gross production by all the bacterial substance and the second the total rate of loss. The latter will be proportional to the concentration prevailing, and also to the number of cells, since, if loss is by diffusion, then the rate is proportional to the area of wall, which in turn is proportional to n. Loss by irrelevant reactions will also be proportional to n.

The first term on the right is derived from equation (1), and expresses the condition that the enzyme must yield its diffusible products in the course of the whole set of operations which result in its apparent autosynthesis. These two operations being proportional but not identical, the constant k_μ is replaced by k'_μ.

For the whole sequence of reactions, therefore, we shall have sets of equations of which the following are typical:

$$\frac{de_{\mu-1}}{dt} = k_{\mu-1} e_{\mu-1}, \tag{3}$$

$$n\frac{dc_{\mu-1}}{dt} = k'_{\mu-1} e_{\mu-1} - K_{\mu-1} c_{\mu-1} n, \tag{4}$$

$$\frac{de_\mu}{dt} = k_\mu e_\mu c_{\mu-1}. \tag{5}$$

These link the growth of the μth enzyme with that of the $(\mu-1)$th.

In (3) it is assumed that the enzyme is saturated with the substrate derived from preceding processes, whereas in (5) linear dependence of rate on substrate concentration is assumed. This assumption is not essential, of course, but it expresses the particular case which it will be useful to develop in this section.

When the steady state is established, that is during the logarithmic phase of growth, the concentrations of the various intermediates will assume stationary values in the sense discussed in Chapter I (p. 12). We shall have, therefore, equations such as the following:

$$\frac{dc_{\mu-1}}{dt} = 0,$$

whence from (4) $k'_{\mu-1} e_{\mu-1} - K_{\mu-1} c_{\mu-1} n = 0.$ (6)

(b) Expression of a condition for cell division

At this stage we have to consider the relation between the total amount of enzyme and the number of cells, n. Cell division depends upon factors which have yet to be discussed. All we shall now assume is that there is some cell component or group of components which must be built up to some necessary minimum before the cell is ready to divide. Let the subscript μ apply to a component upon the full complement of which the division waits. Then there will be direct proportionality between n and e_μ. This being so, $n = \beta e_\mu,$ (7)

where β is a constant.

(c) Proportions of enzymes

From (6) and (7),

$$k'_{\mu-1} e_{\mu-1} - K_{\mu-1} c_{\mu-1} \beta e_\mu = 0,$$

whence $$c_{\mu-1} = \frac{k'_{\mu-1} e_{\mu-1}}{\beta K_{\mu-1} e_\mu}.$$ (8)

Integration of (3) gives

$$e_{\mu-1} = (e_{\mu-1})_0 e^{k_{\mu-1} t},$$ (9)

where $(e_{\mu-1})_0$ is the amount present at the time zero.

Inserting (8) and (9) in (5), we find

$$\frac{de_\mu}{dt} = \frac{k_\mu k'_{\mu-1} e_{\mu-1}}{\beta K_{\mu-1} e_\mu} e_\mu$$ (10)

$$= \frac{k_\mu k'_{\mu-1}}{\beta K_{\mu-1}} e_{\mu-1},$$

i.e. $$\frac{de_\mu}{dt} = \frac{k_\mu k'_{\mu-1}}{\beta K_{\mu-1}} (e_{\mu-1})_0 e^{k_{\mu-1} t}.$$ (10 a)

Integration of (10 a) gives

$$\frac{e_\mu - (e_\mu)_0}{e_{\mu-1} - (e_{\mu-1})_0} = \frac{k_\mu k'_{\mu-1}}{\beta K_{\mu-1} k_{\mu-1}}.$$ (11)

(d) *Logarithmic growth phase*

When growth has proceeded for long enough for the amount of new substance to outweigh that present at time zero, the left-hand side of (11) approaches more and more closely to $e_\mu/e_{\mu-1}$. In other words, in the normal steady state the ratio of the amounts of the two enzymes is constant:

$$\frac{e_\mu}{e_{\mu-1}} = \frac{k_\mu k'_{\mu-1}}{\beta K_{\mu-1} k_{\mu-1}} = \gamma. \tag{12}$$

It should be observed, however, that although the ratio is constant during logarithmic growth, nevertheless γ changes with the value of the constants in (12). Any influence which modifies the values of these will cause a change in the balance of the enzymes. This will prove to be of great importance in the further discussion of adaptive processes.

In equation (3) the enzyme is assumed saturated with respect to its substrate. Had this not been postulated, the concentration $c_{\mu-2}$ would have had to be derived from an earlier equation of the series. This process might have had to be repeated a number of times. Eventually, however, one of the enzymes is encountered for which the introduction of a c term is unnecessary. In the last resort this must apply to the enzymes responsible for the utilization of the primary nutrient substances provided by the medium. Equation (12) may therefore be regarded as generally applicable during the logarithmic phase.

Equation (9) states

$$e_{\mu-1} = (e_{\mu-1})_0 e^{k_{\mu-1} t},$$

and equation (10) may be written

$$\frac{1}{e_\mu} \frac{de_\mu}{dt} = \frac{k_\mu k'_{\mu-1}}{\beta K_{\mu-1}} \frac{e_{\mu-1}}{e_\mu}. \tag{13}$$

After growth has been proceeding for some time

$$\frac{e_\mu}{e_{\mu-1}} = \frac{k_\mu k'_{\mu-1}}{\beta K_{\mu-1} k_{\mu-1}}, \quad \text{from (12).}$$

Therefore

$$\frac{1}{e_\mu} \frac{de_\mu}{dt} = k_{\mu-1}$$

or

$$e_\mu = (e_\mu)_0 e^{k_{\mu-1} t}, \tag{14}$$

and if we choose formally to write

$$e_\mu = (e_\mu)_0 e^{\chi_\mu t},$$

then

$$\chi_\mu = k_{\mu-1}.$$

In other words, the exponential constants for the enzymes are equal.

This is only true so long as we are able to replace $e_{\mu-1}/e_{\mu}$ in (10) by the value γ which it attains after continued growth. If $(e_\mu)_0$ and $(e_{\mu-1})_0$ in (11) had *arbitrary* values, it would be some time before (9) and (14) were simultaneously applicable.

If, however, a culture has been maintained in a given medium for some time, then on serial subculture during the logarithmic phase, the value of $(e_\mu)_0/(e_{\mu-1})_0$ for the new period of growth is the same as $(e_\mu)_\infty/(e_{\mu-1})_\infty$ for the old, and (9) and (14) apply from the beginning, since now $\{e_\mu-(e_\mu)_0\}/\{e_{\mu-1}-(e_{\mu-1})_0\} = \gamma$ throughout.

Logarithmic growth cannot be expected if the value of γ is seriously different in the new medium from what it was in the old: nor will this mode of growth set in immediately if the ratio of the enzymes at the time of subculture differs from that established during the previous logarithmic phase in the same medium. The former case will be considered later in connexion with adaptation. The latter is clearly related to the lag phase.

(e) *Simple model of lag phase depending upon enzyme decay*

During the stationary phase some of the enzymes decay. For the purposes of this discussion we shall take the case where one particular enzyme has decayed much more than the others. Let this one be the $(\mu-1)$th. Since the $(\mu-1)$th is present in much less than normal amount, the functioning of the μth will be affected, and division will be delayed. This delay will constitute one form of lag, which has something in common with the lags actually observed.

In the calculation which follows it will be assumed that the decayed enzyme begins to recover at the normal rate as soon as transfer to the new medium occurs, no other disorganization of the reaction sequence having occurred. This assumption is likely to represent only part of the truth, but the consequences to which it leads will be typical of lags in general.

The growth equations are given by (3), (4), and (5). Since we shall be concerned with the period preceding the first cell division, n will be n_0 throughout, n_0 being the number of cells in the inoculum taken from the old medium and transferred to the new at time zero. To simplify notation $(\mu-1)$ will now be written as 1 and μ as 2.

We have then:

$$de_1/dt = k_1 e_1, \tag{15}$$

$$n_0\, dc_1/dt = k_1' e_1 - K_1 c_1 n_0, \tag{16}$$

$$de_2/dt = k_2 e_2 c_1. \tag{17}$$

(15) gives $$e_1 = (e_1)_0\, e^{k_1 t},$$

so that (16) becomes†

$$n_0 \frac{dc_1}{dt} + K_1 n_0 c_1 = k_1'(e_1)_0\, e^{k_1 t}.$$

The solution of this last equation is

$$c_1 = (c_1)_0\, e^{-K_1 t} + \frac{k_1'(e_1)_0}{n_0(k_1+K_1)} \{e^{k_1 t} - e^{-K_1 t}\}, \tag{18 a}$$

where $(c_1)_0$ is the value of c_1 at $t = 0$.

(17) now becomes

$$\frac{de_2}{dt} = k_2 e_2 \left[(c_1)_0\, e^{-K_1 t} + \frac{k_1'(e_1)_0}{n_0(k_1+K_1)} \{e^{k_1 t} - e^{-K_1 t}\} \right],$$

which by integration yields

$$\ln \frac{e_2}{(e_2)_0} = \frac{k_2(c_1)_0}{K_1}(1 - e^{-K_1 t}) + \frac{k_2 k_1'(e_1)_0}{n_0(k_1+K_1)} \left(\frac{e^{k_1 t}-1}{k_1} + \frac{e^{-K_1 t}-1}{K_1} \right), \tag{18 b}$$

where $(e_2)_0$ is the amount of e_2 at $t = 0$.

If the inoculum comes from an old culture, the intermediates will have diffused out of the cells and $(c_1)_0$ will be nearly zero. In this case the first term on the right-hand side of (18 b) may be neglected.

According to our postulated conditions $(e_1)_0$ is small compared with the normal complement, while $(e_2)_0$ starts at the standard value. The lag will end when $(e_2)_0$ has increased to $2(e_2)_0$. Up to this point n will remain constant at n_0. $(e_1)_0$ being small, t must be considerable, so that (18 b) may be written in the approximate form

$$\ln \frac{e_2}{(e_2)_0} = \frac{k_2 k_1'(e_1)_0}{k_1 n_0(k_1+K_1)}\, e^{k_1 t},$$

or, if L is the lag, $$\ln 2 = \frac{k_2 k_1'(e_1)_0}{k_1 n_0(k_1+K_1)}\, e^{k_1 L}.$$

Since from (7) and (12) respectively

$$n_0 = \beta(e_2)_0 \quad \text{and} \quad (e_2)_0/(e_1)_{0\,\text{normal}} = k_2 k_1'/\beta K_1 k_1,$$

we obtain $$\ln 2 = \left\{ \frac{K_1}{(k_1+K_1)} \frac{(e_1)_0}{(e_1)_{0\,\text{normal}}} \right\} e^{k_1 L}.$$

---

† K_1, the constant governing the rate of loss of intermediate by diffusion, will in fact vary slightly as the lag ends and the cells begin to grow larger. An average value may, however, be assumed for the present purpose without serious error.

If the age of the cells used for the inoculum be denoted by S, the simplest expression for $(e_1)_0$ is

$$(e_1)_0 = (e_1)_{0 \text{ normal}} e^{-\lambda S},$$

λ being a decay constant.

The last equation then becomes

$$k_1 L = \lambda S + \ln\left\{\frac{0 \cdot 693(k_1 + K_1)}{K_1}\right\}. \tag{19}$$

According to this the lag would increase linearly with the age of the cells. In practice such behaviour may be observed over a certain range. Usually, however, the lag increases rather rapidly at first and then more slowly.[11] There was in fact no imperative necessity to assume a simple exponential decay law for the enzyme: more complex laws are expressible by the introduction of a variable λ. If, for example, the enzyme decayed not according to the assumed first order law, but, as is conceivable, according to a second order law, then λ would diminish with decreasing e_1 and the lag would increase with age at a rate which decreased as time went on.

4. Cyclically linked enzyme model

One very important class of linked reactions is typified by the following simple system:

$$
\begin{array}{ccc}
\text{Enzyme} & c_1 & \text{Enzyme} \\
\longrightarrow \text{I} & \longrightarrow & \text{II} \longrightarrow \\
& \underleftarrow{c_2} &
\end{array}
$$

which illustrates some of the essentials of the problem. It is supposed that one of the later enzymes of the sequence produces a diffusible intermediate which plays a necessary part in the functioning of one of the earlier enzymes—acting, for example, in conjunction with another substrate provided by the external medium. The synthesis and operation of enzyme I in the diagram is here supposed to require the intermediate from II: and the set of equations which now applies is taken to be

$$de_1/dt = k_1 c_2 e_1, \tag{1}$$

$$ndc_1/dt = k_1' c_2 e_1 - K_1 c_1 n, \tag{2}$$

$$de_2/dt = k_2 c_1 e_2, \tag{3}$$

$$ndc_2/dt = k_2' c_1 e_2 - K_2 c_2 n. \tag{4}$$

These equations differ from the set (15), (16), and (17) on p. 120 by the addition of the last, and by the introduction of the factor c_2 into

(1) and (2). Enzyme I may, of course, require substrates other than that returned from enzyme II, but its rate of synthesis and action is assumed independent of their concentration.

The most interesting consequence of these new equations is in connexion with the lag phase. In the last section we were concerned with the development of lag caused by the decay of enzymes. We may now consider more closely the lag which might arise as a result of disturbances, by loss during the stationary phase, of the steady concentrations of the various diffusible intermediates.

From the equation (18 a) of the last section it is obvious that if $(c_1)_0$ is zero, that is if all the intermediate has been dispersed from the cells before they are transferred to the new medium, then

$$c_1 = \frac{k_1'(e_1)_0}{n_0(k_1+K_1)} \{e^{k_1 t} - e^{-K_1 t}\},$$

and the rate at which the new concentration is built up depends, apart from the constants k_1 and K_1, only on the initial amount of the *enzyme*. The regeneration of c_1 is independent of $(c_1)_0$. Therefore no very long lag can be expected unless there has been an appreciable decay of the enzymes themselves.

The matter is quite different according to the new set of equations (1) and (4).

During the lag n remains constant at n_0. Moreover, since we are considering dispersal of intermediates rather than decay of enzymes, we may take, with a good degree of approximation, $e_1 = (e_1)_0$ and $e_2 = (e_2)_0$ during most of the lag.

Therefore (2) and (4) become:

$$\frac{dc_1}{dt} = \frac{k_1'}{n_0}(e_1)_0 c_2 - K_1 c_1, \tag{5}$$

$$\frac{dc_2}{dt} = \frac{k_2'}{n_0}(e_2)_0 c_1 - K_2 c_2. \tag{6}$$

The solution of these equations gives

$$c_1 = Ae^{\alpha t} + Be^{\beta t},$$

where α and β are the roots of the equation

$$m^2 + (K_1+K_2)m + K_1 K_2 - \frac{k_1'}{n_0}(e_1)_0 \frac{k_2'}{n_0}(e_2)_0 = 0.$$

When $t = 0$, $c_1 = (c_1)_0$ and $c_2 = (c_2)_0$, whence

$$c_1 = \frac{(c_2)_0(k_1'/n_0)(e_1)_0 - (c_1)_0(K_1+\beta)}{\alpha-\beta}\, e^{\alpha t} + \frac{(c_2)_0(k_1'/n_0)(e_1)_0 - (c_1)_0(K_1+\alpha)}{\beta-\alpha}\, e^{\beta t},$$

with a corresponding expression for c_2.

The important fact here is that the factors multiplying the exponential terms are both linear functions of $(c_1)_0$ and $(c_2)_0$, not merely, as before, of $(e_1)_0$ or $(e_2)_0$. Thus if $(c_1)_0$ and $(c_2)_0$ were both zero, c_1 and c_2 would remain zero for all time. The essential result is more clearly seen if we introduce the simplification that

$$K_1 = K_2 \quad \text{and} \quad k_1'(e_1)_0/n_0 = k_2'(e_2)_0/n_0.$$

We have then

$$c_1 = \frac{(c_1)_0+(c_2)_0}{2}\, e^{\{k_1'(e_1)_0/n_0 - K_1\}t} + \frac{(c_1)_0-(c_2)_0}{2}\, e^{-\{k_1'(e_1)_0/n_0 + K_1\}t},$$

$$c_2 = \frac{(c_1)_0+(c_2)_0}{2}\, e^{\{k_1'(e_1)_0/n_0 - K_1\}t} - \frac{(c_1)_0-(c_2)_0}{2}\, e^{-\{k_1'(e_1)_0/n_0 + K_1\}t}.$$

These last equations differ from equation (18 a) of the last section in that the rate of restoration of c_1 and c_2 depends very much upon $(c_1)_0$ and $(c_2)_0$. Both of these appear in the multipliers of the exponential terms. With the initial values zero there is no recovery. If the initial values are small enough, then recovery may require a time which can be made as great as we please. Thus any value of the lag, up to infinity, could be accounted for in terms of the loss of intermediates. The cyclical mechanism postulated here is not at all improbable in itself. The consequences of its operation are such that recovery from a serious disturbance of the steady state is very much more difficult than it would be with a non-cyclical mechanism. Naturally the example which has just been discussed has been simplified in the most extreme degree possible, but one can see quite clearly that the same kind of result must apply to more elaborately coupled systems. There is, of course, an analogy between the slow and difficult recovery predicted for the chemical systems constituting the cell economy and the extreme tardiness with which complex interlocking national economies can right themselves after the dislocations of supply resulting from events like wars.

From quite a different point of view it is interesting to note that, according to equations (2) and (4) there is no necessary steady concentration of the intermediates during actual growth. If we equate dc_1/dt and dc_2/dt to zero for a steady state, then we only obtain a value for the ratio c_1/c_2. This result differs from that given by the expression (16) of the last section which, equated to zero, defines c_1. Thus, as far as the present equations go, c_1 and c_2 could both continue to increase indefinitely, each stimulating the further increase of the other. But, in fact, one or other must reach such a value that the corresponding enzyme is saturated with substrate. Thus a stationary state will be imposed by conditions other than equations (2) and (4). It will correspond to a condition where one of the enzymes is just working at its maximum possible rate. This result may be very significant in connexion with the considerations advanced on pp. 156 and 190.

As far as the considerations of this section and of the last in respect of the lag go, we may summarize by saying that the decay of enzymes may give as long a lag as we need to account for: dispersal of intermediates will also do this when we postulate some form of cyclic mechanism in the complete reaction sequence.

5. Rate-determining steps: steady states

It has sometimes been the custom to speak of a 'master reaction' which is rate-determining for a whole chain of consecutive processes, such as occur in cells. This is not strictly valid. The velocity of a series of consecutive reactions is certainly not governed in general by that of the slowest. This is easily seen by considering a simple example, namely a series of consecutive first-order reactions, familiar in connexion with radioactive disintegrations:

$$A \longrightarrow B \longrightarrow C.$$

From the equations

$$-\frac{dA}{dt} = k_A A, \qquad \frac{dB}{dt} = k_A A - k_B B, \qquad \frac{dC}{dt} = k_B B,$$

one obtains

$$C = A_0 \left\{ 1 - \frac{1}{k_A - k_B} (k_A e^{-k_B t} - k_B e^{-k_A t}) \right\},$$

from which it is obvious that the rate of production of C depends both upon k_A and upon k_B and not upon either of them separately.

On the other hand, if k_B can be assumed to be very much greater than k_A, the value of C approximates closely to the form

$$C = A_0 \left\{ 1 + \frac{1}{k_B} (0 - k_B e^{-k_A t}) \right\}$$
$$= A_0 (1 - e^{-k_A t}) = A_0 - A.$$

That is to say, provided that k_B can be regarded as very great compared with k_A, then the rate of formation of C can be taken as independent of its precise value. Examples are common enough in chemistry where one of the velocity constants is so great that its exact value need not be taken into consideration. But this is only true in special circumstances. It is not enough merely for one reaction to be slower than the others for it to become a rate-determining step.

It will now be useful to consider how far the simple model which was discussed in the last section will be subject to a master-reaction or rate-determining step. For this purpose the equations of section 3 will be rewritten in a rather more general form:

$$\frac{de_{\mu-1}}{dt} = k_{\mu-1} e_{\mu-1} f_{\mu-1}(c_{\mu-2}), \tag{1}$$

$$n \frac{dc_{\mu-1}}{dt} = k'_{\mu-1} e_{\mu-1} f_{\mu-1}(c_{\mu-1}) - K_{\mu-1} c_{\mu-1} n - k_{\mu} e_{\mu} f_{\mu}(c_{\mu-1}) = 0, \tag{2}$$

$$\frac{de_{\mu}}{dt} = k_{\mu} e_{\mu} f_{\mu}(c_{\mu-1}). \tag{3}$$

These differ from the previous set in two ways: first, the influence of the substrate concentration on the speed of the enzyme reaction is expressed by the unspecified function f:† secondly, in (2) the loss of intermediate by diffusion is no longer assumed to play the principal part in balancing its production. The third term on the right of (2) represents the rate of consumption of the intermediate by the following enzyme of the sequence. Otherwise the assumptions and symbols are the same as those of the previous sections.

Introducing certain abbreviations, we may rewrite (2)

$$a \frac{de_{\mu-1}}{dt} - Zn - \frac{de_{\mu}}{dt} = 0, \tag{4}$$

where $a = k'_{\mu-1}/k_{\mu-1}$ and $Z = K_{\mu-1} c_{\mu-1}$.

Integration gives

$$a\{(e_{\mu-1}) - (e_{\mu-1})_0\} - Z \int n \, dt - \{(e_{\mu}) - (e_{\mu})_0\} = 0. \tag{5}$$

In the present example let the $(\mu-1)$th enzyme be that which bears a constant ratio to n. Then

$$e_{\mu-1} = (e_{\mu-1})_0 e^{k_{\mu-1} t} \quad \text{and} \quad n = n_0 e^{k_{\mu-1} t}.$$

With $Z' = Z/k_{\mu-1}$, (5) therefore becomes

$$e_{\mu} - (e_{\mu})_0 = \{a(e_{\mu-1})_0 - Z' n_0\} e^{k_{\mu-1} t} - a(e_{\mu-1})_0 + Z' n_0$$

† It will be convenient to express the function f in such a way that it becomes unity when the enzyme is saturated and the rate independent of substrate: this saves the introduction of extra proportionality constants, but is otherwise trivial.

which, when the actual values considerably outweigh the initial values, reduces to

$$e_\mu = \{a(e_{\mu-1})_0 - Z'n_0\}e^{k_{\mu-1}t}. \tag{6}$$

This is required by the equation (2) which expresses the possibility of a steady state. But according to (3)

$$\frac{1}{e_\mu}\frac{de_\mu}{dt} = k_\mu f_\mu(c_{\mu-1}),$$

whence

$$e_\mu = (e_\mu)_0 e^{k_\mu f_\mu(c_{\mu-1})t}.$$

Thus the condition for a steady state is that

$$k_\mu f_\mu(c_{\mu-1}) = k_{\mu-1}.$$

This is attainable in one of two ways. If the enzyme is saturated with substrate, so that f_μ is unity, then a stable steady state is only possible under the condition that $k_\mu = k_{\mu-1}$.

On the other hand, if the enzyme is not saturated, and its rate is responsive to changes in $c_{\mu-1}$, then $c_{\mu-1}$ will adjust itself to such a value that the steady state is established.

Thus the relations of the $(\mu-1)$th and the μth enzyme may be envisaged as follows. If the second is inherently capable of much more rapid growth than the first, then it will keep the substrate concentration near zero and its own expansion can only occur at an absolute rate governed by the material which the first passes on to it. Its own formation must settle down to bear a constant ratio to that of the first, determined by a purely stoicheiometric factor. From the point of view of equation (2) this is not a steady state, but from the point of view of cell economy it maintains constancy of composition. If the second enzyme increases more slowly than the first, even when saturated with intermediate, no steady state is possible and it will be eliminated on further growth. The most important case, however, is that where the second enzyme increases more slowly than the first at very small values of c, and faster for high values. Then as increase in bacterial mass occurs, the first may tend to increase relatively to the second: this increases c, which in turn causes more rapid growth of the second, so that a steady state is established and can be maintained indefinitely, as long as the conditions are kept constant.

Having considered the relations of the $(\mu-1)$th and the μth enzymes, we must now give some attention to those of the $(\mu-1)$th to its precursors.

If all the enzymes of the sequence are linked in the way described, and all are responsive to the concentrations of the intermediate substrates, then just as the μth comes to be formed in a constant ratio to the $(\mu-1)$th, so the $(\mu-1)$th does to the $(\mu-2)$th and so on back to the first of the series. The rate of formation of the first will, of course, be a function of external concentrations of foodstuffs. Thus the whole set of enzymes will tend to settle down to constant proportions. If at any stage of the sequence there is an enzyme whose inherent rate is so great that it consumes all the substrate which can be supplied, then this only makes its proportion still more dependent upon the previous members of the series. If, on the other hand, there were one whose rate was so small that no increase in its substrate concentration could cause it to keep pace, then it, and all subsequent members of the series, would be eliminated: and the postulated sequence would not play any part in bacterial processes.

In a certain sense it might be permissible to regard the first step of the sort of sequence described above as a master reaction: though it by no means determines the proportions of the individual enzymes. However, a further possibility must be borne in mind, and this suggests even greater reserve about the use of the term. We have, where convenient, treated enzyme processes as though they constituted one single sequence. Discussions based upon this idea may serve as useful general guides, but they certainly represent an over-simplification. What, in principle, must occur is that the product of one of the later enzymes of a sequence should itself participate, in conjunction with other substrates, in the operation of one of the earlier enzymes, the cell economy as a whole being the totally integrated system discussed in the earlier part of this chapter.

6. Some applications of the models

(a) Enzyme proportions and activities in cells

In an established and prolonged logarithmic growth phase, if external conditions remain constant, the enzymes (and nucleic acids and so on) must settle down to constant ratios, and their activities should reach and retain steady values. But, under normal conditions of growth, the logarithmic phase is not indefinitely prolonged, and the external conditions change. Nutrient materials become exhausted, toxic products accumulate, and the pH changes. The values of the individual constants in the equations of the previous sections themselves change, so that a true steady state is only reached in continuous culture. Otherwise the cells tend always to be moving from one steady state towards another.

This is particularly true when large inocula of old cultures are sub-cultured into new medium not capable of supporting very heavy growth. Before the true steady-state proportions of cell material, seriously disturbed by decay during the stationary phase, are re-established in logarithmic growth, the disturbances due to the approach to a new stationary phase begin to manifest themselves. In such circumstances it is hard for the culture ever to become truly stabilized. The proper conditions for stabilization are repeated subculture into fresh medium of small inocula never allowed to age, or continuous culture.

(b) Adaptive phenomena

When cells which have reached a stable condition in one medium are transferred to another, the constants of many of the separate processes are likely to have changed values. A new stable state has to be established. It will be shown that this readjustment is, in all probability, closely connected with the adaptive phenomena exhibited by bacteria when they are grown in changed media. The whole matter will be discussed more fully in a later chapter, and a few preliminary observations are all that will be made here.

Suppose under the changed conditions the value of the constant k_μ has a smaller value. This would tend at first to cause an increase in the amount of the $(\mu-1)$th enzyme relatively to the amount of the μth. But this increase will cause a rise in $c_{\mu-1}$, which can in turn stimulate more growth of the μth. In such a case adaptation would occur and would be accompanied by a change in one or more of the intermediate concentrations. In the case where the steady state depended upon the absolute equality of $k_{\mu-1}$ and k_μ (see p. 127), this automatic regulation by way of the intermediate concentration could not occur: any adaptation would involve an actual change in the value of k_μ. This could only come about as a result of a modification in the texture of the enzyme itself. In principle we must be prepared to envisage two kinds of adaptive change: one dependent upon mere changed proportions of components, the other associated with actual structural modifications.

(c) Drug action

Drugs may modify specifically any of the constants of the growth equations. If the rate of the primary nutrient utilization is cut down, no automatic adaptive response can be predicted from the foregoing considerations. If, however, the principal influence is exerted upon the operation of the μth enzyme of the sequence, then an expansion of the

$(\mu-1)$th enzyme can give an increased intermediate concentration which can counteract the inhibition due to the drug. Partial or complete resistance of the cells may then develop. This matter will be discussed more fully in a subsequent chapter.

(d) Simple formulation of an automatic adjustment in a system involving two enzymes in series

It will be useful now to give a simple mathematical formulation of the kind of automatic adjustment that can occur.

Suppose enzyme I works to produce a diffusible metabolite which attains a concentration c in the region between I and a second enzyme II which utilizes the intermediate. At time t let the total amounts of I and II be X_1 and X_2 respectively, and, if the cell count is n, the amounts per cell will be X_1/n and X_2/n.

The value of c will be determined by an equation of the type

$$dc/dt = A(X_1/n) - B(X_2/n)c - Cc = 0,$$

A, B, and C being constants, and the three corresponding terms representing formation by I, consumption by II, and loss in processes irrelevant to the operation of II. We have also

$$dX_1/dt = k_1 X_1,$$
$$dX_2/dt = k_2 X_2 c.$$

We further assume that division is provoked by a critical amount of X_2, so that $n = \beta X_2$ where β is another constant.

Thus $$c = \alpha X_1/X_2,$$

α being a new constant.

Thus $$dX_2/dt = k_2 \alpha X_1.$$

Let $$X_1/X_2 = v,$$

$$\frac{dv}{dt} = \frac{X_2(dX_1/dt) - X_1(dX_2/dt)}{X_2^2} = v(k_1 - k_2 \alpha v).$$

If $k_2 \alpha v$ starts small and less than k_1 then dv/dt is positive and the ratio of enzyme I to enzyme II, that is v, increases, but as this happens dv/dt falls and presently becomes zero, after which no further change takes place. The ratio X_1/X_2 is now constant and $k_2 \alpha v = k_1$.

As long as the medium conditions are now maintained constant X_1 and X_2 both increase exponentially with the same rate constant.

If an agency such as a drug interferes with c a further automatic adjustment will set in.

7. Cyclical changes in bacterial properties

In the light of the foregoing discussion it is convenient to consider one possible cause of a phenomenon which has from time to time excited comment and curiosity, and which at first sight seems like a manifestation of an arbitrary quality of living matter. When bacteria are subjected to serial subculture in a given medium, they sometimes give the impression of passing through rather irregular cyclical variations. For example, after growing for a number of subcultures in the form of a suspension of well-separated cells, a pronounced tendency to form clumps may develop, the culture showing under the microscope the appearance of matted groups of cells. As the subculturing process is continued, this habit is lost again. Or again, the enzyme activity of cells in respect of a particular enzyme reaction may, even at a standard age of the culture, show a certain fluctuation from one serial subculture to the next.

Now the normal practice in making serial subcultures is to effect a transfer at standard intervals, for example, every 24 hours. Let us now consider the course of events starting from a given point in the series. In general, at the moment of transfer the cells will have shown some decline, even if a small one, from the maximum enzyme activities of the constituents: and this decline, since the decay constants for the various enzymes will be specific properties of the individuals, will have progressed to varying degrees in different parts of the cell substance. During the next phase of growth the enzyme ratios will tend to return to the standard equilibrium values, and will reach them if the logarithmic multiplication continues long enough. Since, however, the logarithmic phase is of finite extent, the original proportions will be only approximately and not exactly re-established. If, for example, the amount of bacterial substance increased tenfold during the growth, then about 90 per cent of the substance should be of the standard composition and 10 per cent might still depart from it. (This assumes for simplicity what is probably not correct, namely, that no repair of the material or rectification of proportions occurs during the lag phase: but the general argument is not affected by the neglect of this consideration.) An additional factor now comes in: if considerable decay of enzyme substance has occurred before our first subculture, the lag will be correspondingly great. For this very reason, the grown culture will be younger at the 24-hour stage than it would have been had the lag been shorter. Thus we shall automatically start the next subculture with more nearly the standard enzyme ratios, and during the subsequent growth still further return to normality occurs. But, since the lag this time has been shorter, there is more time for the culture to age before the next 24-hour transfer, so that greater opportunity for relapse is provided. Once again, the relapse differs in seriousness with different enzymes. We thus have an alternation of decay and restitution going on with a periodicity which not only is irregular but possesses a different kind of irregularity for various parts of the cell. The result is a complicated, though roughly cyclical, variation in certain enzyme proportions, and, correspondingly, one may well believe, in certain specific properties of the cells. The irregularities will be the more marked the shorter the logarithmic growth phase: because with a very long logarithmic phase, one would always have complete restitution of the true equilibrium proportions. If the latter are never given a real opportunity to re-establish themselves, then the cyclical variations referred to will not, strictly speaking, be closed ones, since it is unlikely that the various periodicities created by the subculturing procedure stand in any precise relation to one another. In such an event the cell would show irregular fluctuations in properties with secular trends towards ever new ones. The latter, fortunately, are slow enough, or unimportant enough, not to remove bacteriology from the realms of quantitative science. The former may well account for the many references in the descriptive literature to 'life cycles'. Since the properties showing the fluctuations which we have been discussing include those which determine morphology, the erratic appearance of short rods, filaments, and so on can be understood. The assumption that these represent an ordered sequence of forms through which each individual passes at the appropriate stage, as with certain more complex organisms, seems not to be necessary, at any rate in general. Consideration of the much more subtle and difficult question of code changes in nucleic acids or actual changes in the primary structures of enzyme proteins will be deferred.

8. New forms of integration

The principle of total integration envisages changes in the proportions of various types of nucleic acid in the cell, corresponding to the changes in the various enzymes. The basic equations of the network theorem apply to all cell constituents (although in the immediately foregoing paragraphs we have found it convenient to exemplify the argument by reference to sequences of enzymes). Reference was made in passing to the possibility that, as a result of certain less probable modes of reaction, the actual structure of a nucleic acid might occasionally be modified. Such an event would constitute virtually a mutation of the genetic code and is further discussed in Chapter XIII. If this kind of modification occurs, and the cell can still grow and function, a new pattern of integration is established.

New patterns of integration can be established in other important ways. In the sexual or quasi-sexual conjugation of cells and in the phenomenon of transduction (p. 29) elements from two cells become fitted into a single system. When cells develop what is called 'drug dependence' (p. 175) a new organization comes into being into which the drug itself enters, and an analogous widening of the integrated system occurs when the so-called resistance transfer factors (RTF) pass from one cell to another (p. 31).

In this connexion the relation of a bacterial cell to a bacteriophage (p. 21) is of special interest, since in this example the new integration can be stable or unstable according to circumstances.

The phage enters the cell and a new order of things comes about where the cell machinery, or an important part of it, is geared to the manufacture of fresh phage according to the information contained in the structure of this invader. The upheaval is often inconsistent with the continued normal growth of the cell, which suffers lysis and destruction. On the other hand, a stable new integration may prove possible in which phage and cell are both harmoniously reproduced. The community set up in this way may resemble a normal cell so closely that the presence of the virus element remains undetected until some external disturbance breaks the rhythm of the joint reproduction, and lysis of the cell sets in. In these so-called lysogenic systems two codes of information play parts in determining what happens. Both may remain integrated or, in certain circumstances, they may, as it were, factorize out and compete, that of the virus winning. (In connexion with competing codes compare the remarks on sporulation on p. 408.)

The nature of the disturbance which converts a stable symbiotic relation to an unstable one and causes the phage to become 'virulent', is an interesting one. Presumably the cell machinery is called upon to adapt itself to changed conditions and the consequent adjustments prove incompatible with the maintenance of the balance between cell and phage.

Some cells can adapt themselves to prevent the multiplication of an invading virus. Animal cells when infected produce, in some circumstances, a substance (or class of substances) which enables them to resist the further multiplication of the virus.

A profound question is posed by the origin of bacteriophages. If they are simply parasites of independent origin which meet their hosts and victims by chance, a very difficult problem indeed arises as to their own earlier evolution. In many ways it seems much easier to accept the suggestion that the phages (or viruses in general) are remnants of broken-down cells, still capable of being reintegrated, stably or unstably, into other cells. It has been claimed, especially by Japanese workers, that the formation of viruses in cells can be induced by certain chemical agents which interfere with normal metabolism. The subject is a controversial one in so far as some prefer to regard the apparent induction of the virus as the activation of one already present in a latent condition.

The whole group of phenomena which have been referred to in this section suggest that a cell, as it may become known to us at the present stage of evolution, may be, as it were, a conflation of potentially independent elements, in fact itself a mixed community in which separate modes of integration have been replaced by a common one.†

REFERENCES

1. See J. Brachet, *Nova Acta Leopoldina*, **26**, 17 (1963).
2. P. C. Zamecnik, *Pontif. Acad. Sci. Scripta Varia*, **22**, 431 (1962). (Semaine d'étude sur le problème des macromolécules d'intérêt biologique.)
3. Jean Apgar, R. W. Holley, and Susan H. Merrill, *J. biol. Chem.* **237**, 796 (1962); J. Goldstein, T. P. Bennett, and L. C. Craig, *Proc. natn. Acad. Sci. U.S.A.* **51**, 119 (1964); see G. L. Brown and Sheila Lee, *Br. med. Bull.* **21**, 236 (1965).
4. Elizabeth Work, *J. gen. Microbiol.* **25**, 167 (1961); H. J. Rogers, *Symp. Soc. gen. Microbiol.* **15**, 186 (1965); C. S. Cummins, *Int. Rev. Cytol.* **5**, 25 (1956); H. R. Perkins, *Bact. Rev.* **27**, 18 (1963); M. R. J. Salton, *The Bacterial Cell Wall*, Elsevier, Amsterdam (1964); J. T. Park, *Symp. Soc. gen. Microbiol.* **8**, 49 (1958).
5. See G. N. Cohen and J. Monod, *Bact. Rev.* **21**, 169 (1957); R. J. Britten, *Symp. Soc. gen. Microbiol.* **15**, 57 (1965).
6. C. B. Afinsen, *Pontif. Acad. Sci. Scripta Varia*, **22**, 5 (1962); see also, however, N. H. Martin, *Biochem. J.* **88**, 3P (1963).
7. F. H. C. Crick, *Symp. Soc. exp. Biol.* **12**, 138 (1958).
8. See F. H. C. Crick in *Les Prix Nobel en 1962*, p. 179, Imprimerie Royale, P.A. Norstedt und Söner, Stockholm (1963).
9. F. Jacob and E. L. Wollman, *Sexuality and the Genetics of Bacteria*, Academic Press, New York (1961).
10. S. Benzer in *The Chemical Basis of Heredity*, edited by W. D. McElroy and B. Glass, p. 70, The Johns Hopkins Press, Baltimore (1957).

† For further discussion of the ideas contained in this chapter see the references numbered 12, 13, and 14.

11. A. M. James and C. N. Hinshelwood, *Trans. Faraday Soc.* **44**, 967 (1948); E. H. Cole and C. N. Hinshelwood, ibid. **43**, 266 (1947).
12. Sir Cyril Hinshelwood, *J. chem. Soc.*, p. 745 (1952); pp. 1304, 1947 (1953).
13. A. C. R. Dean and Sir Cyril Hinshelwood, *Progr. Biophys. biophys. Chem*, edited by J. A. V. Butler and J. T. Randall, Pergamon Press, London, **5**, 1 (1955).
14. A. C. R. Dean and Sir Cyril Hinshelwood, *Nature, Lond.* **199**, 7 (1963); **201**, 232 (1964); **202**, 1046 (1964); **206**, 546 (1965).

VI

ADAPTATION TO DRUGS

1. Introduction

THE term drug is not a very precisely defined one. It means essentially a substance, other than a normal intermediate metabolite, which influences the growth and function of a cell, and in this sense both stimulant and inhibiting compounds would be included. The distinction between a stimulant and a growth factor or even an effective nutrient is rather indefinite and we shall chiefly be concerned with inhibitory actions.

Depending as it does on a very complex pattern of linked chemical actions, mediated by enzymes which in turn are built up on information supplied by nucleic acids, the cell function is susceptible to interference in a great many different ways and at a great many different points.

The class of inhibitory agents known as antibiotics is of special interest from this point of view. They are substances produced by one type of living cell as part of its normal metabolism.[1] For this reason they are not at all unlikely to enter at some stage into the reaction pattern of another type of cell, and when this has its own reaction pattern which does not agree with that of the first type, the result of the intervention may be to disrupt the normal harmony of the functioning and give rise to inhibition.

From the kinetic point of view one of the most interesting aspects of drug action is the way in which cells can become resistant to substances which were originally inhibitory or lethal, and, with antibiotics, resistance may even in the end become associated with actual dependence for growth upon the antibiotic itself.

The influence of drugs, then, on bacteria is varied. Some drugs act simply as general protoplasmic poisons, while others have a specific effect on particular members of the complete sequence of enzyme reactions. Some may interfere with nucleic acid replication, and may even conceivably change a genetic code, though, as we have seen, nucleic acid replication and the activity of the enzymes concerned in it are not so sharply separable as some ways of speaking about the matter suggest.

As far as observable effects on a culture are concerned the action of an inhibitor may reveal itself variously as an effect specifically on the lag, on the rate of growth in the phase of logarithmic increase, on the cell division probability, or even on the total bacterial population supportable by the medium.

A distinction, upon which stress was once laid, is that between bacteriostatic and bactericidal action. Since all bacteria die sooner or later if they are not allowed to multiply, the distinction is one of degree rather than one of kind, but for some practical purposes it may be useful.

As regards the relation of drug action and chemical structure, two effects have to be recognized. On the one hand, the partition of the drug between the medium in which the cells grow and the part of the cell where the action is exerted will depend upon the chemical properties of the drug. In particular, the partition coefficient will show more or less regular variations with such changes in the chemical structure of the drug molecule as increasing length of carbon chain, or replacement of one substituent group by another.[2] Many quite important quantitative differences in pharmacological action can be accounted for in terms of varying phase distributions: and when the actions are compared at equivalent chemical potentials, they are seen to be much more nearly equal.[3] The inhibitory action of substituted phenols on the growth of *Aerobacter aerogenes* has been shown to be parallel with the solubility of the particular phenol in olive oil,[4] which it is not impossible to imagine as a crude model of certain parts of the interior of the cell. The inhibitory action of straight chain aliphatic alcohols increases by a constant factor from one member of the homologous series to the next higher one.[5]

Partition effects, on the other hand, can hardly be invoked to explain the enormous differences in antibacterial action of such classes of compound as sulphonamides, acridine derivatives, triphenylmethane dyes, potassium tellurite, and antibiotics such as the various penicillins, streptomycin and chloramphenicol, to mention only a few of the many specifically inhibitory substances. Such differences depend upon the fact that the drugs in question intervene at particular stages of the reaction sequences involved in growth.

In so far as drugs interfere with specific cell reactions, their effects will depend upon the way in which they are taken up by particular parts of the bacterial substance. Even when the concentration of the drug inside the cell is proportional to that in the solution outside, the amount taken up by the protein or other structures will be usually related to this concentration by an equation of the same general nature as an adsorption isotherm, that is one involving specific constants.

In special circumstances the effect of the drug may depend upon the rate of penetration into the cell from outside. With some kinds of cell, and with more complex tissues, penetration may play an all important part. It varies widely and is highly specific but a decisive effect of penetration does not seem to have been forced upon the attention of workers with bacterial cells, and certain observations suggest that it is not usually a limiting factor. For example, cells of *Propionibacterium pentosaceum* were immunized to the action of sodium fluoride by cultivation in its presence. The immunity might have been ascribed to decreased permeability to the fluoride. Yet the resistance was not overcome by a 7-hour contact with fluoride solution before the other substances required for the test were added to the system.[6] Another observation of a somewhat similar kind is the following: if sulphanilamide is left in contact with *Aerobacter aerogenes* for an hour or two before the carbon source required for growth is added, the effect is not greater than when carbon source and drug are added simultaneously.[7] Some of the quantitative results to be discussed in the next chapter would be rather difficult to interpret in terms of penetration rates, but can be coherently treated on the assumption that penetration is rapid. We shall in fact meet one example at least where resistant cells do not take up drug but this will be contrasted with an example where the resistant cells take up more drug than sensitive ones.

In some respects, as we have said, the most interesting and striking of all the phenomena relating to the influence of drugs on bacteria is that of adaptation. When cultivated in presence of antibacterial substances at a concentration insufficient entirely to prevent multiplication, the cells frequently acquire the capacity to grow normally under conditions which initially would have permitted only very feeble growth. After successive periods of growth at increasing concentrations, strains can be obtained showing immunity to hundreds of times the amounts of drug which initially would have caused complete arrest. The production of resistance in this way is sometimes called 'training'.

The interest of the phenomenon for the purposes of the thesis examined in this book is that quite considerable progress can be made in understanding its nature in terms of kinetic models, and indeed that in some examples drug resistance arises simply by the operation of the regulatory mechanisms which reflect the total integration of the cell. As is well known, an alternative explanation of all adaptive changes exists: that, namely, based upon natural selection. According to this, cells of every degree of drug resistance exist. They can arise by chance or by the direct action of agencies such as radiation and mutagenic chemicals. Those which are best equipped to grow in any given environment outgrow their less well-endowed competitors.

In the treatment of adaptive phenomena we shall first discuss examples which conform best to the hypothesis that the observed changes do indeed represent automatic responses to the new environment; in short, that with altered relative reaction velocities, new enzyme balances are established, and that the properties of the adapted cells are explicable in terms of these. We do this because our primary object is the understanding of the cell machinery. Subsequently, the role of natural selection will be considered.

We shall conclude that there are many phenomena which receive their simplest and most economical explanation, and indeed sometimes their only possible explanation, in terms of a regulatory response of the individual cells. The opposition which this conclusion has sometimes met is the more remarkable in that the result is precisely what would be expected from the essential character of living cells and the integrated nature of their activity.

We shall, however, describe examples, probably exceptional, where pre-existent forms, less susceptible to interference, are selected in presence of the drug. In the most clear-cut of these examples the resistant forms have arisen by the action of natural radiation, and have in some degree lost the capacity for taking up the drug. Detailed study (and detailed study alone) reveals very clear differences between the behaviour shown in this kind of example and that shown in direct self-regulating response.

We shall see that the tenacity with which cells hold drug resistance varies according to a very complex pattern, the discussion of which will lead on to a deeper consideration of cell structure and organization. The question whether imposed changes in nucleic acid codes can ever play any part in this will then arise.

2. Specific interference with cell reactions by drugs

The work of Fildes and others provided evidence that certain substances may block the whole process of growth by interference at definite stages of the reaction sequence. Fildes[8] showed that the antibacterial action of mercury compounds may be quantitatively neutralized by compounds containing —SH groups: the addition of glutathione, for example, titrates the toxic effect of mercury in such a way that 2 moles —SH are equivalent to 1 Hg. The conclusion drawn was that the inhibitory action of the mercury depends upon the blocking of sulph-hydryl groups in cell metabolites or enzymes.

The general idea emerged that specific inhibitory actions may be exerted by substances structurally related to the normal metabolites of the cell. These substances are then taken up by enzymes in competition with their own normal substrates, but, being useless for further parts of the reaction sequence, block the subsequent steps, and so arrest the growth. Woods[9] suggested that sulphonamides interfere with the metabolism of p-amino-benzoic acid in the cell. The utilization rather than the synthesis of this compound was taken to be impeded, since if the latter occurred, addition of p-amino-benzoic acid in excess of a certain minimum requirement should give growth independent of sulphonamide concentration. Such a relation was not in fact found, the observed one corresponding to an actual competition of the two substances over the whole range of concentrations.

McIlwain[10] studied inhibition of growth by pyridine-3-sulphonic acid and its amide. These substances can be supposed to act in competition with the nicotinic acid of normal metabolism. The inhibitors can replace the nicotinic acid in the first stage of its use by the cell, but not in later stages. The amino-sulphonic acid analogues of some natural amino-carboxylic acids have an analogous action,[11] inhibition being observed especially with *Proteus* and with *Staphylococcus*. The antibacterial action is removed by the addition of extra α-amino-carboxylic acid to the medium. When *Staphylococcus* is made independent of added amino-carboxylic acids in the medium, as can be done by training, the amino-sulphonic acids no longer exert their inhibitory action. Pantothenic acid analogues also have antibacterial actions,[12] pantoyltaurine, for example, being antistreptococcal.

Another example of the operation of the same principle is found in the action of indole acrylic acid which is thought to inhibit some stage in the synthesis of tryptophan.[13] In contrast with what might have been suggested by the amino-benzoic acid-sulphonamide antagonism, the addition of traces of tryptophan does not neutralize the inhibitor: thus it is not the actual utilization but the formation of the tryptophan which the indole derivative impedes.

A somewhat similar principle was invoked to explain some results found by Gladstone[14] on growth in presence of amino-acids. Excess of one amino-acid may put out of action the centres involved in the synthesis of another related one, so that growth is only possible if that other one is provided in the medium. For example, valine, leucine, or isoleucine added singly to a mixture which supported growth of *Bacillus anthracis* inhibited the growth. Added together they improved and accelerated it.

These various observations are all examples of the way in which specific intervention of inhibitory substances occurs in the sequence of cell reactions. The theory based on them offered hope of a rational basis for the prediction of possible therapeutic agents. It is not true, however, that all drug actions depend upon structural analogies with normal metabolites: such a statement would not apply to the example of mercury. Again, Wood and Austrian[15] found that with *Staphylococcus aureus* in a synthetic medium, nicotinamide and cozymase antagonize not only sulphapyridine but quite unrelated drugs also, and from this they concluded that there is no evidence that sulphapyridine interferes necessarily with something chemically related to it.

Another class of observations closely connected with the intervention of drugs at specific stages of the reaction sequence is that relating to the phenomenon of 'cross adaptation'. For example, *Aerobacter aerogenes* can be trained to resist the action of amino-acridines, which are normally powerful inhibitors. The trained cells also show increased resistance to the antibacterial action of methylene blue,[16] but not to the action of sulphonamides. Training to sulphanilamide gives immunity to sulpha-guanidine and vice versa[17] and reciprocal cross resistance is also in evidence with Terramycin and chloramphenicol.[18] Sulphonamide training, however, does not give immunity to proflavine.[16] *Staphylococci* show cross training to some acridine compounds and to propamidine.[19] Where two drugs act at the same stage of the reaction sequence we may expect cross adaptation: where they act at different stages, none (see also p. 199).

3. Specific influence on different parts of the growth cycle

From what has been said, we should expect various drugs to have different relative influences on lag, generation time, stationary bacterial population, cell division probability, and so on. This expectation is fully confirmed.

Occasionally cells seem to grow at the normal rate up to a critical concentration of drug above which they fail to grow at all. The explanation seems to be as follows: the drug acts primarily on the lag, but has little effect on the mean generation time. At higher concentrations the drug lengthens the lag to such an extent that the cells all die before growth sets in: if, however, it does set in, as becomes possible at lower drug concentrations, it occurs more or less normally.

Sometimes there is a fairly close parallel between the effect of the drug on the lag and its effect on the generation time. This is found with *Aerobacter aerogenes* and methylene blue, and in certain other cases, but the parallelism is not exact. The difficulty about obtaining more definite information is that precisely in the more interesting examples growth of the cells is accompanied by adaptation to the drug, so that the unmodified value of the generation time is almost impossible to determine with exactness. Furthermore, the lag is a function of the age of the inoculum, while the generation time, from its nature, is not. This again makes comparison in numerical terms difficult.

Different drugs have rather widely different effects on the total population. For varying concentrations of the same drug, however, the total population may change in parallel with the growth rate, a result which can be accounted for by a calculation based upon quite simple assumptions.[20]

Another important specific action of certain drugs is on the cell division probability. Where this is much reduced without a corresponding reduction in the rate of the synthetic processes, the cells may grow to great length and assume the form of filaments. This effect may be so pronounced that the whole culture appears in the form of a few enormously long tangled threads (see Chapter XIV).

4. Influence of drug concentration

This subject is best dealt with in relation to individual examples. First, however, certain general results will be indicated.

The earlier literature is to a considerable extent concerned with the question of 'disinfection'. Many of the results are based upon experiments in which the concentration necessary to suppress visible growth in a standard test is determined. Other measurements relate to the rate at which cells die when exposed to a given concentration of the antiseptic. One of the standard ways of expressing results has been to set the disinfectant action proportional to c^n, n being a power of the concentration, c, of the substance under test.[21] This power law, however, is in need of a rational interpretation, since n often comes out to be quite considerable, 3, 4, or 5, a result which can hardly have a real theoretical significance. n, moreover, is not necessarily integral: and it would therefore seem that the power law must be an approximation for a law of a different form.

Suppose a certain concentration c_0 of the drug can be tolerated by the cell, as a result of the operation of neutralizing mechanisms of some kind. The antibacterial action will then be proportional to $c-c_0$. Representing this action by D, we shall have

$$D = a(c-c_0),$$
$$\ln D = \ln a + \ln(c-c_0),$$
$$d\ln D/dc = 1/(c-c_0).$$

If we also choose to write $\quad D = bc^n,$

we have $\quad\quad\quad\quad \ln D = \ln b + n\ln c,$

$$d\ln D/dc = n/c,$$

and to make the two methods consistent we must set

$$n/c = 1/(c-c_0),$$
or $\quad\quad\quad\quad n = c/(c-c_0).$

Now suppose c_0 is considerable, then $c-c_0$ may be quite small compared with c over the range where the drug action first begins to be marked, and n will appear large. It will not, however, appear constant, though the range of c values in which D rises from zero to practically infinity may be very small and make these variations in n difficult to observe.

Tolerance to concentrations up to a fairly well-defined threshold, followed by a very steep rise in the antibacterial action, is in fact quite often observed. The different types of concentration-action curve found for *Aerobacter* may be summarized by the diagrams in Fig. 35.[20] The initial tolerance is shown in type 2.

As will appear more clearly later, an initial tolerance is sometimes to be expected theoretically. It will be expedient here to refer in anticipation to the results obtained with strains of *Aerobacter aerogenes* trained to various concentrations of proflavine. Figure 55 (p. 189) shows the lag of each strain as a function of the proflavine concentration. It is evident that up to a certain threshold there is little effect, after which the lag rises rapidly towards indefinitely great values. The explanation of this type of behaviour, which we shall develop later, depends upon the idea that the drug interferes with the provision of the intermediate metabolite for a certain cell enzyme system. The rate of functioning of this particular system is related to the concentration of the intermediate according to a curve resembling that in Fig. 36. Normally the concentration of the intermediate in the cell has a value such as $A_1, A_2,...$; it can be reduced to B before the inhibition by the drug is manifest.

For different strains, therefore, there will be tolerances proportional to $A_1 B, A_2 B,...$; but higher drug concentrations cause a fall to some such point as C, the observed inhibition increasing steeply as we pass from B to C. If the value for the normal cells were B, then the value of n in the power expression would be small: as we pass from B to $A_1, A_2,...$ the value of n must rise rapidly. To quote a single numerical example:

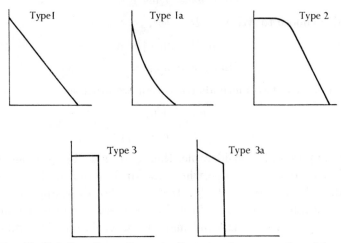

FIG. 35. Relation of growth rate (ordinates) and concentration of drug.

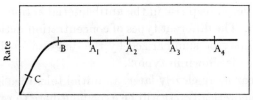

FIG. 36. Growth rate and intermediate concentration.

with a certain strain of cells, 100 mg/l. proflavine causes an increase in the lag in the ratio of 1·0 to 1·1; 150 mg/l., i.e. an extra 50 mg/l., then increases the lag in the ratio 1 : 10. This could be interpreted as indicating a value of n between 5 and 6, which would have no rational basis. The example quoted is an extreme one, since it refers to an artificially resistant strain of cells. But cells possess sometimes a degree of natural resistance to particular antibacterial agents, determined by their species character, or by their history. *Corynebacterium diphtheriae* strains show varying degrees of resistance to pantoyltaurine. Some strains require for their growth the addition of pantothenate to the medium: these are the most sensitive. Some can be trained to dispense with the added pantothenate: these prove to be naturally resistant to the pantoyltaurine, even though they have never been actually trained to growth in its presence.[22]

When there is no threshold concentration it is rather remarkable that the effect of the drug is often given by a simple linear relation, as in Fig. 35, type 1. For example, the action of alcohols on the growth rate of *Aerobacter aerogenes* is given by

$$k = k_0 - ap,$$

where k_0 is the growth rate constant found in the absence of alcohol, and k that found at concentration p, a being constant.[5] This is illustrated in Fig. 37. If the association of the drug and the cell material is governed by an adsorption isotherm, one would expect a linear relation to hold over a certain range, but perhaps not quite so well as appears, for example, in Fig. 37. On this point two comments may, however, be made. In the first place, the relation is not always linear, but may conform rather to type 1 (*a*) of Fig. 35. In the second place, we must perhaps envisage the possibility that the functioning of the cell is reduced to zero before the material upon which the drug is taken up is saturated with adsorbed molecules. If in Fig. 38 the level *AB* represents that at which adsorbed drug reduces the activity of some enzyme to zero, it is evident that the linear relation for the drug action does not necessarily imply that the isotherm remains linear up to saturation. A rather naïve interpretation of this behaviour could be suggested. If the normal substrate molecules, whose access to the enzyme substance the drug impedes, were large compared with the drug molecules themselves, the adsorption of the former could be completely prevented while there was still accommodation left for the latter.

With reference once more to Fig. 35, type 3 represents the case where the drug inhibits a lag phase reaction, so that the cell may die before growth can set in: this case was considered in the last section. Type 3 (*a*) represents a combination of type 1 and type 3.

In connexion with the relation between bacterial growth and drug concentration, reference must be made to a special kind of relation encountered, for example, in the action of sulphanilamide or sulphaguanidine on *Aerobacter aerogenes*. The growth rate falls with increasing drug concentration to a limit below which no amount of drug will reduce it. There seem to be some growth centres unaffected by or inaccessible to the drug. On the face of it, there are two possible explanations. We might here have the inverse of the case discussed above. If the drug molecules are larger than the normal substrate molecules, the surface of the enzyme might refuse to accept more of them, while still having spaces for the normal substrate. On the other hand, what is more likely

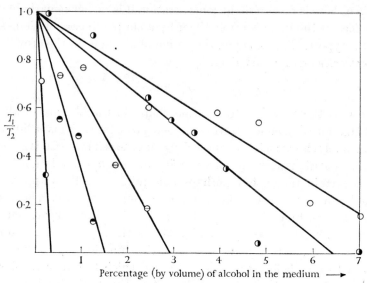

FIG. 37. Reduction in growth rate by alcohols.
○ methyl, ◑ ethyl, ⊖ n-propyl, ◓ n-butyl and ◐ n-hexyl alcohols.

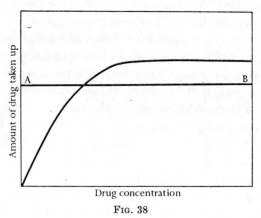

FIG. 38

is that there are really two alternative mechanisms by which growth occurs, and that one is less sensitive to the sulphonamide action than the other.

The further consideration of the relation of drug action to concentration will be deferred until we deal with the subject of adaptation.

5. Behaviour of homologous series of alcohols

This theme is introduced here because it brings us some information about the mode of interaction of the alcohol and the bacterial substance.

In Fig. 39 are plotted three sets of results for the inhibiting power of alcohols as a function of the number of carbon atoms which they contain. The results refer to the toxic effect on potato tissue,[23] on *Salmonella*

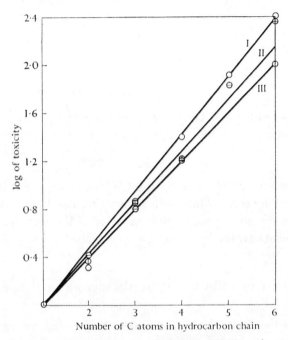

FIG. 39. Relation between the number of carbon atoms in various alcohols and the toxic action.

I, *Salmonella typhi*; II, Potato tissue; III, *Aerobacter aerogenes*.

typhi,[24] and on the growth rate of *Aerobacter aerogenes*.[5] For the latter, the inhibiting power is measured by the value of the constant a of the formula on p. 145. It is evident that there is an accurate linear relation between the logarithm of the inhibiting power and the number of carbon atoms in the chain. This can be accounted for if we make the basic assumption that there is an interaction between each individual —CH_2 group of the alcohol and some structural element of the bacterial substance. Hydrocarbons do not dissolve in water: alcohols do. Therefore the interaction between water and an alcohol may be referred to the hydroxyl group. To remove an alcohol molecule from water will require expenditure of an energy, E, approximately independent of the chain length. The number of alcohol molecules able to leave an aqueous phase in a given time will therefore be proportional to $e^{-E/RT}$. On the other hand, hydroxylic substances as such do not inhibit bacterial growth (compare carbohydrates): therefore the inhibition must be referred to the hydrocarbon chain. If each element of this is individually attached to the cell substance it will require an activation energy nQ to detach the alcohol molecule, n being the number of CH_2 groups, and Q the energy required to detach each one. If c_1 and c_2, respectively, are the concentrations of alcohol in water and in the organism, we have as a condition of equilibrium:

$$A_1 c_1 e^{-E/RT} = A_2 c_2 e^{-nQ/RT},$$

whence
$$c_2/c_1 = \text{const.}\, e^{-E/RT} e^{nQ/RT}.$$

For a given value of c_1 the toxicity will depend upon c_2, and denoting it by θ we have
$$\theta \propto e^{nQ/RT},$$

or
$$\ln \theta \propto n.$$

The independent attachment of each CH_2 unit means that the blocking power of the long chain compounds is **very** considerable. It is interesting to reflect on the growth-sustaining capacity of the corresponding compounds which possess a hydroxyl group attached to most of the carbon atoms.

6. Adaptation of cells to resist the action of drugs. General survey

One of the most remarkable phenomena in the whole range of bacteriology is the completeness, rapidity, and, in some examples, persistence with which cells may become resistant to the further action of drugs after they have been grown in their presence.

The adaptive process, although very common, does not invariably operate. Thus *Aerobacter aerogenes*, although it rapidly acquires resistance to sulphonamides, acridine derivatives, propamidine, potassium tellurite, triphenylmethane dyes, methylene blue, chloramphenicol, streptomycin, Terramycin, thymol, and other inhibitors, may be subcultured as much as 100 times in presence of a partially inhibitory concentration of phenol without showing any appreciable recovery towards a normal growth rate.

Innumerable examples of acquired resistance are recorded in the literature, and range over organisms of every type, and over inorganic substances such as mercury, arsenic, and copper salts, lysozyme of tears or sputum, organic substances of most varied structure, including penicillins and other well-known chemotherapeutic agents.

The speed of adaptation varies, but may be very great: thus Fleming and Allison[25] found that one single subculture was enough to give *Mycobacterium lysodeikticus* a high degree of resistance to the bacteriolytic action of tissues containing lysozyme. *Aerobacter aerogenes* acquires moderate degrees of resistance to proflavine with great ease. It can also acquire enormously high degrees of resistance, though these are only attained after long-continued subculture in presence of the drug.

Adaptation, once acquired, may be retained tenaciously during repeated subcultures in complete absence of any drug to keep the cells in training: on the other hand, it may be lost, sometimes rapidly, sometimes slowly: sometimes as a result of a specific treatment of the cells and sometimes in what appears to be a spontaneous or even unpredictable manner. Long ago Penfold,[26] speaking of acquired fermentative properties of bacteria, observed that the longer a character is impressed the longer it is retained, and that the more easily the cells take on a new character, the longer they retain it. The same, as we shall see, is generally true of drug resistance. This general pattern of adaptation and its retention or loss becomes clearer in the light of quantitative measurements, and will be seen to reflect an essential character of living matter. For the quantitative investigation of adaptive phenomena in liquid media it is convenient to measure lag, mean generation time, and total bacterial population as a function of the serial number in a set of subcultures made in presence of drug at a chosen fixed concentration. Since the lag is a function of the inoculum age, it is also useful to determine the lag-age relationship for the successive subcultures. When the cells have been trained as completely as possible at a given drug concentration, $\bar{m}$, it is informative to test the trained cells at a whole range of drug concentrations, using for the purpose cells of such an age that the lag has, for a given value of the drug concentration, the minimum possible value. This is done for a whole series of values of $\bar{m}$ itself, and the results yield a complete family of lag-concentration curves for the various trained strains.

Many drugs have been examined in this way with *Aerobacter aerogenes* as the test organism, and a general, although somewhat arbitrary, classification of the shapes of the curves so obtained, is represented diagrammatically in Fig. 40. Type *a* has been found with proflavine,[27] 5-amino-acridine,[28] 2,7 diamino-acridine,[28] 2,4 dinitrophenol,[29] crystal violet,[7] and propamidine.[28] Results with potassium tellurite,[28] chloramphenicol,[30] Terramycin,[18] and thymol[31] correspond to type *b* and those for methylene blue[32] to type *c*. The pattern of behaviour may of course vary from organism to organism. For example, the action of 2:4 dinitrophenol on yeast cells[33] corresponds more closely to type *b* than to the type *a* response observed with *Aerobacter aerogenes*.[29]

It is convenient to prepare drug-trained cells by inoculation first into a medium with a concentration of drug giving a lag of about 12 to 24 hours. On the second subculture at the same concentration the lag seldom reappears, but many transfers are necessary before the optimum

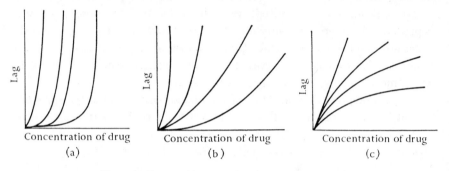

Fig. 40. Types of lag–concentration relationships.

rate of growth at the particular concentration is reached. If, on the other hand, drug is added gradually to an actively growing culture, growth may continue at an appreciable rate at concentrations of drug, which, had they been added in one portion at the beginning of the experiment, would have caused a very long, if not infinite, lag. The procedure forms the basis of the technique known as 'accelerated training' which is discussed in detail in section 14. Sometimes a drug, over a wide range of concentrations, affects only the growth rate of the cells without inducing a lag at all. A good example of this type of behaviour has been found with ethylenediamine tetra-acetic acid and *Aerobacter aerogenes* (section 11). The action of streptomycin on *Aerobacter aerogenes* presents a special case since here a first step in the development of resistance does entail the selection of a special type of cell at low concentrations of the antibiotic. Once selected, however, these cells, although capable of growth without lag at considerably higher concentrations, still show a lag at even higher ones (section 12), to which they need further direct adaptation.

The families of lag-concentration curves can be analysed quantitatively in terms of an adaptive theory of drug resistance. This aspect will be treated in detail in the next chapter where experimental results will be illustrated.

When adapted strains have been tested, it is usually informative to carry out experiments on *reversion*. The strain is subcultured serially in the absence of any drug, and, at appropriate intervals, is retested at various drug concentrations. If spontaneous reversion does not occur, various means of inducing it may be tried, cells trained to one drug being grown in presence of others.

As an alternative to training in liquid media the process can also be carried out on solid media containing drugs. In this connexion a very informative method consists in first of all plating out a small number of sensitive cells on drug-agar plates at a concentration of drug low enough still to allow 100 per cent survival. A colony is then picked from the plate, suspended in a medium such as saline or phosphate buffer, after which suitable dilutions are spread on new drug plates. In this way training can be achieved by a gradual increase of the drug concentration. Important aspects of this method, which will become apparent in further discussion (section 13), are that the survival can be kept at a high level throughout and also that no growth takes place except on the drug-plates themselves.

Sometimes it is important to know if the original culture contains any fully resistant cells at all, or what spectrum of resistance is shown by the cells which it does contain. This information is readily obtained by a comparison of the time-number relations observed after plating various trained and untrained strains on drug-agar (section 15). Some standard colony size may be defined, and α_t, the fraction of the cells plated which have given colonies of this size at time t can be plotted against this time.

Another very important question is that of the extent to which drug-adapted cells may differ from normal cells in respects other than drug resistance. The enzymatic properties of the adapted strains can be investigated in various ways. Definite differences are, in certain examples, detectable, and these have an important bearing on the theoretical interpretation of the changes which occur during the training process (see next chapter).

7. The action of proflavine (2,8 diamino acridine) on *Aerobacter aerogenes*

In this section and in Chapter VII the results of detailed studies on the action of acridines will be considered. First of all, however, some comment should be made on the mutagenic action of these compounds. Nucleic acids form complexes with acridines,[34, 35, 36] and it has been reported that proflavine inhibits DNA-dependent RNA synthesis.[37] It also destroys the infectivity of several viruses[36] though it has been claimed that the mutagenic action, in general, is confined to the even-numbered members of the T-group of bacteriophages, and that in other groups and in bacteria the acridines are not mutagenic.[38] In experiments *in vitro*, acridines may become intercalated between adjacent nucleotide-pair layers in DNA by extension and unwinding of the deoxyribose-phosphate backbone. The overall result of this, as shown by X-ray crystallographic studies, could be to force adjacent base pairs 6·8 Å apart instead of the usual distance of 3·4 Å.[35] It has been claimed that if this happened on one chain of the DNA during replication and not on the other, it could easily lead to the addition or deletion of a base.[35, 39] Such a mutation, however, would be an event which there would be no reason whatsoever to correlate with resistance to the acridines. To suppose that there were any such relation would, incidentally, be rather naïvely 'Lamarckian'. In any event, the relation between intercalation and mutagenesis is not quite clear since some acridines which are inter-calated in DNA are not mutagenic.[38]

The experimental evidence from studies with proflavine will now be considered,[16, 27, 32, 40] the development of resistance to this drug being in all probability something quite different from and additional to the problematical mutagenic action.

In a medium of glucose, ammonium sulphate, phosphate, and magnesium sulphate the mean generation time of *Aerobacter aerogenes* at 40° C is 33 minutes. The influence of proflavine at concentrations of 43 mg/l. is initially to increase the value markedly. Successive sub-cultures are attended by a rapid return to near normal.

Serial subculture number	Mean generation time (minutes)
0	55
11	41
16	36
32	34

During the first subculture in presence of the drug long filamentous cells are often formed, which show that the drug has a specifically inhibitory effect on division (see Chapter XIV). After the first few subcultures the tendency to give abnormal forms vanishes. The total bacterial population is reduced by the drug, and even when the cells are completely trained in other respects, the total population remains low compared with the normal. Thus it seems that a secondary action of the proflavine is to impair the mechanism whereby the cells usually deal with their toxic metabolic products. Resistance to this action does not appear to be acquired. It appears in fact that the resistant cells have switched their metabolism in presence of the drug to some extent to an anaerobic route in which the consumption of carbohydrate and the production of acid for a given amount of growth has become much greater.[41]

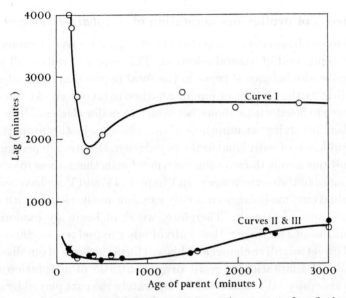

FIG. 41. Lag-age curves of *Aerobacter aerogenes* in presence of proflavine.

Curve I, Untrained cells: 43 mg/l.
Curve II, No drug
Curve III, Trained cells: 43 mg/l.

The most striking effect of the proflavine is upon the lag, which is much increased, rising steeply when the concentration exceeds about 20 mg/l. On subculture of the bacteria in presence of the drug the lag soon returns to a normal value. Some typical results are shown in Fig. 41. Curve I refers to the untrained cells grown in presence of 43 mg/l. of proflavine, curve II to normal cells in absence of drug, and curve III to the trained cells tested, after thirty-two passages, in 43 mg/l. proflavine. The coincidence of curves II and III shows the completeness of the adaptation, at least in respect of the lag.

The lag-concentration curves for a series of adapted strains are given in Fig. 55 of the next chapter. They are seen to constitute a related family, the spacing between successive curves being equal to the difference between the corresponding concentrations of drug used in training. The discussion of this family of curves is deferred until we deal with the quantitative theory of the adaptation.

Adaptation to proflavine is associated with 'cross adaptation' to methylene blue, to other acridine derivatives, and to propamidine (partially). This subject will be more thoroughly discussed in the next chapter.

8. Theory of proflavine-adaptation of *Aerobacter aerogenes*

The most obvious hypothesis to apply to any adaptive phenomenon is, at first sight, that of natural selection. This supposes cells of all possible properties, the balance of types in the total population being adjustable according as the growth of one or another is favoured. At the outset, then, we are faced with a choice between two major classes of hypothesis: one class involving assumptions about changes in the proportions of different kinds of individual in the population, the other depending upon assumptions about the way the individual cells themselves may change in response to the environment. In Chapters IV and V we have seen that individual enzyme balances not only can, but must, change with change in conditions of growth. Therefore, we shall begin by exploring the possibilities of the theory that individuals themselves are the primary seat of direct adaptive changes. This will form the basis of our discussion, not only of adaptation to resist drugs, but also of adaptation to new media generally. We shall consider separately the part played by natural selection. This will be done under two heads: first, the idea that natural selection alone will account for the facts—which we shall not accept as a universal explanation: and secondly, that natural selection superposes itself on direct adaptive changes (which, of course, is inevitable if such changes occur) with results that are detectable by experiment.

The simple model of adaptation to proflavine which will now be considered is based upon the idea that the drug inhibits the action of some part of the enzyme system responsible for the production of necessary growth intermediates. If the inhibition occurs at a specific stage in a sequence of processes, those members of the sequence which precede the one affected will be able to operate at their normal rate, while those which come later will be retarded, since the enzymes concerned will be starved of their normal supply of raw materials. If the formation of the intermediates required for growth is held up, the lag must be lengthened: the mean generation time will also be adversely affected. During the lag the retarded mechanisms build up the necessary concentrations of the various substances needed to bring about division, and eventually growth starts. This does not mean, however, that the cells have become adapted: it only means that a retarded mechanism has been able to do its normal work when given increased time to do it in. Once actual growth begins, however, the proportions of the various enzymes in the cell will change. We shall suppose that those enzymes whose formation is retarded as a result of the action of the drug are mostly essential to the cell: and that, for this reason, division of the cell does not occur

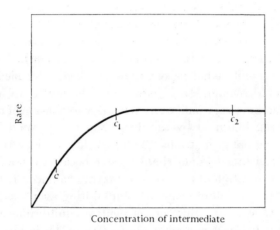

Concentration of intermediate

FIG. 42. Rate and intermediate concentration.

until they have been synthesized in approximately the normal standard amount. By the time this has happened the uninhibited parts of the enzyme system will have been formed in considerably more than the normal amount per cell. When the new material synthesized is enough to outweigh the original amount, there will have been established an entirely new enzyme balance. The increased amount of one group of enzymes leads to the increased concentration in the cell of an intermediate substrate utilizable by the first enzyme of the set whose growth is inhibited. Quantitative calculations, which are developed in the next chapter, show that the enzyme balance can change until this increased concentration restores the growth rate of the inhibited set to normal. The cells are now fully adapted to resist the action of the drug. The changes in the concentration of the key intermediate are shown in Fig. 42. Before the drug acts it is c_1; while the drug acts and the cells are untrained it is c; after adaptation it returns to c_1, so long as the drug continues to act. If the cells are transferred to a medium containing no drug, the increased amounts of certain of the enzymes cause the intermediate concentration to rise to c_2.

From the experimental fact that the trained cells show no greater activity in the normal medium than the original untrained cells, we must infer that c_1 already corresponds to nearly the limiting rate, and that further increase to c_2 does not cause any corresponding increase in the rate of operation of the enzyme system. This is not surprising in cells which have presumably evolved to grow with near maximum efficiency in the absence of drug.

It follows that trained strains might show some reluctance to revert. The increased production from the expanded part of the enzyme system does not stimulate an increase in the specific synthesis rate of the unexpanded part. The new enzyme balance established in presence of the drug is therefore not necessarily disturbed. This means that the resistance would remain. If c_1 were below the horizontal part of the curve, the increase to c_2 would cause a relative expansion of the enzymes which had been inhibited by the drug, and there would be a return towards the original proportions. As far as this consideration goes, the retention of resistance would simply occur because there is no active reason for a restoration of the original enzyme balance. If the cells are subjected to the action of some other inhibiting agent, acting upon a different set of enzymes, this sort of neutral equilibrium may well be actively disturbed and reversion may occur. The induced reversion which sometimes results from growth in phenol[16] or cresol[40] might well be regarded as an example of the working of this kind of process.

According to this picture, adaptation should occur with considerable rapidity. This, in considerable measure, is true. Our hypothesis, then, predicts speed, completeness, and possible stability of adaptation to the appropriate antibacterial agent. The observed phenomena do indeed exhibit these characters on occasion, but they exhibit others as well, which show that the picture we have sketched is only a first approximation—assuming it to be true at all. Adaptation may be complete without being stable, and stability only seems to be acquired when the training has been continued for a much longer time than is required for mere renovation of cell material. The discussion of this matter is part of a larger question which will be dealt with in Chapter X. Here we will simply mention one possible hypothesis which seems to have several arguments in its favour.

The changed enzyme balance envisaged by the simple view outlined above must have certain secondary consequences. In the first place, all parts of the cell material form, probably, one structural unity. Expansion of one part can hardly occur without producing some effect, possibly actual mechanical strain, upon others. Secondly, a changed enzyme balance directed solely to the correction of a disturbance caused by a drug must have certain secondary influences on the supply and demand relations of other cell functions. One can, therefore, imagine a cell, adapted to resist the drug, still incompletely adapted in respect of the various secondary consequences. The series of secondary adjustments will probably require a much longer and subtler process of training than the primary enzyme expansion: and only when they are completed will the adaptation be stable (see p. 264).

The elementary theory given above is a specific and simple illustration of the more general theorem discussed in Chapter V under the heading of total integration. According to this theorem the growth rate in presence of the drug assumes the best value possible in the circumstances, while in the process of adjustment the balance of enzymes changes, and the predominant reaction pattern itself may be modified. As a general consequence the enzyme balance of adapted or 'trained' cells should differ in various ways from that of the original sensitive ones. The detection of all the possible complex changes is a difficult matter in view of the enormous numbers of enzymes whose activity would have to be tested. Nevertheless there is experimental evidence that the balance does change in a way suggesting a coordinated pattern. *Aerobacter aerogenes* adapted to resist proflavine shows a lowered activity of various oxidative enzymes with, on the other hand, a marked increase of the asparagine deaminase typical of the nitrogen metabolism. Training of the same strain of bacteria to streptomycin or to crystal violet leads to an expansion of the enzymes concerned in the breakdown of carbon sources.[41]

9. The action of sulphonamides on *Aerobacter aerogenes*[42]

The action of sulphanilamide or of sulphaguanidine on the growth of *Aerobacter aerogenes* reveals a number of rather important contrasts with that described for the same organism and proflavine.[17]

Sulphanilamide lengthens the lag, and decreases the growth rate: it has little adverse effect on the total population, which may in certain circumstances even be increased by the action of the drug.

In some respects the most interesting difference is in the form of the growth curves which, for the first subculture in presence of the sulphonamide, assume the composite form illustrated in Fig. 43. A mean generation time can be read off from each section of the curve: and the values corresponding respectively to the earlier and later stages of growth may be referred to as m.g.t. I and m.g.t. II. The point of intersection of the two parts of the curve will be termed the transition point.

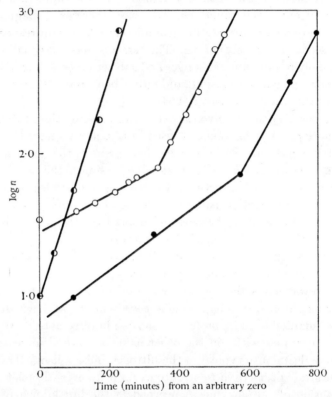

FIG. 43. Growth in presence of sulphonamide (showing characteristic composite form of growth curve).

◐   Normal growth curve.
○, ●   Typical growth curves in presence of sulphonamide.

For untrained cells both m.g.t. I and m.g.t. II increase (that is, the growth rate falls) with increasing drug concentration, but not indefinitely. For both, a well-defined limit is reached, as shown in Fig. 44, which gives the results obtained with sulphanilamide (SA) and with sulphaguanidine (SG). The ordinates represent the ratio of the normal mean generation time to that measured in presence of the drug: that is, the relative growth rate.

When the cells are subcultured serially in presence of the drug, adaptation occurs, and takes the following course. The slopes of the two sections of the growth curve increase, but, more important, the transition point occurs earlier and earlier, soon passing below the range of convenient measurement. The whole curve then assumes the normal form. In the earlier stages of adaptation the resistance is incomplete (even although the abnormal shape of the growth curve is no longer shown): the resistance is specific to the particular sulphonamide to

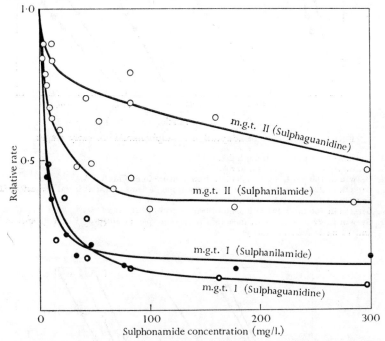

FIG. 44. Growth rate and sulphonamide concentration.

which the training is occurring, and it is readily lost on subculture in a sulphonamide-free medium (Figs. 45 and 46). After about thirty subcultures, however, the growth rate returns to the value observed in the absence of the drug; the resistance is non-specific, training to sulphanilamide giving resistance to sulphaguanidine and vice versa; and it is stable to many subcultures in the drug-free medium.

Loss of resistance may, however, be induced artificially in the stably adapted strain by culture in presence of proflavine. This induced reversion only occurs in cells which have not had any previous opportunity of adaptation to proflavine. If they are first adapted to proflavine and then to sulphonamide, the adaptation to both may be stably retained, and that to sulphonamide will survive subculture at even higher concentrations of proflavine than that originally employed.[43]

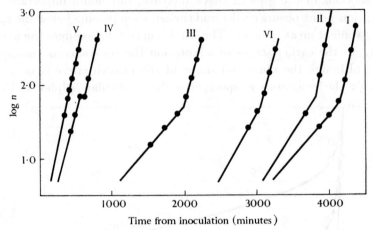

Fig. 45. Specificity of adaptation to sulphonamide in early stages.

    I. Untrained culture in 160 mg/l. SG.
   II. Untrained culture in 218 mg/l. SA.
  III. Growth in 160 mg/l. SG of inoculum from culture in 225 mg/l. SA.
  IV. Growth in 225 mg/l. SA of inoculum from same parent culture as in III (transfers III
      and IV made simultaneously).
   V. Growth in 160 mg/l. SG of inoculum from culture in 160 mg/l. SG.
  VI. Growth in 225 mg/l. SA of inoculum from same parent culture as in V (transfers V
      and VI made simultaneously).

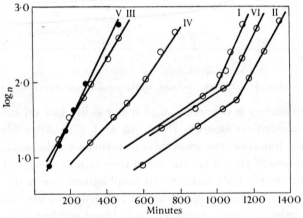

Fig. 46. Development and decay of adaptation in early stages.
All cultures in 218 mg/l. sulphanilamide.

    I. First culture (time zero 2000 minutes from origin).
   II. Second culture in SA inoculated at transition point.
  III. Second culture in SA inoculated at onset of stationary phase.
  IV. Second culture in SA inoculated 800 minutes after onset of stationary phase.
   V. Strain trained by three passages through SA, inoculated at onset of stationary phase.
  VI. Strain from V as parent whose adaptation has been lost after passage through drug-
      free medium.

The antagonism of sulphonamides and p-amino-benzoic acid has already been mentioned. The addition of the latter substance to the medium restores the growth rate in presence of sulphanilamide completely to normal.[9]

The study of the lag relationships is complicated by a specialized effect: namely, that when cells of a parent culture which would show only a short lag in the normal medium are transferred to the medium containing sulphonamide, there is a short immediate burst of growth, which then slows up, as though the drug had required a finite time to begin to exert its action.[44] Then there is a fresh lag period, after which the definite growth phase begins. For quantitative measurements it is simpler to work with cells showing a definite lag in the drug-free medium, and to study the increase in lag over this standard value as a function of the drug concentration.

The lag-concentration curves form a family rather different from that given by *Aerobacter aerogenes* and proflavine (p. 189). Training to a fairly low concentration of sulphanilamide gives a considerable degree of resistance to much higher concentrations. The curves show, over a considerable range, quite a large measure of independence of the drug concentration, $\bar{m}$, at which the training process is carried out. This is illustrated in Fig. 47, where it is seen that cells trained at 56, 110, and 213 mg/l. behave almost identically.

10. Discussion of results on sulphonamide-adaptation

The progress of the adaptation through the stages of incompleteness and instability to completeness and stability corresponds to what is found with proflavine, and, in itself, requires no further comment at the present juncture.

But the story is rather more complex than just this. In the earlier stages the adaptation is specific: cells trained to sulphaguanidine are not trained to sulphanilamide, nor vice versa. Thus the first response of the cell seems to be to develop a mechanism which is qualitatively different from that which is finally brought into play. In the final state, one may well assume that there has been an expansion of those enzymes necessary to manufacture an effective sulphonamide antagonist. This idea is consistent with the fact that the resistance is then non-specific and complete. At the earlier stage, an alternative mode of growth seems to be used by the cell. Bacteria can almost certainly achieve their synthetic processes by many alternative routes. If one of these is blocked at a certain point, the obstruction can be by-passed, though the by-passing may depend upon the bringing into action of enzymes not normally in use. The form of the growth curves found for the first subcultures in media, containing sulphonamides are very suggestive of such a situation. The matter may be made clearer by reference to Fig. 48. There are two alternative growth processes, one, the slower, possessing a lag AB: the other, the faster, possessing a lag AC. Now suppose these could operate side by side and independently. (How this could happen is a matter

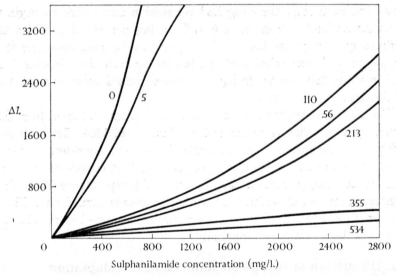

FIG. 47. Family of lag-concentration curves for *Aerobacter aerogenes* in sulphanilamide. The numbers on the curves indicate the concentration (mg/l.) at which the various strains were trained.

for further consideration.) The observed growth curve would follow the continuous line and, in the case where the faster growth mode had the longer lag, there would be a transition point as shown in the first two of the three small diagrams.

We could account formally for the behaviour during the initial stages of sulphonamide adaptation if we suppose that there exists an alternative to the normal mode of growth and that this alternative is considerably less inhibited by sulphonamides than the normal one. Initially, however, this new mode is subject to a long lag, since the necessary intermediates are not present. Ordinarily it would never have a chance to operate and develop, because growth by its more efficient competitor would be complete before it had a chance. But the presence of the drug reverses the relative efficiencies, and the new one supersedes the old at the point T.

According to this, AB is the lag, in presence of the sulphonamide of the normal growth mechanism, and AC that of the alternative. The slope of the line BT is the rate of the normal mechanism inhibited by sulphonamide, and the slope of the line CT that of the relatively insensitive alternative mechanism (CT is steeper than BT but less steep than the normal growth rate in absence of drug). As training proceeds, the lag of the alternative mechanism becomes shorter relatively to that of the normal (inhibited) one. T therefore moves downward, and finally disappears, when AC just becomes less than AB.

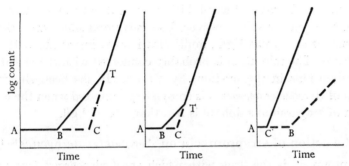

FIG. 48. Training of alternative mechanism.

The sequence of curves shown by the continuous lines in the three diagrams corresponds to a well-established pattern of bacterial training, not only to sulphonamides, but also to certain changes of medium (see Chapter VIII). The idea of the alternative mechanisms seems, therefore, to be of rather general applicability. It must be pointed out, however, that Fig. 48 represents an over-simplification, since the two modes of growth could hardly be treated as quite unconnected, and in practice the operation of one could hardly fail to influence the lag of the other. Indeed, the idea of two independent lags is itself not without difficulty. Nevertheless the phenomenon of broken growth curves and transition points seems to demand some such interpretation (see p. 201).

What has been said is far from giving a complete account of the sulphonamide adaptation. We do not know, for example, whether the final maximum resistance represents simply the perfection of the alternative growth mechanism we have been considering, or whether it depends upon a different one. There are qualitative changes which accompany the completion of the training (specificity to non-specificity) and these might suggest a completely new mechanism. But they might, on the other hand, do no more than show that the quantitative development of certain enzymes goes hand in hand with a qualitative change in their chemical texture. This question must be left open for the present.

11. The action of ethylenediamine NNN'N' tetra-acetate (EDTA) on *Aerobacter aerogenes*[29]

Over a wide range of concentrations EDTA affects the growth rate without inducing a lag at all. The progressive nature of the reduction in the growth rate as the concentration is increased is shown in Figs. 49a and 49b. There is always an increase of about twofold in the cell mass before the inhibitory effect sets in. Repeated subculture at a given concentration decreases the inhibition without entirely eliminating it. Long continued growth, however, becomes impossible when the concentration is as high as 1 g/l., multiplication ceasing at about the third subculture. The inhibition is probably connected with the chelation of magnesium ions in the medium by EDTA. It has been shown that growth of *Aerobacter aerogenes* is completely inhibited when the concentration of magnesium sulphate is less than 2×10^{-6} g/l.

12. The action of streptomycin on *Aerobacter aerogenes*[45, 46, 47]

Streptomycin is the drug with which the Lederbergs[48] first applied their method of 'replica' plating. By this technique pre-existing mutants, if they are present at all, may be selected without their ever having come into contact with the drug. A drug-free agar plate is inoculated with a heavy suspension of organisms and incubated until confluent growth just appears. A velvet pad supported on a wooden block is then pressed lightly on the surface of the growth so as to transfer organisms to the pad, which is then pressed in turn on to the surface of control plates containing no drug and then on to plates containing drug. The plates, which are marked with a reference grid, are then incubated and any growth on those with drug can be identified with the corresponding site on the drug-free controls. The cells on this site are picked off, in a fairly generous manner so as not to miss the mutants, and after suitable dilution are used to inoculate another drug-free plate. By repetition of this cycle many times any resistant mutants may be obtained in a pure state, never having come into contact with the drug. In this way the Lederbergs obtained streptomycin-resistant organisms.

The replica-plating experiment might easily lead to the conclusion that all streptomycin resistance depended on the pre-existent mutants, but this would be an unjustifiable over-simplification. Quantitative studies lead to a quite different conclusion.[45, 46, 47]

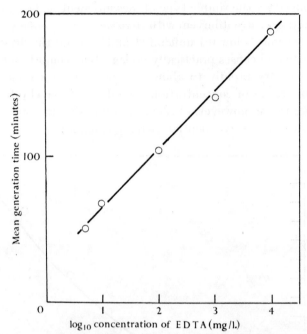

FIG. 49a. Plot of mean generation time against the logarithm of the concentration of EDTA (sodium salt).

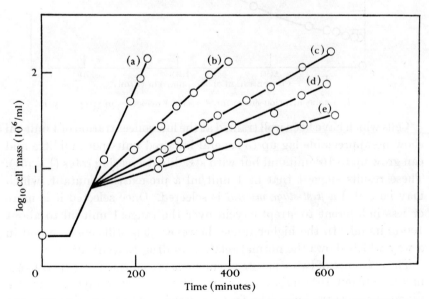

FIG. 49b. Growth curves for cultures containing (a) 0, (b) 10, (c) 100, (d) 1000, and (e) 10 000 mg/l. of EDTA (sodium salt).

Even judged by the simple type of measurement on lags and growth rates the action of streptomycin with *Aerobacter aerogenes* is exceptional. At concentrations below 0·1 unit/ml (1 unit = 1 μg) the drug has little effect on rate and causes practically no lag. Between 0·1 and 1 unit/ml the lag rises very rapidly to about 14 hours and then shows over a considerable range of concentration a tendency to level off. Over the much wider range, however, of about 100 units/ml to 1500 units/ml it shows a more or less exponential increase (Fig. 50).

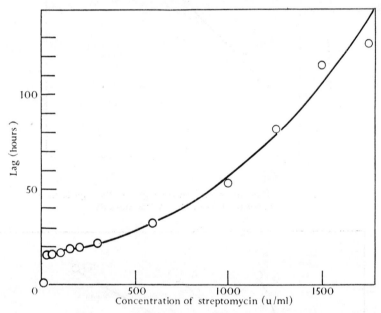

Fig. 50. Lag-concentration curve for *Aerobacter aerogenes* in streptomycin.

Cells which have been well trained at the low concentration of 1 unit/ml show no appreciable lag up to several hundred units per millilitre and can grow up to 10^3 units/ml but with steadily decreasing rates (Fig. 51). These results suggest that at 1 unit/ml a pre-existing mutant, which may be called a *first-stage mutant* is selected. Once selected it is more or less indifferent to streptomycin over the range 1 unit/ml to about 100 units/ml. In the higher range, however, it is still sensitive and in a way which shows the normal relation to drug concentration.[45]

The existence of two separate phenomena is confirmed by experiments in which about 10^9 sensitive cells are plated on streptomycin-agar at a range of concentrations. The fraction surviving to give colonies drops rapidly to about 5×10^{-8} by the time the concentration is 1 unit/ml and remains at this level up to about 2000 units/ml. Here again any cells which can survive at 1 unit/ml, the selected mutants, can survive over the whole range of concentrations, though the time required for the colonies to form increases just as the growth rate in liquid medium (Fig. 51) falls.[45]

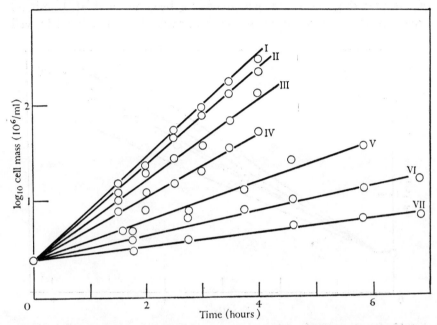

Fig. 51. Growth curves for cultures in streptomycin medium of a strain of *Aerobacter aerogenes* previously subcultured at 1 unit/ml of streptomycin.

Streptomycin concentration in test: (I) 0, (II) 1, (III) 50, (IV) 100, (V) 300, (VI) 600, and (VII) 1000 units/ml

The existence of the first-stage mutants has been confirmed by the replica-plating technique itself. Strains of *Aerobacter aerogenes* resistant to the lower ranges of streptomycin concentration, though still sensitive to the higher ranges, were obtained in this way.[47]

Mutants essentially similar in character were obtained in greatly increased number by irradiation with ultraviolet light. Isolation of single colonies well screened from radiation led, on the other hand, to cultures with a much lower proportion of first-stage mutants. It would seem, therefore, that the origin of these mutants in normal culture is quite possibly to be looked for in the action of the natural radiation to which they are always subjected.[46]

The behaviour of this first-stage mutant at higher concentrations of drug has in all respects the characteristics of an adaptive response by the majority of the cells in the culture. The evidence is as follows. The fan-shaped family of curves given at higher concentrations of drug by a strain which has grown once in 1 unit/ml (Fig. 51) gradually and progressively closes up as the cells are subcultured at 1000 units/ml (Fig. 52). This is in sharp contrast with the 'all or nothing' behaviour of the first-stage mutants, which having been selected at 1 unit/ml grow almost indifferently at any concentration from 1 unit/ml to well

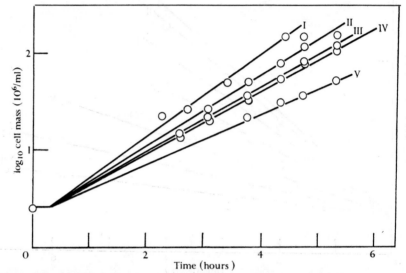

FIG. 52. Growth curves for cultures in streptomycin medium of a strain of *Aerobacter aerogenes* previously subcultured at 1000 units/ml of streptomycin.

Streptomycin concentration in test (I) 0, (II) 50, (III) 150, (IV) 1000, and (V) 8000 units/ml.

over 100 units/ml. It might perhaps be argued that the progressive variation depends upon the gradual selection from a whole range of mutant types. This idea is rendered very unlikely by an experiment in which a large number of cells is spread on an agar plate with 1000 units/ml and a histogram is constructed of the colony diameters at a standard time (a measure, that is, virtually of growth rates). The histogram shows the median value and the distribution of the resistance. Several of the largest and several of the smallest colonies, that is, of the most resistant and the least resistant, are taken off, diluted, and replated, so that new histograms are obtained. This process is repeated successively and as it goes on the median resistance moves steadily up towards a limit. The distribution, however, remains of the same breadth, and remains of the same form whether the most or the least resistant of the preceding set of colonies has been used. At each stage there is 100 per cent survival on the plate of the cells inoculated.[45] It is therefore extremely difficult to see how any selection whatever can have occurred. Considerable interest attaches in general to the statistical analysis of rates of development of colonies and this is dealt with in Chapter XI.

Various theories concerning the biochemical events leading to streptomycin resistance have been put forward from time to time.[49-52] In connexion with the formation of first-stage mutants by radiation, which is generally destructive, it is significant that streptomycin-resistant cells have sometimes been found to take up the drug less readily than sensitive cells.[53]

In conclusion it may be remarked that the replica-plating method has given clear proof of the presence of mutants possessing some degree of resistance to streptomycin and of others resistant to bacteriophage. The tacit assumption, however, which sometimes appears to be made, that if the technique were applied to all other examples the result would be the same, is seen, in the light of the detailed study of *Aerobacter* and streptomycin, to be more than dubious.

13. The training of *Aerobacter aerogenes* to chloramphenicol in non-selective conditions[54]

While first-stage streptomycin-resistant mutants can be selected without contact with the drug, on the other hand, in other examples drug-resistant forms can be produced in conditions which preclude selection.

When inocula of about 100 cells are spread on the surface of agar plates containing the ingredients necessary for growth, these cells all give rise to clearly separated colonies. If drugs are incorporated in the agar the fraction of cells which survive to do so is a function of the concentration but some drug level can usually be found at which all the cells still form colonies. One of these colonies may now be picked off from the drug plate, resuspended in a diluent such as isotonic saline or phosphate buffer, and suitable dilutions again plated on agar containing a range of concentrations of drug. A colony can be chosen from the highest level at which all the cells in the inoculum still survive and the cycle may now be repeated. This is the basis of a technique by which *Aerobacter aerogenes* was gradually trained to resist the antibiotic chloramphenicol under conditions in which selection of rare mutant types could not play a major role. The acquisition of resistance to chloramphenicol proceeds by a series of small steps, in sharp contrast with streptomycin, and when the technique of replica plating has been attempted only trivial increases in resistance have been obtained.

A typical experiment is summarized in Table 2, and it should be emphasized that at each cycle the survival, which was ascertained by a direct comparison of similar inocula on drug-free plates and drug-plates respectively, was high and that no intervening period of growth was

TABLE 2

Resistance of Aerobacter aerogenes *on serial subculture on chloramphenicol-agar*

	α_∞ at the given concentration (mg/l.)							
Cycle	5	10	15	20	25	40	50	60
1	*0·9*	(10⁻⁴)						
2	0·9	*1·0*						
3		*1·0*	0·7					
4		*1·0*	0·2					
5		1·0	1·0	*1·0*				
6			1·0	1·0	*1·0*			
7					*0·9*	1·0		
8					*1·0*			
9					1·0	*1·0*		
10						*1·0*		
11						0·5		
12						1·0	*0·9*	
13					*1·0*		0·4	0·4
14					0·8	*0·8*	0·5	
15					1·0	1·0	*0·9*	
16						0·5	*0·6*	0·2
17							*0·4*	0·2
18							*0·3*	
19						1·0	1·0	0·9

Note. The value italicized means that this plate was the source of the colony used in the next cycle.

allowed betwen cycles. α_∞ is the fraction of the inoculum which survived to form colonies on the plates. The conclusion that a ten- to twelvefold increase in resistance has taken place is inescapable. Further experiments in which strains trained in liquid medium to resist 50 and 160 mg/l. of drug respectively were used showed that an overall increase in resistance of at least 40-fold and probably 160- to 200-fold was possible.

14. Accelerated training to drugs

When drug is added gradually to an actively growing culture of bacteria growth may sometimes continue up to concentrations far higher than those which would be completely inhibitory to a culture inoculated in the normal way. The entire experiment may be completed in a time interval far too short to allow of any appreciable selection of pre-existing types of resistant cell. Moreover, under favourable conditions the growth rate remains high enough to bear witness that the response involves the majority of the cells in the culture. The technique has been successfully applied with *Aerobacter aerogenes* and the drugs proflavine,[55] 5-amino-acridine,[56] and propamidine.[57] Some typical results are given in Table 3. In the control experiments of the last column the

TABLE 3

Accelerated training of Aerobacter aerogenes *to drugs*

Medium	Final drug concentration (mg/l.)	pH		Total duration of experiment (min)	Lag in control experiment (min)
		Initial	Final		
A. *Experiments with 5-amino-acridine*					
1. Concentrated glucose	49	7·12	6·72	183	2600
2. Dilute glucose	51	7·12	6·88	135	1600
3. Malate	24	7·10	7·25	105	1440
4. Dilute glucose with triple strength buffer	39	7·10	7·10	70	3000
B. *Experiments with propamidine isethionate*					
1. Dilute glucose	260	6·95	6·80	125	418
2. Concentrated glucose	208†	6·97	6·98	325	3400

† pH kept constant by an autotitrator assembly.

lag was measured of an inoculum introduced into the corresponding medium adjusted to the final pH (column 4) and containing drug at the final concentration in column 2.

The large difference between the lag observed when untrained cells are inoculated directly into the control medium and the time taken for the experiment itself shows that rapid adaptation has taken place and is not connected with any change in the pH of the culture.† Acridines and propamidine, it is true, are inactivated by acids (see p. 203) but this factor has been allowed for in the control. Moreover, similar results have been obtained not only when neutrality was maintained by the use of an autotitrator-regulator assembly, but also under conditions in which the drug used becomes progressively *more* active as growth continues and the medium tends towards alkalinity.

The progress of the adaptation can be followed by withdrawal of samples at intervals and the plating of about 100 cells on drug-agar and on control plates so that α_∞, the fraction of the inoculum which ever forms

---

† In view of these results it is surprising that a mistaken criticism of Sinai and Yudkin[58] (based upon experiments not strictly relevant to the issue) should be repeated by Fisher.[59]

colonies, can be obtained. Some results obtained with propamidine isethionate are given below (Table 4).

The large increase in resistance is again apparent, and it takes place under conditions where the majority of the cells survive, since the ratio of the viable count to the total (microscope) count remains throughout at a level not far short of unity. Moreover, size distributions of the cells were essentially unimodal although there were indications of filament

TABLE 4

Progress of the accelerated training to propamidine isethionate

Time (min)	Cell mass (10⁶/ml)	Concentration of drug in liquid medium (mg/l.)	σ†	Viable count / Microscope count	α_∞ on agar containing 250 mg/l. of drug‡
0	26	0	0·63	0·98	$4·4 \times 10^{-4}$
90	68	70	0·62	0·85	0·47
205	123	127	0·72	0·83	0·56
325	265	208	0·61	0·84	0·55

† Cell mass/cell number—a measure of cell size.
‡ Seven days' incubation of plates.

Note. Cell mass is measured in terms of the corresponding *number* of cells of standard size.

TABLE 5

The stability of the accelerated training to 5-amino-acridine

History of culture	Fraction of inoculum which formed colonies on drug-agar (50 mg/l.)
(a) Control 1	$3·2 \times 10^{-3}$
(b) After 1 accelerated training followed by 1 subculture in drug-free medium	$9·5 \times 10^{-3}$
(c) After 4 accelerated trainings each followed by 1 subculture in drug-free medium	0·58
(d) Control 2	$8·8 \times 10^{-3}$

formation. The large increase in resistance early in the experiment when the drug concentration had reached 70 mg/l. is of interest and is similar to that observed in tests with proflavine in liquid medium.

The rapidly gained resistance is unstable. One subculture in the absence of drug usually leads to a more or less complete loss of that conferred by one spell of accelerated training. If, however, the procedure is repeated several times a greater stability is reached as shown in Table 5, which gives some results obtained with 5-amino-acridine. The 'trainings' were carried out in dilute glucose medium and the final drug concentrations were similar to those shown in Table 3. On more prolonged subculture in drug-free medium even this increased stability is lost.

15. Time–number relationships

When bacteria are plated on a solid medium, such as an agar gel, containing a drug, the fraction (α_∞) of the inoculum which ever form colonies varies with the concentration of the drug, and may range from

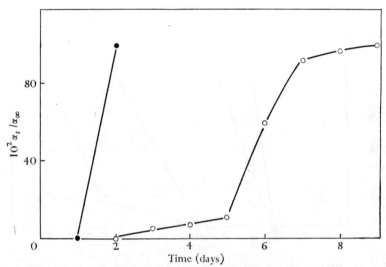

FIG. 53. Rate of development of colonies of *Escherichia coli mutabile* on chloramphenicol-agar (10 mg/l.).

○   Untrained strain, $\alpha_\infty = 1\cdot1 \times 10^{-6}$
●   Trained strain, $\alpha_\infty = 1\cdot0$

almost 100 per cent to a very minute fraction. If α_t is the fraction which have formed colonies of a standard size by the end of a time interval t, the rate of development of the colonies can be represented by a plot of α_t/α_∞ against t. When *Escherichia coli mutabile* was plated on chloramphenicol-agar the results given in Fig. 53 were obtained,[60] and with *Aerobacter aerogenes* and Terramycin those shown in Fig. 54.[18] There can be little doubt that fully resistant forms were absent from the original inoculum since even the few members of the population that were going to survive to form colonies did so on the first occasion much more slowly than normal, but at a more nearly normal rate after training. Similar results have been obtained with *Aerobacter aerogenes* and brilliant green,[60] proflavine,[60] streptomycin[60] (high concentrations), and dinitrophenol,[29] with *Escherichia coli mutabile* and propamidine,[60] and with the yeast *Saccharomyces cerevisiae* and dinitrophenol,[33] Janus black,[61] and crystal violet.[62]

When α_∞ is minute, large inocula have to be used to get any colonies at all and in these circumstances it is sometimes alleged that the great excess of sensitive cells delays the time of appearance of colonies from the resistant ones. Direct experiment, however, in which mixtures of a large number of sensitive cells and a few resistant cells were plated

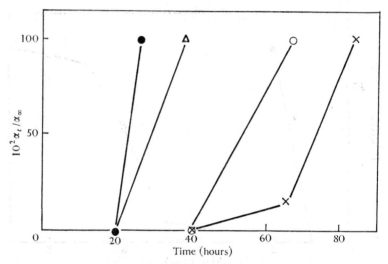

Fig. 54. Rate of development of colonies of *Aerobacter aerogenes* on Terramycin (oxytetracycline)-agar.

●   Untrained strain, no drug on plate, $\alpha_\infty = 1\cdot0$
○   Untrained strain, 1 mg/l. of drug on plate, $\alpha_\infty = 0\cdot89$
×   Untrained strain, 2 mg/l. of drug on plate, $\alpha_\infty = 0\cdot14$
△   Strain trained to 2 mg/l. of drug, 2 mg/l. of drug on plate, $\alpha_\infty = 1\cdot0$

in the presence, severally, of all the drugs mentioned above has shown that this interference does not occur. In any event α_∞ in some of the examples was not far short of $1\cdot0$ (Fig. 54) and the measurement had only entailed an inoculum of about 100 cells (see section 13).[18]

16. Mechanisms for destroying drugs, penicillinases

The discovery and purification of penicillin by Fleming[63] and by Florey and his associates[64] marked the initiation of all modern work on antibiotics. In general, penicillin is more active against Gram-positive than against Gram-negative organisms and at quite an early stage resistant strains were encountered. These were found to contain an enzyme capable of destroying the drug. This enzyme, called penicillinase[65] or more recently penicillin β-lactamase,[66] is widely distributed among bacterial species and much work has been carried out on it.[67] The production of penicillinase is not, however, the only mechanism involved in penicillin resistance since resistant bacteria which do not contain the enzyme are known.[68] Moreover, in non-penicillinase-producing strains tolerance can be produced by 'training' without the appearance of the enzyme.

A major problem in medicine is presented by penicillin-resistant staphylococci, and here again, although naturally occurring resistant strains have been found to produce penicillinase, those produced artificially do not. The latter have been stated to lose their resistance readily while the former do not, but statements of this kind should be regarded in the light of what will be said in Chapter X.

To solve the problem posed by the naturally occurring resistant staphylococci the structure of the penicillin molecule has been varied in such a way that the enzyme would have no affinity for it. Penicillin has a nucleus, 6-amino-penicillanic acid, and a side chain. In the common benzyl penicillin the side chain is derived from phenylacetic acid, and new penicillins having different side chains have been produced.[68] Two examples are dimethoxyphenyl-penicillin[69] and 3-phenyl-5-methyl-4-isoxazolyl penicillin[70] which are almost completely unaffected by staphylococcal penicillinase. They also inhibit staphylococci which are resistant to benzyl penicillin. Resistance to these new penicillins can be obtained by 'training' at increasing concentrations of drug.[69] Penicillinase is not produced.

The cephalosporins, another group of penicillins, are also of considerable interest, especially since the introduction of the semi-synthetic antibiotic cephaloridine.[71] It was produced from cephalosporin C which is not decomposed by staphylococcal penicillinase.

17. Drug dependence

With some drugs, particularly streptomycin, some of the resistant forms which grow successfully when the drug itself is present show a phenomenon called drug dependence.[72] When deprived of the drug their growth is abnormal, and long filaments often arise.[73] In *Salmonella* this inhibition of cell division is said to be due to an inability to form the septa which in normal circumstances separate the cells. When streptomycin is added again, normal septation accompanied by synchronous growth occurs. It was concluded that the drug in this example was necessary not only for normal septation but also to maintain a heritable system responsible for it.[74] Sometimes drug dependence is associated with a requirement for a specific amino-acid.[75]

A detailed study[49] with *Escherichia coli* showed that some dependent strains only grew at the maximum rate in the presence of relatively high concentrations (greater than 100 units/ml) of streptomycin, and that in these conditions the macromolecular composition of the cells was more or less normal. As the drug concentration was reduced, however, both the growth rate and the macromolecular composition changed in a progressive manner, slower growth being associated with a reduced protein content and an enhanced RNA content of the cells. At low drug levels the DNA content was slightly subnormal. When dependent cells which had been grown in a medium containing more than the critical amount of streptomycin were separated, washed, and resuspended in drug-free medium an interesting sequence of events took place. The cells continued to divide for a time and the number of divisions undergone appeared to be a function of the concentration of drug to which they were previously exposed. During this time the cell mass had been increasing exponentially at the maximum rate. Growth then slowed off over a period of 1 to 2 hours and then continued in an arithmetic manner for the next 16 to 20 hours during which a sixfold increase in cell mass occurred. Division had stopped, however, and the cells became larger. The viable count did not begin to decline until several hours after the stationary phase had been reached. During deprivation of streptomycin the synthesis of some enzymes was virtually abolished while that of others proceeded at almost the normal rate. The dependent cells were found to bind a small amount of drug.

The theoretical implications of drug dependence are discussed on p. 266.

REFERENCES

1. H. W. Florey, E. Chain, N. G. Heatley, Margaret A. Jennings, A. G. Sanders, E. P. Abraham, and Mary E. Florey, *Antibiotics*, Oxford University Press, London, 1949; Mary Barber and L. P. Garrod, *Antibiotics and Chemotherapy*, Livingstone, Edinburgh, 1963.
2. K. H. Meyer, *Trans. Faraday Soc.* **33**, 1062 (1937).
3. J. Ferguson, *Proc. R. Soc.* B **127**, 387 (1939).
4. A. H. Fogg and R. M. Lodge, *Trans. Faraday Soc.* **41**, 359 (1945).
5. S. Dagley and C. N. Hinshelwood, *J. chem. Soc.*, p. 1942 (1938).
6. W. P. Wiggert and C. H. Werkman, *Biochem. J.* **33**, 1061 (1939).
7. D. S. Davies, C. N. Hinshelwood, and A. M. James, *Trans. Faraday Soc.* **43**, 138 (1947).

8. P. Fildes, *Br. J. exp. Path.* **21**, 67 (1940).

9. D. D. Woods, *Br. J. exp. Path.* **21**, 74 (1940).

10. H. McIlwain, *Br. J. exp. Path.* **21**, 25, 136 (1940).

11. H. McIlwain, *Br. J. exp. Path.* **22**, 148 (1941).

12. H. McIlwain, *Biochem. J.* **36**, 417 (1942).

13. P. Fildes, *Br. J. exp. Path.* **22**, 293 (1941).

14. G. P. Gladstone, *Br. J. exp. Path.* **20**, 189 (1939).

15. W. B. Wood and R. Austrian, *J. exp. Med.* **75**, 383 (1942).

16. D. S. Davies, C. N. Hinshelwood, and J. M. Pryce, *Trans. Faraday Soc.* **40**, 397 (1944).

17. D. S. Davies and C. N. Hinshelwood, *Trans. Faraday Soc.* **39**, 431 (1943).

18. A. C. R. Dean and B. L. Giordan, *Proc. R. Soc.* B **161**, 571 (1964).

19. J. McIntosh and F. R. Selbie, *Br. J. exp. Path.* **24**, 246 (1943).

20. Anne Poole and C. N. Hinshelwood, *J. chem. Soc.*, p. 1565 (1940).

21. W. W. C. Topley and G. S. Wilson, *Principles of Bacteriology and Immunity*, 1st ed., 4th imp., Arnold, London (1934); W. Burrows, *Textbook of Microbiology*, Saunders, Philadelphia (1954).

22. H. McIlwain, *Biochem. J.* **37**, xiii (meeting abstract) (1943); *Br. J. exp. Path.* **24**, 203, 212 (1943).

23. W. S. Stiles, *An Introduction to the Principles of Plant Physiology*, p. 92, Methuen, London (1950); W. Stiles and M. L. L. Stirk, *Protoplasma*, **13**, 1 (1931).

24. F. W. Tilley and J. M. Schaffer, *J. Bact.* **12**, 303 (1926).

25. A. Fleming and V. D. Allison, *Br. J. exp. Path.* **8**, 214 (1927)

26. W. J. Penfold, *J. Path. Bact.* **14**, 406 (1910).

27. D. S. Davies, C. N. Hinshelwood, and J. M. Pryce, *Trans. Faraday Soc.* **41**, 163 (1945).

28. J. M. Pryce and C. N. Hinshelwood, *Trans. Faraday Soc.* **43**, 742 (1947).

29. B. J. McCarthy and Sir Cyril Hinshelwood, *J. chem. Soc.*, p. 2269 (1958).

30. J. B. Woof and Sir Cyril Hinshelwood, *Proc. R. Soc.* B **153**, 321 (1960).

31. L. S. Phillips and Sir Cyril Hinshelwood, *J. chem. Soc.*, p. 3679 (1953).

32. J. M. G. Pryce, D. S. Davies, and C. N. Hinshelwood, *Trans. Faraday Soc.*, **41**, 465 (1945).

33. D. G. Wild and Sir Cyril Hinshelwood, *Proc. R. Soc.* B **144**, 287 (1955).

34. Harriett G. Heilweil and Q. Van Winkle, *J. phys. Chem.* **59**, 939 (1955); A. R. Peacocke and J. N. H. Skerrett, *Trans. Faraday Soc.* **52**, 261 (1956); E. S. Anderson, J. A. Armstrong, and Janet S. F. Niven, *Symp. Soc. gen. Microbiol.* **9**, 224 (1959).

35. L. S. Lerman, *J. molec. Biol.* **3**, 18 (1961); *J. cell. comp. Physiol.* **64**, Suppl. 1, 1 (1964).

36. C. Scholtissek and R. Rott, *Nature, Lond.* **204**, 39 (1964).

37. J. Hurwitz, J. J. Furth, M. Malamy, and M. Alexander, *Proc. natn. Acad. Sci. U.S.A.* **48**, 1222 (1962).

38. See R. Dulbecco, *J. cell. comp. Physiol.* **64**, Suppl. 1, 181 (1964).

39. S. Brenner, L. Barnett, F. H. C. Crick, and Alice Orgel, *J. molec. Biol.* **3**, 121 (1961).

40. D. S. Davies, C. N. Hinshelwood, and J. M. G. Pryce, *Trans. Faraday Soc.* **41**, 778 (1945).

41. D. J. W. Grant and Sir Cyril Hinshelwood, *Proc. R. Soc.* B **160**, 42 (1964).

42. For general information see D. D. Woods, *J. gen. Microbiol.* **29**, 687 (1962); and Mary Barber and L. P. Garrod, *Antibiotics and Chemotherapy*, Chapters 2 and 3, Livingstone, Edinburgh (1963).

43. A. M. James and C. N. Hinshelwood, *Trans. Faraday Soc.* **43**, 274 (1947).

44. Edna R. Main, L. E. Shinn, and R. R. Mellon, *Proc. Soc. exp. Biol. Med.* **39**, 272, 591 (1938); **42**, 115 (1939); **43**, 593 (1940); but see also p. 138 of this book.

45. W. T. Drabble and Sir Cyril Hinshelwood, *Proc. R. Soc.* B **154**, 449 (1961).

46. W. T. Drabble and Sir Cyril Hinshelwood, *Proc. R. Soc.* B **155**, 433 (1961).

47. W. T. Drabble, *Proc. R. Soc.* B **154**, 571 (1961).

48. J. Lederberg and Esther M. Lederberg, *J. Bact.* **63**, 399 (1952).

49. C. R. Spotts and R. Y. Stanier, *Nature, Lond.* **192**, 633 (1961).

50. Janet L. Stern and S. S. Cohen, *Proc. natn. Acad. Sci. U.S.A.* **51**, 859 (1964).

51. P. D. Bragg and W. J. Polglase, *J. Bact.* **84**, 370 (1962); **86**, 544 (1963); **88**, 1399 (1964); **89**, 1158 (1965).

52. C. R. Spotts, *J. gen. Microbiol.* **28**, 347 (1962).

53. See reference 46 for details.

54. A. C. R. Dean, *Proc. R. Soc.* B **153**, 329 (1960).

55. A. C. Baskett, *Proc. R. Soc.* B **139**, 251 (1952).

56. A. C. R. Dean and P. H. Broadbridge, *Proc. R. Soc.* B **158**, 279 (1963).

57. A. C. R. Dean and T. M. Warman, unpublished observations.

58. J. Sinai and J. Yudkin, *J. gen. Microbiol.* **20**, 373 (1959).

59. K. W. Fisher, *Br. med. Bull.* **21**, 277 (1965).

60. A. C. R. Dean and Sir Cyril Hinshelwood, *Proc. R. Soc.* B **144**, 297 (1955).

61. D. G. Wild and Sir Cyril Hinshelwood, *Proc. R. Soc.* B **145**, 32 (1956).

62. D. G. Wild and Sir Cyril Hinshelwood, *Proc. R. Soc.* B **145**, 24 (1956).

63. A. Fleming, *Br. J. exp. Path.* **10**, 226 (1929).

64. E. B. Chain, H. W. Florey, A. D. Gardner, N. G. Heatley, Margaret A. Jennings, J. Orr-Ewing, and A. G. Sanders, *Lancet*, **2**, 226 (1940); E. P. Abraham, E. B. Chain, C. M. Fletcher, A. D. Gardner, N. G. Heatley, and Margaret A. Jennings, *Lancet*, **2**, 177 (1941).

65. E. P. Abraham and E. B. Chain, *Nature, Lond.* **146**, 837 (1940).

66. See F. R. Batchelor, E. B. Chain, M. Richards, and G. N. Rolinson, *Proc. R. Soc.* B **154**, 522 (1961).

67. See, for example, M. R. Pollock in *The Enzymes*, edited by P. D. Boyer, H. Lardy, and K. Myrbäck, 2nd ed., Academic Press, New York, **4**, 269 (1960); M. R. Pollock in Ciba Foundation Study Group No. 13, *Resistance of Bacteria to the Penicillins*, edited by A. V. S. De Reuck and Margaret P. Cameron, p. 56, Churchill, London (1962).

68. E. B. Chain in Ciba Foundation Study Group No. 13 as above, p. 3; J. A. P. Trafford, D. M. McLaren, D. A. Lillicrap, R. D. S. Barnes, J. C. Houston, and R. Knox, *Lancet*, **1**, 987 (1962); compare also R. Sutherland, *J. gen. Microbiol.* **34**, 85 (1964).

69. G. N. Rolinson, Shirley Stevens, F. R. Batchelor, J. Cameron-Wood, and E. B. Chain, *Lancet*, **2**, 564 (1960).

70. J. H. C. Nayler, A. A. W. Long, D. M. Brown, P. Acred, G. N. Rolinson, F. R. Batchelor, Shirley Stevens, and R. Sutherland, *Nature, Lond.* **195**, 1264 (1962).

71. See E. P. Abraham, *New Scient.* **24**, 430 (1964).

72. H. B. Newcombe and R. Hawirko, *J. Bact.* **57**, 565 (1949).
73. J. Lederberg and Jacqueline St. Clair, *J. Bact.* **75**, 143 (1958); T. F. Paine and M. Finland, *J. Bact.* **56**, 207 (1948); P. Schaeffer, *Biochim. Biophys. Acta* **9**, 563 (1952).
74. O. E. Landman and W. Burchard, *Proc. natn. Acad. Sci. U.S.A.* **48**, 219 (1962).
75. E. P. Goldschmidt, T. S. Matney, and H. T. Bausum, *Genetics*, **47**, 1475 (1962).

VII

QUANTITATIVE RELATION OF DRUG CONCENTRATION TO LAG AND GROWTH RATE IN ADAPTATION

1. Introduction

THE principle of total integration discussed in an earlier chapter gives strong reasons for supposing that the tendency of cells to develop drug resistance should be very general. Experimental investigations, of which some examples have been given in the last chapter, show that in fact direct adaptation is a demonstrable phenomenon. The kinds of evidence may be conveniently summarized here.

In the first place, in examples such as *Aerobacter aerogenes* with proflavine[1] or chloramphenicol[2] the level of resistance is nicely adjusted to the concentration of the drug at which the cells have been 'trained'. Selection will account for this result only if extremely improbable systems of polygenes are postulated. The first-stage mutants resistant to streptomycin, which are clearly demonstrable in the original culture, once selected show a degree of resistance practically independent of the drug concentration, as would be expected. On the other hand, when much higher degrees of resistance are concerned the level attained is once more closely related to the streptomycin concentration employed in the training, and there is no direct evidence from any source of pre-existing fully resistant forms.[3]

With some drugs at moderate concentration all the cells spread on an agar-drug plate form colonies, though initially they do so much more slowly than normally. The rate of growth increases on consecutive transfers to new plates, and, if the drug concentration is gradually raised, high levels of resistance may be reached with almost complete survival of the cells plated at each stage.[4]

In carefully managed conditions drug can be added to a growing culture in such a way that a high, though transitory, resistance develops too rapidly to be accounted for by selection.[5, 6]

Other kinds of evidence will be given in the next chapter to show that direct adaptation of cells to new substrates occurs. This shows in principle that processes other than pure selection may operate, and since growth in presence of a drug is not essentially different from growth in a medium with unfamiliar nutrients, the evidence of substrate adaptation bears more or less directly on that of drug adaptation.

There is no justification for any kind of partisan attitude on this matter. There can be no question whatever of 'selection versus adaptation'. Both processes can be foreseen, and both can be demonstrated, in appropriate examples, to occur. The nature of cell organization is such that adaptive responses can hardly fail to occur: they are part of the order of nature. If, on the other hand, some cells have been changed by the action of radiation or by 'errors' in the synthesis of their nucleic acids to have abnormal properties, they cannot help being selected in conditions where these deviations happen to be advantageous.

On the whole we believe that direct adaptation is much commoner than the selection of mutants. The reason may well be that mutations, however caused, are more often deleterious than advantageous, though it must be admitted that what constitutes a disability in normal conditions may just happen to help survival in difficulties.

A quite possible point of view is that there are two kinds of drug resistance, negative and positive. In the negative kind the cell would be protected by failure to take up the drug, and its inability to do so would be due to a destructive action of an agency such as radiation on receptors. In the positive kind the cell develops a reaction pattern which by-passes or involves antagonists to the action of the drug.

2. Simple quantitative treatment of lag-concentration relations

Reproducible quantitative relations can be found between lags, and growth rates, on the one hand, and drug concentrations on the other. Each relation is characteristic of a given strain of cells, and when the bacteria are trained in presence of drug at a given concentration, $\bar{m}$, there are definite quantitative connexions between $\bar{m}$ and the properties of the strain of cells produced. An attempt at an elementary mathematical formulation of these relations is now desirable. What follows will be more specific and detailed, and therefore involves more assumptions than the general considerations of Chapter V which have already indicated the general character of the phenomena.

The fundamental assumptions remain the same. Cell material is supposed to be synthesized by a series of interdependent processes, as a result of which in the steady state all the constituents increase according to an autocatalytic law. We shall start, as before, with equations which refer to the whole mass of living matter present, not simply to that in one cell, and introduce some condition about cell division as an auxiliary hypothesis. The division condition is, however, an essential element in the whole treatment, in so far as the constants of the equations could not remain at nearly steady values unless periodic division were in fact occurring.

For simplicity it will be convenient to fix our attention on certain enzymes of a series in which consecutive reactions of the whole pattern occur. We assume that each enzyme increases according to the auto-catalytic law, which it must do in the steady state, and continues to do so nearly enough, during the movement from one steady state to another which the addition of a drug to the system will occasion. We shall further introduce the condition that the rate of accretion of substance to an enzyme at any moment is a function of the concentration of the intermediate derived from a preceding member of the series. This function is given the form of an adsorption isotherm, so that the rate varies linearly at lower values of the concentration and becomes constant at higher values.

For the division condition we shall make the simplest postulate that some cell constituent must reach a critical amount. The best candidate for this role in general is some form of DNA, but since this has to be built up by enzymes, certain of these (directly responsible for DNA) might also assume the function. For our particular purpose here, how-ever, we can make do with a simpler condition. The drug is supposed to slow down various processes, and we shall assume, what can hardly be very far wrong, namely that division must await until the most slowly increasing of a relevant group of enzymes has been able to reach some standard amount.

Now we shall suppose that the drug somehow interrupts the reaction sequence at a stage between two particular enzymes of the series: either by interfering with the action of the $(\mu-1)$th enzyme, or with the inter-mediate produced by it, or by a direct action on the functioning of the μth enzyme. To simplify the notation we shall now refer to the $(\mu-1)$th enzyme as enzyme 1 and to the μth as enzyme 2. Their amounts at time t will be represented by x_1 and x_2 respectively.

Corresponding to the equations on pp. 117 and 126 we have now:

$$\frac{dx_1}{dt} = k_1 x_1, \tag{1}$$

$$n\frac{dc}{dt} = k_1' x_1 - Kcn - k_2 x_2 f(c) = 0, \tag{2}$$

$$\frac{dx_2}{dt} = k_2 x_2 f(c). \tag{3}$$

We shall suppose that division of the cell occurs when a standard amount of enzyme 2 is formed per cell, so that

$$n = \beta x_2.$$

Moreover, in the circumstances which we shall be considering, $f(c)$ will be taken to be almost linear, so that we shall replace it by c, ignoring any proportionality factor (which can be regarded as absorbed in the other constants). Equation (2) then gives

$$c = \frac{k_1' x_1}{k_2 x_2 + K\beta x_2} = \frac{x_1}{x_2}\left(\frac{k_1'}{k_2 + K\beta}\right). \qquad (2\,a)$$

From (3), $$\frac{dx_2}{dt} = \frac{k_2 k_1'}{(k_2 + K\beta)} x_1;$$

but $$x_1 = (x_1)_0 e^{k_1 t},$$

so that $$\frac{dx_2}{dt} = \frac{k_2 k_1'}{k_2 + K\beta} (x_1)_0 e^{k_1 t};$$

whence, by integration,

$$x_2 - (x_2)_0 = \frac{k_2 k_1'}{k_1(k_2 + K\beta)} \{(x_1) - (x_1)_0\},$$

$(x_1)_0$ and $(x_2)_0$ being the amounts at $t = 0$. Thus

$$\frac{x_2 - (x_2)_0}{x_1 - (x_1)_0} = \frac{k_2 k_1'}{k_1(k_2 + K\beta)} = \gamma. \qquad (4)$$

The ratio x_2/x_1 tends to the limit γ, which is approached as soon as the new matter synthesized outweighs sufficiently that in the inoculum.

The drug will affect the value of γ, which we assume to be changed to γ'. The effect may consist in a lowering of the ratio k_1'/k_1, a lowering of k_2, or an increase in K. The first represents a reduction in the yield of active intermediate per unit amount of the enzyme 1 synthesized. The second represents a direct impairment of the functioning of enzyme 2, while the third is a waste of intermediate in reactions other than the synthesis of enzyme 2. For the moment all we need note is the reduction in the value of γ. From equation (4) it follows that x_2/x_1 will settle down in presence of the drug to a new ratio, and, since the amount of x_2 per cell is, on the average, kept constant by the division condition, the amount of x_1 per cell will increase.

We now consider the initial growth rate of an inoculum transferred to a medium containing drug. First, we suppose the inoculum to be taken from drug-free medium, so that

$$(x_2)_0/(x_1)_0 = \gamma.$$

But in the presence of the drug, from (4),

$$\frac{dx_2}{dx_1} = \gamma',$$

or

$$\frac{dx_2}{dt} = \gamma' \frac{dx_1}{dt};$$

therefore

$$\frac{1}{(x_2)_0} \frac{dx_2}{dt} = \frac{\gamma'}{(x_2)_0} \frac{dx_1}{dt} = \frac{\gamma'}{\gamma} \frac{1}{(x_1)_0} \frac{dx_1}{dt} = \frac{\gamma'}{\gamma} k_1.$$

Since the division of the cell keeps pace with x_2, the term $(1/x_2)_0 \, dx_2/dt$ represents the overall growth rate, which is seen to be reduced by the drug in the ratio γ'/γ.

Secondly, we suppose the cells to have been grown in presence of drug for some time. For the inoculum we now have

$$(x_2)_0/(x_1)_0 = \gamma', \qquad \frac{dx_2}{dt} = \gamma' \frac{dx_1}{dt},$$

$$\frac{1}{(x_2)_0} \frac{dx_2}{dt} = \frac{\gamma'}{(x_2)_0} \frac{dx_1}{dt} = \frac{\gamma'}{\gamma'} \frac{1}{(x_1)_0} \frac{dx_1}{dt} = k_1.$$

In other words, the reduction in growth rate caused by the drug has now been compensated by the change in the ratio x_2/x_1. This corresponds to a complete adaptation.

For future reference it will be convenient to note here what happens to the intermediate concentration, c, in various circumstances. From equation (2 a) it is evident that if the reduction in γ is due to a lowering of k_1' or to an increase in K, then the immediate effect of the drug is to lower c. Adaptation increases x_1/x_2 and restores c to its normal value. If, on the other hand, the drug acts by lowering k_2, then c is immediately increased according to (2 a) and, after adaptation, increased still more. (If K is large, the first increase is unimportant.)

The two important cases thus are: (1) the drug lowers c, and adaptation, through an increase in the ratio x_1/x_2, restores c to normal; (2) the drug lowers k_2 but the effect of this is counteracted by an increase in c which occurs on adaptation through the expansion of enzyme 1.

We now turn to the consideration of the ways in which the drug does, in fact, affect γ. If the ratio of k_1'/k_1 is reduced, it means that the drug does not impede the synthesis of the basal material of enzyme 1, but interferes with the production of the intermediate which would normally be formed. In other words, the course of the reactions occurring at enzyme 1 is deflected. This is by no means an improbability. The basal structure of the enzyme is of a protein-like character, and may be associated with prosthetic groups. One possible action of the drug might be to displace these, giving a modified protein.

In this connexion one might quote the view of Albert that there is a competition between acridine drugs and hydrogen ions for negatively charged sites on protein surfaces, an idea introduced to account for the influence of pH on the effectiveness of the drugs of this class (p. 203). K would be changed if the drug combined with the active intermediate. Such an interference would be particularly likely to occur if the intermediate consisted of some molecule of very great chemical reactivity, or indeed of a free radical. The reduction of k_2 could easily be brought about by adsorption of the drug on the surface of enzyme 2, or by the formation of a drug-enzyme compound.

By which of the various means γ is changed is not relevant to the mechanism of the actual adaptive process, though of interest to the general theory of drug action. In fact the mode of action of various drugs seems to be very different, highly specific and occasionally multiple.

To quote only one example, the penicillins sometimes inhibit the formation of mucopeptides in the cell wall and this probably plays an important part in their selective toxic action: benzyl penicillin is stated to inhibit ribitol teichoic acid formation.[7] For our present purpose these highly individual actions should not obscure the general principles underlying all of them.

For the discussion of adaptive phenomena, therefore, we shall adopt an empirical expression for the drug action, which can, when convenient, be compared with any given theoretical form. We shall consider separately the two cases mentioned above, the first being where c is reduced by the initial action of the drug and restored to normal by the adaptive change: and the second where k_2 is reduced, and the rate of growth of enzyme 2 restored to normal by the increase in c resulting from the expansion of enzyme 1.

Case 1. Let the normal value of c for unadapted cells in the absence of the drug be c_1. Then we write

$$c = c_1 - \phi(m).$$

The function $\phi(m)$ of the drug concentration, m, will characterize the drug for this purpose.

After adaptation, c will have returned to c_1 even in presence of the drug. If, therefore, the cells are transferred to a medium containing no drug, there will be an immediate increase to a value given by

$$c = c_1 + \phi(m).$$

If the cells are first adapted to a concentration $\bar{m}$ and then transferred to a concentration m, the value will be given by

$$c = c_1 + \phi(\bar{m}) - \phi(m). \tag{5}$$

Case 2. Here drug and substrate compete for the surface of the enzyme. As before, let c_1 be the normal value of c for the unadapted cells in the absence of drug; in the adapted cells c will have risen to c_2, so that if $\bar{m}$ is the concentration of drug at which training occurs

$$\psi(c_1, 0) = \psi(c_2, \bar{m}), \tag{6}$$

where
$$\psi(c_1, 0) = k_2 f(c_1).$$

$\psi(c, m)$ is the function which replaces $k_2 f(c)$ when intermediate and drug are acting jointly on enzyme 2.

The total rate of functioning of enzyme 2 may be expressed

$$\text{rate} = R = R_0\{1 - \chi_1(m) + \chi_2(c)\}. \tag{7}$$

Equation (6) then becomes

$$R_0\{1 + \chi_2(c_1)\} = R_0\{1 - \chi_1(\bar{m}) + \chi_2(c_2)\}.$$

Therefore
$$\chi_2(c_2) = \chi_2(c_1) + \chi_1(\bar{m})$$

so that for trained cells transferred to another concentration m, we have

$$\text{rate} = R_0\{1 + \chi_1(\bar{m}) - \chi_1(m) + \chi_2(c_1)\}.$$

$\chi_2(c_1)$ is a constant, since c_1 is the standard value for unadapted cells in the absence of drug. We therefore write

$$R = R_0\{\text{constant} + \chi_1(\bar{m}) - \chi_1(m)\}, \tag{8}$$

which is formally similar to (5). It must be emphasized, however, that the expression (7) where the actions of drug and intermediate are represented by two independent functions can only hold over limited ranges and with express understandings about the limits of its applicability. For example, if drug has lowered R much below normal, it is reasonable to suppose that increase in c raises it again. In the absence of drug, when R was normal, a corresponding increase of c might well have less effect. (7) and (8) are therefore only taken to apply over the range where drug and intermediate are in competition. For the subsequent discussion case 1 will be the more satisfactory to handle.

3. Influence of drugs on lag and on growth rate

The discussion of the last section dealt with the rate of growth and operation of a certain enzyme referred to for the purposes of the model as enzyme 2. It would not be any serious extension of the hypothesis to transfer the whole consideration to the growth of the entire cell: in fact the treatment adopted tells us directly, subject only to the validity of the assumptions, what will happen to the mean generation time of the cells on adaptation.

But for experimental studies of adaptive processes the mean generation time is not the most convenient quantity to handle. From its very nature, it can only be determined by experiments in which increase in cell material takes place: and, as we have seen, any serious increase in mass is likely to be attended by the occurrence of adaptation. Thus the measurements will always refer to cells which have already undergone some degree of adaptation.

With the lag, on the other hand, this difficulty does not arise. Up to almost the end of the lag phase there is little increase in cell mass, and none at all during the major part of the time. Thus the lag is characteristic of the cell in the particular state of adaptation prevailing at the time when the transfer to the new medium is made.

The question arises, then, of the relation of the lag to the rate of enzyme action which has so far formed the basis of our calculations. In the following pages we shall make the explicit assumption that the minimum value of the lag (that is, the value which is determined by the presence of the drug alone, and is not increased by ageing of the cells) is inversely proportional to the rate of an enzyme process similar to that of enzyme 2 in the model described. Actually this rate itself will probably vary during the lag period and the expression

$$\text{lag} = L = \frac{A}{\text{rate of enzyme process}} = \frac{A}{R},$$

where A is a constant, would be more correctly replaced by

$$\int_0^L R \, dt = \text{constant.}$$

We shall, nevertheless, use the simpler form which should serve as a reasonable working hypothesis.

4. Families of lag-concentration curves

We consider cells which have been grown repeatedly at a drug concentration $\bar{m}$, and then are tested for their lag at a whole series of concentrations. For each value of $\bar{m}$ there will be a characteristic curve relating m, the test concentration, to the corresponding lag. The lag, as we have seen, depends upon the age of the inoculum: we shall consider its minimum value. That is to say, for all the tests we shall suppose a culture to be used of such age that in the absence of any drug the lag would tend to zero. The lag-concentration curve which will be considered will be that showing ΔL as a function of the test concentration m, ΔL being the difference between the lag observed in presence of the drug and that shown by an identical inoculum in the drug-free medium.

Some typical families of curves are shown in Figs. 55, 57, 58, 59, 60, 61, and 63.

In discussing the form and spacing of the curves in these families, we shall adopt as the basic hypothesis the idea that the resistance is achieved by a change in the enzyme balance in the cells. Other modes of resistance will be discussed separately.

We shall also adopt the assumption of the last section that the lag is expressible in the form

$$L = \frac{A}{R}, \tag{1}$$

where A is a constant (for a given type of organism and a given medium) and R is the rate of operation of an enzyme process.

R itself will depend upon the concentration, c, of the substrate which the enzyme employs, in a manner expressible approximately by a Langmuir isotherm:

$$R = \frac{kc}{1+bc}, \tag{2}$$

where k and b are constants.

The influence of the drug will be taken to change c in accordance with the discussion on p. 186:

$$c = c_1 + \phi(\bar{m}) - \phi(m), \tag{3}$$

where c_1 is the value characteristic of the unadapted cells in the absence of the drug.

Although it is an assumption that (1), (2), and (3) have these precise forms, there can be little doubt about the general shape of these expressions, so that the discussion which follows probably possesses a more general validity than the detailed arguments which have led up to it.

Substituting (3) and (2) in (1) we obtain

$$L = \frac{A}{k}\left\{\frac{1}{c_1 + \phi(\bar{m}) - \phi(m)} + b\right\}.$$

If L_0 is the value of L when $m = 0$,

$$\Delta L = L - L_0 = \frac{A}{k}\left\{\frac{1}{c_1 + \phi(\bar{m}) - \phi(m)} - \frac{1}{c_1 + \phi(\bar{m})}\right\}. \tag{4}$$

Equation (4) gives the family of lag-concentration curves for the series of strains which have been adapted to various drug concentrations.

5. Discussion of a typical example of a family of lag-concentration curves

One of the more thoroughly studied examples is that of *Aerobacter aerogenes* adapted to various concentrations of proflavine (2,8 di-amino-acridine).[1, 8, 9] The family of curves is shown in Fig. 55. The general form

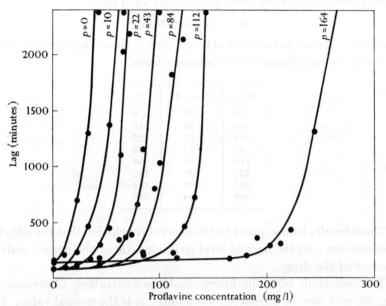

FIG. 55. Family of lag-concentration curves for trained strains of *Aerobacter aerogenes* in proflavine.

The value of p indicates the concentration at which the cells were trained.

of the individual curves is in accordance with the requirement of equation (4) of the last section, the lag remaining low until m exceeds $\bar{m}$ by a certain amount, after which the lag rises steeply towards infinite values.

Furthermore, the spacing of the separate curves of the family is well accounted for if $\phi(m)$ is taken to be a simple linear function of m: $\phi(m) = fm$ where f is a constant. The curves in Fig. 55 are reproduced quite reasonably well by the formula

$$\frac{1}{L-L_0} = 1 \cdot 0 \times 10^{-4}\{(\bar{m}+54)^2/m-(\bar{m}+54)\},$$

which is derived from equation (4) of the last section by writing $\phi(m) = fm$, and $c_1 = 54f$.

The mode of spacing of the curves can be seen from equation (4) itself. L becomes infinite when $c_1 + \phi(\bar{m}) - \phi(m) = 0$; that is to say: in the present example when $c_1 + f\bar{m} = fm$, or when $m = 54 + \bar{m}$. If L is large compared with L_0, without actually becoming infinite, we shall have approximately:

$$L = \frac{\text{constant}}{c_1 + f\bar{m} - fm},$$

and if m_s is the drug concentration at which the lag attains some assigned large value, for example 1000 minutes, we shall have

$$m_s - \bar{m} = \text{constant}.$$

That this relation is rather closely satisfied is shown by the agreement of the last two columns of the following table.

m_{1000}	$m_{1000} - 40$	$\bar{m}$
30	-10	0
50	10	10
62	22	22
84	42	43
114	74	84
137	97	112
242	202	164
490	450	430

These results lend support to the general conclusion that the adaptation restores c to the normal level characteristic of the normal cells in absence of the drug.

The behaviour of c, the intermediate concentration, illustrated by Fig. 56, may now be considered more fully. c_1 is the normal value. The action of the drug lowers it to c_2. Adaptation restores it to a point which will be provisionally indicated by c_2'. In the drug-free medium the adapted cells develop a concentration c_1', but, from the nature of the isotherm, this enhanced value produces no corresponding increase of growth rate. The interval c_1 to c_1', while not representing any increased speed of action (decreased lag) in the ordinary medium, corresponds to a considerable degree of tolerance to the drug.

The point c_1, as previously suggested, must lie just near the shoulder of the curve since, on the one hand, trained cells show no advantage over untrained cells when transferred to drug-free medium and, on the other hand, untrained cells show little tolerance to the drug before the lag begins to rise. The former fact shows that c_1 cannot lie far down the sloping portion of the curve: the latter that it cannot lie far along the horizontal part.

Furthermore, it now seems that the point c_2' is in fact coincident with c_1. This was tacitly assumed in the previous discussion, but is now confirmed by the experimental fact that all the curves, including that for the untrained cells, constitute a unique family, as shown by the above table.

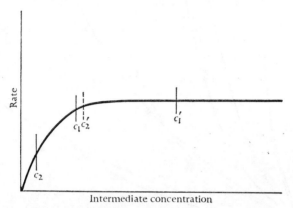

FIG. 56. Intermediate concentration and rate.

6. Form and spacing of the curves in a family

With *Aerobacter aerogenes* and proflavine, both the form of the individual curves and the actual spacing of the various members of the family are fairly satisfactorily accounted for with the help of the assumption that $\phi(m)$ is a linear function of m. The spacing is exactly adjusted to the value of $\bar{m}$, the concentration at which the cells are trained. Thus if m_s is the drug concentration which causes a lag of s (s being large) then $(m_s - \bar{m})$ is constant throughout the family.

This pattern, however, is not always observed. For example, with *Aerobacter aerogenes* and potassium tellurite[10] the curves become more and more widely separated with successive equal increments in $\bar{m}$ (Fig. 57). For lags of 1000 minutes it is found that

$$m_s = 7 \cdot 1\bar{m} + 6.$$

Another example of this type of behaviour is seen with *Aerobacter aerogenes* and chloramphenicol (Fig. 58), and for a lag of 600 minutes the formula is $m_s = 8 \cdot 1\bar{m} - 37$. The curve for the untrained strain, moreover, has a small but distinct anomaly in the shape of an unusual step at a concentration of about 10 mg/l.[2] Marked cross-resistance exists between chloramphenicol and Terramycin, and in general form the lag-concentration curves are similar. Terramycin, however, is the more active drug and in this example the empirical equation for a lag

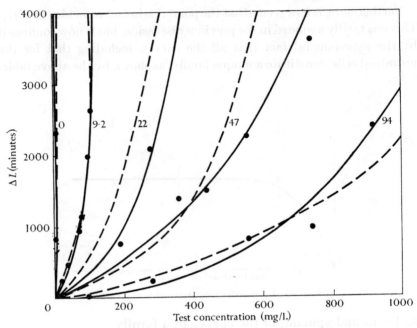

Fig. 57. Family of lag-concentration curves for trained strains of *Aerobacter aerogenes* in potassium tellurite. The dotted lines were calculated from

$$\frac{1}{\Delta L} = 0.0029\left[\frac{\{1.16+\ln(1+\bar{m})\}^2}{\ln(1+m)} - \{1.16+\ln(1+\bar{m})\}\right] \quad \text{(See ref. 10).}$$

The figures on the curves indicate the concentrations at which the cells were trained.

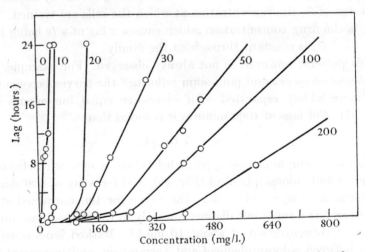

Fig. 58. Family of lag-concentration curves for trained strains of *Aerobacter aerogenes* in chloramphenicol.

The figures on the curves indicate the concentrations at which the cells were trained.

of 2000 minutes is $m_s = 2 \cdot 3\bar{m} + 18$ (Fig. 59).[11] With some drugs the adaptive capacity of the cells appears to be limited and attempts to increase $\bar{m}$ become more and more difficult. This is illustrated in Fig. 60 which gives results for *Aerobacter aerogenes* and propamidine. The successive curves of the family crowd together.[10]

The family of curves obtained for the adaptation of *Aerobacter aerogenes* to crystal violet is shown in Fig. 61 and is of an intermediate form.[12]

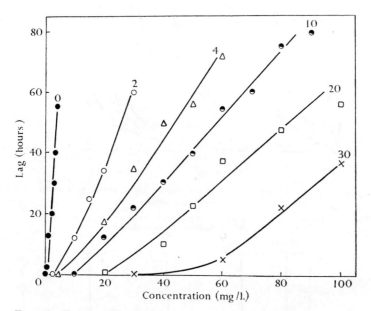

FIG. 59. Family of lag-concentration curves for trained strains of *Aerobacter aerogenes* in Terramycin (oxytetracycline).

The figures on the curves indicate the concentrations at which the cells were trained.

Both the form and the spacing of the curves are determined by the function $\phi(m)$. Since the lag is given by

$$\Delta L = \text{constant} \left\{ \frac{1}{c_1 + \phi(\bar{m}) - \phi(m)} - \frac{1}{c_1 + \phi(\bar{m})} \right\}$$

we may write, when ΔL is fairly large,

$$\Delta L = \frac{B}{c_1 + \phi(\bar{m}) - \phi(m)}.$$

If m_s is the concentration of drug which causes a lag s, then for the various strains of trained cells we have

$$c_1 + \phi(\bar{m}) - \phi(m_s) = \text{constant} = E.$$

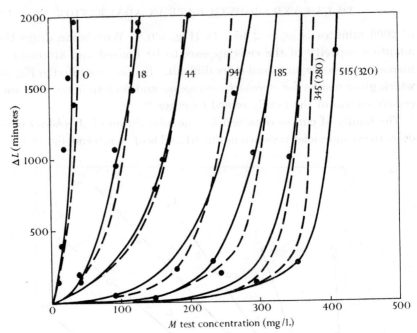

FIG. 60. Family of lag-concentration curves for trained strains of *Aerobacter aerogenes* in propamidine.

The figures on the curves indicate the concentrations at which the strains were trained.
The dotted lines are calculated.

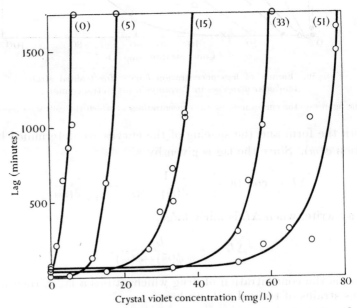

FIG. 61. Family of lag-concentration curves for trained strains of *Aerobacter aerogenes* in crystal violet.

The figures on the curves indicate the concentrations at which the strains were trained.

Now let $\phi(m)$ be expressed empirically as a power series

$$\phi(m) = \alpha m + \beta m^2 + \gamma m^3 + \dots,$$

α, β, and γ being constants. Then,

$$\alpha m_s + \beta m_s^2 + \gamma m_s^3 = E + \alpha \bar{m} + \beta \bar{m}^2 + \gamma \bar{m}^3,$$

$$\alpha \frac{dm_s}{d\bar{m}} + 2m_s\beta \frac{dm_s}{d\bar{m}} + 3\gamma m_s^2 \frac{dm_s}{d\bar{m}} = \alpha + 2\beta \bar{m} + 3\gamma \bar{m}^2,$$

$$\frac{dm_s}{d\bar{m}} = \frac{\alpha + 2\beta \bar{m} + 3\gamma \bar{m}^2}{\alpha + 2\beta m_s + 3\gamma m_s^2}.$$

The various patterns of behaviour which have been illustrated correspond to different forms of the $\phi(m)$ function.

1. If β and γ are zero, then $dm_s/d\bar{m} = 1$, and the spacing is uniform with that of the values of $\bar{m}$.

2. If α is positive and the joint effect of the others negative, then, since m_s is greater than $\bar{m}$, the value of $dm_s/d\bar{m}$ is greater than unity. This means that the spacing increases as $\bar{m}$ increases.

3. If the joint effect of the β and γ terms is positive, then $dm_s/d\bar{m}$ is less than unity and successive curves tend to crowd together with increase of $\bar{m}$.

To the extent that the $\phi(m)$ function is empirical this classification is only a formal one. But what is more significant is that the same $\phi(m)$ function which describes the spacing of the curves in a family also describes certain important properties of the individual curves themselves.

From the expression

$$\Delta L = \frac{B}{c_1 + \phi(\bar{m}) - \phi(m)},$$

we find by differentiation

$$-\frac{B}{(\Delta L)^2} \frac{\partial(\Delta L)}{\partial m} = -\phi'(m) = -(\alpha + 2\beta m + 3\gamma m^2),$$

$$\frac{\partial(\Delta L)}{\partial m} = \frac{(\Delta L)^2}{B}(\alpha + 2\beta m + 3\gamma m^2).$$

Now consider the slope of the curve of ΔL against m, measured at a standard value of ΔL. In families of the proflavine type, β and γ are zero, and therefore, for a given value of ΔL, the slope $\partial(\Delta L)/\partial m$ should be constant. That this is approximately true is shown by the numbers which follow:

$\bar{m}$ ($mg/l.$)	$\partial m/\partial(\Delta L) \times 10^2$ $mg/l./min$ at $\Delta L = 1000$
0	1·16
10	1·10
22	0·97
43	1·10
84	1·12
112	1·06

In families of the potassium tellurite type, $\alpha+2\beta m+3\gamma m^2$ decreases with increase of m. The greater $\bar{m}$, the greater the value of m required to produce a given value of ΔL, and, therefore, the slope $\partial(\Delta L)/\partial m$ decreases as $\bar{m}$ increases. That successive curves of the family are of decreasing steepness is shown in Fig. 57.

For *Aerobacter aerogenes* and potassium tellurite, $\phi(m)$ can be empirically represented by

$$\phi(m) = a \ln(1+1 \cdot 0m).$$

This is obtained from the spacing of the curves. Since

$$\frac{B}{(\Delta L)^2} \frac{\partial(\Delta L)}{\partial m} = \phi'(m) = \frac{1 \cdot 0a}{1+1 \cdot 0m},$$

$$\frac{\partial m}{\partial(\Delta L)} = \frac{B}{(\Delta L)^2} \frac{(1+1 \cdot 0m)}{a}.$$

The inverse slope $\partial m/\partial(\Delta L)$ should increase linearly with m, the value of the drug concentration needed to produce the standard lag. The following table shows that this prediction is approximately fulfilled.

$\bar{m}$	m_{1000}	$(\partial m/\partial \Delta L)_{1000} \times 10^3$	$(3+0 \cdot 45m_{1000})$
0	4	5	5
9·2	75	30	37
22	200	93	93
47	320	230	147
94	650	295	295

A family of curves of the type 3 is illustrated by the lag-concentration curves for various adapted strains of *Aerobacter aerogenes* tested in propamidine. From the variation of m_s with $\bar{m}$ the $\phi(m)$ function can be found graphically (see next section). The curve of $\phi(m)$ against m shows an inflexion. At this point the second differential coefficient of $\phi(m)$ is zero. But since $\phi'(m)$ is proportional to $\partial(\Delta L)/\partial m$, $\phi''(m)$ is proportional to $\partial^2 \Delta L/\partial m^2$. Thus at the value of m corresponding to the point of inflexion in the $\phi(m)$, m curve the slope of the ΔL, m curve should show a maximum or minimum value—actually a minimum.

For $\Delta L = 1000$ this minimum occurs at about $m = 200$. The decrease and subsequent increase in the steepness of the curves at $\Delta L = 1000$ can be seen in Fig. 62. The slopes are recorded in the following table.

$\overline{m}$	m_{1000}	$(\partial \Delta L/\partial m)_{1000}$
0	26	133
18	96	23
44	165	18
94	245	17
185	292	17
280	342	33
320	395	48

The position of the minimum is not very well defined, but the results are consistent with its being more or less in the predicted region of $m_{1000} = 200$.

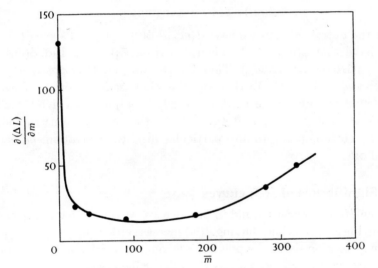

FIG. 62. Slopes of lag-concentration curves.

7. Determination of $\phi(m)$ curves

The foregoing discussion shows that the spacing of the members of a family of lag-concentration curves on the one hand, and the forms of the individual curves on the other, can be satisfactorily correlated with the aid of the $\phi(m)$, m function for the system. The methods of determining it may now be indicated.

Some standard value of ΔL is chosen and the corresponding drug concentration m_s is read off from the lag-concentration curves for each value of $\bar{m}$. If possible the relation of m_s and $\bar{m}$ is expressed by a convenient empirical equation, such as that used above for the potassium tellurite experiments:

$$m_s = 7 \cdot 1 \bar{m} + 6. \tag{1}$$

For a constant value of the lag, the general equation shows that $\phi(m) - \phi(\bar{m}) = $ constant. Thus

$$\phi(m_s) - \phi(\bar{m}) = \text{const.} \tag{2}$$

It is sometimes possible to find a simple form for $\phi(m)$ such that (1) follows directly from (2). This will, of course, be the form required. In the present example $\phi(m) = a \ln(1 + bm)$ satisfies the conditions, as may easily be verified by substitution in (2).

When an algebraical method is not convenient a graphical method may be used. If m_s is plotted against $\bar{m}$, a series of pairs of values $m_{s1}, \bar{m}_1; m_{s2}, \bar{m}_2, \ldots$ can be read off such that $\bar{m}_j = m_{s,j-1}$. But

$$\phi(m_s) - \phi(\bar{m}) = \text{constant} = C.$$

For the untrained cells we have $\phi(m_{s0}) - \phi(0) = C$, and since $\phi(0) = 0$, we have that $\phi(m_{s0}) = C$. Then $\phi(m_{s1}) - \phi(\bar{m}_1) = C$. But $\phi(\bar{m}_1)$ was chosen to be equal to $\phi(m_{s0})$. Thus $\phi(m_{s1}) - \phi(m_{s0}) = C$, or $\phi(m_{s1}) - C = C$, whence $\phi(m_{s1}) = 2C$. In this way the whole series of $\phi(m)$ values can be found as multiples of C. C can easily be adjusted to give the whole $\phi(m)$, m curve the required scale. From the curve so constructed the values corresponding to any particular drug concentration, m, can be read off.

8. Significance of $\phi(m)$ curves

The $\phi(m)$, m curves found in practice are of varied shape, sometimes being linear, sometimes having $\phi(m)$ increase either more or less rapidly than m, or even showing a point of inflexion, at which a more than linear increase with m succeeds a less than linear increase.

We must now inquire briefly into the possible meaning of such behaviour.

From equation (2 a) of section 2 we have

$$c = (x_1/x_2)\{k_1'/(k_2 + K\beta)\},$$

and since $x_2/x_1 = \gamma$ by equation (4) of that section, it follows that

$$c_1 = \frac{1}{\gamma_1} \frac{k_1'}{k_2 + K\beta},$$

where γ_1 is the value of γ for normal cells.

In presence of the drug k_1' will be assumed to be reduced (case 1, p. 185) so that

$$(k_1')_m = k_1' - \psi(m).$$

Therefore
$$c_1 - c = \frac{1}{\gamma_1(k_2 + K\beta)} \{k_1' - (k_1')_m\} = \frac{\psi(m)}{\text{constant}}.$$

Since, therefore,
$$c = c_1 - \frac{\psi(m)}{\text{constant}}$$

and
$$c = c_1 - \phi(m),$$

$\psi(m)$ is proportional to $\phi(m)$.

A linear course of the $\phi(m)$, m curve, therefore, corresponds to a linear reduction of k_1' with drug concentration. Such linear relations are not at all uncommon and conform to known types of adsorption isotherm. When $\phi(m)$ increases more than linearly with m it would appear that the reduction of k_1' depends upon a kind of adsorption (of drug on the enzyme surface) where co-operative effects between the drug molecules occur. Less than linear proportionality suggests that adsorption of a certain amount of drug impedes the adsorption of more drug to a greater extent than it impedes the adsorption of the competing substrate. This might well occur if the drug molecules were large and the substrate molecules small. For a point of inflexion in the $\phi(m)$, m curve, the condition would be that the two effects just referred to should be present in competition with one another.

9. Cross adaptation

Cells of *Aerobacter aerogenes* which have become adapted to proflavine show increased resistance to inhibition by methylene blue and vice versa. Training to proflavine confers some degree of resistance to other acridines. Indeed, training to various members of the acridine group, 2,8 diamino-acridine, 5-amino-acridine, and 2,7 diamino-acridine shows a set of reciprocal relations which are approximately quantitative.

Certain results found with *Aerobacter aerogenes* for proflavine and methylene blue will be summarized as an illustration of the kind of relations which are characteristic of cross adaptation.[9]

Methylene blue increases the lag of the cells in a synthetic medium: for untrained cells the empirical relation

$$L - L_0 = 30m \tag{1}$$

is approximately followed.

Various adapted strains give a series of lag-concentration curves which crowd together as $\bar{m}$ increases, that is to say, there is a limit to the adaptation which can occur.

Each of the trained strains, tested in proflavine, shows resistance to this drug corresponding to what it would have acquired by direct adaptation at a concentration P'. The equivalent proflavine concentration, P', plotted against the methylene blue training concentration $\bar{m}$, gives a curve which is markedly concave to the $\bar{m}$ axis, that is to say, the equivalent proflavine resistance increases much less rapidly than $\bar{m}$. This stands in an obvious qualitative connexion with the fact that the methylene blue resistance itself tends to a limit.

It is of interest to inquire how far a quantitative relation exists.

From the equation (4) of section 4 we have

$$L - L_0 = \frac{A}{k} \left\{ \frac{1}{c_1 + \phi(\bar{m}) - \phi(m)} - \frac{1}{c_1 + \phi(\bar{m})} \right\}. \tag{2}$$

The constants A/k and c_1 are obtained by experiments *with proflavine alone*. Then by comparison of equation (1) above, with (2) for $\bar{m} = 0$, a series of values of $\phi(m)$ may be found and plotted against m. The resulting curve is concave to the m axis. We now have the constants of equation (2) and the $\phi(m)$, m relation from experiments in which no methylene blue-adapted strains of the organism have been used at all. From the results, however, we are in a position to predict the behaviour of the methylene blue-trained strains both in methylene blue and in proflavine. The basic assumption of this procedure is that the modes of attack of the two drugs on the cells are comparable.

The results of the attempted prediction are as follows.

1. Cells trained at the highest possible concentration of methylene blue are calculated to show an equivalent proflavine resistance which should never exceed that corresponding to training at 54 mg/l., i.e. P' should have a limiting value of 54. Experimentally the limiting value of P' was found to be 30.

2. The calculated lag-concentration curves for the methylene blue-trained strains crowd together in the correct manner, but the shape of the individual curves is not very well reproduced. The comparison of the calculated and the observed results is shown in Fig. 63.

The results of the calculations reveal a significant correspondence between the behaviour of proflavine and that of methylene blue, and allow the semi-quantitative prediction of one type of behaviour from the other. Better numerical agreement might be obtained with more accurate results, but it is more likely that superposed on the common actions of the two drugs, there are specific actions to which the theory is inapplicable.

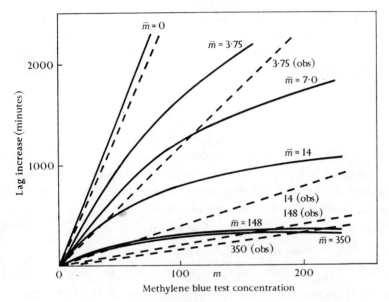

FIG. 63. Family of lag-concentration curves for trained strains in methylene blue.

10. Development of alternative mechanisms

In the example of adaptation of *Aerobacter aerogenes* to sulphonamides the experimental results suggested that the development of an alternative growth mechanism is a possibility. In this section a simplified and hypothetical but more specific model of such a process will be considered.[12]

Suppose we have the following relation of enzymes:

$$I \longrightarrow M_1 \longrightarrow II \longrightarrow M_2 \atop c \qquad\qquad c' \searrow III \atop IV \longrightarrow M_2 \nearrow$$

Enzyme I produces the intermediate M_1 which attains in the cell the steady concentration c and which is the substrate for enzyme II. Enzymes II and IV are alternative sources of M_2 which is utilized by enzyme III. The steady concentration of M_2 is c', to which, normally, II makes a much greater contribution than IV.

If c drops, c' will drop in consequence of the lowered contribution which II will then be able to make.

Let the drug interfere with the production of M_1, thereby cutting down the supply of M_2 from II and making III relatively more dependent on IV. We assume III to be an important constituent of the cell, so that division has to await the formation of the standard amount of it.

In a medium where a steady state has been reached I and IV maintain a constant ratio. If their amounts are x_1 and x_4 respectively, then

$$x_1 = (x_1)_0 e^{Kt} \quad \text{and} \quad x_4 = (x_4)_0 e^{Kt},$$

K being the overall growth constant. Also

$$x_4/x_1 = \gamma. \tag{1}$$

The concentrations c and c' are determined by the factors which have been discussed before; but to simplify the calculation we are now going to neglect the loss by diffusion from the region of the enzymes. The essential result will not be changed by this.

Now
$$dc/dt = k_1' x_1 - k_2 x_2 c = 0, \tag{2}$$
$$dc'/dt = k_2 x_2 c + k_4' x_4 - k_3 x_3 c' = 0,$$
or
$$dc'/dt = k_1' x_1 + k_4' x_4 - k_3 x_3 c' = 0. \tag{3}$$

(2) and (3) assume the synthesis and functioning of II to be completely linked. To avoid the introduction of extra symbols, the formation of M_2 is equated to the formation of x_2.

$$dx_3/dt = k_3 x_3 c' = k_1' x_1 + k_4' x_4 \quad \text{from (3)}$$

and since $dx_1/dt = Kx_1$, we have

$$dx_3/dx_1 = (k_1' x_1 + k_4' x_4)/Kx_1 = k_1'/K + k_4' \gamma/K. \tag{4}$$

For a culture growing under constant conditions x_3/x_1 must settle down to the same value as dx_3/dx_1, and thus for an inoculum taken from such a culture trained to a drug concentration $\bar{m}$,

$$(x_3)_0/(x_1)_0 = (k_{1(\bar{m})}' + k_4' \gamma)/K = A_{(\bar{m})}. \tag{5}$$

If this inoculum is transferred to another drug concentration, m, it will grow in such a way that x_3/x_1 tends to a new value A_m. But *initially* the rate of growth of x_3 will be given by

$$(dx_3/dt)_0 = k_{1(m)}'(x_1)_0 + k_4' \gamma(x_1)_0 = K_m(x_3)_0.$$

Thus
$$K_m = k_{1(m)}' \left\{ \frac{(x_1)_0}{(x_3)_0} \right\}_{(\bar{m})} + k_4' \gamma \left\{ \frac{(x_1)_0}{(x_3)_0} \right\}_{(\bar{m})},$$

or
$$K_m = \left\{ \frac{(x_1)_0}{(x_3)_0} \right\}_{(\text{training})} \{k_{1(\text{test})}' + k_4' \gamma\}, \tag{6}$$

the subscripts 'training' and 'test' being more explicit ways of writing $\bar{m}$ and m respectively.

k_1' is the quantity assumed to be affected by the drug. When it is reduced there is a depression in growth rate according to (6). According to (5), however, $(x_3)_0/(x_1)_0$ will adjust itself to a new value, so that eventually $\{(x_3)_0/(x_1)_0\}_{(\bar{m})}$ becomes $(k_{1(m)}' + k_4'\gamma)/K$

since the cells are now trained at the test concentration.

$K_{(m)}$ now equals K once more and complete adaptation has occurred.

So far, the present case differs little from that considered earlier, but when we come to consider the behaviour of the cells in still higher concentrations of the drug the difference appears. The smaller the factor $(k_1' + k_4'\gamma)$, the greater is the relative importance of $k_4'\gamma$, since it is k_1' which is sensitive to the drug. (5) and (6) may be written in the form

$$\frac{K_m}{K} = \frac{k_{1(\text{test})}' + k_4'\gamma}{k_{1(\text{training})}' + k_4'\gamma} = \frac{F(m) + B}{F(\bar{m}) + B}, \tag{7}$$

where F represents a function of the drug concentration and B is independent of the drug. As soon as $F(m)$ is small compared with B, the further reduction in $F(m)/F(\bar{m})$ is of no consequence. This means that there is a value of the training concentration $\bar{m}$ which will give complete resistance even to vastly greater values of m.

As we have seen, strains of *Aerobacter aerogenes* trained to sulphonamide tend to behave in a manner which, over a certain range at least, is more or less independent of the training concentration. The composite growth curves found with sulphonamides favour some sort of alternative mechanism theory for the training. But they require an alternative mechanism theory of a rather different form, which will be best considered in relation to adaptation to change of nutrients.

11. Influence of pH on the action of proflavine

The effect of pH on the bacteriostatic action of acridine derivatives with *Escherichia coli* has been studied by Albert and others.[13] The drugs are much less effective in acid than in neutral solutions. The active molecular species is the positively charged acridinium ion. Over the range of pH in which the bacteriostatic action shows very great changes there is little change in the degree of ionization of the drug, which corresponds throughout to a great preponderance of the cationic form. The influence of the hydrogen ion concentration would seem, therefore, to be exerted, not on the drug itself, but on the proteins of the cell.

Albert supposes a competition between hydrogen ions and acridinium ions for various negative centres in the protein.

The following is a simple treatment of such an effect. Let the negative centres in the cell material be represented by X^-. Then for the acid dissociation we have

$$\frac{[X^-][H^+]}{[XH]} = K_1,$$

and for the combination of the protein material with the acridinium cations,

$$\frac{[X^-][AH^+]}{[XAH]} = K_2.$$

Since nearly all the drug is present in solution as cation we may write $AH^+ = m$. From the equations, we then find

$$\frac{[XH]}{[XAH]} = \left(\frac{K_2}{K_1}\right)\frac{[H^+]}{m}.$$

If XH be regarded as the active surface of the protein and XAH as the inactive surface, then the last expression is $s/(1-s)$, whence

$$s = \left(\frac{K_2}{K_1}\right)\frac{[H^+]}{m} \Big/ \left\{1 + \left(\frac{K_2}{K_1}\right)\frac{[H^+]}{m}\right\}.$$

It seems reasonable to assume that, for equal drug effects, s should be constant, which means that $[H^+]$ should vary linearly with m. In other words, the concentration of the drug required to produce a standard degree of inhibition should increase in direct proportion to the hydrogen ion concentration. Albert and collaborators found for *Escherichia coli* that a tenfold change in m corresponds to a shift of 1·2 pH units, instead of 1·0 as the simple expression just derived would demand.[13] With *Aerobacter aerogenes*, in synthetic media m varies with a power of the hydrogen ion concentration of about 0·7. This power does not change detectably when the cells have been previously adapted to moderately high concentrations of the drug (Fig. 64).[14] The influence of the buffer salts on the dissociation constant of the protein and upon the adsorption of the acridine derivatives will be far from negligible and may account for the deviations.

12. Further observations on the changes in enzymatic properties of cells brought about by adaptation to drugs

The basis of the preceding discussions of adaptation is that a change in the enzyme balance of the cells occurs during growth in the new environment. The question whether such changed enzyme balance is susceptible to direct demonstration—by methods other than inference from the altered growth rates themselves is partially answered by the work of Grant and Hinshelwood described on p. 157. Quite a number of other suggestive observations are on record. Smirnow[15] made various qualitative experiments on changes in fermentative properties of bacteria. Kruger[16] stated that the culture of *Bacterium enteridis* (Gartner) on agar containing malachite green gave rise to changes in the enzymes, but led to no permanent acquisition of new properties.

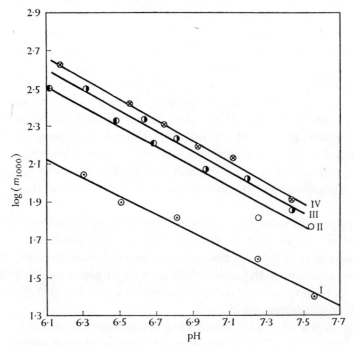

FIG. 64. Influence of pH on the action of proflavine. m_{1000} is the concentration of proflavine required to increase the lag by 1000 minutes.

I, Untrained cells; II, cells trained to 21 mg/l.; III, cells trained to 44 mg/l.; IV, cells trained to 71 mg/l.

Sulphapyridine-resistant strains of *Pneumococcus* are stated to have changed in their metabolic activities: peroxide and dehydrogenase are much reduced.[17] Variants have been obtained from *Pneumococcus*, under the influence of sulphonamides, showing a range of different metabolic activities—in forming hydrogen peroxide, fermenting inulin, and displaying different degrees of virulence.[18]

A good deal of effort has been expended in discovering whether sulphonamide-trained bacteria produce increased supplies of the natural sulphonamide antagonist, para-amino-benzoic acid. The results differ from strain to strain, or, at any rate, according to the conditions of the experiments. Sulphathiazole-resistant strains of *Staphylococcus aureus* were stated to produce more than the parent strain from which they were derived.[19] Housewright and Koser[20] found that sulphonamide-resistant *Staphylococcus aureus* produced 10 to 1000 times as much as the non-resistant parent strain, but that the trained strains of *Pneumococcus* and *Shigella paradysenteriae* showed no increase in p-amino-benzoic acid synthesis. Lemberg, Tandy, and Goldsworthy[21] found no increased production when a strain of *Escherichia coli* was trained to lower concentrations of sulphathiazole, but an increase when higher concentrations were employed. They quote the results of other observers as revealing extra production with *Staphylococcus*, *Gonococcus*, and *Pneumococcus*, and no extra production with *Escherichia coli*.

The behaviour of *Aerobacter aerogenes* trained to various drugs has already been mentioned. Other observations showed that when trained to high concentrations of crystal violet the dehydrogenase activity of this organism towards glycerol was found to be much lowered, and this change was reflected in an increased difficulty of growth in glycerol media. Training to high concentrations of proflavine had the opposite effect.[22]

The induced loss of sulphonamide adaptation of *Aerobacter aerogenes* when grown in presence of proflavine has also been referred to. In this connexion it is of interest that training to sulphonamide enhances the catalase activity of the cells, while growth in presence of proflavine lowers it, both for normal cells and for cells which have previously been trained to sulphonamide.[23]

When repeatedly subcultured at a pH removed from the optimum value *Escherichia coli* does not show adaptation: the pH optimum and the limits of tolerance remain unchanged. The enzyme content of the cells, however, may show changes with the pH prevailing during growth.[24] One group of enzymes, including urease, and catalase, change in amount with the pH of growth in such a way that the effective activity remains constant. For example, if the pH is remote from the optimum, more enzyme is formed, the increased amount just compensating for the decreased activity at the adverse pH. This means that cells grown at an adverse pH and tested at a favourable one show a higher activity than those grown and tested at the favourable one.

Further reference to the changes in enzyme activities accompanying adaptation will be made in connexion with training to new sources of nutrient material.

REFERENCES

1. D. S. Davies, C. N. Hinshelwood, and J. M. Pryce, *Trans. Faraday Soc.* **41**, 163 (1945).

2. J. B. Woof and Sir Cyril Hinshelwood, *Proc. R. Soc.* B **153**, 321 (1960).

3. W. T. Drabble and Sir Cyril Hinshelwood, *Proc. R. Soc.* B **154**, 449 (1961).

4. A. C. R. Dean, *Proc. R. Soc.* B **153**, 329 (1960).

5. A. C. Baskett, *Proc. R. Soc.* B **139**, 251 (1952).

6. A. C. R. Dean and P. H. Broadbridge, *Proc. R. Soc.* B **158**, 279 (1963).

7. See for details H. J. Rogers in Ciba Foundation Study Group No. 13, *Resistance of Bacteria to the Penicillins*, edited by A. V. S. De Reuck and Margaret P. Cameron, p. 25, Churchill, London (1962).

8. D. S. Davies, C. N. Hinshelwood, and J. M. Pryce, *Trans. Faraday Soc.* **40**, 397 (1944); **41**, 778 (1945).

9. J. M. G. Pryce, D. S. Davies, and C. N. Hinshelwood, *Trans. Faraday Soc.* **41**, 465 (1945).

10. J. M. Pryce and C. N. Hinshelwood, *Trans. Faraday Soc.* **43**, 742 (1947).

11. A. C. R. Dean and B. L. Giordan, *Proc. R. Soc.* B **161**, 571 (1964).

12. D. S. Davies, C. N. Hinshelwood, and A. M. James, *Trans. Faraday Soc.* **43**, 138 (1947).

13. A. Albert, S. D. Rubbo, R. J. Goldacre, M. E. Davey, and J. D. Stone, *Br. J. exp. Path.* **26**, 160 (1945).

14. A. R. Peacocke and Sir Cyril Hinshelwood, *J. chem. Soc.*, p. 1235 (1948).

15. M. R. Smirnow, *J. Bact.* **1**, 385 (1916).

16. H. Kruger, *Zentbl. Bakt.* **141**, 77 (1938).

17. C. M. MacLeod, *Proc. Soc. exp. Biol. Med.* **41**, 215 (1939).

18. Ruth A. McKinney and R. R. Mellon, *J. infect. Dis.* **68**, 233 (1941).

19. M. Landy, N. W. Larkum, Elizabeth J. Oswald, and F. Streightoff, *Science*, **97**, 265 (1943).

20. R. D. Housewright and S. A. Koser, *J. infect. Dis.* **75**, 113 (1944).

21. R. Lemberg, D. Tandy, and N. E. Goldsworthy, *Nature, Lond.* **157**, 103 (1946).

22. D. S. Davies and C. N. Hinshelwood, *Trans. Faraday Soc.* **43**, 257 (1947); see also A. M. James and C. N. Hinshelwood, *Trans. Faraday Soc.* **44**, 967 (1948), and references therein.

23. E. H. Cole and C. N. Hinshelwood, *Trans. Faraday Soc.* **43**, 266 (1947).

24. E. F. Gale and Helen M. R. Epps, *Biochem. J.* **36**, 600 (1942).

VIII

THE RESPONSE OF BACTERIAL CELLS TO NEW SOURCES OF CARBON AND NITROGEN

1. Introduction

IF the source from which cells are to derive their carbon or their nitrogen is varied, at least one reaction, and possibly a number of other reactions, in the total pattern must be changed. In the simplest example all that may be necessary is the addition of an extra step. Thus if cells have been utilizing glucose and are called upon to use lactose instead, it could be enough for them first to hydrolyse this disaccharide to give glucose and galactose (though this is by no means the only way in which lactose could be attacked). In general, however, the reaction pattern will have to be more radically reorganized. In all these circumstances the behaviour to be expected is that discussed in Chapter V, namely some initial reluctance and then a fairly rapid response.

The literature of bacteriology abounds in references to the adaptation of bacteria to new sources of nutrient. Cells of a given species are frequently unable to utilize a given carbon or nitrogen source with maximum efficiency until they have, as it were, become acclimatized to it. For example, some strains of *Escherichia coli*, although they grow readily in a medium containing glucose and asparagine as carbon and nitrogen sources respectively, multiply slowly, if at all, when the asparagine is replaced by ammonium sulphate.[1] They can, however, be 'trained' to utilize ammonium sulphate as sole nitrogen source by successive culturing (serial subculture) in media in which the amount of asparagine is reduced and that of the ammonium sulphate increased progressively. While this method seldom fails in the adaptation of coliform organisms to utilize ammonia, the presence of a carbon source to which the cells are well conditioned may actually inhibit the use of a new sugar. For example, glucose inhibits the formation of the enzyme β-galactosidase which is a necessary step in the metabolism of lactose. This is the so-called 'glucose-effect' (Chapter IX) and in the adaptation to new sources of carbon the standard practice is to introduce the cells into a medium containing the substance under test as the sole source of carbon and to allow events to run their course.

Biochemical tests such as the ability to ferment a given sugar are often used in the classification of bacteria, and the media employed usually contain peptone as well as the sugar.[2] On this basis strains of *Escherichia coli* which do not ferment sucrose or lactose are referred to as sucrose-negative or lactose-negative while *Aerobacter aerogenes* is dulcitol-negative. As will be seen later, however, if these strains are inoculated into a simple defined medium containing the substance under test as the sole source of carbon, growth may eventually take place after a lag of varying length. The explanation in the case of the peptone-sugar media would appear to be that the negative strains utilize the peptone for their requirements of both carbon and nitrogen and when the latter is exhausted further growth on the sugar is impossible or at any rate delayed. The corresponding positive strains (those which ferment the substance under test), on the other hand, are capable of attacking both the peptone and the added carbon source simultaneously.

In what follows much reference will be made to the behaviour of *Aerobacter aerogenes*. Some strains of *Escherichia coli*, in particular the strain referred to as *Escherichia coli mutabile* (*Bacterium coli mutabile*), originally so called on account of its initial reluctance and subsequent readiness to metabolize lactose, and some yeast strains will also be considered. First of all, however, some comment on the kind of substrates which are attacked by bacteria is desirable.

2. Substances supporting growth

Although the versatility of bacteria may appear to be enormous, not all carbon- or nitrogen-containing compounds are potential sources of carbon or nitrogen. This is clearly seen in the intensive studies of den Dooren de Jong[3] who recorded the presence or absence of growth with various species of bacteria and a wide range of compounds. The results of a more detailed study with fewer substances, lags, growth rates, and total populations being determined, are summarized in Table 6. The list, which refers to carbon substrates for *Aerobacter aerogenes*, is by no means exhaustive but with these substrates the entire range of types of behaviour is exemplified.[4] A list of nitrogen sources would include ammonium salts, nitrates, and amino-acids, the latter incidentally being rather poor sources of carbon for coliform organisms.

The substances in Table 6 which do not support growth call for little comment, and with those to which the cells are already fully adapted on transfer from a glucose medium the rate of growth is not necessarily as rapid as in the glucose medium. For example, although the mean generation time during the first subculture in L-arabinose or D-xylose medium is the same as in glucose medium (33 minutes), in pyruvate medium it is 45 minutes and does not improve on subsequent subculture.

TABLE 6

Behaviour of Aerobacter aerogenes *with various substances as sole sources of carbon*

Compounds towards which the cells are already fully adapted on transfer from a glucose medium	Compounds towards which the cells undergo adaptation	Compounds failing to support growth
glyceric acid	acetic acid	formic acid
pyruvic acid	glycerol	oxalic acid
lactic acid	malonic acid	propionic acid
DL-malic acid	succinic acid	tartronic acid
L-arabinose	fumaric acid	erythritol
D-xylose	D-tartaric acid	L-tartaric acid
glucose	meso-tartaric acid	
cellobiose	glutaric acid	
inositol	α-keto-glutaric acid	
citric acid	adipic acid	
cis-aconitic acid	lactose	
	maltose	
	sucrose	
	dulcitol	
	D-arabinose	
	glycine	

With the substances to which adaptation takes place a lag is usually observed on the first exposure and may range from a few hours to several days, but once it has been traversed it seldom reappears. Growth, when it eventually takes place, is slow but improves with continued subculture and during this process composite growth curves (section 3) are often observed. Typical examples illustrating these aspects will be dealt with in turn.

In the studies referred to the cells were always thoroughly conditioned to a simple defined medium, containing glucose as the carbon source, by many serial transfers before introduction into the new medium where the substance under test was the sole source of carbon or nitrogen. It is evident that it had to be utilized by the cells if growth was to occur at all. A quite different approach has been used by Monod and his associates in the study of enzyme induction where, by the addition of suitable inducers to cells already growing in a complete medium, the production of enzymes not necessary for continued growth in that medium is stimulated (see Chapter IX).

As has been seen, the range of available carbon sources for *Aerobacter aerogenes* and *Escherichia coli*, though wide, is not unlimited. Bacteria, however, taken as a whole group, show very remarkable catholicity, strains being known which will utilize hydrocarbons, including methane, and others which can derive their nitrogen from atmospheric nitrogen. *Aerobacter aerogenes* can seldom be induced to perform such feats.

3. Composite growth curves

In one type of behaviour the growth curves assume the broken form shown in Fig. 65. In successive subcultures the transition from the

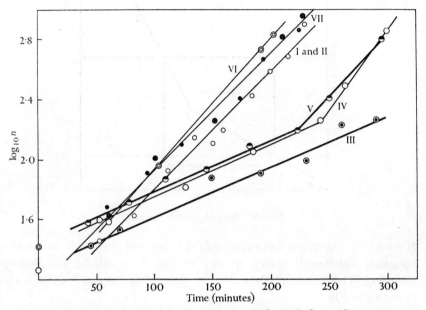

FIG. 65. Adaptation in glycerol and its reversal—typical growth curves.

I and II, cells trained by 7 and 9 passages respectively; III, 9 training passages, 1 reversion passage; IV, 9 training passages, 2 reversion passages; V, 6 training passages, 2 reversion passages; VI, 9 training passages, 2 reversions, followed by 1 training passage; VII, 6 training passages, 2 reversions, followed by 3 training passages; the time origins are adjusted to avoid inconvenient overlapping of curves. (Note composite form of certain of the curves and compare with Fig. 43.)

slower to the faster mode of growth occurs at a progressively earlier stage. Analogous behaviour has already been encountered in the example of the training of *Aerobacter aerogenes* to resist sulphonamides.

(*a*) Aerobacter aerogenes *and glycerol*[5, 6]

An excellent example of this kind of behaviour is shown by the adaptation of *Aerobacter aerogenes* to glycerol. Typical growth curves obtained during the training of the cells to glycerol (after transfer from a corresponding medium containing glucose) are shown in Fig. 65.

When the growth curve is of the form shown, the progress of adaptation cannot be represented by changes in the value of the mean generation time. In Fig. 66, for example, the adaptation might occur by a combination of three effects: an increase in the slope of AB, an increase in the slope of BC, or the downward movement of B. For a numerical measure the most convenient quantity to record is the *time* taken for

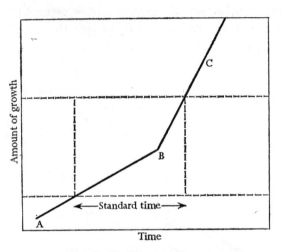

FIG. 66. Broken growth curves.

the count to increase from a standard value well below B to another standard value well above B: any of the three effects are thereby included. The course of adaptation to glycerol in successive subcultures is shown in Fig. 67.

If the glycerol-trained cells are passed through a glycerol-free medium (containing glucose as carbon source) soon after they have reached the limiting degree of adaptation (maximum growth rate), a reversion occurs at about the same rate as the original adaptation. Reversion is dealt with in detail in the next chapter but some preliminary comments will not be out of place here. It can be revealed by periodic tests in glycerol as illustrated in Fig. 67. The final 'reverted' state is not necessarily identical, in respect of growth rate in glycerol, with the original, but different original strains of the same species vary a good deal in this respect among themselves. When the training to glycerol has been very prolonged, however, the adapted strain no longer shows reversion even after fifty subcultures in a medium containing none, and may be taken

to be stable. When the training has been carried through an intermediate number of subcultures, a phenomenon which may be termed
delayed reversion is observable. On passage through the glycerol-free
medium, the strain retains its full glycerol adaptation (as shown by
separate tests in glycerol) for a certain number of subcultures and then
more or less rapidly reverts. The course of events is shown in Fig. 68
and is exactly parallel with that found for lactose adaptation (see below).

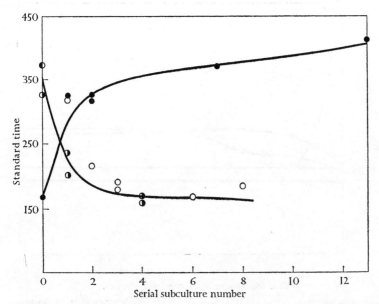

FIG. 67. Adaptation in glycerol and its reversal. Passages through glycerol
medium—falling curve: through glucose medium—rising curve (all measurements in glycerol medium).

Open circles—training; filled-in circles—reversion; half-shaded circles—retraining after
reversion. The number of training passages before the reversion tests was 6 or 9. (N.B. *Short*
times signify *high* degree of adaptation to glycerol.)

(b) Aerobacter aerogenes *and glycine (as nitrogen source)*[5]

This example resembles the previous one, except that the first segment
of the growth curve is more sharply separated from the second. Growth
by the first mode reaches its stationary phase before that by the second
overtakes it. Actual growth curves are shown in Fig. 69 and the relation
between these and the curves of Fig. 65 is suggested by Fig. 70.

In its earlier stages, the adaptation to glycine is reversible, but, from
analogy with other cases, it can probably be presumed to become stable
on long-continued training. The full stabilization was not observed
experimentally but the training was probably not carried on for long

enough for it to be established. A certain progress towards it was, however, detected after fifteen passages.

4. Shortening of mean generation time

The break in the growth curves, as described under section 3, is not
always in evidence, though when it is not observed it may have occurred

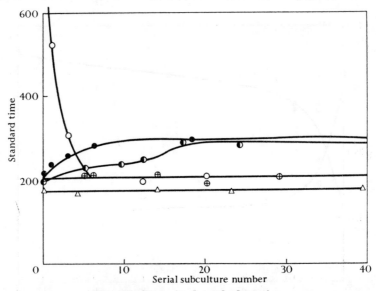

FIG. 68. Stages in glycerol adaptation.

○ adaptation	⊕ stable strain after 49 passages
● reversion after 5 passages	△ stable strain after 71 passages
◑ delayed reversion after 12 passages	

before the bacterial counts came into the range of convenient measurement. At all events in the usual range of measurement all that is
observable is a progressive decrease in the mean generation time.

(a) Aerobacter aerogenes *and lactose*[7]

There is no specially great lag when *Aerobacter aerogenes* adapted to
glucose is transferred to a corresponding lactose medium. On the first
occasion it is about 6 hours longer than in a parallel subculture into
glucose. On subsequent subcultures the difference vanishes. After a
few subcultures the mean generation times, initially about 100 minutes,
attain the same value as in glucose, namely about 33 minutes. If the
cells are removed from the lactose medium at this stage and returned
to glucose, rapid reversion occurs. If transferred after a longer training

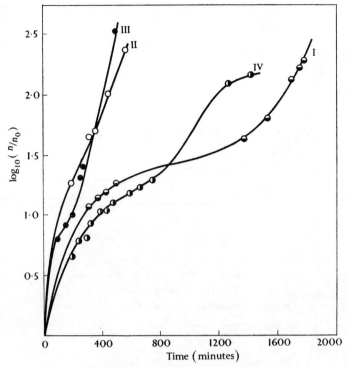

FIG. 69. Form of growth curves in glycine medium.
I, Untrained; II, trained; III, trained (washed cells); IV, after 9 reversion
passages.

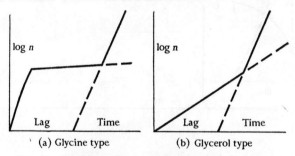

FIG. 70. Schematic, illustrating relation of glycine-type
and glycerol-type growth curves.

in lactose, there may still be reversion, but it is not observable until
after a delay of quite a number of subcultures, during which it appears
to remain in suspense. Finally, after very thorough training, the lactose
adaptation becomes stable enough to persist even after 30 to 40 subcultures in absence of any lactose. The training-reversion relations are

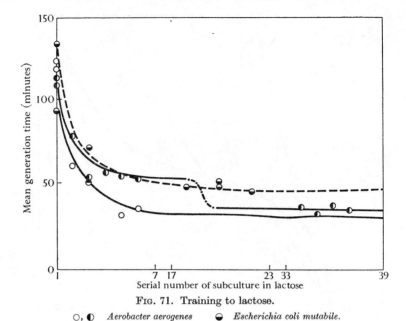

FIG. 71. Training to lactose.

○, ◑   *Aerobacter aerogenes*   ◗   *Escherichia coli mutabile.*

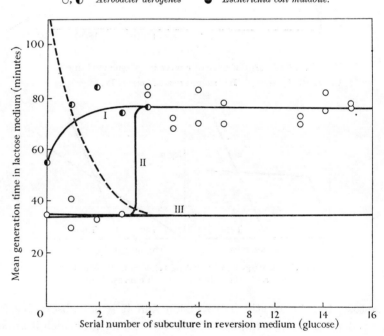

FIG. 72. Loss of lactose adaptation.

I, 5 training passages: rapid reversion   II, 31 training passages: delayed reversion
III, 100 training passages: no reversion
    Broken line shows curve of adaptation (cf. Fig. 71) for comparison.

shown in Figs. 71 and 72. The behaviour of the enzyme β-galactosidase during these processes of training and reversion is discussed on p. 242.

(b) Aerobacter aerogenes *and other disaccharides*[7]

The training of *Aerobacter aerogenes* to maltose and sucrose conforms to the same scheme as the training to lactose. The adapted strains all grow with a mean generation time equal to that found in glucose. Cells trained to glucose are, for certain strains at least, found to be already adapted to cellobiose.

Adaptation is not reciprocal, in the sense that cells trained to one of the three disaccharides, lactose (L-strain), maltose (M-strain), or sucrose (S-strain) are not adapted to the other two. By successive training, however, strains adapted to any pair (LM, MS, LS), or to all three (LMS), can be obtained from the original glucose-adapted strain. The relationships of the mean generation times are shown in the following table:

	Mean generation times (minutes) for strain tested in		
Strain trained to	Lactose	Maltose	Sucrose
Glucose	100	110	60
Lactose	33	84	46
Maltose	77	32	42
Sucrose	97	109	33
Lactose + sucrose	33	..	31
Lactose + sucrose + maltose	31	35	34

Long-continued serial subculture in lactose (and presumably in any of the other disaccharides) causes no loss in the capacity of the cells to grow with maximum efficiency in glucose.

It should be mentioned, however, that a lactose-trained strain, in the intermediate state where it is stable to 10 or 20—though not to an indefinite number—of subcultures in glucose, suffers a rapid induced reversion if it is grown in maltose.

(c) Aerobacter aerogenes *and carboxylic acids and some other compounds*

Some carboxylic acids are effective as sole sources of carbon, others are not (Table 6). To those which do support growth glucose-grown cells are either already fully adapted or require training. With the acids of the latter class lags, in general, are of a few hours' duration and the training process consists again in a shortening of the mean generation time. All the acids related to the well-known tricarboxylic acid cycle, a scheme for the oxidation of pyruvic acid, support growth, but differences in response exist. For example, although *Aerobacter aerogenes* requires no adaptation to pyruvate, malate, *cis*-aconitate and citrate, it does to succinate, fumarate, and α-ketoglutarate. In all these substrates, however, growth remains slower than in glucose even after many subcultures. The growth curves in media containing citrate or *cis*-aconitate have complex forms suggesting alternative sequences of

TABLE 7

Training of Aerobacter aerogenes *to acetate as sole carbon source*

Serial number of subculture	Mean generation time (minutes)
10	200
17	48
23	43/162†
28	62
36	102/40†
44	87
53	63
63	82
73	56
83	69
92	82
102	91/51†
111	53
128	52

† Composite growth curve (see section 3).

reactions,[4] and this is also found in an acetate medium where during the course of long-continued subculture considerable fluctuations in growth rate are observed (Table 7).[8] Training to an earlier member of the sequence, acetate, succinate and fumarate results in adaptation to a later member but not vice versa.[4] This observation gives an indication of the order in which these substances occur in the reaction pattern of the cells.

The carboxylic acids are of interest in another connexion. If, after growth has ceased in a medium containing the full complement of glucose, cells of *Aerobacter aerogenes* are allowed to age in the exhausted solution, they exhibit a long lag on subsequent transfer to a new glucose medium. The addition of small amounts of carboxylic acids (neutralized to pH 7·12) shortens this lag, the most effective acids being in order—malic, citric, succinic and fumaric, and *cis*-aconitic acid. Combinations of acids are no more effective than the individuals, and none has as pronounced an action as heart-broth. Acetic acid does not shorten the lag much and has an inhibiting influence on growth which the others have not.[4]

The importance of molecular configuration is illustrated in Table 6. L-tartaric acid does not support growth but adaptation takes place to the D-isomer. In media containing L-arabinose as the sole source of carbon both the lag and the growth rate are the same as in glucose, but on the first exposure of *Aerobacter aerogenes* to D-arabinose the lag is several days and is followed by slow growth. Exceptionally long lag on first transfer is the subject of the next section, and since much work has been carried out with the system *Aerobacter aerogenes*—D-arabinose, in order to determine whether the adaptation is due to the selection of a small number of specially endowed pre-existent cells or to a response by the majority, it will be dealt with in detail. The adaptations of *Escherichia coli mutabile* (*Bacterium coli mutabile*) to lactose and of the yeast *Saccharomyces cerevisiae* to galactose will also receive attention.

5. Exceptionally long lag on first transfer

(a) Aerobacter aerogenes *and* D-*arabinose*[6, 9-11]

When glucose-adapted cells are introduced into a medium containing D-arabinose as the sole source of carbon the lag before growth begins is influenced to a considerable extent by the age of the inoculum. For example, cells whose lag in a fresh glucose medium would be less than an hour usually grow in D-arabinose medium after 2 or 3 days, whereas if the lag in glucose medium is 5 to 10 hours, growth seldom takes place at all in D-arabinose. Once the long lag has been traversed it does not reappear in subsequent subcultures.

An essential condition for utilization of the sugar is that the resting cells should remain in contact with D-arabinose for a given total time. This can be shown by the following experiment.[9] A number of inocula are made in parallel into D-arabinose medium. Some are left until growth has occurred and from these the initial lag L_0 is obtained. To others, after given times, T, have elapsed, a small amount of glucose or L-arabinose is added and growth allowed to take place until the added sugar is just exhausted. Inocula are then retransferred into the D-arabinose medium and the lags L are determined. Within the range of experimental error it is found that $L = L_0 - T$, that is the total lag may be interrupted by a period of growth in another sugar but its total value remains constant. Moreover, continuous growth in a mixture of D-arabinose and another more readily utilizable sugar, such as glucose or

L-arabinose, prevents the utilization of the former. On continued sub-culture in D-arabinose medium the growth rate improves up to a limit (Fig. 73).[12]

An exceptionally long lag may be the time taken by the majority of the cells in the population to adjust themselves to the new conditions

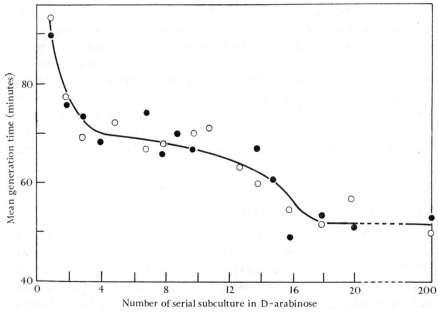

FIG. 73. Effect of 'training' on the mean generation time of *Aerobacter aerogenes* in D-arabinose.

○ series 1   ● series 2

or alternatively it may represent no more than the time interval necessary for a minute proportion of specially endowed cells in the original inoculum to multiply up to the limit of measurability.

It would appear at first sight that a simple method to distinguish between these alternatives would be to plate out on a solid medium, containing D-arabinose as the only carbon source, about 100 cells and to see whether or not all eventually formed colonies. Under these conditions the yield is indeed found to be 100 per cent, but it has been pointed out that bacteriological media, even when prepared from specially purified ingredients, contain traces of impurities which may be sufficient to support the multiplication on solid media of single cells until micro-colonies containing about 10^6 to 10^7 cells are formed.[13] If the frequency of mutations were of this order, it could be argued that each microcolony might, whether visible or not, contain at least one mutant capable of utilizing D-arabinose. This mutant would then multiply and its progeny overgrow the microcolony. While some impurity growth does undoubtedly occur, the explanation just given is ruled out by the following type of experiment. It involves the withdrawing of samples at intervals from a culture lagging in a liquid D-arabinose medium. Suitable dilutions of these samples are prepared so that about 100 cells can be plated on to D-arabinose-agar plates and the time taken for the colonies to reach a standard 'positive' size is recorded. This size is chosen to be much larger than that reachable by impurity growth alone and corresponds to that reached after two days' incubation from cells well adapted to D-arabinose. What has been found in numerous experiments with *Aerobacter aerogenes* and D-arabinose and with other systems is this; the longer has been the period of sojourn in the liquid medium the shorter is the time required for the positive size to be reached on the plate. In other words, the progress of the lag in the liquid has done something to shorten the delay time on the solid medium. If growth on the plate depended on the spontaneous appearance of appropriate mutants during microcolony formation, the time of development of the major colony would be more or less constant and would certainly bear no relation whatever to the previous history of the culture in the liquid medium.[14]

Apart from *Aerobacter aerogenes* and D-arabinose the systems *Escherichia coli mutabile*-lactose, and *Escherichia coli* K12 with dulcitol and with D-arabinose have been studied in this way. Of a series of seventeen experiments eight gave a definite positive result. In the others reduction of the lag observed on the plate occurred in the usual way but at a stage too close to the active growth of the parent liquid culture for the result to be conclusive.[15]

The conclusion that the majority of the cells of *Aerobacter aerogenes* participate in the response to D-arabinose is strengthened by the measurement during the lag phase of cell mass, by a turbidimetric method, and cell number, by counting under the microscope. In a typical experiment of this sort the mass increased by 40 per cent before any change in number was observed at all (Fig. 74 and Table 8).[14]

That the response is not due to selection is further confirmed in the following way. If a small amount of glucose is added to the culture after a few divisions have occurred in D-arabinose rapid growth ensues and after this no cells stably adapted to D-arabinose can be detected at all. This loss of adaptation happens in a time interval too short for the complete reselection of arabinose-negative cells.[14]

The first step in the utilization of D-arabinose is its conversion to D-ribulose by the enzyme ribulose isomerase. Unadapted cells grown in a glucose medium have a low enzyme content which increases about

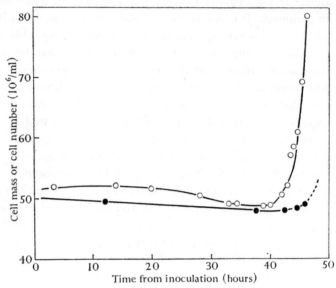

FIG. 74. Demonstration that increase in bacterial mass of culture of *Aerobacter aerogenes* in D-arabinose medium precedes detectable multiplication of numbers.

   ○   cell mass (determined turbidimetrically)
   ●   cell number (determined by direct microscope counting)

TABLE 8

Accuracy of microscope counts recorded in Fig. 74

Ordinal number of sample	Mean count over four squares at various chamber fillings	Average of means	% increase in cell mass
1	50·0, 49·0	49·5	0
2	49·5, 47·0, 46·2, 46·4, 48·1, 48·6, 49·5	47·9	0
3	47·3, 47·3, 49·2	48·0	7
4	48·5, 48·9, 47·3, 49·1, 47·8	48·4	18
5	50·6, 49·1, 47·3	49·0	40

a hundred-fold on adaptation to D-arabinose. Unadapted cells are, however, unable to degrade pentose and it would appear that, although they possess ribulose isomerase in small quantity, they do not have the complete enzyme pathway necessary to convert the sugar to a nonpentose form. An investigation of ribulose isomerase activity during the first stage of growth in a D-arabinose medium has provided further striking evidence against an explanation in terms of mutation-selection. For example, the activity begins to increase only after the first increases in cell number are discernible, and a 2 per cent rise in cell number was associated with a thirty-fold rise in activity of the enzyme (Figs. 75 and 76). If this change is to be explained in terms of a mutant population

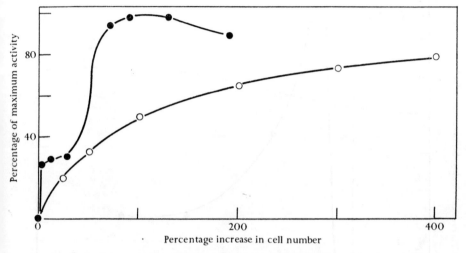

FIG. 75. Variation in percentage increase in cell mass and percentage of maximum ribulose isomerase activity found in the culture.

● observed values, ○ theoretical values assuming mutation and selection. The percentage of the maximum activity was calculated from that obtained from a culture of the same strain in D-arabinose with a starting count of 80×10^6/ml, in its first growth cycle.

overgrowing the quiescent non-mutants, then these mutants must at the moment when they are just coming into prominence be assumed to possess a ribulose isomerase activity very much greater than they ever do again, since the calculated specific value, referred to the newly formed cell substance, is greater than is ever found in the most fully adapted organisms. This paradoxical situation does not arise if the measured activity is calculated by reference to all the cells in the culture.[12]

There exists the possibility that during the course of a long lag in liquid medium some of the cell population may be undergoing death followed by the lysis of the dead cells. If the lysis proceeded far enough, the living cells in the culture could grow and might even divide by consuming the lysate. In this way a turnover of cells accompanied by the emergence of D-arabinose-utilizing mutants would appear to be possible. This idea, however, does not stand up to critical examination. First of all, in the experiment of Fig. 74 the turbidity of the culture, which was continuously stirred by a stream of sterile air, never decreased appreciably, and in other examples it has remained constant until just before division sets in. If lysis with resynthesis were taking place under these conditions, it would have to be a remarkably efficient process,

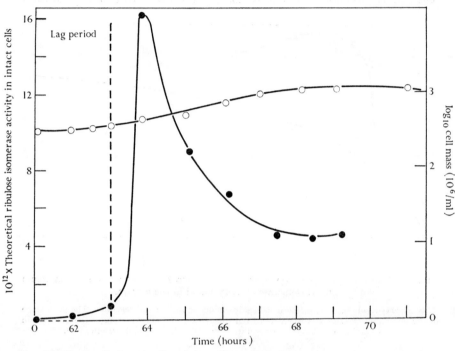

FIG. 76. Changes in intact cell activity of hypothetical mutants necessary to reconcile the two curves in Fig. 75.

○ log$_{10}$ cell mass.   ● theoretical mutant cell enzyme activity.

especially considering that much of the carbon in the bacterial cell is present in macromolecular compounds such as polysaccharides, proteins and nucleic acids which would need to undergo a very rapid degradation into readily assimilable fragments.

The question of this kind of turnover was studied by Ryan[16] in a somewhat analogous situation involving a strain of *Escherichia coli* unable to synthesize histidine from the constituents of a simple salts–glucose medium. He found that in media devoid of histidine, the presence of glucose or lactose (if the cells had been previously adapted to it) led to slow death of the cells. At the same time some of the bacteria became able to grow without added histidine. This was clearly an example where growth at the expense of lysed dead cells seemed possible. Ryan decided, however, against the hypothesis of lysis and resynthesis on the following grounds.

(1) If mixtures of h⁻ lac⁺ cells (requiring histidine and able to grow readily in its presence in lactose) and h⁻ lac⁻ cells (long lag before growth in lactose) are kept in lactose without histidine, the lac⁺ should increase relatively to the lac⁻ by growing on histidine liberated by the lysis into the medium. This shift did not occur.

(2) The enzyme β-galactosidase should have been lost to the medium from lac⁺ cells in the absence of lactose and should have developed in lac⁻ cells in a lactose medium at predictable rates which were not found.

(3) If any 'cryptic' growth were occurring, the addition of penicillin, which has an enhanced action on growing cells, should increase the death-rate, and this did not happen.

(4) Lysis might possibly have been observable on an agar surface, and was not.

None of the observations quoted mean that intracellular, as distinct from population turnover, is not occurring. Indeed, in 'division without growth' DNA is formed at the expense of RNA (p. 95) and in conditions of nutrient deficiency the rate of turnover of protein (or RNA) has been given as about 5 per cent per hour, which means that in 6 to 8 hours about one-third of the protein in the non-growing cells will have passed through the free amino-acid pool.[17] An internal reorganization of this kind may well be happening during the lag in D-arabinose, since it is only at the end that the disappearance of pentose from the medium becomes detectable.

(b) Escherichia coli mutabile *and lactose*

This example has been often investigated.[13, 18] Much of the work has used complex agar media based on peptone and lactose together with dyes such as eosin or methylene blue. When cells of *Escherichia coli mutabile* are spread on the surface of such a medium they grow at the expense of the peptone and colourless, translucent colonies arise. On further incubation secondary growths (or papillae) appear on these colonies and the cells in this new growth ferment the lactose so that the dye changes colour and the papillae acquire a characteristic appearance. The random nature of the occurrence of papillae in situations such as this has led to the belief that they are dependent on lactose-utilizing mutants arising spontaneously during the growth on the peptone. Reasons will, however, be given later in support of the view that papilla formation is not in itself by any means unambiguous evidence for mutation (Chapter XII).

The adaptation of *Escherichia coli mutabile* to utilize lactose as the sole source of carbon in a chemically defined liquid medium conforms to a pattern very similar to that found with *Aerobacter aerogenes* and D-arabinose. There is a lag of two to three days before growth begins and the growth rate improves on serial transfer. If a small number of cells is plated they all eventually form colonies on lactose–agar plates, and if samples are withdrawn at intervals from a lagging culture, then the longer the time spent in the liquid medium the shorter that necessary for development of the colonies on lactose–agar plates. An increase in cell mass before any division sets in can again be demonstrated.[19] It will be seen, therefore, that the arguments just presented in support of a response of the majority of the cells to D-arabinose can also be advanced here.

It has been claimed that at a certain stage of the incubation in a liquid lactose or D-arabinose medium the plating of samples on the appropriate solid medium gives rise to two types of colony which can be designated as 'positive' or 'negative' respectively. The 'positives' are assumed to have arisen by the overgrowing of the 'negatives' by pre-existent mutants present in minute proportion in the original culture. From a cursory visual examination of Fig. 77 the conclusion could easily be drawn that a separate 'positive' class existed. Figure 77, however, is not a photograph of colonies on an agar plate but of a drawing[20] constructed to fit the Gaussian distribution $y = (h/\sqrt{\pi})e^{-h^2x^2}$ where $h = 2$.

Bimodal distributions of colony diameters, which two separate classes would give, were, at any rate in one extended series of researches,[15, 19, 21] never seen in the platings of samples taken during the actual lag phase in the liquid D-arabinose or lactose media. They can, however, sometimes be observed after both cell mass and cell number have increased.[20] Although an adaptation may make considerable progress during a lag phase it is far from complete at its end and, as has been seen, this applies even when the lag is short. On this basis bimodal distributions in no way conflict with an adaptive interpretation, since at the end of the lag some members of the population may quite easily be more nearly organized for division than others. Since adaptation proceeds still further when division takes place, those cells which divide first would have an advantage when plated and in extreme cases a bimodal distribution of colony diameters at a given time could result. More often, however, a distribution broadened at the upper end is observed (see Chapter XI).

If the age of the cells is carefully controlled, the lags on the first exposure of a standard inoculum of *Escherichia coli mutabile* to lactose or of *Aerobacter aerogenes* to D-arabinose are more or less reproducible. If these lags, in spite of the evidence just given, are regarded simply as the times necessary for the multiplication of the appropriate mutants

Fig. 77. Gaussian distribution of sizes, $h = 2$.

then a simple calculation shows in what constant small proportion these mutants must have been present in the original population. Presumably they must be assumed to be formed continuously during the growth in the glucose medium and if, indeed, they are, the proportion of the 'positive' mutants would be expected to increase steadily. Since it does not (the lag on first transfer always being observable), it is pertinent to inquire into the mechanisms which maintain the equilibrium level. The simplest explanation would postulate a low rate of forward mutation coupled with a very high rate of reverse mutation. Direct experiment, however, has shown that the fully adapted strains do not revert at all easily.[11, 19] Nor do large differences in growth rates provide a simple explanation, since fully adapted and unadapted strains are indistinguishable in this respect. Mean generation times of about 40 min, which is the value usually found for lactose-adapted and lactose-unadapted strains in glucose medium, are hard to determine with a precision better than 1 to 2 min and so minor differences may exist. Selection on this basis, however, would be far too slow a process. For example, if equal proportions of two strains with mean generation times of 40 and 42 min respectively were grown together, twenty-five subcultures of eight generations each would be necessary before the first strain outnumbered the second by about a thousandfold.[22]

These difficulties only arise if, in the face of so much contrary evidence, an explanation based on mutation and selection is insisted on.

In a similar situation Attwood, Schneider, and Ryan proposed a solution based on a concept called 'periodic selection'.[23] They investigated the change in proportions which took place when two strains of *Escherichia coli* which differed in their histidine requirement were grown together. They suggested that the strain present in the greatest proportion in a mixture could undergo mutations, quite unrelated to the histidine requirement, which favoured its predominance in a particular environment. They appreciated, nevertheless, that this process could not continue indefinitely.

Escherichia coli mutabile is reluctant to utilize ammonium sulphate as source of nitrogen when first transferred from a rich medium (such as nutrient broth) to a glucose–salts medium, and many subcultures are necessary before the optimum rate of growth is reached. In a series of experiments in which lactose-adapted and lactose-unadapted strains of this organism were mixed in various proportions and were then grown together in glucose–salts medium results were obtained which did not agree with those predicted by periodic selection. It was observed that, irrespective of the initial proportions, the strain which had previously received the most thorough training to the basal medium predominated in the end.[22] Similar results were obtained with *Aerobacter aerogenes* and D-arabinose and with a strain of *Escherichia coli* and D-arabinose.[24]

6. *Saccharomyces cerevisiae* in various carbon sources

Many of the phenomena described in the foregoing sections for bacteria are found in the study of yeast cells.

Yeasts such as *Saccharomyces cerevisiae* can exist in two states called haploid and diploid respectively. In the diploid the number of chromosomes is double that in the haploid, and haploids, provided they are of compatible mating types, can be induced to undergo recombination. This process, unlike the unidirectional transfer of information found with some bacteria (p. 30), involves the fusion of the two cells, and the resulting diploid can sometimes now undergo further changes called sporulation resulting in an *ascus* containing four spores. These spores can be separated by micro-dissection and the properties of cultures derived from them investigated.

Yeasts grow more slowly than bacteria in chemically defined media, and mean generation times of 199 to 399 minutes are commonly observed at the optimum temperature, even after serial transfer for some time. The medium itself, usually buffered to pH 5·0, needs to be more complex than that which satisfies the less exacting bacteria. Salts such as calcium chloride and potassium iodide, together with a wide range of trace metals, are often added, and sometimes small amounts of growth factors such as aneurin are necessary, although some strains can be adapted to dispense with them.

Typical adaptive responses are shown. For example, when a haploid strain derived from a spore isolate was inoculated into minimal medium supplemented by aneurin there was no lag, while in the absence of the aneurin the lag was considerable. The growth rate was slow and improved gradually over many subcultures. Towards the end of the lag there was a considerable increase in cell mass before any division set in.[25] A similar effect was observed when certain diploid strains were inoculated into media containing either raffinose[25] or galactose[26] as the sole source of carbon (Fig. 78).

Thus even with cells as highly organized as yeast a response by the bulk of the population is in evidence (compare sections 5a, 5b). It is borne out by a series of experiments on the adaptation of a *Saccharomyces* strain to a galactose medium (Fig. 79). In a 'reconstruction' experiment some cells which had already been fully adapted to the galactose were mixed with completely untrained cells in the proportion of 1 in 10^6, thus giving a population simulating a normal culture containing about the number of spontaneous mutants commonly assumed. Successive growth curves were then determined. The behaviour of the artificial mixture in no way approximated to that of the original strain. With the artificially prepared population the galactose-positive cells (the 'mutants') have already risen to complete dominance by the second subculture, where the growth rate is already optimal. In sharp contrast, the training of the initially negative strain is reflected in a much more gradual and progressive increase in growth rate.[26] Similar results have been found in other examples.[25]

Yeasts show adaptive relations towards compounds of the tricarboxylic acid cycle, sometimes resembling and sometimes contrasting with those of *Aerobacter aerogenes* and *Escherichia coli*. The relative rates of growth of fully adapted organisms in the various compounds change from one strain to another, and sometimes cross adaptations are observed.[27]

One interesting technical advantage possessed by yeasts is that sometimes observations on Mendelian segregations can be combined with

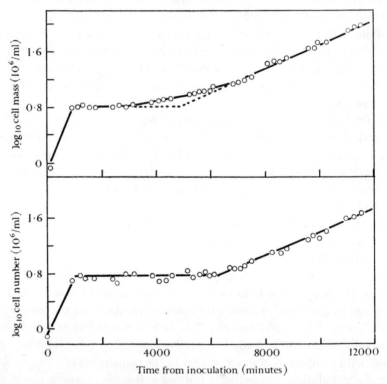

Fig. 78. Increase in cell mass before cell number towards the end of the lag phase of *Saccharomyces cerevisiae* during the first subculture in galactose medium.

Upper curve—cell mass; lower curve—cell number (microscope count).

adaptive studies. Thus a certain strain of *Saccharomyces cerevisiae* forms an ascus from which substrains can be derived as already described. Two of the four utilize galactose well, the other two with reluctance. But even so, the 'positive' strains still need considerable training before they will develop their optimum growth rate in galactose, and in this process the characteristic adaptive phenomena are seen.[26, 28] This fact illustrates the inappropriateness of statements which seek to represent 'adaptation' and 'genetic control' as somehow incompatible ideas. They are, of course, complementary.

Unfortunately the training of yeasts to drugs, which occurs fairly readily, almost always causes loss of the power to sporulate, so that what should be very interesting experiments are frustrated.

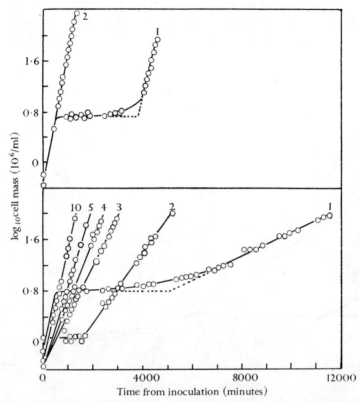

FIG. 79. Comparison of the selection of adapted cells from a mixture containing a fraction 10^{-6} of adapted cells (upper part of figure) with the actual behaviour observed during serial subculture of an initially unadapted strain of *Saccharomyces cerevisiae* in galactose (lower part of figure).

The numbers on the curves indicate the number of subcultures.

7. *Aerobacter aerogenes* and *Escherichia coli* in media containing nitrate and nitrite[29]

Except in the experiments involving glycine (section 3), ammonium sulphate was the source of nitrogen in all the various examples cited so far in this chapter. *Aerobacter aerogenes* can, however, also obtain its nitrogen from inorganic nitrate. When a strain which has been thoroughly conditioned to a glucose–ammonium sulphate medium is introduced for the first time into glucose–sodium nitrate medium growth is slow, but there is no lag. On successive subculture in the nitrate the growth rate improves. There is no lag on retest in ammonium sulphate. In the first subculture in a nitrite medium growth even slower than in nitrate is observed (Fig. 80). Since growth in nitrite is slower than in nitrate, it might appear that the former cannot be an inter- mediate in the metabolism of the latter. But at the concentration normally employed nitrite has an inhibitory effect on growth. When

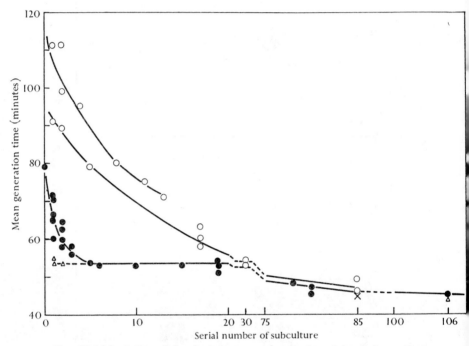

FIG. 80. Adaptation of *Aerobacter aerogenes* in nitrate and in nitrite media.

○	Trained in nitrite, tested in nitrite.	△	Trained in nitrate, tested in dilute nitrite.
●	Trained in nitrate, tested in nitrate.	×	Trained in nitrite, tested in dilute nitrite.

sufficiently dilute solutions are used the optimum rate is obtained in the first subculture, so that the training in Fig. 80 really represents an adaptation to resist the specific drug action of the nitrite itself. Serial subculture in nitrate confers some resistance to nitrite, 105 passages in the former being roughly equivalent to 25 in the latter. Nitrate has no inhibitory effect comparable to that of nitrite, and when it is added to an ammonium sulphate medium the growth rate is unaffected.

In sharp contrast to *Aerobacter aerogenes*, strains of *Escherichia coli* often require considerable training to ammonium sulphate before growth at the optimum rate occurs, and adaptation to ammonium sulphate does not involve that to nitrate, a culture just trained to the former requiring a considerable number of further subcultures in the latter. On the other hand, direct training to nitrate, by gradual elimination of asparagine from a nitrate–asparagine mixture (see section 1), gives adaptation to both nitrate and ammonia.

If a culture of *Aerobacter aerogenes* is growing in nitrate and ammonium sulphate is added, the nitrate reduction ceases immediately and is only

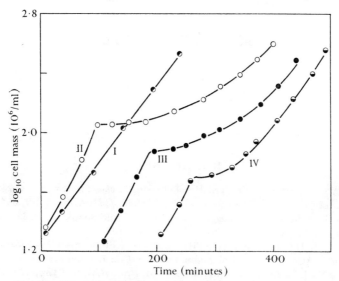

FIG. 81. Effect of adding ammonium sulphate to actively growing cultures in nitrate medium.

I, No ammonium sulphate added
II, 100 mg/l. ammonium sulphate added at time = 0
III, 60 mg/l. ammonium sulphate added at time = 100 minutes
IV, 30 mg/l. ammonium sulphate added at time = 200 minutes

resumed after the ammonia has been completely consumed. Figure 81 shows how nitrate utilization is delayed by the initial presence of ammonia, a remarkable example of the phenomenon discussed on p. 278.

8. Failure of adaptive response

Sometimes attempts to evoke an adaptive response are quite negative. The following example illustrates a simple method of testing, based upon the training procedure of gradually replacing the old by the new substrate.

Aerobacter aerogenes was inoculated simultaneously into two mixtures, one containing 200 mg erythritol and x mg of glucose, the other containing x mg of glucose alone. In successive sub-cultures x was reduced. The total bacterial population n_s produced in each of the parallel cultures was measured. If there were no adaptation to the erythritol, n_s would drop in proportion to x, and would remain the same for the two tubes. If adaptation occurred, n_s would remain higher in the medium containing the erythritol. The numbers below show that the former alternative corresponds to the actual course of events.

mg glucose	50	15	5	5	5	0
n_s		320	58	65	74	0

In a similar experiment with arabinose the results were:

mg arabinose	25	10	2	2
n_s	++	++	+	83
omitting erythritol				97

REFERENCES

1. G. A. Morrison and Sir Cyril Hinshelwood, *J. chem. Soc.* p. 372 (1949).
2. See, for example, S. T. Cowan and K. J. Steel, *J. Hyg., Camb.* **59**, 357 (1961); and *Medical Microbiology*, edited by R. Cruickshank, J. P. Duguid, and R. H. A. Swain, Livingstone, Edinburgh (1965).
3. L. E. den Dooren de Jong (1926); see Margery Stephenson, *Bacterial Metabolism*, 3rd ed., p. 184, Longmans Green & Co., London (1949).
4. A. C. Baskett and Sir Cyril Hinshelwood, *Proc. R. Soc.* B **136**, 520 (1950).
5. R. M. Lodge and C. N. Hinshelwood, *Trans. Faraday Soc.* **40**, 571 (1944).
6. E. G. Cooke and C. N. Hinshelwood, *Trans. Faraday Soc.* **43**, 733 (1947).
7. J. R. Postgate and C. N. Hinshelwood, *Trans. Faraday Soc.* **42**, 45 (1946).
8. A. C. R. Dean and Sir Cyril Hinshelwood, *Proc. R. Soc.* B **142**, 45 (1954).
9. S. Jackson and C. N. Hinshelwood, *Trans. Faraday Soc.* **44**, 568 (1948).
10. S. Jackson and Sir Cyril Hinshelwood, *Proc. R. Soc.* B **136**, 562 (1949).
11. Sir Cyril Hinshelwood and S. Jackson, *Proc. R. Soc.* B **137**, 88 (1950).
12. J. E. M. Midgley, *Proc. R. Soc.* B **153**, 250 (1960).
13. F. J. Ryan, *J. gen. Microbiol.* **7**, 69 (1952).
14. A. C. Baskett and Sir Cyril Hinshelwood, *Proc. R. Soc.* B **139**, 58 (1951).
15. A. C. R. Dean, *Proc. R. Soc.* B **147**, 247 (1957).
16. F. J. Ryan, *J. gen. Microbiol.* **21**, 530 (1959).
17. See J. Mandelstam, *Bact. Rev.* **24**, 289 (1960) and references therein.
18. R. Massini, *Arch. Hyg. Bakt.* **61**, 250 (1907); K. Baerthlein, *Zentbl. Bakt.* **66**, 21 (1912); I. M. Lewis, *J. Bact.* **28**, 619 (1934); J. Monod, *Schweiz. Z. Path. Bakt.* **15**, 407 (1952).
19. A. C. R. Dean and Sir Cyril Hinshelwood, *Proc. R. Soc.* B **142**, 225 (1954).
20. A. C. R. Dean and Sir Cyril Hinshelwood, *Proc. R. Soc.* B **151**, 435 (1960).
21. A. C. R. Dean and Sir Cyril Hinshelwood, *Proc. R. Soc.* B **146**, 109 (1956).
22. A. C. R. Dean and Sir Cyril Hinshelwood, *Proc. R. Soc.* B **142**, 471 (1954).
23. K. C. Attwood, Lilian K. Schneider, and F. J. Ryan, *Proc. natn. Acad Sci. U.S.A.* **37**, 146 (1951).

24. J. R. Cross and Sir Cyril Hinshelwood, *Proc. R. Soc.* B **145**, 507 (1956).
25. B. C. Kilkenny and Sir Cyril Hinshelwood, *Proc. R. Soc.* B **139**, 575 (1952).
26. B. C. Kilkenny and Sir Cyril Hinshelwood, *Proc. R. Soc.* B **139**, 73 (1951).
27. S. Jackson and B. C. Kilkenny, *J. chem. Soc.* p. 1561 (1951).
28. B. C. Kilkenny and Sir Cyril Hinshelwood, *Proc. R. Soc.* B **140**, 352 (1952).
29. P. R. Lewis and C. N. Hinshelwood, *J. chem. Soc.* pp. 824, 833, 841, 845 (1948).

IX

ENZYMATIC CHANGES ACCOMPANYING
ADAPTATION TO NEW SUBSTRATES

1. Introduction

DRUG resistance is often accompanied by detectable changes in the enzyme balance in cells. Occasionally there is an increase in some enzyme capable of destroying or inactivating the drug, as exemplified in the penicillinase which is formed in considerable amount in certain types of penicillin-resistant bacteria.[1] More often, however, the changes in the enzymes are complex and reflect the switch of the whole metabolism to a route which is less interfered with by the drug. Some examples of this kind of shift were referred to on pp. 157 and 204.

Adaptation to new substrates, however, is normally revealed by a much more obvious change in the enzyme balance, some examples of which are discussed in what follows.

2. Dehydrogenase activity

Dehydrogenases are enzymes concerned in the oxidation of the carbon substrate. This activity can be measured in non-growing suspensions of cells by a variety of techniques in which the reduction of dyes such as methylene blue or 2,3,5 triphenyl tetrazolium chloride serves to indicate the course of the redox reactions.

During the adaptation of *Aerobacter aerogenes* to utilize a given carbon substrate the dehydrogenase activity towards this same compound increases in parallel with the growth rate. For a series of different substrates, although the optimum growth rates may vary perhaps four-fold, there are only small variations in the dehydrogenase activity of the fully adapted cells.[2]

These results are illustrated in Figs. 82 and 83, in which R is a measure of the dehydrogenase activity in a standard test.

The close connexion between adaptation and the development of the enzyme activity is clear. The rough constancy of the optimal activity suggests that oxygen uptake can on occasion become a limiting factor.

There is, however, no simple one-to-one correspondence governing the whole adaptive process. *Aerobacter aerogenes* shows a very long lag when

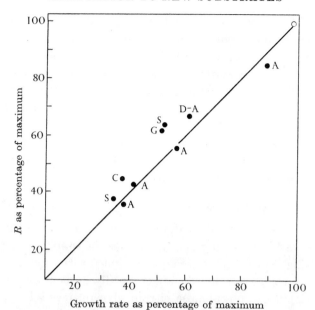

Growth rate as percentage of maximum

FIG. 82. The parallel development of R and the growth rate during the course of training to various substrates.

alues for cultures containing (A) acetate, (C) citrate, (D–A) D-arabinose, (G) glycerol, and (S) succinate.

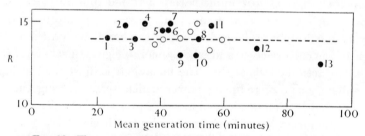

Mean generation time (minutes)

FIG. 83. The constancy of R in fully adapted cultures at 40° C.

Carbon sources: (1) glucose-amino-acids 'A'; (2) glucose-amino-acids 'B'; (3) glucose; (4) glycerol; (5) DL-malate; (6) pyruvate; (7) fumarate; (8) D-arabinose; (9) succinate; (10) L-glutamate; (11) DL-lactate; (12) α-ketoglutarate; (13) acetate. The unfilled circles represent citrate cultures growing under various conditions. Amino-acids 'A' is the combination of amino-acids, except cystine and cysteine, found to give the optimum rate of growth in aerobic defined media (see reference 30, Chapter III) and amino-acids 'B' is a sub-optimal combination.

first grown in succinate as sole carbon source. When growth begins it is accompanied by a rapid rise in the succinic dehydrogenase activity, and after a number of serial subcultures in succinate this activity reaches its optimum. On retransfer of the cells to a medium containing glucose in place of succinate, the cells rapidly lose their high succinic dehydrogenase activity, but the lag in the succinate medium returns only gradually[3] (cf. Chapter X). Thus the succinic dehydrogenase activity, although important, is not the sole determinant, and indeed there is no one governing factor other than the complete reaction pattern. The complex interaction of different factors is illustrated by the fact that in the earliest stages of adaptation to succinate *Aerobacter aerogenes* shows an abnormal increase in asparagine deaminase, which no longer occurs in the fully adapted cells.[3]

In a somewhat similar way specific deaminases increase in amount in cells which depend for their nitrogen on the compounds from which these enzymes can remove ammonia.

3. Aerobic–anaerobic transitions[4]

In some measure related to the above phenomena are those which occur when cultures growing in oxygen have the supply cut off or when those growing anaerobically are again supplied with oxygen.

Aerobacter aerogenes will grow anaerobically in media where the carbon source is glucose, D-arabinose, citrate, glycerol, inositol, or pyruvate. When the air supply is removed growth fails in acetate, fumarate, α-ketoglutarate, lactate, succinate, or malate. If the air supply is suddenly cut off from a culture growing in one of the first group of media, growth is almost immediately arrested, but after a variable period of delay is resumed again. In the second group of media the delay is indefinitely prolonged. During the arrest period the reducing power of the culture rises, and when anaerobic growth sets in, if it does set in, the activity falls again. The behaviour is illustrated in Fig. 84. The enhancement of reducing power which occurs during the initial stages of deprivation of air demands the presence of a nitrogen source to allow the formation of fresh enzyme by synthesis. During anaerobic growth the consumption of the carbon substrate, to give a unit increase in bacterial mass, rises steeply.

In the absence of oxygen a new mechanism must be developed. In this the reduced hydrogen carriers, which would normally be reoxidized by molecular oxygen, are now dealt with by a new process involving a more wasteful consumption of the carbon source. When glucose is the source of carbon the production of acid is greatly increased as a result.

When cells which have been growing anaerobically are supplied with molecular oxygen once more, the growth rate rises: there is no delay and the molecular oxygen is consumed from the start with full efficiency. The fermentative production of acid from glucose ceases immediately the aeration is resumed.

The lack of symmetry in the transition from aerobic to anaerobic growth and vice versa can be interpreted in a simple way. The metabolism can be taken to involve hydrogen carriers, which may be denoted XH_2, and which in aerobic growth are reoxidized ultimately by molecular oxygen. If the oxygen supply fails, a new mechanism for the reoxidation must be developed and this involves enzyme synthesis, which takes time.

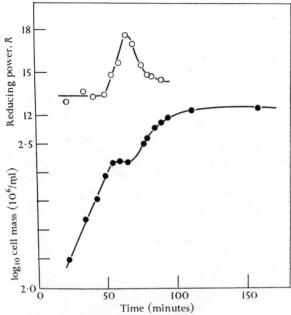

FIG. 84. Detail of the aerobic–anaerobic transition in glucose medium.

At the transition the cell mass was equivalent to 275×10^6/ml standard cells.

On the other hand, when oxygen is available again it can at once deal with XH_2 as before. The development of the anaerobic mechanism apparently involves several stages. First, absence of oxygen to reoxidize XH_2 leads to arrest. A first adjustment leads to the development of a route in which YH_2 is produced, and its accumulation leads to the rise in reducing power of the culture shown in Fig. 85. A further adaptive change, the ease of which varies with the substrate, and which may fail to occur at all, leads to the establishment of the major processes utilizing YH_2. The reducing power of the culture drops as anaerobic growth is resumed, the consumption of substrate now being increased.

These phenomena are related to the effect first observed by Pasteur[5] and known by his name. In this, oxygen lowers the actual consumption of the carbon substrate by the organism which depends upon it for growth. In other words, the more economical aerobic process inhibits the more wasteful anaerobic degradation. There has been much discussion of the Pasteur effect and many detailed mechanisms have been suggested for its operation in particular systems.[6] The essential nature

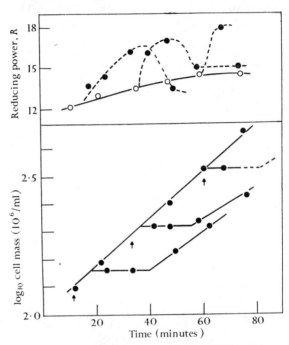

Fig. 85. Aerobic–anaerobic transitions at different stages of growth in glucose–salts medium.

At points marked by arrows portions of the aerobic culture were removed and made anaerobic. R and the cell mass were determined both in the main aerobic culture and in the anaerobic portions.

● R in anaerobic cultures   ○ R in aerobic cultures

of the phenomenon would seem to be as follows. Anaerobic growth demands the development of a new system for the reoxidation of certain reduced intermediates normally handled by molecular oxygen. In the newly established system there is a redox pair, XH_2/X, which is exposed competitively to reaction with molecular oxygen or in its absence to reactions ultimately involving the consumption of more substrate. If the oxygen reaction is the more efficient it automatically reduces the ratio XH_2/X and so inhibits the competing reaction. This, whatever the complexity of detail may be, is in the last resort an example of the competitive inhibitions referred to in Chapter V. Aerobic growth is more rapid than anaerobic growth, and here too that route is followed which allows the optimum rate. Indeed, the whole range of phenomena, whatever their complexity of detail, exemplify in general the operation of the principles of the network theorem of the earlier discussions.

4. Changes occurring during adaptation to nitrate

Coliform bacteria in general and *Aerobacter aerogenes* in particular reduce nitrate to nitrite and use the nitrite in growth. The rates of enzyme attack on nitrate and nitrite respectively can be separately

TABLE 9

The proportionality between the growth rate in nitrate medium and the rate of nitrite consumption[7]

Organism	Rate of nitrite consumption in separate test	M.g.t. in nitrate	Product
Escherichia coli mutabile	66	82	$5 \cdot 41 \times 10^3$
	118	45	$5 \cdot 31 \times 10^3$
	138	38	$5 \cdot 24 \times 10^3$
			mean $5 \cdot 3 \times 10^3$
Escherichia coli	99	53	$5 \cdot 25 \times 10^3$
Aerobacter aerogenes	86	53	$4 \cdot 56 \times 10^3$
	87	52	$4 \cdot 52 \times 10^3$
	90	51	$4 \cdot 59 \times 10^3$
	95	49	$4 \cdot 65 \times 10^3$
	102	54	$4 \cdot 59 \times 10^3$
			mean $4 \cdot 6 \times 10^3$

measured with suspensions of bacteria. The relative rates vary considerably. When *Aerobacter aerogenes* has not been adapted to nitrate the reduction of this may be the slowest step, but the rate then increases on training and eventually many strains grow in nitrate at a rate determined by the rate of consumption of *nitrite*, the product of rate of nitrite consumption and mean generation time becoming approximately constant, as shown in Table 9.

With untrained *Aerobacter aerogenes* the product of the nitrate reduction rate and the mean generation time in nitrate was $4 \cdot 6 \times 10^3$ in the particular experimental units used in Table 9. When nitrate is reduced more rapidly than nitrite is consumed, nitrite can be shown to accumulate in the medium.

There is naturally a complex interlocking of different parts of the reaction pattern. Thus, if we start with a strain of *Escherichia coli* not yet fully adapted to utilize ammonium sulphate as a source of nitrogen, then training to a glucose–ammonium sulphate medium in the absence of any nitrate already confers some measure of increased adaptation to nitrate.

Competitive actions are much in evidence in experiments where the oxygen supply is lowered. In these conditions the rate of reduction of

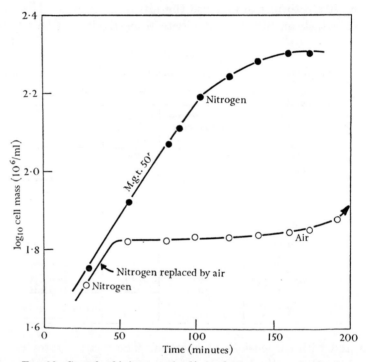

Fig. 86. Growth of 'nitrate-trained' *Aerobacter aerogenes* in nitrate medium with discontinuous aeration changes.

nitrate and nitrite by *Aerobacter aerogenes* increases, as it were, in response to need for a source of oxygen (cf. p. 243). If an anaerobic culture in nitrate is suddenly aerated there is a catastrophic fall in the nitrate–nitrite reduction rates, as growth is arrested (see Fig. 86).[8]

5. Formation of β-galactosidase

β-galactosidase is the enzyme which mediates the hydrolytic splitting of the kind of linkage uniting the glucose and galactose units in lactose. Cells of *Aerobacter aerogenes*, which have not been adapted to growth in lactose show very little β-galactosidase activity when samples taken from a culture are washed and tested (the test depending on the release of coloured o-nitro phenol from o-nitrophenyl-β-D-galactoside). During the early stages of growth in a medium containing lactose as the carbon source there is a rapid increase in the amount of enzyme detectable in the cells. After several subcultures in lactose the cells reach a maximum of enzyme activity although even after this has occurred the growth rate continues to increase. During an individual growth cycle the enzyme activity goes through characteristic variations, and this pattern itself changes as the serial subculture is prolonged.[9]

The enzyme formed during growth in lactose is diluted out during subsequent growth in glucose, and, if the period of adaptation has been short, falls to its original level. As the adaptation is continued, however, the dilution process occurring in absence of lactose ceases to be complete, and a considerable residue of activity, much higher than that of un-adapted cells, is left. The cells now synthesize appreciable amounts of the enzyme even in the absence of lactose.[9] The question of the stability and persistence of adaptations in general is discussed more fully in the following chapter.

With adapted cells of *Aerobacter aerogenes* the β-galactosidase activity remains more or less constant per unit mass of material during a considerable part of the logarithmic phase. Towards the end, however, it frequently tends to show a rapid rise and may reach a maximum shortly after the end of the logarithmic period. If cells in this state of maximum activity are reinoculated into a new medium, the value rapidly falls to normal. The rise is not due to pH change, but is due to a tendency for the oxygen supply to run short, since it is delayed or prevented when the air stream normally provided for the culture is replaced by oxygen. If the culture is grown in a stream of nitrogen the enzyme activity is greater throughout.[9] These effects illustrate once more the formation of enzymes in an automatic fashion in apparent response to a need. In absence of oxygen anaerobic mechanisms come into play and the carbohydrate is much less efficiently used. The growth rate tends to drop on this account and it would do so more than it actually does were it not for the compensation whereby new proportions of cell constituents establish themselves in accordance with the principles of Chapter V. There will be no steady state until such adjustments have occurred that enough enzyme has accumulated to handle the extra lactose needed. Until then lack of the enzyme would hold up all processes dependent on it relatively to its own formation.

6. Permeability relations

When bacterial cells are disrupted, by exposure, for example, to ultrasonic vibrations or by treatment with benzene, certain enzyme activities
may be quite markedly increased.[10, 11] The meaning of this seems clear,
namely that sometimes the activity of the enzyme is limited by the rate
at which substrate can reach it, by some kind of permeability effect.
The breaking up of the cell renders accessible regions of enzyme activity
to which entry was previously restricted. The most obvious barrier to
free access would seem to be the cell wall or membrane. A good deal
has been said about what has been called 'active transport' across cell
boundaries,[12] and for certain examples, notably that of β-galactosidase,
Monod has argued that the access of substrate may be mediated by a
specific enzyme called a 'permease'.[10]

With *Aerobacter aerogenes* the permeability relations are quite complex.
There are two types of behaviour shown when cells are subjected to
disruptive treatments. In one the enzyme activity falls throughout.
In the other it first shows a rise, which may on occasion be considerable,
and then eventually shows a progressive decline as the disintegrating
treatment is prolonged. β-galactosidase and asparagine deaminase, for
example, rise rapidly to a maximum, catalase falls from the start.
Dehydrogenases are all rapidly inactivated by benzene treatment of the
cells. When, however, ultrasonic vibrations are used to break them up,
their enzyme activity shows a different pattern of variation according
to the state of mobilization of the dehydrogenases themselves. When
the cells are fully adapted to the substrate, and the relevant dehydrogenase may be deemed fully mobilized, its activity falls during exposure.
Dehydrogenases, however, which are present in the 'non-induced' or
incompletely mobilized state (for example, succinic dehydrogenase of
cells grown in glucose) show a rise to a maximum.[13]

Thus it is evident that rate of access may or may not be a limiting
factor. When no enhancement of activity at all can be detected, we
might suppose that the concurrent deactivation is so great as to mask it,
or that the enzyme is very easily satisfied by very small supplies of
substrate, or else that the enzyme itself is actually located in or near
the cell boundary. The first possibility is rendered unlikely by the
relatively slow decrease from the maximum in examples where one
occurs, so that the destructive effects are seen in general not to be severe
enough to be likely to mask an appreciable rise. Catalase, which does
not show any enhancement of activity,[13] would, if it were actually

located very near the surface, there be in the best position for protecting the cell against access of the toxic hydrogen peroxide from the medium: but, on the other hand, hydrogen peroxide could well be formed internally. Mitchell[14] put forward the interesting idea of 'translocation catalysis', whereby, for example, fully mobilized dehydrogenases might act on their substrates outside the cell and release the products inside. The destructive action of benzene, in contrast with that of ultrasonic vibrations, acts chiefly on the outer layers of the cell, and its complete destruction of dehydrogenases might perhaps be consistent with the idea that they are located in the surface. During the growth cycle of *Aerobacter aerogenes* in lactose the ratio of β-galactosidase activities for intact and disrupted cells varies in a way which shows them to be separate functions: the ratio also varies during the course of adaptive training to lactose, a matter to which further reference will be made later.

The utility of conceptions such as that of active transport and of the working of specific permeases is a matter for debate. All that will be said for the moment is that such phenomena may be simulated by other effects. If there is inside a cell any substance or structure possessing a strong chemical or adsorptive affinity for a constituent of the medium then this constituent will be drawn into the cell up to a total concentration far exceeding that outside. This is a plain matter of physical chemistry and needs no specific mechanism at the cell boundary. Moreover, the separate variations of enzyme activity during growth, adaptation, or crossing of cells, while it may be conveniently described in terms of two entities, the enzyme and the corresponding permease, does not absolutely demand this distinction. The distribution, as well as the amount of an enzyme, can change. Indeed the experiments of Holt et al.[15] show that redistribution of enzymes may occur even in the course of a cell cycle.

The assumption of a specific enzyme, or permease governing the access of a given reagent to the cell is based upon evidence of two kinds. One sort is exemplified by the fact that the mechanism whereby certain strains of *Escherichia coli* can accumulate β-galactosides in the cell is inhibited by dinitrophenol or by sodium azide and this is taken to suggest that some active enzymatic process underlies the phenomenon. When cells are exposed to a high enough concentration of some reagent inducing β-galactosidase formation (see following section) the ratio of increase in enzyme to increase in bacterial mass is maximal from the start. With lower concentration of the reagent, however, there is an initial period of acceleration. If cells which have been 'induced' for several hours are washed, grown again in medium, and a low concentration of inducer is now added, enzyme synthesis starts immediately at a constant rate. Thus during the acceleration phase the sensitivity of the cell to low concentrations of inducer seems to increase, and the postulate is made that this sensitivity is controlled by a factor which increases during induction. This is the 'permease'.[10, 16] The other kinds of evidence depend upon the study of mutants and on the crossing of bacterial strains which are thought to support the idea that the presence or absence of a permease is a genetically controlled factor.[17]

Whatever may be the descriptive utility of this point of view, it must not be forgotten that according to quite general dynamical laws of cell growth, cells not in a steady state in relation to their environment may temporarily show every kind of relative rate in the synthesis of different components (see p. 108). Further, as already remarked (p. 32), crossing experiments in which results are 'scored' as + and − may easily create the impression of discrete factors whose physical reality is open to doubt.

7. Non-metabolizable inducers

According to some workers on the subject the use of lactose to 'induce' the formation of β-galactosidase gives results which are too complex to handle satisfactorily. They believe that the functions of inducer of the specific enzyme, on the one hand, and metabolic substrate, on the other, are separable. Various thiogalactosides prove to be capable of inducing β-galactosidase formation in *Escherichia coli* when this is growing on another substrate such as maltose. Methyl-β-D-thiogalactoside is a much used inducer of this type. It has been stated that with this substance as the sole source of carbon no growth occurs. Nor does it occur with phenyl-β-D-galactoside as sole carbon source, but with a mixture of the two growth does occur. This is explained by the statement that one substance is an inducer but not a substrate, while the other is a substrate but not an inducer.[18]

In the absence of the inducing galactoside only small amounts of enzyme are formed and, in general, substances other than galactosides do not bring about the induction, although L-arabinose has been reported to be a weak inducer.[11] The results obtained on the kinetics of the enzyme formation in presence of the inducer may be quite complex, because the inducing action is superposed on all the other effects which play a part in protein synthesis, and, as we have already pointed out, cells prepared for specific types of enzyme test may or may not be in a steady state in relation to their environment. Conditions, moreover, need to be found where permeability effects are no longer limiting. When the appropriate conditions are established the ratio of β-galactosidase synthesized to total protein formed in unit time ('differential rate of synthesis') increases linearly with time over a certain range. This differential synthesis sets in immediately the inducer is added[18, 19, 20] (though this does not mean that in various circumstances the formation of total protein may not lag).

This kind of behaviour is very much what might be expected from the consideration of branching networks described in Chapter V. When there is a 'modulation' from one reaction pattern to another certain enzyme ratios change to new values, and they begin to do so as soon as the conditions demand it. This would apply, for example, to the ratio Y_1/X_j in the equation on p. 112.

The mode of action of the specific inducer raises very interesting questions. The 'non-metabolizable inducers' are in some ways reminiscent of those metabolic analogues which inhibit cell processes because they are structurally similar enough to metabolites to have affinity for active sites while being different enough not to be effective substitutes for the metabolites themselves. Monod[18] states that probably the thiogalactosides undergo neither hydrolysis nor transglycosidic reactions *in vivo*, at least in *Escherichia coli*; Zabin, Kepes, and Monod[21] say that the 'major fraction' of the thiogalactoside is found unchanged. Nevertheless the thiogalactoside causes a small change in respiration of the cells,[22] and some of it may become acetylated.[21] Cohen and Rickenberg[23] showed that the thiogalactoside is 'fixed' or absorbed in the cells, but that this fixation is negligible with uninduced bacteria and increases with the amount of enzyme which they contain.

The thiogalactosides, being capable of 'fixation' and of affecting respiration and of entering into acetylation reactions, evidently intervene in some way or other in the reaction patterns of the cell, even if their effect on the growth rate in maltose is not considerable. Glucose, it should be noted, antagonizes their inducing action quite markedly.[18] The lipopolysaccharides of *Escherichia coli* mostly contain a galactose component (7 out of 8 listed by Stacey and Barker[24]). In some circumstances the galactose residue will very probably be built into the macromolecular structure by the kind of linkage which β-galactosidase splits. Since, by thermodynamical principles, enzymes should catalyse the inverse of any reversible reaction they mediate, the same enzyme can play a part in forming such linkages. Thus in the normal metabolism of *Escherichia coli*, even in the absence of added galactoside, there can well be a small part for β-galactosidase to play. Now if the fixation of the inducer inhibits this action, it will temporarily distort the reaction pattern until an increase in the amount of the enzyme establishes a new dynamic balance. This adjustment will only occur during the functioning of the cell and will be reflected in a gradual shift in the ratio of β-galactosidase to the whole cell material. During this time there is no need for the overall growth, say in maltose, to be seriously impaired, since a substitute, though second best, pattern of polysaccharide formation can well serve in the interval. The polysaccharides of cells grown under varying conditions of induction and adaptation are worthy of detailed study. Some mode of action of the thio compounds of this general type would place the induction phenomenon in the same general perspective as training to new substrates and the development of drug resistance.

A quite different kind of explanation, however, is widely assumed, especially by those primarily interested in genetics. According to this, structural genes are responsible for each type of protein. They assemble ribonucleotides into a specific messenger RNA which conveys the information to the ribosomes where the polypeptide chains are synthesized. There are other genes which act as regulators and determine the formation of 'repressors'. These substances may combine with operator genes and prevent the actions to which the information contained in them would otherwise lead. An inducer, on this view, is assumed not to exert a positive action of its own but to cancel the action of a repressor, thereby allowing the synthesis of the appropriate messenger RNA and subsequently the specific enzyme.[25, 26]

If we accept the view that all other effects on the cell of a non-metabolizable inducer are entirely trivial and secondary, then a purely negative action of this kind would indeed seem to follow. This would mean, however, that the regulator gene had no real function other than to cut off a normally quite unnecessary process, namely the formation of the inducible enzyme. If it has no other function, then natural selection would seem to have done its work very badly, leaving two genes with no function but to frustrate one another. Such a state of affairs would be surprisingly wasteful.

If the regulator gene does have other functions, then it is not strictly correct to say that the inducer in interfering with its action does not have any adverse effect on metabolism to which a normal adaptive reaction could be expected.

The distinction of structural and regulator genes, and the statement that the regulatory mechanism operates 'at the genetic level' might seem at first sight to stand in sharp contrast with the theorems about regulatory response formulated in Chapter V. There is in fact no necessary conflict. Genes, whether structural or regulatory, are built up under the influence of enzymes: enzymes are synthesized under the guidance of nucleic acids related to genes. The network of mutual dependences with its branchings and alternatives must always be there. The theory about non-metabolizable inducers which we have just discussed cannot, of course, dispense with the conception of overall cell integration. Where it differs from possible alternative views is in the particular constants in the network equations which the inducer is assumed to modify. It postulates an effect of the inducer on the constants of a gene action, whereas the alternative view might postulate an effect on the constants of some enzyme actions.

An interesting possibility arises in this connexion. If the non-metabolizable inducer, for example the thiogalactoside, had an adverse effect on the cell so that the increased production of enzyme afforded a more effective overall reaction pattern, then the response would be expected to show itself as often as the cells were exposed to the inducer, unless eventually a more radically different reaction pattern could establish itself which by-passed the action of the thiogalactoside altogether. The study of long-imposed adaptive phenomena (see Chapter X) shows that quite profound secondary adjustments can indeed follow the primary adaptive response. If this occurred in the present example, then after long repeated exposure to the thiogalactoside, the cells might lose their response to it. In other words, they might show a gradual training to what amounts to the drug action of the inducer. There would, of course, be no such possibility with the metabolizable inducers themselves. Even if the action of the thiogalactoside is thought of as 'derepression' with no other effect, the fact would remain that there is an overproduction of enzyme for which no use exists. The balance of material and energy is thus less favourable than it might be, and this reaction pattern should gradually be superseded by a less wasteful one, if such exists. Here again, according to the general principle, a gradual training to 'resist' the inducer is conceivable.

Though we offer it with some diffidence, perhaps one last comment is permissible in the context of adaptation and induction generally. On the basis of general laws of growth, such as those outlined in Chapter V, or indeed of improved or elaborated versions of them, these phenomena seem to follow as something to be rather widely and generally expected. The control of genes by appropriate repressors, waiting for the inducer like the Sleeping Beauty waiting for the kiss of the prince, seems to demand a special hypothesis for each separate example, at least until some more complete theory of why so many should be repressed for so much of the time, and yet have survived long ages of evolution.

8. Superposition of adaptations—multiple substrates, substrates and drugs

Aerobacter aerogenes may be trained by serial subculture successively in lactose, maltose, and sucrose to show simultaneously an optimum growth rate in each of them severally, and when it is in this state it shows no impairment of its power to grow at an optimum rate in glucose.[27] Generally, however, the attempt to pile up multiple adaptations results in a partial loss of some of those first imposed. The degree of compatibility probably depends upon the similarity of the metabolic routes by which the substrates are utilized. If these are rather different the final result has to be some sort of compromise.

With lactose and D-arabinose, for example, the kind of compromise reached is illustrated by the following figures. A strain which originally showed a mean generation time of over 200 minutes in D-arabinose and 65 in lactose, grew after thorough training to the former with a m.g.t. of 58 minutes and, after training to lactose alone, of 35 minutes. The mean generation times after 46 subcultures in D-arabinose followed by 80 in lactose were 77 minutes in the former and 35 minutes in the latter, whereas after 40 in lactose followed by 59 in D-arabinose they were 49 minutes in the former and 47 minutes in the latter.[28]

If training to succinate is superimposed on that to lactose and arabinose the disorganization is considerable, the mean generation times in both D-arabinose and lactose increasing several times over (to more than 200 minutes) by the time that in succinate has dropped to 37 minutes.

Drug adaptations and substrate adaptations can be held at the same time, but here again there is a tendency for compromise or even for severe loss of adaptation as new demands are added. A strain of *Aerobacter aerogenes*, for example, was trained to proflavine, sulphanilamide, succinate, glycerol, and lactose, in this order. Eventually the mean generation times in the appropriate media were, in the order just given, 85 (45), 45 (33), 58 (35), 42 (35), and 200 (33) where the optimum value for a single adaptation is given in brackets. All these values, except that for lactose in which little adaptive response is evident, are better than those for untrained strains, but well below the individual optima.[28]

In another series of experiments in which a strain of *Aerobacter aerogenes* was trained *in succession* to streptomycin (1 unit/ml), sulphanilamide (1000 mg/l.) and chloramphenicol (30 mg/l.) full resistance to all three drugs was obtained. The resistance to streptomycin proved to be the most stable and that to chloramphenicol the least. Although the *simultaneous* training to all three drugs was not possible, growth did occur in the presence of any two of them. Streptomycin with sulphanilamide was the most inhibitory combination and streptomycin with chloramphenicol the least.[29] The pattern of behaviour in the latter mixture, however, provides further evidence about the origin of resistance to chloramphenicol. This is dealt with in Chapter XIII.

9. Some approximate mathematical considerations

In general, adaptation is a growth-linked process in which changes in the material proportions, including the enzyme balance, of the cell occur. It is not inseparably linked with division, at any rate in its earlier stages, since, as we have seen, mass may increase appreciably before the cells begin to divide. (Nor are all lag phases necessarily adaptive, since the enzymes may be intact but the pools of diffusible metabolites may have escaped from the cells and need to accumulate once more, or toxic substances may need to be removed. Here the factors operating are similar to those which cause induction periods in ordinary *in vitro* chemical reactions.) According to the principles set out in Chapter V, growth-linked adaptations involve the whole reaction pattern of the cell, and the facts referred to in the foregoing section confirm this idea. The handling of the general equations is, however, difficult, and for certain purposes simpler approximate treatments, which fix attention on individual parts of the complete reaction pattern, have their uses. We append, therefore, simple approximate treatments of some of the effects described in earlier chapters and in the first part of the present one.

1. *Increase of growth rate*

As, for example, in the adaptation of *Aerobacter aerogenes* to lactose, there is initially a moderate growth rate which, on serial subculture, improves rapidly to an optimum value.[27]

No new function is acquired, though the capacity of an existing one improves on use. The enzyme capable of using the new substrate must therefore be formed even from the normal substrate. It might be regarded as a by-product of the normal functioning of the cell or it may play some minor role. We shall schematize this by assuming an enzyme j, the amount of which, x_j, is a constant fraction of the amount of enzyme 1, and which is capable of performing the function to be trained.

As on p. 117 we write the equations

$$dx_1/dt = k_1 x_1,$$

$$n\, dc/dt = k_1' x_1 - Kcn = 0,$$

$$dx_2/dt = k_2 x_2 c,$$

$$n = \beta x_2,$$

where the symbols have the same meaning as before, and similar assumptions are made. We now add, however,

$$x_j = \gamma x_1.$$

It follows from these equations by integration that

$$x_j - (x_j)_0 = (\gamma \beta K k_1 / k_2 k_1')\{x_2 - (x_2)_0\},$$

where $(x_j)_0$ and $(x_2)_0$ are the amounts present at time zero. On prolonged growth the enzyme ratios settle down to the values given by

$$(x_j) = (\gamma \beta K k_1 / k_2 k_1')(x_2) = A(x_2), \tag{1}$$

where (x_2) is the standard amount of enzyme 2 per cell.

When the cells are transferred to the new medium enzyme j, instead of being of secondary importance, becomes the seat of the key process. We now have it formed not as a by-product or minor constituent but at a rate determined ultimately by the new substrate. Accordingly we write

$$dx_j/dt = k_j x_j.$$

Either directly or indirectly, the products of its working lead to the synthesis of enzyme 2 as before. To simplify the equations we suppose this to occur directly (though the essential result does not depend upon this) and write

$$n\, dc_j/dt = k_j' x_j - K_j c_j n = 0,$$

$$dx_2/dt = k_2^* x_2 c_j,$$

whence, as before, we obtain the steady amount of x_j in a cell to be

$$x_j - (x_j)_0 = (\beta K_j k_j / k_2^* k_j')\{x_2 - (x_2)_0\} = A_j\{x_2 - (x_2)_0\},$$

which, as soon as the new material outweighs the old, becomes

$$(x_j) = A_j(x_2). \tag{2}$$

The initial growth rate of the cells just transferred from the old medium will be $k_j A(x_2)$, while that of the adapted cells will be $k_j A_j(x_2)$ by equations (1) and (2) respectively. A may be as small as we please, since γ may be very small. The growth rate will then increase to a steady new value as enzyme j expands to its new proportion.

2. *Composite growth curves*

As has been explained, the curves in Figs. 65 and 69 can be formally interpreted in terms of two competing processes, one with a greater growth rate but initially longer lag, the other with a lower rate and shorter lag. The adaptation consists in the relative shortening of the lag of the former. If there were present in the system two quite independent groups of cells with the characteristics postulated, then such behaviour would be readily understandable. Indeed, at first sight, the not infrequent occurrence of composite growth curves might seem to lend support to the view that what we observe in such examples is simply the outgrowing of one sub-species of bacteria by another sub-species in an initially inhomogeneous culture. It will be more convenient to consider the part played by selection under one single heading later. At the present juncture we shall consider what alternative explanations are possible. We suppose that there exist two alternative reaction sequences, one favoured in presence of the original substrate, the other favoured in presence of the new substrate. The two substrates will be referred to as A and B and the two sequences as I and II respectively. Suppose growth has been occurring for a long time by sequence I with substrate A. The enzymes of sequence II are in fact formed to some extent but do not exist in any specially favourable proportions for the occurrence of sequence II. Some of them may, indeed, be present in very small amounts. If now the cells are transferred to substrate B, growth by sequence II, although chemically the optimum, may not be able to set in for some time, since the proportions of some of the essential enzymes may correspond to what would in effect be equivalent to a very aged and decayed state had B been the usual medium. A long lag is therefore necessary before even the first cell division is ready to occur. If in the meantime no growth can occur by sequence I, all that we shall observe will be a long lag in the new medium followed by growth by sequence II. If, however, substrate B can be utilized at low efficiency by sequence I (as might sometimes happen) then, since the enzymes for I are fully mobilized there will be no abnormal lag, but simply slow growth. The question now arises as to what happens if the two processes are combined. If the total bacterial substance can be slowly increasing by the inefficient combination (B, I) while the deficient enzymes of the more efficient process (B, II) are being built up to the required amounts, then we shall observe a growth curve with a transition point as in Figs. 65 and 69. The transition point will occur at the moment when the lag of the (B, II) process comes to an end.

The idea of a lag existing with respect to one process in a mass of matter increasing all the time by another requires some further explanation. The following considerations seem, however, to show it to be reasonable. We suppose the bacterial mass to be increasing by the operation of sequence I in presence of substrate B, the overall rate constant being k. Enzymes 1, 2,... are present at time t in total amounts $(x_1)_0 e^{kt}$, $(x_2)_0 e^{kt}$,.... . The enzyme j, necessary for the initiation of the sequence II, is formed in quite small amount. This we express by writing dx_j/dt with a term equal to $\gamma dx_1/dt$. As long as this is the only source of j, the amount per cell remains a fraction of the amount of 1. But in a medium containing substrate B, j is formed as a major element of the reaction pattern, the rate at time t being given by $k_j x_j$. Thus the total rate of production of j throughout the whole bacterial mass is given by the equation

$$dx_j/dt = \gamma dx_1/dt + k_j x_j$$
$$= \gamma k x_1 + k_j x_j$$
$$= \gamma k (x_1)_0 e^{kt} + k_j x_j$$

or $$dx_j/dt - k_j x_j = \gamma k (x_1)_0 e^{kt}.$$

This linear differential equation holds irrespective of the cell division. The solution is

$$x_j = (x_j)_0 e^{k_j t} + \frac{\gamma k (x_1)_0}{(k_j - k)} \{e^{k_j t} - e^{kt}\}.$$

When t is great enough, the first term on the right outweighs the second, since by the conditions of the problem k_j is greater than k and γ is small. Eventually, therefore, we shall have an exponential rate of production of j with a rate constant k_j: and sequence II will take control. (What then happens to enzyme I is a matter for separate consideration.) But $(x_j)_0$ is very small compared with $(x_1)_0$. Therefore the amount per cell, $(x_j)_0/n$, is small compared with the standard amount which would normally provoke a division. Cell division is determined by x_1/n until x_j/n has passed a critical value given by $(x_j)/n$ where (x_j) is considerably greater than $(x_j)_0$. At this point growth by sequence II will supersede that by sequence I, and the overall rate constant k_j will replace that characteristic of the growth mode (I, B), namely k.

According to this view, growth proceeds by the relatively inefficient mechanism (I, B) during the time which is required for the small initial supply of enzyme $(x_j)_0$ to build up by an alternative process to the value

(x_j). This can be properly termed the 'lag' of the alternative process even though n is increasing steadily. In the present sense the lag of the process II is the time required for x_j/n to attain a threshold value. From the point of view of each cell, enzyme j starts at a very small value and attains the standard value at the end of the lag. That the number of cells has meanwhile been increasing is irrelevant, and merely represents a continuous change of scale of the phenomenon studied: it is as though we observed the induction period of a chemical reaction in a vessel which, as we watched, was filled fuller and fuller of the same reaction mixture.

As regards those parts of the cell substance which are built up by the joint action of enzymes I and j, their rate of formation will be approximately the sum of terms proportional respectively to dx_1/dt and dx_j/dt. While x_j is small this will be very nearly equivalent to saying that the total mass increases proportionally to e^{kt}, and subsequently, soon after x_j has passed the threshold, to e^{k_jt}. For the total mass, X, we may write approximately

$$X = ae^{kt} + be^{k_jt},$$

where k_j is greater than k but a is greater than b. In the usual way of plotting growth curves $\log X$ is expressed as a function of t. For small values of t the above equation gives a straight line of slope nearly equal to k, and in a certain region there is a rapid transition to a line of greater slope. Values of the function

$$100e^t + be^{3t}$$

are shown in Fig. 87 with $b = 10$, 1, and 0·1 respectively. The resemblance of the curves to those shown in Figs. 43, 65, and 66 is obvious.

3. *Exceptionally long initial lag*

This phenomenon is exemplified by *Escherichia coli mutabile* and lactose (see p. 225). There is no absolute need, as far as the explanation of the lag goes, to seek beyond the principles outlined in the previous paragraph. If $(x_j)_0$ were extremely small, and if, further, during the consequent lag of the sequence (II, B) the makeshift sequence (I, B) were unable to operate at all (that is, if the enzyme which normally deals with the substrate A were unable to deal with B at all), then the essential fact would be accounted for.

Account must always of course be taken of the possibility of the production of mutants. When a cell multiplies there may be, for various reasons, imperfect replication resulting in a mutant possessing special properties. If the properties which thus arise are favourable to growth in the medium in which the cell happens to be, then preferential multiplication of the privileged types must occur. According to this view, the long lag would be the time of waiting for favourable mutations or that required for the mutants to multiply if they are already present.

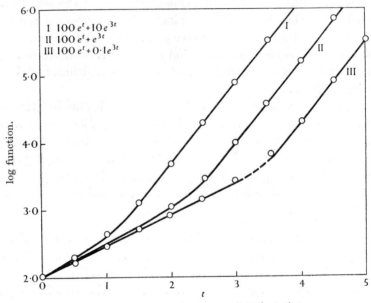

FIG. 87. Curves of the function $100e^t + be^{3t}$.

This whole matter will be more fully discussed in Chapter XIII. Here it will only be observed that the idea of random mutations seems better suited to explain the appearance of unexpected properties in cells which have been subjected to influences such as short-wave radiation or chemical 'mutagens', than to account for those examples where the properties acquired are nicely adjusted to the requirements of optimum growth in complex and specific ways. *Aerobacter aerogenes*, as has been stated, can be trained to grow optimally in any combination of the sugars, lactose, sucrose, and maltose (taken singly or in pairs): it can acquire drug resistance precisely graded to the particular concentration of drug in which it has been grown. It is assigning a very heavy role to chance to attribute the initiation of all these adaptations to random variations.

10. Loss of properties

According to the theorems of Chapter V, adaptations to new substrates should be reversible. In principle they are, but the rate of reversion and the stability of the adapted state constitute a problem of great complexity and subtlety to which the whole of the next chapter will be devoted.

For enzyme systems to expand adaptively according to the processes envisaged in the network equations there must of course be some minimal amount present initially: in other words, the branch of the total reaction pattern in which the enzyme in question is concerned must bear a minimal amount of traffic at all times. Otherwise after a period of growth

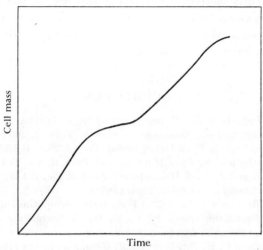

FIG. 88. Diphasic growth.

in which other parts of the cell substance were expanding exponentially and this one not at all, the individual enzyme would be diluted out altogether. Complete loss of properties occurs rarely if ever in the course of normal culturing in media unless these contain destructive agents. According, moreover, to the theories which envisage 'repressors' and 'derepressors', the essential genes remain permanently available.

Nevertheless a drastic loss of particular activities, reflected in inability to grow without specific additions to the medium, occurs when cells are exposed to radiation and to certain types of drug. These represent an actual destruction, partial or even in the last limit permanent, of parts of the cell structure. They constitute one kind of mutation (Chapter XIII).

11. The phenomenon of diphasic growth

The competitive use of substrates and the superseding or 'repression' of less efficient processes by more efficient ones has already been discussed. It is well exemplified in the phenomenon which is conveniently called diphasic growth.[30] If bacteria are grown in mixtures of two carbohydrates under conditions where the exhaustion of the carbon source limits growth, a curve of the type shown in Fig. 88 may be found.

The two parts correspond to the successive utilization of the two sugars. All the carbohydrates which show delayed susceptibility to attack belong to the class for which adaptation is necessary but previous adaptation does not remove the arrest, so that growth in the first and preferred sugar is evidently actively preventing the use of the second. This phenomenon is clearly connected with that of enzyme repression, which will be discussed at the end of the next chapter after the reversibility of adaptations has been considered.

REFERENCES

1. See M. R. Pollock in *The Enzymes*, edited by P. D. Boyer, H. Lardy, and K. Myrbäck, 2nd ed., Academic Press, New York, **4**, 269 (1960).
2. A. C. Baskett and Sir Cyril Hinshelwood, *Proc. R. Soc.* B **137**, 524 (1950).
3. B. J. McCarthy and Sir Cyril Hinshelwood, *Proc. R. Soc.* B **150**, 410 (1959).
4. A. C. Baskett and Sir Cyril Hinshelwood, *Proc. R. Soc.* B **138**, 75, 88 (1951).
5. L. Pasteur, *Études sur la Bière*, Paris (1875).
6. See for details reference 4 and Ciba Foundation Symposium on the *Regulation of Cell Metabolism*, edited by G. E. W. Wolstenholme and Cecilia M. O'Connor, Churchill, London (1959).
7. P. R. Lewis and C. N. Hinshelwood, *J. chem. Soc.* p. 824 (1948).
8. P. R. Lewis and C. N. Hinshelwood, *J. chem. Soc.* p. 833 (1948).
9. N. Richards and Sir Cyril Hinshelwood, *Proc. R. Soc.* B **154**, 463 (1961); B **156**, 20 (1962).
10. See for details G. N. Cohen and J. Monod, *Bact. Rev.* **21**, 169 (1957); I. Zabin, A. Kepes, and J. Monod, *J. Biol. Chem.* **237**, 253 (1962).
11. B. Rotman, *J. Bact.* **76**, 1 (1958).
12. See for details R. J. Britten, *Symp. Soc. gen. Microbiol.* **15**, 57 (1965).
13. D. J. W. Grant and Sir Cyril Hinshelwood, *Proc. R. Soc.* B **160**, 25 (1964).
14. P. Mitchell, in 1st Int. Union of Biochemistry and Int. Union of Biological Science, Stockholm Symposium on *Biological Structure and Function*, edited by T. W. Goodwin and O. Lindberg, Academic Press, New York, **2**, 581 (1961).
15. S. J. Holt and D. G. O'Sullivan, *Proc. R. Soc.* B **148**, 465 (1958).
16. A. Kepes and G. N. Cohen in *The Bacteria*, edited by I. C. Gunsalus and R. Y. Stanier, Academic Press, New York, **4**, 179 (1962).
17. See A. B. Pardee, F. Jacob, and J. Monod, *J. molec. Biol.* **1**, 165 (1959).
18. J. Monod in *Enzymes, Units of Biological Structure and Function*, edited by O. H. Gaebler, p. 7, Academic Press, New York (1956).
19. J. Monod, *Rec. Trav. chim. Pays-Bas Belg.* **77**, 569 (1958).
20. M. Cohn, *Bact. Rev.* **21**, 140 (1957).
21. I. Zabin, A. Kepes, and J. Monod, *Biochem. biophys. Res. Commun.* **1**, 289 (1959).

22. A. Kepes, *C. r. hebd. Séanc. Acad. Sci., Paris* **244**, 1550 (1957).

23. G. Cohen and H. V. Rickenberg, *C. r. hebd. Séanc. Acad. Sci., Paris* **240**, 466 (1955).

24. M. Stacey and S. A. Barker, *Polysaccharides of Micro-organisms,* Clarendon Press, Oxford (1960).

25. J. Monod, *Angew. Chem.* **71**, 685 (1959); F. Jacob and J. Monod, *Cold Spring Harbor Symp. quant. Biol.* **26**, 193, 389 (1961); J. Monod, J. P. Changeux, and F. Jacob, *J. molec. Biol.* **6**, 306 (1963); F. Jacob and J. Monod, *Pontif. Acad. Sci. Scripta Varia, Semaine d'Étude sur le Problème des Macro-molécules d'Intérêt Biologique* **22**, 85 (1961).

26. See S. Brenner, *Br. med. Bull.* **21**, 244 (1965).

27. J. R. Postgate and C. N. Hinshelwood, *Trans. Faraday Soc.* **42**, 45 (1946).

28. A. W. Scopes and Sir Cyril Hinshelwood, *J. chem. Soc.* p. 1838 (1952).

29. A. C. R. Dean and P. J. Rodgers, unpublished observations.

30. J. Monod, *A. Rev. Microbiol.* **3**, 371 (1949).

X

THE REVERSIBILITY OF ADAPTIVE CHANGES

1. Introduction

THE stability of an adaptive change, as has emerged in part during the discussion of some individual examples, varies. The evidence will be gathered together in a later section, and in preparation for this we shall return to the theme of the fundamental properties of living cells.

In general it may be said that when adaptations are first imposed they are very readily lost. When cells which have just been adapted to a new medium, B, are returned to the old, A, a rapid reversion occurs, and if they are now tested in B, the process of adjustment has to be gone through as though it had not been enacted before. Metaphorically speaking, the cells show little memory of their previous experience. When the adaptation has been maintained for a long time it becomes stable, and a very prolonged cultivation in the original environment is needed before the apparent memory is lost.

Sometimes the stability or persistence of the adaptation is very great, and one frequently expressed view is that adaptation in such examples consists in nothing other than the selection of a mutant form with a stable heredity. This view, however, oversimplifies the problem and does not do justice to the actual factual evidence. It also fails to recognize a very important general character of living matter.

In his book *Brain, Memory, Learning*, W. Ritchie Russell[1] observes, 'All living matter shows features that may be considered a form of memory. It all shows spontaneous activities that tend to form patterns which are at first relatively simple, but show a strong tendency to repeat.' Some phenomena of this sort would indeed appear to occur in the brain cells concerned with memory itself. The first impress of what is to be remembered appears to be evanescent but capable of stabilization to a high degree. Dr. H. R. Ing[2] has pointed out that probably in addiction to drugs such as morphine or heroin the reaction network (see p. 106) of some unidentified cells in the brain is altered. These cells then require the drug for their normal working. If it is withdrawn suddenly severe symptoms develop in the patient, whereas a more gradual withdrawal allows the brain-cells to return to their normal network.

According to the theorems about reaction patterns and networks and the principle of total integration, the amounts of various cell components change in a given environment until they become consistent with an optimum rate of increase of the cell material as a whole. Change of medium causes the proportions to modulate to other values. The simple treatments already given of these phenomena predict that the adaptive adjustments should be rapidly reversible when the cells are returned to their original environment. This corresponds to the very earliest stages of many observed adaptations. These results, however, are based upon a theory which describes in effect the organization of the cell in time: its organization in space must also be taken into account. So far the geometry of the cell has entered only in an indirect way into the equations of the network theorem. The values of the constants α_1, α_2,... (p. 109) must themselves be functions of the cell geometry in so far as they involve the lengths of diffusion paths and other factors affecting internal transfer of intermediate metabolites.

2. Architectonics of the cell

The genetic information in a cell is ultimately translated into a spatial distribution of matter, that, primarily, of the different macromolecular substances in the cell itself, and, secondarily, of the various types of cell in tissues and organs of differentiated living things. We shall here be concerned with the first part only of the problem.

The basic idea in the translation of genetic information into structure is relatively simple. The units of information are arranged in space, for example along the chain of DNA. They govern, in some way or other, chemical processes of various kinds, and the products of these processes must diffuse away to enter into further reactions elsewhere. Thus the concentrations of the chemical intermediates in the cell must form spatial patterns, and for the multiplicity of substances involved these concentrations have values at different points which are functions of the spatial coordinates. The possible rates of further stages of synthesis (or degradation) will thus themselves be functions of these concentrations, and so in turn of the spatial coordinates.

Numerous labile substances will play their part in the total pattern of cell reactions, and some will be exposed to the possibility of alternative fates, such as useless destruction, unless the appropriate reaction partner is available at the opportune moment. And this availability is itself a function of the path which the partner or its precursor has had to travel, right back to the point at which the essential genetic information guided some initiating stage in a sequence. Thus we may say that the spatial organization of a living cell is closely connected with the presence of the right substance in the right place at the right time.

Since diffusion paths may be of decisive importance in determining reaction rates, both absolute and relative, we see that they constitute an essential link between the reaction pattern on the one hand and the geometry of the cell on the other.

3. The internal map

A bacterial cell, as many writers have recognized, must have some kind of internal structure of its own. The interior is not a homogeneous mass, but rather resembles a three-dimensional semi-fluid mosaic, in which, moreover, a constellation of discrete particulate matter can be discerned.

The interior has been described in various ways. Needham[3] referred to a 'cytoskeleton', though Peters made the reservation that this term must not be taken to imply any rigidity and referred himself to 'some tenuous network by the action of which the cell's enzymic activities are coordinated'.[4] Monné has referred to 'cytoplasmic fibrils'[5] and Dickens[6] to 'cellular compartments' for various components or functions. Sissakian[7] has spoken in more general terms of the heterogeneity of the protoplasm and the localization of the biochemical functions. Weiss[8] observed that the 'countless chemical workshops' of the cell continue to function even after the viscous cytoplasm has been stirred or submitted to centrifuging, and he envisages fields of organization, perhaps controlled by the conditions at surfaces.

The lack of rigidity in the cell structure might seem at first sight to conflict with any idea of referring diffusion paths and other kinetic determinants to spatial coordinates. But it need not necessarily do so. These coordinates, even if for some purposes we treat them as ordinary Cartesian coordinates, could in principle be some quite complicated system having reference to those elements in the cell structures whose relation is not destroyed in any permissible distortion. To take a simple analogy, the movement of adsorbed molecules over the surface of a deformable adsorbant could be described in a way which largely eliminated the elastic distortion of that surface.

By differential centrifugation discrete submicroscopic particles known as ribosomes can be separated from cells, other fractions of the centrifugate containing cell wall, nuclear material and in some types of cell, *mitochondria*. The ribosomes, which show considerable variations in size and aggregation, are the seat of complex physical and chemical changes and important centres of protein synthesis.[9]

Some experimenters have been much concerned with the 'pools' of metabolites which form in functioning cells, for example the pools of amino-acids or nucleotides, and which can be studied with the help of radioactive tracers. The concentrations of particular constituents rise and fall according to circumstances in a way which allows inferences to be made about the details of reaction patterns. Sometimes the substances in the pool are derived from outside but often represent intermediates on their way from one processing department of the cell to another.[9]

We see, therefore, that several models of the cell may have a limited validity and be useful in the analysis of particular problems. In the first place, there is the reaction network which we have previously discussed. This, however, does not deal explicitly with the spatial organization. Further, the cell can be regarded as presenting a spatial map with a sort of mosaic structure of its macromolecular components and spaces where pools of metabolites may form. Again, the cell can be thought of for some purposes as a constellation of discrete particles subject to some kind of field of force which imposes an order on it. In one sense the cell is a polarized structure. There may be a congregation of DNA molecules in certain special *nuclear regions* with a coded structure. The surface layers of the cell contain a complex assembly of polysaccharides, mucopeptides, and so on, the structure of which is also in some degree ordered, and is highly specific. Long-chain molecules thread the intervening regions. They are themselves coiled and folded through the action of different kinds of chemical forces, hydrogen bonding, electrostatic, and van der Waals forces. Thus some kind of polarization will exist between the central and the peripheral regions. The enzymes localized in the surface layers themselves must be arranged in a sort of chart which guides the release of appropriate metabolites into the interior. The so-called permeases[10] would be included under this heading.

Whether the cell is regarded as a constellation of particles in a polarizing field, or whether it is looked on as a mosaic of folded and packed macromolecules, the question arises about the mechanical stability of the whole system. Some arrangements and dispositions will be freer from strain and will possess a lower potential energy than others. And it is into a condition with a relative minimum of potential energy that the whole structure must tend to settle down.

The change in geometrical configuration is not likely to be very easy, the mosaic being in some respects a close-packed one. On the other hand, profound reorganization is observed each time the cell divides, and one field of polarized structure gives rise to two nearly identical halves. The discussion of cell division is deferred till later, but it is evidently an orderly and far from random process. It must presumably involve some degree of loosening of the whole mosaic structure, so that periods of cell division would seem to be the times most favourable for any refoldings or repackings calculated to give a greater mechanical stability. Suppose a cell to be in an adequately functional state but with an overall geometrical configuration of its parts not yet consistent with the minimum of potential energy required for mechanical stability. It can well be imagined to approach closer and closer to this state during the course of a series of successive cell divisions.

4. Interplay of reaction network and spatial map

The two tendencies, that, on the one hand, to establish the optimum proportion of cell constituents according to the network theorem, and that, on the other, to achieve a maximum stability of the spatial map, interact with one another in a complex manner.

When transferred to a new environment, whether one demanding the development of enzymes to metabolize new nutrients, or one containing a toxic substance the action of which must be antagonized or circumvented, the cells develop a new reaction pattern which involves changed proportions of various components. But this state will probably no longer allow the old spatial map to be preserved without strain and distortion, since it is extremely unlikely that the two separate sets of proportions both correspond to maxima of mechanical stability.

Thus the new proportions create a demand for still further adjustment. During the succeeding cell divisions the strain created can gradually be relieved, and only when this has happened can the adaptation to the new conditions be regarded as truly complete. But the whole process is far from simple. Suppose a reaction network which we will designate $N(1)$ changes to $N(2)$ on transfer of the cells to a new environment. The original spatial map may be designated $M(1)$, and at first is retained so that a state we may call $N(1)M(1)$ becomes $N(2)M(1)$ with the creation of mechanical instability. $M(1)$ is thereby caused gradually to change to $M(2)$. But $N(2)$, which was the best possible reaction network for $M(1)$, is no longer quite the best for $M(2)$. The changed spatial map has altered *inter alia* various diffusion paths and so affected the rates of certain of the chemical reaction steps. Further changes in $N(2)$ now occur, and these in turn demand further changes in $M(2)$, until we reach a limit, $N'(2) M'(2)$, where both reaction network and spatial map are simultaneously optimal.

The establishment of new spatial maps is a complex repacking of a system in which there is by no means unlimited freedom of manœuvre. In some ways it could probably be visualized as somewhat akin to a recrystallization, or the phase change of a polymorphic substance. We may therefore predict that the initial course of an adjustment, that is the transition from $N(1) M(1)$ to $N(2) M(1)$, will be rapid, but that the state so achieved will not correspond to complete adaptation. The completion, through a series of stages ending up at $N'(2) M'(2)$ may well be quite lengthy, and indeed sometimes the final state may be approached with great slowness and only after repeated culturing of the cells.

In general these predictions are fully confirmed by observations on adaptive processes.

In the light of the principles outlined above the question of the reversibility of adaptations assumes a much more complicated aspect than would be suggested by the network theorem alone. If the first stage only of adaptation has occurred after transfer from environment I to environment II, so that $N(1) M(1)$ has become $N(2) M(1)$, then return to the original condition, I, should result in a rapid reversion to $N(1) M(1)$, that is to say the adaptation is readily lost.

But now suppose that the mutual accommodation of reaction network and spatial map has progressed through its sequence of stages to $N'(2) M'(2)$. The loss of this adaptation on return to the original environment, I, will now no longer be anything like a simple reversal of the sequence traversed in the forward direction. For on transfer from II back to I, the first stage will be the re-establishment of a reaction network appropriate to I, the spatial map remaining for the time being almost unchanged. That is to say the first stage of the return journey will be to $N'(1) M'(2)$ and this, it should be observed, is a state in which the cells have never existed before and through which they did not pass during the adaptive process. Even if we neglect the differences between $N'(1)$ and $N(1)$ and between $M'(2)$ and $M(2)$ and so on, we see that while the course of adaptation is by the sequence $N(1) M(1)$, $N(2) M(1)$, $N(2) M(2)$, that of de-adaptation is from $N(2) M(2)$ to $N(1) M(2)$ to $N(1) M(1)$, and the return involves a state not passed through in the forward process. When, moreover, the whole sequence of successive approximations of reaction network and spatial map to their optima is taken into account, we see that during de-adaptation there will be a whole series of states passed through in which the cells have not been before.

Now although $N(1) M(1)$ may be much more favourable for growth in environment I than is $N'(2) M'(2)$ as finally established in environment II, nevertheless $N'(2) M'(2)$ itself may be more favourable for growth even in I than some of the hitherto unexplored intermediate stages of the reversion path. When this is so the cells will remain with the organization $N'(2) M'(2)$ or at any rate an organization on the same side as this of an intermediate barrier condition. A barrier is always constituted by an intervening state less favourable than the initial one, as is illustrated by the analogy of those states of higher energy which have to be passed through in chemical reactions and which usually limit the rate of the change.

Reversion of an adaptation may, therefore, sometimes be quite slow. There are, moreover, reasons why on occasion it should be very slow indeed or almost indefinitely delayed. Let the medium we have called I be a growth medium and II be the same medium with the addition of a toxic drug. The first stage in the development of drug resistance will be the establishment of any reaction network which allows any improved growth at all. This first stage of adaptation would, as we have seen, be easily reversed on growth in a drug-free medium. Gradually, however, the adaptation becomes more complete, and the state we have referred to as $N'(2) M'(2)$ is achieved. The basal medium, it must be remembered, is the same whether the drug is present or not, so that $N'(2) M'(2)$ must normally be compatible with reasonably efficient growth in the drug-free environment. If it happens to be nearly as good as the original then there will be only a quite small tendency to revert. If it is better than some intermediate state which would, as the foregoing discussion indicated, have to be passed through during reversion, then at any rate a considerable proportion of the drug resistance would be held tenaciously in spite of cultivation of the cells in the drug-free medium.

In special circumstances another and even more striking phenomenon is possible. Some antibiotics are metabolic products of specific organisms, and so in principle are not incapable of entering into the actual reaction networks themselves. In a drug medium the resistant cells develop a growth mechanism which not only suffers minimum interference by the drug but, as in the case just considered, allows optimum utilization of the basal medium itself. In certain circumstances the most advantageous reaction scheme is one in which the antibiotic substance itself participates, perhaps with a role not wholly unlike that which it plays in the type of organism from which it is derived. Once a scheme involving the drug as an actual metabolite is well established it may, for the kind of reason already discussed, be rather persistent. If and when this happens an actual need for the presence of the drug is observed, and we have the phenomenon known as 'drug dependence', which was described in Chapter VI (p. 175).

5. Some special circumstances leading to stability or persistence of adaptive changes

The interplay of reaction network and spatial map shows that the pattern of stability relations can be expected to be a complex one. Other special circumstances can also affect the stability.

According to the general principles of cell organization that combination of processes is selected which gives an optimum rate of growth. As we have pointed out, many alternatives exist, and switches can occur from one to another when required, as trains on a railway network may be diverted from one branch to another to avoid an obstruction.

For growth in a given medium, then, alternative reaction patterns will exist, one normally more efficient than the others. We will confine our attention to that which is the most efficient and to one other. Suppose there is a component playing an important part in the one sequence of reactions and present in total amount X (in the whole culture) and a second component, present in total amount Y, which is involved in the alternative, competing sequence. Suppose further that the Y component requires for its action (enzymatic, information-bearing, or other) a certain metabolite, which has an intracellular concentration c, but that this metabolite can be destroyed by the X component or metabolized in some way which is not useful for the overall growth process.

The concentration, c, of this intermediate metabolite is determined by an equation of the form

$$dc/dt = A - Bc - CcX/n = 0,$$

where A, B, and C are constants. A gives the rate of formation in any given cell, Bc the loss from the reaction region by diffusion, and CcX/n the rate of destruction by the X component, present in each cell in amount X/n.

Thus
$$c = \frac{A/B}{1+(C/B)(X/n)} = \frac{A/B}{1+\gamma X/n},$$
$$dY/dt = kYc = k_y Y/(1+\gamma X/n),$$

where k_y is a new constant. Then since dX/dt may be written $k_x X$, we find that

$$\frac{1}{(Y/X)}\frac{d(Y/X)}{dt} = \frac{d\ln(Y/X)}{dt} = \frac{k_y}{1+\gamma X/n} - k_x.$$

This relatively simple model, analogues of which could easily exist in real cells, has very interesting properties. Suppose we start with $d\ln(Y/X)/dt$ negative, as it could be if at $t = 0$ the value of X_0/n were large. Then the proportion of the Y component gets less and less with time and no effective use of the Y route will be possible at all. If, on the other hand, X_0/n were small $k_y/(1+\gamma X_0/n)$ could be $> k_x$ so that the differential coefficient is positive and Y/X begins to increase. X and Y are parts of possible metabolic routes, and we may have the division condition approximating either to $X = \beta n$ or $Y = \beta' n$ according to the route which is being followed. Suppose X_0/n is so small that Y/n reaches β' before X/n reaches β, then division will occur and the value of $k_y/(1+\gamma X/n)$ will now be $k_y/(1+\beta'\gamma X/Y)$. Then we have

$$\frac{d\ln(Y/X)}{dt} = \frac{k_y}{1+\beta'\gamma(X/Y)} - k_x.$$

If this last expression is positive, Y/X continues to increase and the Y route becomes the sole effective one.

The important result here is that the final upshot is dependent on the initial ratio X_0/Y_0. If the X route is well established it inhibits the development of its rival (even though this rival route might be inherently faster). Thus we might have the phenomenon of an established adaptation persisting in spite of the existence of a more effective alternative which is not able to obtain an initial foothold. Once this initial opportunity were provided, the faster route would capture the traffic. What could upset the initial state of affairs and destroy, as it were, the vested interest of the existing route, would be a general but differential decay in enzyme activity, as occurs when cells age. The initial advantage of the established route could then be lost, and, given a start on equal terms, the more efficient route would win.

If it so happens that k_x and $k_y/(1+\gamma X_0/n)$ are nearly equal, then a general ageing process interrupted by short periods of renewed growth could lead to the appearance of extremely unstable and erratic behaviour, with the growth rate of the cells strongly influenced by their immediately past history. Such erratic changes are indeed observed in some circumstances (p. 218).

Another special mechanism which may give rise to almost indefinitely slow reversion from an adaptive change is discussed in connexion with lag-concentration curves on p. 156.

6. Survey of experimental findings on stability of drug resistance

From the foregoing discussion adaptations possessing a wide range of stabilities would be expected, and this indeed has been observed in detailed studies with drugs. The following general conclusions may be drawn.

1. A marked degree of resistance is often reached after a relatively short period of growth in presence of the drug, but this resistance is easily lost on growth in the drug-free medium.

2. A more stable resistance results from longer periods of growth in the presence of the drug, and there is a direct correlation between the stability of the resistance and the duration of this 'training'. As would be expected, there is considerable variation from drug to drug with a given organism, and even with the same drug under different circumstances, but within any given set of standardized experiments the correlation holds.

3. After thorough 'training' the resistance usually declines in a very gradual manner during a large number of generations in drug-free medium. In the majority of examples, however, the end result is a strain of bacteria practically as sensitive as the original one.

4. Resistance to very high concentrations of a drug is usually less stable than resistance to lower concentrations.

These general statements have been arrived at from the consideration of a large number of experiments with many antibacterial agents. All that can be given here is a representative collection which illustrates the essential points. The results are presented in the form of a summary in Table 10.

Before the findings are discussed in more detail some general comments on experimental techniques are necessary. A 'subculture' usually involved about eight cell generations, and when a fractional number is given it means that tests were made after only two or three generations of growth had taken place in the drug medium. The experiments were all carried out in liquid medium and the degree of resistance was determined by measurement of the lag or the mean generation time or both. When proflavine at 43 mg/l., Terramycin at 2 mg/l., or sulphanilamide at 218 mg/l. were used, the stated concentrations of drug were the first the cells had ever been exposed to. With streptomycin, for reasons already stated (p. 164), cells already given a low grade of resistance by

T A B L E 10

Effect of growth in drug-free medium on the resistance
of Aerobacter aerogenes *to drugs*

Drug	Concentration (mg/l.)	Number of sub-cultures in drug		Number of subsequent sub-cultures in drug-free medium	Extent of reversion	Ref.
Proflavine		*a*	0·3	1 to 2	Considerable	
	43	*b*	15	8	Partial	11
		c	15	20	Partial, less than *b*	
		a	105	63	None	
	195	*b*	105	70	Partial	
		c	105	87	Almost complete†	12
		a	203	21	None	
	214	*b*	203	29	Partial	
		c	203	34	Partial, greater than *b*	12
		d	203	75	Complete	
Streptomycin		*a*	3	15	Complete	
	1000	*b*	6	30	Partial	13
		c	6	77	Almost complete	
		d	19	82	None	
Thymol		*a*	1	5	Almost complete	
	140	*b*	4	5	Partial	14
		c	10	5	Less than *b*	
		d	27	5	Less than *c*	
Sulphanilamide	218		3	1	Almost complete	15
Chloramphenicol		*a*	79	18	None	
	37	*b*	79	55	Partial	12
		c	79	82	Complete	
		a	114	11	None	
		b	114	22	Partial	
	69	*c*	114	46	Partial, greater than *b*	12
		d	114	71	Complete‡	
Propamidine isethionate	267	*a*	102	24	None	
		b	102	43	Partial	12
		c	102	203	Partial, greater than *b*	
Terramycin		*a*	1	37	Partial	
	2	*b*	1	87	Same as *a*	16
		c	20	66	Same as *a*	

† Resistance largely lost to 100 and 50 mg/l. also.
‡ Resistance largely lost to 37 mg./l also.

selective growth at 1 mg/l. were introduced into 1000 mg/l., and in all
the other examples the cells were 'trained' by serial subculture in
gradually increasing concentrations of drug until the stated level had
been reached.

The extent of reversion in Table 10 is described in general terms such
as 'partial' or 'almost complete', but the progress of events was followed

in considerable detail as will be seen in Table 11 where the complete data for some of the examples are recorded.

In the cells of micro-organisms such as the yeast *Saccharomyces cerevisiae* and the fungus *Penicillium roquefortii*, which may possibly be regarded as more highly organized, resistance to drugs develops at least as rapidly as in bacteria but is lost much more readily.[17] At times,

TABLE 11

'Detraining' of drug-resistant Aerobacter aerogenes *by serial subculture in drug-free medium*

Drug	Concentration (mg/l.)	Number of subcultures in drug	Number of subsequent subcultures in drug-free medium	Behaviour in drug medium†	
				Lag (h)	m.g.t. (min)
Proflavine	214	203	7	2·3	44
			21	1·0	61/32
			29	9 to 24	—
			34	12 to 24	—
			50	No growth in 1 week	—
			62	36 to 48	—
			75, 89	No growth in 1 week	—
Chloramphenicol	69	114	11	1·7	39
			22	6·3	40
			34	8·4	67
			46	12 to 24	—
			58	26 to 31	—
			71	No growth in 1 week	—
Thymol	140	0	—	16·0	—
		1	5	15·0	—
		4	5	12·2	—
		10	5	3·3	—
		27	5	2·5	—

† At 'training' concentration.

instead of a return to the fully sensitive state there is a rapid drop in resistance to an equilibrium state intermediate between full resistance and sensitivity, and the cells may remain in this state for a very considerable time. An example of this behaviour is seen with *Saccharomyces cerevisiae* and dinitrophenol (Fig. 89).[18]

A sort of equilibrium state is also not uncommonly reached during the growth of drug-trained bacteria in drug-free medium, and indeed after *Aerobacter aerogenes* had received only one subculture in 2 mg/l.

of Terramycin it rapidly reverted to an intermediate state which persisted during more than 400 generations in the absence of the drug.[16]

7. Stability of adaptations to new substrates

Adaptations of bacteria to utilize new carbon sources (when these form the sole source of carbon) may on occasion be even more stable than adaptations to drugs, and an 'equilibrium state', which may

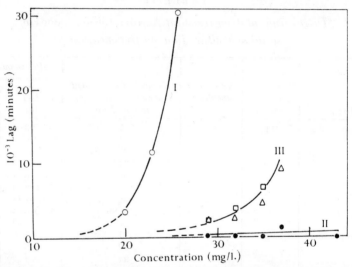

FIG. 89. Lag-concentration relations for untrained, trained, and partially reverted strains of *Saccharomyces cerevisiae* in presence of 2,4-dinitrophenol.

○ untrained; ● trained; △ trained strain after six subcultures in drug-free medium; □ trained strain after 112 subcultures in drug-free medium.

persist for a considerable time, is also often observed. Usually, however, this equilibrium state is not far enough removed from the 'fully trained' state to be easily and accurately evaluated by the usual tests in liquid medium. A convenient method of testing consists in plating a dilution of the culture containing a number of cells (which must not be too large or the test is invalidated, see p. 289) on agar media containing the substance under test as the only source of carbon. Under these conditions cells from a fully adapted organism will form colonies of a size which can be adopted as standard after about two days of incubation. The state of adaptation of a culture which has been grown in a 'detraining' medium can then be ascertained if a careful record is made of colony diameter against time of incubation. After a strain of *Escherichia coli mutabile* had passed through about 180 generations of growth in lactose medium, 16 generations in glucose medium were sufficient to induce a very slight degree of reversion, which remained practically unchanged for at least the next 600 generations.[19] A similar situation was found with *Aerobacter aerogenes* and the sugar D-arabinose. The behaviour is shown in Table 12, which illustrates the kind of results obtained with the quantitative technique just described.[20]

TABLE 12

Reversion in glucose–salts medium of Aerobacter aerogenes *'trained' in* D-arabinose *medium*

Number of subcultures in D-arabinose medium	Number of subsequent subcultures in glucose medium	Number of cells plated	Number of viable cells on D-arabinose	% of cells viable on D-arabinose which formed colonies of the standard size after incubation for			
				2 d	3 d	4 d	5 d
32	0	75	70	100	—	—	—
	1	200	200	100	—	—	—
	8	46	47	100	—	—	—
	21	53	58	57	85	100	—
	36	68	70	0	100	—	—
	117	218	232	0	100	—	—
	131	60	53	0	93	93	—
	170	58	41	0	90	90	—
	274	149	126	0	78	80	80
	419	90	70	0	0	0	0

On the other hand, if after only a few generations of growth in the D-arabinose medium glucose is added to a culture of *Aerobacter aerogenes* so that growth continues, rapid reversion during which no stably adapted cells can be detected takes place.[21] A strain which had received sixty-five subcultures in an acetate medium required sixty-two culturings in the glucose medium before the 'training' to acetate was lost, and during the course of this 'detraining' the following stages were observed: (1) fairly rapid growth in acetate: slow growth in glucose with considerable fluctuations in both rates; (2) considerable improvement in glucose growth rate without much impairment in acetate rate; (3) still further improvement in glucose accompanied by a decline in acetate; (4) optimum rate in glucose: acetate training lost.[12] The first stage was prolonged and is another example of the 'equilibrium' state. In the adaptation of *Aerobacter aerogenes* to glycerol the stages (1) adaptation complete but unstable, (2) adaptation complete and reversion delayed, and (3) adaptation complete and stable were passed through as serial subculture in glycerol medium was continued.[22] A strain of the yeast *Saccharomyces*

T

cerevisiae given one subculture in galactose (to which it required adaptation) showed delayed reversion during subsequent culture in the original (glucose) medium. If, however, fifteen culturings in galactose were given, the adaptation survived at least 100 subcultures in glucose.[23]

In stability tests it is common practice to return the adapted strain to the medium in which it had been fully conditioned before the adaptation. A variant of this method consists in introducing the strain to yet another medium which sometimes accelerates the process of 'detraining'. For example, the adaptation of *Escherichia coli mutabile* to lactose, which persists in the 'equilibrium' state during the course of many subcultures in a glucose medium, has been reversed by growth in media containing either acetate or succinate as the sole source of carbon,[24] and the adaptation of *Aerobacter aerogenes* to utilize lactose after being fully conditioned to a glucose medium is lost more readily in maltose than in the original glucose.[25] In a similar manner the loss of the proflavine resistance of *Aerobacter aerogenes* has been hastened by growth in the presence of *m*-cresol.[26] The number of stable adaptations which can be impressed in succession on a bacterial strain is dealt with elsewhere (p. 250).

8. Enzyme activities in adaptation and reversion

The adaptation of *Aerobacter aerogenes* to lactose has been much studied in relation to the activity of the enzyme β-galactosidase, responsible for the primary splitting of the lactose molecule into glucose and galactose. Here, too, the course of the adaptation follows the familiar pattern of passage through instability to relative stability. If the cells have been grown on lactose for a short time only and are then transferred to a glucose medium, the β-galactosidase, which has increased very much in amount, is rapidly diluted out until it reaches the level in the original unadapted organisms. But if growth in lactose has been continued long enough, then on return to glucose, although the β-galactosidase activity drops, it remains at a level much higher than that of unadapted organisms. Further, at this stage the cells regenerate the enzyme in lactose far more rapidly than they did originally, whereas in the earlier stages of the lactose adaptation a spell of growth in glucose puts everything, as it were, back to scratch.[27, 28]

Superficially the easiest explanation of adaptation and de-adaptation might seem to be the selection of a mutant type in the one process, and the reselection of the original type in the reversion. Stabilization by long-continued culture might be envisaged as the selection of a mutant strain so purified of the original type that there is none left to be reselected.

The arguments against the belief that all adaptive processes are selective in this sense have already been given, and, where they apply there is no point in attributing the loss of a direct adaptation to anything but the reversal of the process by which it occurred. It would, moreover, seem rather gratuitous to suppose that the cells which eventually grow after a long lag in presence of a drug contain any representatives of the sensitive strain at all: or indeed that any of the non-mutant strain should accompany the cells which eventually grow in D-arabinose after a 7-day lag.

The reversion could be attributed to spontaneous back-mutations, but the quantitative explanation of reversion rates on this basis leads to very serious difficulties with *Aerobacter* and D-arabinose.[29]

If one assumes a mixture of two mutant types, stable and unstable, in the lactose adaptation of *Aerobacter*, further complications arise since, to explain the overall pattern of adaptation and de-adaptation, first the one type and then the other must be assumed to possess the selective advantage.[28]

9. Recovery of bacterial strains damaged by ultra-violet light

Damaged cells show a changed chemical reaction pattern. When they recover during subculture in an appropriate medium the process has obvious analogies with the adaptations and de-adaptations already discussed.

When bacteria are exposed to ultraviolet light, or indeed to X-rays or the radiations of radioactive substances, they suffer varying degrees of damage, and after prolonged subjection to these actions a culture will become completely sterile. The survivors of irradiation may be grown on nutrient plates and allowed to form colonies and so give rise to substrains which may show properties differing from those of the unirradiated parent, and from one another. Almost invariably the change consists in the loss of ability to grow without the addition of specialized constituents to the medium. Commonly a strain which would initially grow with ammonium sulphate as sole source of nitrogen now needs to be provided with one or more specific amino-acids, which it appears to have lost the capacity to build up for itself. Growth, however, is perfectly satisfactory in the presence of the 'required' compound.

These radiation-damaged forms are generally referred to as mutants, and are supposed to have suffered, under the influence of the radiation, destruction of one or more genetic structures which normally provide the information guiding the synthesis of the molecules now required. This interpretation may in some instances be correct, but the matter is more complex than is always realized.

In the first place, one of the commonest methods of testing cultures is to record growth as present (+) or absent (−) after a fixed interval. This procedure, as has been pointed out, virtually imposes a qualitative distinction where what is in fact present is no more than a quantitative difference.[30] If one strain will not grow at all (or only with the utmost difficulty) in the absence of lysine while another grows easily without it, then it is reasonable to call the first a mutant. But the matter is usually not so clear cut as this, as the following observations show. Cultures of *Aerobacter aerogenes* were irradiated with ultraviolet light and sub-strains cultivated from the survivors. Generally speaking these sub-strains showed lags in simple media.

A histogram was then made of the numbers of irradiated strains whose lags in an ammonium sulphate medium without amino-acid addition exceeded by various amounts, ΔL, the lag of the unirradiated strain. Many showed large values of ΔL (reduced to zero by addition of aspara-gine and glutamic acid to the medium), but ΔL varied continuously over a wide range. The distribution corresponded more to a quantitative difference in the activity of certain chemical systems than to the absolute presence or absence of a genetic character. A simple + or − scoring system would have given a completely false picture. When the sub-strains which showed a considerable lag in the ammonium sulphate medium were subcultured several times in it their disability rather rapidly disappeared, and after a few growth cycles the lag was reduced nearly to zero again.[31]

The process of rapid repair of the damage caused by the light, repre-senting as it does the development of the enzyme systems necessary for the rapid utilization of the medium in which the cells find themselves, is strongly reminiscent of the other adaptive processes discussed in earlier chapters.

Mutants of many micro-organisms have been isolated by the action of radiations or chemical 'mutagens' such as proflavine, nitrogen mustard, or Fenton's reagent:[30] they seldom, if ever, show a gain of new characters but simply a loss or impairment of existing ones. They can seldom be isolated except from cultures in which the majority of the cells have been killed altogether. Mutants with specific 'requirements' have been much used for experiments on the crossing of strains and the recombination of genetic characters.[32] In this connexion it is very unfortunate that so little stress is normally laid on the relative nature of most of the requirements, and upon the extreme instability of most of the deficient strains, which, with rather rare exceptions, can easily be induced to dispense with the 'requirements' when called upon by need to do so.

The instability of the biochemical deficiencies caused by mutagenic agents, admitted but not stressed by most workers in the field, has often enough been attributed to spontaneous reverse mutations. In this connexion some further experiments made with *Aerobacter aerogenes* are relevant.[30] A large variety of substrains were prepared by different mutagenic techniques and examined in respect of (*a*) growth rates in a minimal medium, and (*b*) behaviour in fermentation reactions. Growth rates showed a continuous spectrum of values, sugar fermentation reactions were slowed or inhibited in varying degrees. Varying 'requirements' could have been stated according to the conditions of the test by which they were judged. Recovery on subculture was usual and when it occurred complete. When the growth rate had been impaired it improved in successive subcultures in the minimal medium.

Simple theoretical calculation shows that the pattern of recovery should be different according to whether the process depends upon spontaneous reverse mutation or upon an adaptive response of the whole reaction system. If reverse mutants are being selected, the growth rate should improve very rapidly over a comparatively short interval just when the faster-growing forms are gaining ascendancy over their slower competitors, and thereafter the higher growth rate should be permanently established. Actually the effect of 'retraining' declares itself slowly and gradually over very many subcultures, and the rate varies upwards and downwards from one subculture to the next according to the age of the inoculum. If the phenomenon depends upon the reversal of mutations, then those mutations must constitute a complex series of small independent changes rather than one major genetic modification. Gradualness, is, however, just what is predicted from the various types of adaptive reversion described.

Results on nutritional mutants of *Escherichia coli* show a pattern generally similar to that presented by *Aerobacter aerogenes*.[33] Nutritional requirements appear rather more readily than with *Aerobacter*, but there is still an almost continuous spectrum of behaviour both in respect of the requirement developed, and in respect of its persistence. Of seventy-eight changed strains of *Escherichia coli* two only proved to be stable.

All the rest recovered their power of optimum growth in the minimal medium after varying degrees of persuasion.

10. The phenomenon of 'enzyme repression'

As we have seen, the balance of enzymes in bacteria changes during adaptation to new substrates, an enzyme which is specifically required for dealing with a new medium constituent increasing in amount. When the need is no longer present the amount of enzyme decreases again. The way in which this kind of adjustment can occur is clearly indicated by the general kinetic equations of growth.

The literature contains many references to phenomena described respectively as 'end-product inhibition' and 'enzyme repression' [34, 35, 36] and it is now desirable to examine the relation of these to the phenomena discussed in the present and the previous chapters.

In 'end product inhibition' the products of an enzyme action block the functioning of this same enzyme. In 'enzyme repression' one or other of the products inhibits not the specific activity of this enzyme but its actual synthesis in the cell. The first bears no special relation to adaptive or de-adaptive phenomena, but the second does.

As an example of end-product inhibition we may take the action of cytidilic acid in inhibiting the condensation of aspartate and carbamyl phosphate in a mutant of *Escherichia coli*. The inhibitor is the final product of an enzyme pathway initiated by the inhibited enzyme. The inhibition is competitive.[37] Analogies to end-product inhibition, as was pointed out earlier, are quite common in inorganic chemistry. The oxidation of sulphur dioxide on a platinum catalyst is retarded by the sulphur trioxide formed which competes with the reacting substances for adsorptive sites on the metal. The decomposition of ammonia on certain catalysts is similarly retarded by the hydrogen produced, and so is that of nitrous oxide on platinum by the oxygen formed.[38]

The explanation in kinetic terms is, in its general principle, quite simple. The reaction proceeds, as always, by way of a transition state in which the molecules have received enough thermal energy (activation energy) to loosen existing structures and so open the way for the formation of new ones. If there is an affinity between any part of the new structure and the solid surface, the resulting interaction can contribute to the lowering of the activation energy and so facilitate the reaction. In simple terms the pull of the platinum on the oxygen atom of the nitrous oxide contributes a good deal to the reaction

$$N_2O(Pt) \rightarrow N_2 + O(Pt).$$

But this very circumstance means that the product in question will tend to remain adsorbed on the catalyst rather than be released and so it will compete for the places on the surface which might have been occupied by more of the initial reactant. In this way some degree of end-product inhibition should be quite common.

There is, however, the rather special circumstance in the phenomenon of enzyme inhibition that the enzyme acted upon may be not the one which directly causes the formation of the inhibitory product, but an earlier member of the same sequence. The principle, however, is probably the same. Synthetic pathways involve small steps at a time, and, therefore, the substrates S_1, S_2, S_3,... of successive enzymes may have considerable parts of their structure in common. The enzyme has an affinity for its own substrate, S_1, and possesses certain atomic spacings which conform to those of this substrate. Thus on occasion it will have spacings which are not unlikely also to conform to those of some fairly closely similar substrate later in the same sequence.

In any event inhibition by products formed in an enzyme sequence will naturally obtrude itself and be observed, while inhibition by other substances would only be found in very special experiments. The inhibition in some examples may, therefore, be not quite so specific as it appears, and may merely be more easily brought to notice.

'Repression' is a phenomenon of much deeper significance. The formation, as distinct from the action, of β-galactosidase, the enzyme which brings about the hydrolysis of galactosides, is cut down by galactose. Its synthesis is also repressed by the presence of glucose, which can repress that of other enzymes also. Enzymes concerned in arginine synthesis, such as acetyl-ornithinase, are less readily formed in presence of arginine itself. Sometimes several enzymes of a single pathway are repressed at the same time by the same substance, an effect which has been called 'coordinate repression'.[35] Examples are enzymes of the histidine biosynthesis in *Salmonella typhimurium* and those of arginine biosynthesis in *Escherichia coli*.

All these phenomena can probably be summed up in the statement that any substance which by-passes the need for an enzyme tends to repress its formation. Magasanik,[39] discussing the repression of various enzymes by glucose, points out that these all govern the formation of products which the cell could obtain more easily by other reactions direct from glucose itself. McFall and Mandelstam[40] made the following statement, which is very significant, about the repression of β-galacto-sidase: 'the glucose effect is not specific, and any compound that the cells can use as a source of carbon and energy can repress the formation of β-galactosidase. . . . The degree of repression produced by a compound is directly correlated with its effectiveness as a growth substrate.' What these observations very strongly suggest is that the action of the 'repressor' consists less in a specific inhibition than in an effective competition, which, as it were, diverts traffic from the route which involves the use of the repressed enzyme. This is exactly what is predicted by the equations developed in Chapter V.

An explanation of this kind is borne out by numerous other observations. Inorganic phosphate is reported to repress the formation of alkaline phosphatase in *Escherichia coli*, and if the cells are supplied with a mixture of β-glycerophosphate, which requires a phosphatase for its utilization, and inorganic phosphate, which does not, they grow rapidly until they have exhausted the latter, and then show a lag after which a slower growth accompanied by the consumption of the organic phosphate occurs.[41]

Repression is closely related to the phenomenon of diphasic growth (p. 257) where the competitive by-passing of the formation of the less efficient enzyme seems clear.

In general, where growth rates have been measured it appears that the release of a repression is normally followed, at least temporarily, by a slower rate of growth than was possible while the repressor itself was being metabolized.[42, 43]

Phenomena essentially similar in kind are observed in nitrogen metabolism. *Aerobacter aerogenes* can utilize either ammonium sulphate or an inorganic nitrate as a source of its nitrogen, the former more readily than the latter. When an ammonium salt is added to the medium, it will be recalled, nitrate reduction is almost completely stopped, and only begins again, after a period of recovery, when the ammonia has all been used up.[44]

Our own view, it had better be stated clearly, is that all the phenomena which have been described are essentially manifestations, though possibly in a more complex form, of the behaviour shown by the model discussed in Chapter V. The synthesis of enzymes is integrated by the system of closed cycle dependences into the working of the cell: if a given enzyme has no role to play in the prevailing pattern, it will not be formed. If it is present initially in considerable amount it will consequently be diluted out.

The question may arise why certain enzymes are not eliminated altogether, for example, β-galactosidase in cells long grown without any need to hydrolyse lactose for their carbon. But it by no means follows that an enzyme not fulfilling its more obvious role may not nevertheless serve a subsidiary purpose which is always important enough to demand a residual low level of it. This may be illustrated by an example. Micro-organisms contain, in cell walls and elsewhere, a great variety of polysaccharides which they must normally, indeed probably always, synthesize for themselves from monosaccharides. The enzymes which synthesize them will be those which would cause hydrolytic splitting of a corresponding linkage in a disaccharide, since all enzyme actions are in principle reversible. Thus β-galactosidase, even in cells not dependent on lactose for carbon, might be needed in small amounts for incorporating a certain amount of galactose into a polysaccharide ultimately destined for a place in the cell wall. While the enzyme is playing this relatively minor role it remains in small proportion: when it is needed to metabolize major initial sources of carbon it increases in amount in accordance with the general principle.

An alternative view of the whole complex of phenomena related to repression has been put forward. It is superficially at least very different from that outlined above. Any metabolic route, it is said with justice, is under the control of a group of related genes (a statement in no way ignored in the equations of Chapter V). This complex of genes is thought of as being in some way susceptible to a process of being switched on and off. A repressor substance may be produced under the influence of other genes in the cell and this is supposed to switch off or inhibit by blocking it one of the genes controlling a possible metabolic route. An inducer which stimulates the formation of a given enzyme acts by antagonizing a repressor already blocking the use of information carried in a gene. Thus the metabolic route is opened.

This view seems on the face of it to raise again a question which is difficult to answer, why namely there should be in the cell repressed information waiting for the arrival of an inducer which the cell might indeed never have met before in the course of evolution. It would appear much simpler to attribute to the inducer a positive stimulating action rather than the negative one of stopping a repression for which no obvious reason exists. The argument in favour of this view of repression and 'de-repression' is, however, interesting and based upon important observations on the crossing of bacterial strains (p. 29). We will consider in particular the effects of crossing on the activity of β-galacto-sidase. In some coliform cells this enzyme is formed spontaneously whatever the conditions of growth (plus type). In other types of cell it does not develop except under the influence of an inducer (minus type). Now suppose the plus type has a gene X which the minus type lacks. If either of two parent cells can contribute X, then, when they unite, the recombinant should form the enzyme without the action of the inducer. This result, however, was not found. It appeared, on the contrary, that if either of the parents required an inducer then the recombinant required one too. Thus what can come indifferently from either parent is not the gene X, representing a capacity, but the *need* for an inducer. Hence the idea of a repressor as an active, positive agent.[36, 45]

The grave doubt, however, which may be felt about this argument, ingenious as it may be, is that it assumes the combination of the cells to occur virtually without any serious degree of disorganization. When information from one cell has been rapidly injected into another there must be a considerable upheaval and the reaction networks must be greatly changed. Disorganization itself, which is almost inseparable from the recombination process may be regarded as much as a positive factor as the presence of a repressor gene. After the genetic changes associated with recombination there is, in general, evidence for some considerable measure of such disorganization. New characters may only reveal themselves fully after an interval of growth sometimes referred to as 'phenotypic delay',[46] that is to say, a lag between the introduction of a genetic element and its manifestation in the individual or phenotype. Yeasts provide an interesting example. In some circumstances, as explained, they form asci containing four spores which may be dissected by a micromanipulation technique and used to initiate four derivative strains. Sometimes there are clear-cut Mendelian phenomena, two of the strains being positive in some character and the other two negative. But even the positive strains only reveal the character in question to its full extent after a further period of growth and adaptation during which, we may suppose, the disorganization of genetic reshuffling is rectified and the cell integration fully established.[47]

Quite apart from this general consideration, it is doubtful whether the statistical evidence about the occurrence of positive and negative strains in the above sense is abundant enough to establish the repressor gene as a positive entity, even if the characterization of positive and negative were itself less arbitrary than it so frequently is.

REFERENCES

1. W. Ritchie Russell, *Brain, Memory, Learning*, Clarendon Press, Oxford (1959).
2. H. R. Ing, private communication.
3. J. Needham, quoted by R. A. Peters (reference 4).
4. R. A. Peters, *Nature, Lond.* **177**, 426 (1956).
5. L. Monné, *Adv. Enzymol.* **8**, 1 (1948).
6. F. Dickens, in Ciba Foundation Symposium on *Regulation of Cell Metabolism*, edited by G. E. W. Wolstenholme and Cecilia M. O'Connor, p. 353, Churchill, London (1959).
7. N. M. Sissakian, in Rep. Int. Symp. Moscow, *The Origin of Life on the Earth*, p. 235, Acad. Sci. U.S.S.R., Moscow (1957).
8. P. Weiss, 'Differential growth' in *The Chemistry and Physiology of Growth*, edited by A. K. Parpart, p. 135, Princeton Univ. Press, Princeton, N.J. (1949).
9. See Chapter I, section 15, and *Studies of Macromolecular Biosynthesis*, edited by R. B. Roberts, Carnegie Inst. Wash. Publ. 624, Washington, D.C. (1964).
10. See G. N. Cohen and J. Monod, *Bact. Rev.* **21**, 169 (1957); R. J. Britten, *Symp. Soc. Gen. Microbiol.* **15**, 57 (1965).
11. J. M. G. Pryce and C. N. Hinshelwood, *Trans. Faraday Soc.* **43**, 752 (1947).
12. A. C. R. Dean and Sir Cyril Hinshelwood, *Proc. R. Soc.* B **142**, 45 (1954).
13. W. T. Drabble and Sir Cyril Hinshelwood, *Proc. R. Soc.* B **154**, 449 (1961).
14. L. S. Phillips and Sir Cyril Hinshelwood, *J. chem. Soc.* p. 3679 (1953).
15. D. S. Davies and C. N. Hinshelwood, *Trans. Faraday Soc.* **39**, 431 (1943).
16. A. C. R. Dean and B. L. Giordan, *Proc. R. Soc.* B **161**, 571 (1964).
17. *Saccharomyces cerevisiae*—D. G. Wild and Sir Cyril Hinshelwood, *Proc. R. Soc.* B **142**, 427 (1954); B **144**, 287 (1955); B **145**, 14, 24, 32 (1956). *Penicillium roquefortii*—G. W. Bartlett, ibid. B **150**, 120 (1959).
18. D. G. Wild and Sir Cyril Hinshelwood, *Proc. R. Soc.* B **144**, 287 (1955).
19. A. C. R. Dean and Sir Cyril Hinshelwood, *Proc. R. Soc.* B **142**, 225 (1954).
20. J. R. Cross and Sir Cyril Hinshelwood, *Proc. R. Soc.* B **145**, 516 (1956).
21. A. C. Baskett and Sir Cyril Hinshelwood, *Proc. R. Soc.* B **139**, 58 (1951).
22. E. G. Cooke and C. N. Hinshelwood, *Trans. Faraday Soc.* **43**, 733 (1947).
23. A. A. Eddy and Sir Cyril Hinshelwood, *Proc. R. Soc.* B **142**, 32 (1954).
24. A. C. R. Dean, unpublished observations.
25. J. R. Postgate and C. N. Hinshelwood, *Trans. Faraday Soc.* **42**, 45 (1946).
26. D. S. Davies, C. N. Hinshelwood, and J. M. G. Pryce, *Trans. Faraday Soc.* **41**, 778 (1945).
27. N. Richards and Sir Cyril Hinshelwood, *Proc. R. Soc.* B **154**, 463 (1961).
28. N. Richards and Sir Cyril Hinshelwood, *Proc. R. Soc.* B **156**, 20 (1962).
29. S. Jackson and Sir Cyril Hinshelwood, *Proc. R. Soc.* B **136**, 562 (1949); Sir Cyril Hinshelwood and S. Jackson, *Proc. R. Soc.* B **137**, 88 (1950).
30. See also A. C. R. Dean and Sir Cyril Hinshelwood, *J. chem. Soc.* pp. 1157, 1159, 1169, 1173 (1951).
31. A. R. Peacocke and C. N. Hinshelwood, *Proc. R. Soc.* B **135**, 454 (1948).
32. See for details F. Jacob and E. L. Wollman, *Sexuality and the Genetics of Bacteria*, Academic Press, New York (1961).
33. A. C. R. Dean, *J. chem. Soc.* pp. 2817, 2823 (1952); A. C. R. Dean and Sir Cyril Hinshelwood, *J. chem. Soc.* p. 2826 (1952).

34. See general discussion and contributions by B. Magasanik, Adèle K. Magasanik and F. C. Neidhardt and by A. B. Pardee in Ciba Foundation Symp. on *Regulation of Cell Metabolism*, edited by G. E. W. Wolstenholme and Cecilia M. O'Connor, Churchill, London (1959).
35. H. J. Vogel in *Control Mechanisms in Enzyme Synthesis*, edited by D. M. Bonner, p. 23, Ronald Press Co., New York (1961).
36. J. Monod, *Angew. Chem.* **71**, 685 (1959).
37. See A. B. Pardee in reference 34 and R. A. Yates and A. B. Pardee, *J. biol. Chem.* **221**, 757 (1956).
38. G. M. Schwab, H. Noller, and J. Block, *Handbuch der Katalyse*, Springer-Verlag, Wien (1957).
39. B. Magasanik, *Cold Spring Harbor Symp. quant. Biol.* **26**, 249 (1961).
40. Elizabeth McFall and J. Mandelstam, *Biochem. J.* **89**, 391 (1963).
41. Annamaria Torriani, *Biochim. Biophys. Acta* **38**, 460 (1960).
42. H. J. Vogel, *Cold Spring Harbor Symp. quant. Biol.* **26**, 163 (1961).
43. B. N. Ames and Barbara Garry, *Proc. natn. Acad. Sci. U.S.A.* **45**, 1453 (1959).
44. P. R. Lewis and C. N. Hinshelwood, *J. chem. Soc.* p. 833 (1948); Sir Cyril Hinshelwood, *Discovery*, **23/10**, 18 (1962).
45. F. Jacob and J. Monod, *Cold Spring Harbor Symp. quant. Biol.* **26**, 193, 389 (1961); J. Monod, J. P. Changeux, and F. Jacob, *J. molec. Biol.* **6**, 306 (1963); see also S. Brenner, *Br. med. Bull.* **21**, 244 (1965).
46. H. B. Newcombe, *Genetics*, **33**, 447 (1948); **38**, 134 (1953).
47. B. C. Kilkenny and Sir Cyril Hinshelwood, *Proc. R. Soc.* B **139**, 73 (1951); B **140**, 352 (1952).

XI

SOME STATISTICAL CONSIDERATIONS ABOUT THE TIME TAKEN FOR THE DEVELOPMENT OF COLONIES[1,2,3]

1. Introduction

WHEN a sufficiently dilute suspension of bacteria is spread over the surface of a nutrient agar plate each individual cell eventually forms a colony provided that the conditions of growth are favourable and none of the cells die before they have had time to begin multiplying. In these conditions the final number of colonies measures the number of viable cells, unless groups of cells adhere together in the original suspension, when, of course, only one colony forms from the whole group. In many examples, and in particular with *Aerobacter aerogenes* and with *Escherichia coli*, suitably diluted suspensions consist of well-separated cells and so long as the plate is not too heavily inoculated each colony does correspond to a single cell of the initial diluted culture.

When the cells do not die at an appreciable rate and when they are all capable of using the agar medium the 'viable count' inferred from the colony number equals the total count as determined under the microscope in a counting chamber. When, however, some of the cells die before they have begun to form a colony or when some are inherently incapable of utilizing the agar medium as prepared for the experiment, the fraction, α_∞, of the total number which ever form colonies at all is less than unity.

Colonies take time to form and to grow to an assigned size, and if α_t is the fraction of the plated cells which have formed colonies by time t, then α_t/α_∞ is a quantity which can yield very important information.

In Chapter VI the α_t/α_∞ relations for cultures spread on agar plates containing drugs were referred to. These relations will now be examined from a statistical point of view in more detail. The behaviour on the first exposure of *Escherichia coli mutabile* to lactose and of *Aerobacter aerogenes* to D-arabinose as the sole source of carbon will be considered in a similar way.

2. The development of colonies on agar plates containing drugs[1]

In the presence of many drugs the death-rate of unadapted cells is high and in an adaptive process like that represented in Fig. 53

(Chapter VI) only those cells favoured by chance with an exceptionally long survival time form colonies at all. The nature of survival-time curves (see Chapter XV) shows that usually the incidence of death is not far from random. In a dying culture any adaptation depends on the interplay of two statistical factors. On the one hand, there will be a wide distribution of actual survival times and, on the other, a statistical scatter of the lags preceding the growth of those cells which survive at all.

The following theoretical treatment[1] is based on equations which are only approximately true in the quantitative sense. Nevertheless, it leads to a result that will almost certainly remain valid even if the detailed forms of the statistical laws are considerably varied.

Suppose the most probable delay before a cell begins to develop into a colony be L. If the actual delay is t, then this represents a deviation of θ, and

$$\theta = t - L.$$

As a rough approximation we take the deviations to be Gaussian, so that the probability of a deviation between θ and $\theta + d\theta$ is

$$\frac{h}{\sqrt{\pi}} e^{-h^2\theta^2} \, d\theta$$

or if $x = h\theta = h(t-L)$, the probability is

$$\frac{1}{\sqrt{\pi}} e^{-x^2} \, dx.$$

We shall be concerned chiefly with large negative values of x, that is, exceptionally quickly developing cells.

The cells are dying off according to a law which will be taken as roughly exponential (Chapter XV) so that n_t, the number of survivors at time t, conforms to the equation

$$dn_t/dt = -\lambda n_t + f(n_t, t),$$

where λ is the death-rate constant, and $f(n_t, t)$ is the rate at which some cells succeed in dividing and thus escaping the lethal process. In the conditions considered very few do this, so that $f(n_t, t)$ is a small fraction of λn_t. Thus the fraction surviving at time t is nearly $e^{-\lambda t}$.

Of this, the number which make an early start and form colonies in the interval between t and $t+dt$ is a fraction $\dfrac{1}{\sqrt{\pi}} e^{-x^2} \, dx$, where dx is the deviation corresponding to dt. The fraction of the original population which starts to form colonies between t and $t+dt$ is then

$$e^{-\lambda t} \frac{1}{\sqrt{\pi}} e^{-x^2} \, dx = \frac{1}{\sqrt{\pi}} e^{-\lambda(L + x/h)} e^{-x^2} \, dx$$

since $x = -h(L-t)$. The total number which do this from time 0 to time t is

$$\frac{1}{\sqrt{\pi}} \int_{-hL}^{-h(L-t)} e^{-\lambda(L+x/h)} e^{-x^2}\, dx = \frac{e^{-\lambda L}}{\sqrt{\pi}} \int_{-hL}^{-h(L-t)} e^{-(x+\lambda/2h)^2} e^{\lambda^2/4h^2}\, dx,$$

where $-h(L-t)$ and $-hL$ are the limits of x corresponding to $t = t$ and $t = 0$ respectively.

If $y = x+\lambda/2h$ the last integral becomes, with the new limits of y corresponding to the old limits of x,

$$P = \frac{e^{-\lambda t} e^{+\lambda^2/4h^2}}{\sqrt{\pi}} \int_{-hL+\lambda/2h}^{-h(L-t)+\lambda/2h} e^{-y^2}\, dy$$

$$= \frac{e^{-\lambda L} e^{\lambda^2/4h^2}}{\sqrt{\pi}} \left\{ \int_{0}^{hL-\lambda/2h} e^{-y^2}\, dy - \int_{0}^{h(L-t)-\lambda/2h} e^{-y^2}\, dy \right\}$$

$$= \tfrac{1}{2} e^{-\lambda L} e^{+\lambda^2/4h^2} \{ \mathrm{erf}(hL-\lambda/2h) - \mathrm{erf}(hL-\lambda/2h-ht) \}. \tag{1}$$

When $\lambda = 0$ this becomes

$$P = \tfrac{1}{2}\{ \mathrm{erf}(hL) - \mathrm{erf}(hL-ht) \}. \tag{2}$$

When $t > L$ the limits are interchanged and we have

$$P = \tfrac{1}{2}\{ \mathrm{erf}(hL) + \mathrm{erf}(ht-hL) \} \tag{2'}$$

and correspondingly for (1).

As t increases (2′) reaches a limit of unity. The final limit of (1) is

$$e^{-\lambda L} e^{+\lambda^2/4h^2} = \alpha_\infty,$$

the fraction of the cells which eventually form colonies.

α_t, the fraction which has formed colonies at time t, is not directly given by the above formulae, since in these t is the time at which the colony *begins* to form and not that at which it attains a standard size. Nevertheless, the difference between the two times may be taken as a more or less standard value, and the equations will apply to the observed times if the origin of the experimental curves is shifted. In any case t of the equations will give a generally correct model for the behaviour of t_{obs}.

The most interesting consequence of these equations is that the existence of a finite death-rate shortens the value of the most probable delay for those cells which actually do grow to colonies. When $\lambda = 0$, equation (2) gives, as t increases, a limiting value of unity, which corresponds to $\alpha_\infty = 1$. When λ is not zero, α_∞ is $e^{-\lambda L} e^{\lambda^2/4h^2}$, which is less than unity and may be very small indeed. But α_t/α_∞, which is given by the quantity in the curly brackets, rises from 0 to 1 as before, and the most probable value of the delay, that is, the time for α_t/α_∞ to reach the value 0·5, is now no longer L but $L-\lambda/2h^2$, as is clear by inspection.

The magnitude of h for a trained culture (of the kind with which our examples will deal) or for one growing in the absence of drug may be

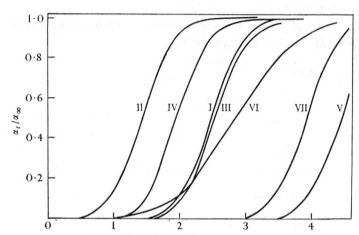

FIG. 90. Theoretical curves of α_t/α_∞ as a function of time.

Curve	h	L	λ	α_∞
I	1·8	2·5	0	1
II	1·8	2·5	7	10^{-6}
III	1·8	3·5	7	10^{-9}
IV	1·8	2·5	3·5	$10^{-3\cdot4}$
V	1·8	5	3·5	$10^{-7\cdot5}$
VI	0·9	5	3·5	10^{-6}
VII	1·8	5	7	$10^{-13\cdot6}$

taken as about 1·8 (with the time unit in days), which corresponds to a spread of about one day between $\alpha_t/\alpha_\infty = 0\cdot1$ and $\alpha_t/\alpha_\infty = 0\cdot9$, as shown in curve I of Fig. 90.

With proflavine at a concentration of 253 mg/l., a culture would be sterilized in a few days, so that λ is in the range 5 to 10 day^{-1}. Thus the reduction in the apparently most probable lag is of the order $7/(2\times1\cdot8^2)$ if h remains unchanged, or about one day.

With $\lambda = 7$ day^{-1}, $L = 2\cdot5$ days, and $h = 1\cdot8$, the value of α_∞ is about 10^{-6}, which is comparable with that observed in many experiments.

In such an experiment L might have been increased by the presence of a drug to about a day more than the normal value in the absence of the drug, and yet $L-\lambda/2h^2$, which gives the apparent value for the survivors, would be nearly the same as that observed with a resistant culture in a drug-free medium. This result is illustrated by a comparison in Fig. 90 of curves I, II, and III.

The value of h itself, however, will be different for trained and untrained cultures. The more scattered the distribution of lags, the smaller the value of h. Curves V and VI in Fig. 90 show the effect of a change in h from 1·8 to 0·9. The difference in the forms of curve I, or any of the curves with $h = 1·8$, and VI ($\lambda = 3·5$, $L = 5$, $h = 0·9$) are in fact comparable with the differences between the α_t/α_∞ against time curves for trained and untrained strains shown in Figs. 53 and 54 and in numerous other examples.[1] It is thus reasonable to assume that h is smaller for the untrained strains and when this is so the effect previously described is much enhanced. A comparison of curve VI with curve I of Fig. 90 shows how a true value of L of 5 days in an untrained strain with $\lambda = 3·5$ and $h = 0·9$ may be replaced by an apparent value of not much more than half of this.

In non-mathematical terms these conclusions can be expressed in the following manner. All properties of populations, particularly physiological properties which vary in a very complex manner during the growth cycle of an individual cell, show a statistical fluctuation about a most probable value. Large deviations from this value are rare and very large ones very rare indeed, but up to a point have an assignable probability. In a plate test where all the cells are expected to grow the inoculum must be restricted to about 10^2 cells (see Chapter VIII, section 5), and then the chances of including anything very far from the average of the population are very small. On a drug plate, however, to obtain a comparable number of survivors one must inoculate something like a million times as many cells of an unadapted culture as would be necessary in the corresponding experiment with a fully adapted strain (or in an experiment without drug). The few of these unadapted cells which survive and form colonies are therefore the extreme tail of a very large population, and since their highly deviant behaviour is being compared with that of an average of the adapted population they might, on occasion, appear to develop into colonies more rapidly than the adapted cells. For this reason in the experiments in which unadapted cells are plated on drug agar some of the survivors may even form colonies more quickly than when fully adapted cells are used. Although this behaviour might suggest the presence of resistant mutants in the sensitive population it is only what is to be expected on purely statistical grounds.

For a proper comparison an inoculum of 10^2 cells of the adapted

U

culture should be plated on 10^4 drug plates and the fastest developing few compared with the survivors obtained from 10^6 sensitive cells. Clearly this is impracticable but it emphasizes the caution required in the interpretation of results.

Another example to which this statistical approach has been applied is that of *Aerobacter aerogenes* and chloramphenicol. The lag-concentration relations have been given earlier (Chapter VII, Fig. 58) and in the

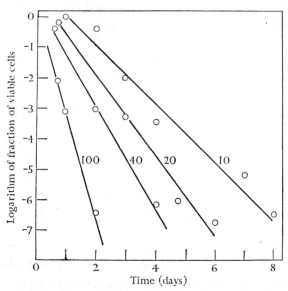

FIG. 91. Death-rate as a function of chloramphenicol concentration.
Numbers on curves indicate the drug concentration in mg/l.

presence of this drug the death-rate is high. The results of some death-rate determinations carried out in the salts–glucose medium, from which a nitrogen source has been left out to prevent growth, are given in Fig. 91. It is apparent that the higher the concentration of drug the more rapid the death.

When α_t/α_∞ is plotted against t for a series of concentrations of chloramphenicol sigmoid curves are obtained (Fig. 92). Here again we see the paradoxical appearance of more rapid development at higher drug concentrations. The dotted lines are calculated from equation (2), with $L' = L - \lambda/2h^2$, so that

$$\frac{\alpha_t}{\alpha_\infty} = P = \tfrac{1}{2}\{\mathrm{erf}(hL') - \mathrm{erf}(hL' - ht)\}, \qquad (3)$$

and the values of h and L' given in Table 13.

L' is the median value of the delay for those colonies which are *actually formed*. L' and h can be calculated from the curves of α_t/α_∞ (Fig. 92) and L is the value of L' when $\alpha_t/\alpha_\infty = 1$. From the values of α_∞ those of λ can be obtained for different concentrations of drug on the plates.

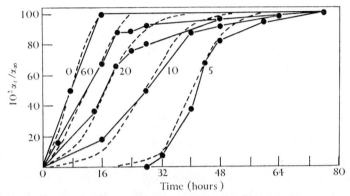

FIG. 92. Gaussian curves for colony development times (untrained strain). Numbers on curves denote drug concentration in mg/l.

TABLE 13

Experimental values of L', h and α_∞ and the calculated values of λ and L for an untrained organism

Chloramphenicol concentration (mg/l.)	L' (h)	α_∞	h	λ (h^{-1})	L (h)
0	8	1	0·16	0	8
5	41	$1\cdot27 \times 10^{-1}$	0·08	0·045	45
10	28	$3\cdot95 \times 10^{-5}$	0·068	0·24	54
20	17	$8\cdot9 \times 10^{-6}$	0·068	0·34	54
40	18	$3\cdot6 \times 10^{-6}$	0·096	0·43	46
50	16	$2\cdot8 \times 10^{-6}$	0·096	0·44	41
60	12	$1\cdot84 \times 10^{-6}$	0·096	0·52	38

Here again it should be noted that when α_∞ is small large numbers of cells must be inoculated on to the drug plates to obtain any survivors at all, and this is precisely what is done in the isolation of mutants. As mentioned previously, however, these apparent mutants may represent no more than rapidly growing cells corresponding to the tail end of a more or less normal distribution of times. At high drug levels the cells in the inoculum which, in more favourable conditions, would have shown more nearly the median time for colony development die before they can develop. The order in which the curves are spaced in Fig. 92 may appear to be just the reverse of what would be expected. This, however, is another example of what can happen when the average of one population is compared with the tail of another. As the drug concentration is increased α_∞ falls and more and more cells must be plated to obtain a countable number of colonies on the drug plates, and as this continues the observed behaviour becomes progressively less representative of that expected from the population as a whole. But α_t is always expressed as a fraction of α_∞ and this scaling procedure may easily make the fastest development appear to occur at the highest drug concentration.

3. The adaptation of bacteria to new sources of carbon

(a) Times required for the formation of colonies of standard size

Statistical considerations can similarly be applied to the utilization of a new substrate as a sole source of carbon. After the cells have been spread on an agar plate containing the substance under test there is a lag and then a period of growth until the colonies reach the diameter chosen as the standard. The sum of the lag plus the growth time will have a series of values $L_1, L_2,..., L_j,...$ for the various cells. Let $\alpha_t/\alpha_\infty = P$, where α_t and α_∞ have the usual meaning. If the values $L_1, L_2,...$ are distributed about a most probable value L in a more or less Gaussian manner then the probability of a value L_j lying between t and $t+dt$ is $\dfrac{h}{\sqrt{\pi}} e^{-h^2(L-t)^2}$ (provided that L is great enough for this expression to be negligibly small when $t = 0$). The number of colonies which reach the standard size between t and $t+dt$ is equal to the number of cells for which the value of L_j lies in this range. The value of P at time t will therefore be given by

$$P = \frac{h}{\sqrt{\pi}} \int_0^t e^{-h^2(L-t)^2} \, dt,$$

whence $\qquad\qquad P = \tfrac{1}{2}\{\mathrm{erf}(hL) - \mathrm{erf}(hL - ht)\} \qquad\qquad (4)$

when $t < L$ or $\qquad\quad P = \tfrac{1}{2}\{\mathrm{erf}(hL) + \mathrm{erf}(ht - hL)\} \qquad\qquad (4')$

when $t > L$.

These formulae, which are identical with formulae (2) and (2') derived earlier, prove reasonably satisfactory for *Aerobacter aerogenes* on nutrient agar or on agar containing glucose or pyruvate as carbon source. They also hold for *Escherichia coli* on lactose agar. Some examples are given in Fig. 93 where the percentages of the colonies which have reached a diameter of 1·0 mm are plotted against time. In Table 14 some typical numerical values (determined by trial fitting of curves) are summarized. The closeness with which the individual colonies conform to the most probable value of L is indicated by the

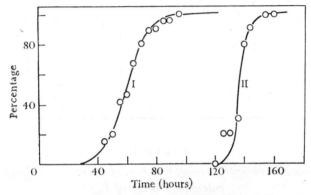

Fig. 93. Numbers of colonies formed at different times.
Curve I. *Aerobacter aerogenes* on nutrient agar at 25° C.
Curve II. *Escherichia coli mutabile* (lac⁻) on lactose-agar at 37° C.

TABLE 14
Distribution of growth times

Bacteria	Medium	Temp. (°C)	L	h
Aerobacter aerogenes	Nutrient agar	25	61	0·059
	Glucose agar	25	54	0·23
	Pyruvate agar	25	47	0·12
Escherichia coli mutabile (lac⁻)	Lactose agar	37	137	0·15

value of h, which varies from trial to trial but does not depend on the size criterion adopted (Table 15).

In the experiments described so far the number of cells inoculated on the plates was small (< 100) so that all would form large colonies. If the number plated is very large only the few colonies which have made an early start succeed in attaining the standard size, the majority being still small when exhaustion of the nutrient, or some other cause, stops growth. This is clearly seen in the behaviour of *Escherichia coli mutabile* on lactose agar at 37° C (Table 16).

The question now arises as to how far the small proportion of early developing colonies in the experiments with the larger inocula can be

TABLE 15

Values of h with different size criteria

Colonies	Standard size adopted as criterion (*mm*)	L	h
Aerobacter aerogenes on nutrient agar at 25° C	1	61	0·06
	0·75	48	0·08
	0·5	34·5	0·14
Aerobacter aerogenes on glucose agar at 25° C	1	54	0·24
	0·75	47	0·24
	0·5	40·5	0·20
Escherichia coli mutabile (lac⁻) on lactose agar at 37° C	1	137	0·15
	0·75	93·5	0·15
	0·5	62·5	0·10

TABLE 16

Inoculation with varying numbers of cells: observed and calculated values of L_{50}

Number of cells plated	Final number of colonies which reached 1·0 mm diameter n_∞	Time (L_{50}) for 50% of the number in the previous column to reach 1·0 mm (*hours*)	L_{50} (*calc.*)
25	25	187	187
360	77	152	157
7200	55	121	124
$1·4 \times 10^5$	56	125	107

With higher inocula there were also uncountable numbers of smaller colonies.

accounted for on the basis of the Gaussian distribution observed when the inoculum is small and all the cells plated can form colonies of the standard size. An approximate estimate can be obtained by using the relation given above,

$$P = \frac{h}{\sqrt{\pi}} \int_0^t e^{-h^2(L-t)^2} \, dt.$$

Let $h(L-t) = y$, then

$$P = -\frac{1}{\sqrt{\pi}} \int_{+hL}^{y} e^{-y^2} \, dy = \frac{1}{\sqrt{\pi}} \int_y^{hL} e^{-y^2} \, dy.$$

We are now concerned with the early developing colonies corresponding to large deviations of t from L ($t \ll L$), and since the value of the integral from the limit $\pm hL$ is numerically almost identical with that from $\pm\infty$,

$$P = \frac{1}{\sqrt{\pi}} \int_{y}^{hL} e^{-v^2}\,dy = \frac{1}{\sqrt{\pi}} \int_{y}^{\infty} e^{-v^2}\,dy.$$

Moreover, when y is large

$$\int_{y}^{\infty} e^{-v^2}\,dy \sim \frac{e^{-v^2}}{2y};$$

hence

$$P = \frac{e^{-h^2(L-t)^2}}{2\sqrt{\pi}\,h(L-t)}. \tag{5}$$

The experimental results are handled in the following manner. From the measurements obtained with the smallest inoculum referred to in Table 16 and from the formulae (4) and (4′), L is found to be 187 and $h = 0.031$. (The distribution calculated from the Gauss formula is compared with the actual experimental results in Fig. 94, curve I.) With these values of L and h and by use of equation (5) or equation (4) as required, the fraction, P, of the much higher inocula which should have formed colonies in times considerably less than L is calculated. From P and the number inoculated, N_0, the actual number, $N_0 P$, which should have appeared at given times is calculated. $N_0 P$ is then expressed as a percentage, not of the number plated, but of the number of cells, n_∞, which have been able to give colonies of the standard size before exhaustion of the plate limits further growth. The quantity $100 N_0 P/n_\infty$ is then plotted against t and from this plot L_{50}, the time for 50 per cent of those colonies which ever do so to reach the standard size, is read off.

A comparison of observed and calculated values of L_{50} is shown in Table 16 and the complete course of the curves obtained when the percentage is plotted against time is given in Fig. 94, where the continuous lines are calculated by the procedure just explained and the experimental observations are represented by the points. (The results for the largest inoculum will be dealt with separately later.) The calculation assumes that the growth conditions remain constant until the plate is exhausted, when a sudden cut-off occurs. Although this is an approximation it is not greatly in error since growth rates do in general remain constant until the nutrient concentration falls almost to zero. The accumulation of toxic products can also result in an abrupt fall in the growth rate, and in the present situation exhaustion of the plate is taken to include this factor also. The general agreement between the experimental and the calculated values in Table 16 and in Fig. 94 does indeed confirm an approximately Gaussian distribution.

At the highest inoculum size the results may be somewhat anomalous. The L_{50} values in Table 16 show that the colonies appeared *later* than expected and this in itself argues against an increasing probability of pre-adapted mutants when N_0 is increased. In tests for mutants large

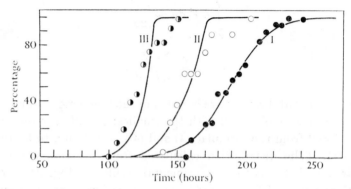

FIG. 94. Colony formation from varying numbers of cells of *Escherichia coli mutabile* on lactose-agar.

Curve I, 25 cells; curve II, 360 cells; curve III, 7200 cells. The percentage is that of the colonies eventually reaching 1 mm diameter which reach that size by the time given in the abscissa.

numbers of cells are often plated in the hope of including a few mutants in the inoculum. But equation (5) shows how easily incorrect conclusions could be drawn. For example, if L for a small inoculum were 187 hours, $h = 0.031$ as found above, and N_0 were 10^9, then when $h(L-t) = 3.85$, $P = 2.7 \times 10^{-8}$. Twenty-seven large colonies might then be expected on the plate at $t = 63$ hours and this is several days earlier than the modal time for small inocula. Exhaustion of the plate by the very numerous minute developing colonies would prevent this number from increasing many times, and the erroneous conclusion might be drawn that these twenty-seven colonies belonged to a special class. This behaviour has something in common with that described earlier for drugs.

(b) Distribution of sizes at various times

So far the discussion has centred on the distribution of the times at which colonies reach a standard diameter. The distribution of sizes at a given time is also not far from Gaussian. This is seen from Fig. 95 which shows the results obtained at different times when a small inoculum of lactose-negative cells of *Escherichia coli mutabile* was plated on lactose-agar. For comparison the same number was plated on glucose-agar to which the cells are already fully adapted. In spite of the large differences

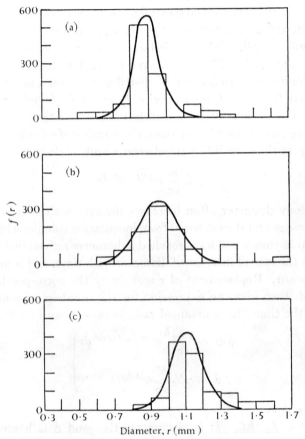

FIG. 95. Diameter distributions of lac⁻ *Escherichia coli mutabile* colonies.

(a) Lactose-agar, 70 cells, 267 hours: $h = 9.82$, $r_0 = 0.89$
(b) Lactose-agar, 70 cells, 292 hours: $h = 6.40$, $r_0 = 0.95$
(c) Glucose-agar, 70 cells, 42 hours: $h = 7.57$, $r_0 = 1.10$

in the time scale between the sets on the two different media, the distribution of sizes is similar and the Gauss curves represent these distributions well except for the incidence of rather more large colonies than would be expected. The curves represent the function

$$f(r) = 100 \frac{h}{\sqrt{\pi}} e^{-h^2(r_0 - r)^2},$$

where r is the diameter and r_0 its modal value. The scale was chosen so that the area under the curves, or of the histograms, is 100. In each case the plate contained seventy cells, so that all had given rise to a colony when the measurements were made.

An approximate theoretical treatment can be given of the size distribution at different times. Suppose N_0 cells are plated and that a fraction γ form colonies at all. Unless N_0 is large, γ approaches unity; its value when less than unity will be considered later. Let the lags which occur before colonies begin to develop be distributed about a modal value L_0. (This differs from the L used previously which included also the time of growth, now to be treated separately.) Then if, as the previous results suggest, the distribution is Gaussian, the number of colonies which start to develop in the time interval between τ and $\tau+d\tau$ is

$$\gamma N_0 \frac{h}{\sqrt{\pi}} e^{-h^2(L_0-\tau)^2} d\tau.$$

The colony diameter often increases linearly with time over a considerable range and thus at time t from inoculation colonies which started to develop at time τ will have reached a diameter r given by $r = k(t-\tau)$, where k is the rate of increase of diameter with time, and is not very far from constant. Replacement of τ and $d\tau$ by the corresponding values of r and dr then gives an expression for the numbers of colonies, $\phi\,dr$, which at the time t have attained radii between r and $r+dr$:

$$\left.\begin{aligned}
\phi\,dr &= \frac{\gamma N_0}{\sqrt{\pi}} \frac{h}{k} e^{-h^2(L_0-t+r/k)^2}\,dr \\[6pt]
\phi &= \gamma N_0 \frac{h'}{\sqrt{\pi}} e^{-h'^2(kL_0-kt+r)^2}
\end{aligned}\right\} , \tag{6}$$

where $h' = h/k$.

While $t < L_0$, kL_0-kt is always positive and ϕ falls steadily as r increases from zero. When $t > L_0$ there is a modal value, r_0, of r given by $kL_0-kt+r = 0$, so that $r_0 = k(t-L_0)$. A series of curves calculated from equation (6) for different values of t, with $L_0 = 50$ hours, $h' = 12\cdot0$, and $k = 10^{-2}$ mm/hour is shown in Fig. 96. N_0 is taken to be 100 and $\gamma = 1\cdot0$. At the shortest time considered there was no maximum. Later a maximum appears and moves to the right as t increases.

Experimental results obtained when seventy cells of *Escherichia coli mutabile* (lactose negative) were spread on lactose-agar are shown in Fig. 97, where the lines were arrived at by drawing smooth curves through the corresponding histograms. It is apparent that similarities exist between Figs. 96 and 97, but in the experimental set the distribution shows a tendency to widen as time goes on and this becomes even more marked at still longer times. The effect is seen in Fig. 98, which records a continuation of the experiment referred to in Fig. 97. The actual histograms are given and they show once more the appearance of colonies larger than expected.

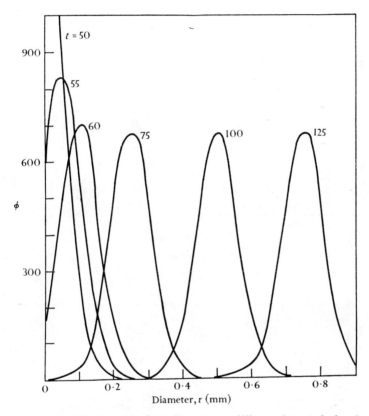

FIG. 96. Distributions of colony diameters at different times, calculated.

In the ideal case (Fig. 96) k is assumed to remain constant until the plate is exhausted, by which time the progress of the curves to the right also stops. In the series of experiments with seventy cells, however, k fell markedly when the mean size approached 0·8 mm and then after a period of slow growth rose again. This could indicate the adaptation to and the subsequent utilization of breakdown products such as fatty acids which the cells would reject while the carbohydrate was in plentiful supply. The great increase in scatter shown in Fig. 98 occurred during this final phase.

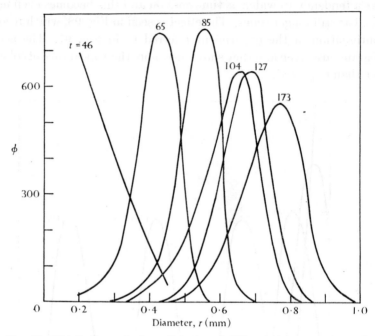

FIG. 97. Distributions of colony diameters at different times, experimental.

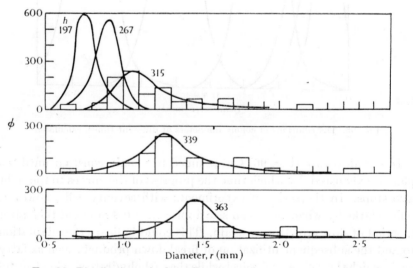

FIG. 98. Distributions of colony diameters at longer times, experimental.

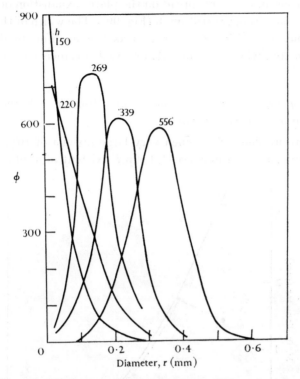

FIG. 99. Distribution of colony diameters with large inocula.

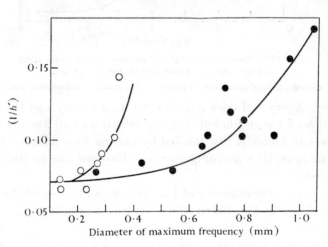

FIG. 100. Variation of $(1/h')$ with modal diameter (r_0).

O   Inoculum 3×10^3 cells   ● inoculum 70 cells

When larger inocula are spread on the plates exhaustion occurs while the colony diameters are still small (Fig. 99). The width of the distribution, as measured by $1/h'$, increases as the medium tends towards exhaustion, and when large inocula are used this increase sets in earlier (Fig. 100).

(c) *Yield of colonies on lactose-agar plates from lac+* Escherichia coli mutabile: *the 'overlap' factor*

A special problem arises when very large inocula of 10^6 to 10^9 cells, such as would be used in a search for pre-existent mutants, are spread

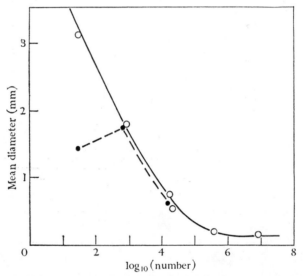

FIG. 101. Mean diameter at full development as a function of the number of cells plated, for lac+ strain.

●·····● 2 days' incubation of plates   ○ 3 days' incubation of plates

on plates. Every cell does not give rise to a colony and the factor γ which allows for some kind of 'overlap' is only a small fraction of unity. The 'overlap' factor is best studied by plating fully adapted lac+ cells on lactose-agar, thus avoiding any complications due to the adaptive process itself.

The mean colony diameter of lac+ cells as a function of the number plated is shown in Fig. 101 in which the continuous line and the points refer to 3 days' incubation and the broken line to 2 days' incubation. Colony diameter drops rapidly down to a limit beyond which a constant small size seems to be reached. With small inocula the full development takes longer since larger colonies are formed.

The yield, (number of colonies formed)/(number of cells plated), as a function of the inoculum size, is given in Fig. 102 and there is no simple relation between size and number. If the colonies were hemispherical and their size limited purely by exhaustion of the nutrient, the function (number)(yield)(diameter)^3 would be constant. This is not found (Table 17) and it would appear that with large colonies growth

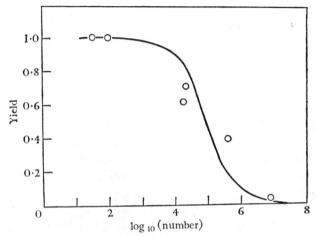

FIG. 102. Final yield of colonies as a function of the number of cells plated.

Circles indicate measurements: line drawn from equation (7).

TABLE 17

Number–size relation

Number plated	(Number)(yield) (diameter)^3
10^2	1720
10^3	4400
10^4	6800
10^5	2900
10^6	990
10^7	980

is limited more by the adverse influence of metabolic products than by failure of nutrient. Moreover, when the colonies are very small the yield is difficult to assess accurately. The variation of the yield with numbers can nevertheless be treated in a reasonably satisfactory approximate way.

Suppose that N_0 cells are plated. The plate may conveniently be assumed to provide S sites, and no more, capable of supporting a distinguishable colony. If more than one of the cells falls within a single site then only one colony will result.

Now let us imagine that the N_0 cells are distributed at random among the S sites. A certain number, S_0, may remain empty, and this can happen in $_SC_{S_0}$ ways. Now let the N_0 cells be assigned to the $(S-S_0)$ occupied sites so that there is at least one for each site. The number of possibilities for such an assignment is that of choosing $(S-S_0-1)$ of the (N_0-1) gaps among N_0 lined-up objects, that is,

$$_{N_0-1}C_{S-S_0-1} = \frac{(N_0-1)!}{(S-S_0-1)!\,(N_0-S+S_0)!}.$$

This expression multiplied by $_SC_{S_0}$ gives for the total number of possible conditions of the plate

$$W = \frac{S!}{S_0!(S-S_0)!}\,\frac{(N_0-1)!}{(S-S_0-1)!\,(N_0-S+S_0)!}.$$

The value of S_0 is required which will make W a maximum, a condition giving the most probable distribution among the sites, and when N_0 and S are large numbers, the state for most plates.

By application of Stirling's approximation to $\ln W$, and by differentiation, the required value of S_0 is found to be

$$S_0 = \frac{S(S-1)}{N_0+S-1} = \frac{S^2}{N_0+S}, \quad \text{very nearly.}$$

The fraction of sites filled is

$$\frac{S-S_0}{S} = 1 - \frac{S_0}{S} = \frac{N_0}{N_0+S}.$$

$$\text{Yield} = \frac{\text{number of colonies}}{\text{number of cells plated}} = \frac{S}{N_0+S}. \tag{7}$$

In Fig. 102 the yield given by equation (7) is shown as a function of N_0 by the continuous line, which is calculated with a value of $S = 10^5$. The points indicated by circles are experimental results.

(d) Plating of very large numbers of lac⁻ cells

To detect pre-existing lac⁺ (lactose utilizing) mutants in a culture of lac⁻ (lactose non-utilizing) *Escherichia coli mutabile*, with an assumed mutation rate of 10^{-7}, 10^9 cells might be plated and 100 mutants might be expected to develop well ahead of any others. From what has already been shown, however, it becomes clear that the following factors must also be taken into account.

1. The total number of colonies expected from an inoculum of 10^9 cells would be about 10^5 and hence γ in equation (6) would be about 10^{-4}.

2. k will tend to rise appreciably on very heavily seeded plates.

3. From this and other causes h' of equation (6) drops and this fall in h' means an increase in the width of the distribution, which is accentuated by the early exhaustion of the plate by the large inoculum.

The early appearance of some relatively large colonies is favoured by these factors and by two others. First there is a tendency for the larger colonies to grow even larger than expected (Figs. 95, 98), as occurs also on a glucose plate, and secondly any traces of cell lysis may permit 'cannibalism' and the development of patches of abnormal growth with so high an inoculum.

The distribution of sizes among the actual colonies formed at 45 hours from inoculation when 1.6×10^9 cells of *Escherichia coli mutabile* were spread on the surface of a lactose-agar plate is given in Fig. 103. A total of 424 colonies were measured at sample areas of the plate, which was estimated to contain about 6×10^4 colonies. A Gaussian distribution which fitted the results between diameters of 0 and 0·15 mm in Fig. 103 would not include the long, fairly even, spread between 0·15 and 0·65 mm. Moreover, only about one cell in 10^4 actually gave rise to an individual developed colony.

If conditions had permitted every cell to give a colony without disturbance by overlapping or by exhaustion and if $L_0 = 40$ hours, $k = 2 \times 10^{-2}$ mm/hour, and $h' = 6.0$ (values suggested by experiments), then the ordinate of the Gauss curve would have been $\dfrac{6.0}{\sqrt{\pi}} e^{-(6.0)^2(r-0.1)^2}$.

The number of colonies with radius greater than r can be found by integration. For large values the approximate integral $e^{-z^2}/2\sqrt{\pi}z$ is convenient, where $z = 6.0(r-0.1)$. The number to be expected with diameters greater than 0·60 mm works out as a fraction 1.2×10^{-5} of the total number. This is a negligible percentage, but the absolute number, i.e. $1.2 \times 10^{-5} \times 1.6 \times 10^9 = 1.9 \times 10^4$, is large. The largest colonies, however, are those which started developing exceptionally early. If these can grow unrestrained by overlap and plate exhaustion until practically full size is reached and if only the later starters are affected by these limitations, then the absolute number of big colonies should be reckoned not as a fraction of 1.6×10^9 but as a fraction of the total number (10^5) actually developing. This would amount to almost 20 per cent.

A complete theoretical treatment taking into account the Gaussian distribution of lag times, the overlap and the plate exhaustion would be very complex. A simplified assessment can be obtained as follows. The ordinates in the Gaussian distribution

$$y = \frac{6 \cdot 0}{\sqrt{\pi}} e^{-(6 \cdot 0)^2 (r - 0 \cdot 1)^2}$$

are now chosen so that the area under the curves is $1 \cdot 0$. Let P be the integral from r to ∞, that is, the fraction of the total with diameters greater than r; then

$$1 \cdot 6 \times 10^9 P = n_\tau,$$

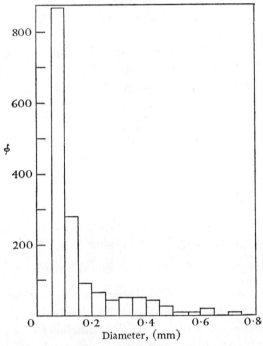

FIG. 103. Distribution of colony diameters with an inoculum of $1 \cdot 6 \times 10^9$ cells of *Escherichia coli mutabile*.

where n_τ is the number which have started to develop before the time τ and so have reached the specified size by the time of observation. We assume that n_τ is also subject to the 'overlap' correction so that

$$n_{\text{obs}} = \frac{n_\tau 10^5}{10^5 + n_\tau}, \tag{8}$$

the total number of colony-developing sites being again taken as 10^5. We now assume that the development of the earliest arising colonies, i.e. those which have reached large sizes and are relatively few in number, has not been appreciably affected by the later starters, an assumption which, although it would not apply to all, must certainly apply to some of them.

n_{obs} has a limit of 10^5, and each value is now expressed as a fraction of this, and from the curve of $n_{obs}/10^5$ against r, the corresponding frequency curve or histogram is obtained by differentiation. In the present example this has the form of an approximately Gaussian distribution with a sharp maximum at about 0·52 mm. This is not yet in agreement with the facts, but plate exhaustion, which sets in early with large inocula, has not so far been allowed for. A rough estimate of the effect of this factor can be obtained by the use of Fig. 101, which gives the diameter of fully developed lac$^+$ colonies as a function of inoculum size. First the number, n_r, with diameter greater than r, is calculated as a function of r from

$$dn_r = 1\cdot6\times10^9 \times \frac{6\cdot0}{\sqrt{\pi}} e^{-(6\cdot0)^2(r-0\cdot1)^2} \, dr,$$

and n_{obs} is obtained by using the value of n_r in equation (8). The plot of $n_{obs}/10^5$ against r is then made. This is shown in curve I of Fig. 104. The values of n_r are known for points on this curve and corresponding to each value of n, a new value, r', of the diameter is obtained from Fig. 101. $n_{obs}/10^5$ is then plotted against the value of r' (curve II, Fig. 104). The approximation has now been made that the colonies which ended their lags soon enough can attain the diameter reached by lac$^+$ colonies in similar circumstances. Curve II has been made to merge into curve I gradually as shown by the broken line but no further corrections have been applied. From curve II the values of $n_{obs}/10^5$ are read off for each small range of r, and from the readings a histogram is constructed (Fig. 105). This histogram shows in a considerably exaggerated form the apparently abnormal frequency of the larger size which was observed in Fig. 103, and the longer the lag and the shorter the actual growth time the more important does this effect become. Indeed, if there were a wide distribution of lags about a large value of L_0, and a very rapid development of colonies once growth eventually started, then the few early starters would have developed into colonies of maximum size before any others could seriously deplete the nutrient in the plate. Fig. 105, which is not based on the existence of special mutant cells, gives the illusion of their presence to a greater extent than the actual experimental distribution shown in Fig. 103.

In a comparable study carried out with *Aerobacter aerogenes* and D-arabinose very similar results were obtained.[4] The conclusions of

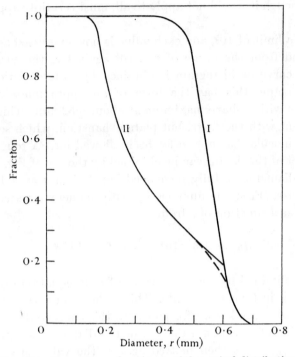

Fig. 104. Stages in rough estimate of theoretical distribution.
I and II see text.

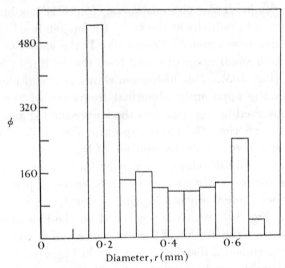

Fig. 105. Rough estimate of possible histogram showing apparent mutants.

this section may thus be summarized as follows. The early appearance of a small number of large colonies on thickly seeded plates is in fact what would be predicted from the Gaussian distribution obtained when the inoculum is small enough for all the cells to develop into large colonies. No necessity arises, therefore, to postulate special mutant types, or to assume any essential discontinuity between those cells which start early and the bulk of the population.

4. Bimodal distributions

In the experiments described in earlier chapters (either with drugs or with new sources of carbon) bimodal distributions of colony diameters

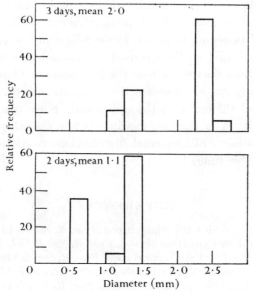

FIG. 106. Bimodal distributions after seven subcultures of *Aerobacter aerogenes* in D-arabinose liquid medium.

The number of days on the plate is indicated in each case.

were not observed, and in this connexion it is worth recalling what has been said earlier (Chapter VIII, Fig. 77) about how deceptive a cursory examination of colonies on a plate can be. Nevertheless, bimodal distributions are found in certain circumstances and, in particular, in experiments in which samples are withdrawn for plating from lagging cultures. The reduction in the plate lag which occurs as the lag in the liquid medium progresses has been discussed (Chapter VIII, section 5). In experiments of this kind bimodal distributions of colony diameters are sometimes seen but never before some growth has taken place in the liquid medium. Up to this point the distribution is Gaussian and relatively narrow. It begins to broaden once growth has begun and develops a 'tail' towards the end of the scale corresponding to larger diameters. It is still far from bimodal but, on occasion, bimodal distributions appear after considerable growth has taken place in the new medium. For example, during the adaptation of *Aerobacter aerogenes* to D-arabinose in liquid medium what might be bimodal distributions were seen at the third subculture and persisted at the seventh subculture.[5] The set from the seventh subculture is given in Fig. 106.

Even if these are truly bimodal distributions they are still compatible with an adaptive interpretation and would arise in the following way. At the end of the lag phase in the liquid medium the adaptation, although it may have made considerable progress, is likely to be far from complete. Once growth has begun, however, those cells which have divided once or twice in the liquid medium constitute a population more advanced in adaptation than the rest. Hence the possibility of a bimodal distribution at this early stage. More usually, however, the observed effect is a broadening of the curve at the upper end. Since many subcultures are often necessary in the new medium before the adaptation is complete, the possibility of abnormal distributions continues to exist for some considerable time.

REFERENCES

1. A. C. R. Dean and Sir Cyril Hinshelwood, *Proc. R. Soc.* B **144,** 297 (1955).
2. J. B. Woof and Sir Cyril Hinshelwood, *Proc. R. Soc.* B **153,** 321 (1960).
3. A. C. R. Dean and Sir Cyril Hinshelwood, *Proc. R. Soc.* B **146,** 109 (1956).
4. B. J. McCarthy and Sir Cyril Hinshelwood, *Proc. R. Soc.* B **153,** 339 (1960).
5. A. C. R. Dean and Sir Cyril Hinshelwood, *Proc. R. Soc.* B **151,** 435 (1960).

XII

COMMUNITIES OF CELLS: COLONIES

1. Introduction

IN the evolution of self-replicating organic matter the acquisition of a boundary wall marks the attainment of individuality and a measure of autonomy by the cell. What is contained within the cell wall has, as has already been pointed out, something of the character of a symbiotic community with its elaborate constellation of ribosomes and its multiplicity of enzymes, all useful but some not essential to survival, and also its capacity to receive into itself information-bearing elements from other cells. The symbiosis of bacterial cells with lysogenic phages, the occurrence of resistance transfer factors and, with cells like yeast, the existence of diploids formed by the fusion of two haploids all reflect the community aspect of the cell itself.

The aspect of autonomy reveals itself in the capacity of a single cell placed thousands of times its own diameter from others on a nutrient agar plate to divide and eventually give rise to a colony. Autonomy, however, in no way implies lack of mutual influence. In a bacterial culture in a liquid medium all the cells send out not only toxic products but useful growth intermediates and even enzymes, thereby exercising a mutual effect which may on occasion become very important. When the cells multiply to form colonies on a solid medium they are forced to respect the mutual restraints of a close-packed community. The colony itself in some respects constitutes an individual, and indeed often has enough character of its own to offer in its size and visual appearance an important clue about the bacterial species from which it arises.

To exaggerate the individuality of bacterial colonies to the point of likening them to organisms would perhaps be far-fetched, but the study of their formation and structure draws attention to various factors which must also play a part in the morphology of multicellular organisms in the true sense.

2. Mutual influences of cells in liquid media

When *Escherichia coli* is inoculated into a medium containing ammonium sulphate as the nitrogen source small amounts of glutamic and aspartic acids are detectable in the medium just before the end of the lag phase.[1] These substances themselves shorten the lag if present in the medium from the start. What would appear to happen is that some of the cells, before the various parts of their reaction patterns have settled down to the harmonious relation of the steady state, are producing these intermediates more rapidly than they are using them, and are allowing them to escape. Once in the medium these intermediates are available for use by other cells which are less advanced in their progress towards the ending of the lag.

In Chapter III we have seen how the lag of cultures of *Aerobacter aerogenes* may be greatly shortened by increase in the size of the inoculum, a fact which is easily intelligible if it is supposed that all the cells present may contribute intermediates to a common pool in the medium. The more cells there are to make their contribution the greater the concentration for the benefit of all. That useful intermediates should escape at all is of course a temporary breakdown of the protective mechanism, by which the cell membrane prevents wholesale dilution of everything important for the synthetic processes organized inside its boundary.

To the extent, however, to which escape does occur the whole culture and not the separate cell becomes the individual. The mutual influences of cells under conditions of high population density, when they are rapidly building up concentrations of toxic products in the medium or are competing for inadequate supplies of oxygen, are obvious and do not call for special comment.

A curious effect is sometimes observed with certain enzyme activities. The phosphatase activity of *Aerobacter aerogenes* reaches a maximum very early in the growth cycle and then declines rapidly as though by simple dilution with new material. The smaller the inoculum the higher is the maximum activity. If there are few cells, each produces more phosphatase than it would were it part of a larger population.[2] The effect is as though a certain total enzyme content were built up per unit volume of the culture taken as a whole. Here again it is the culture which appears as the individual entity. The phenomenon suggests that phosphatase is here concerned in some co-operative process which also involves intermediates diffusing through the medium.

3. Formation of colonies

The bacterial colony, formed by the multiplication of individual cells more or less immobilized on the surface of a solid medium, constitutes a dense and crowded community in which various complex events may occur.

Colonies possess an internal structure of a sort and, as already remarked, vary in their appearance from one bacterial strain to another. Under the microscope dividing cells of *Aerobacter aerogenes* and *Escherichia coli mutabile* are seen to form chains in which newly added members frequently swing round to align themselves exactly parallel with others, there being some degree of mobility possible. The result is at first a close-packed two-dimensional array of rods. At intervals, however, a change of direction occurs, for some reason possibly connected with unevennesses in the surface, and there is a break in the regularity of the hitherto almost crystalline type of pattern. The next result is thus a structure with numerous faults or gaps which occur where the non-parallel alignment arises. Thus we have something vaguely resembling a mosaic of imperfectly crystalline pieces. While the incipient colony is still very small a second layer of cells begins to form at a point where the lateral pressure of the growing cells on one another forces one of them out of the original plane. Meanwhile growth spreads outward giving a more or less circular contour, and the colony as a whole assumes a convex form since the upward growth has had time to proceed further at the centre where the process began than at the periphery.[3] Observations generally similar to these on *Aerobacter* and *Escherichia* have been described by Roelcke and Intlekofer[4] for other organisms.

Thus the colony consists of numerous imperfectly aligned regions of parallel growth like crystalline blocks, with faults and channels running through it in a random manner. These allow the access of nutrients from below to regions above the plane of the solid medium itself. It is clear that the detailed structure depends in a complex way on the size and shape of the individual cells, the surface characteristics of the medium and the surface characteristics of the cells themselves.

In a sense a colony bears a resemblance to a tissue in a plant or animal, and though the organic connexion between its parts is much weaker some does exist and the later evolution of the colony is determined to some extent by transport phenomena carrying nutrients or metabolites through its mass. Thus the morphology of a colony foreshadows in a very rudimentary way that of complex organisms in general.

A phenomenon which used to be called 'bacterial dissociation' is one manifestation of variations affecting the forms of colonies growing on solid media.[5]

The chief forms distinguished are smooth, which are even and glossy, rough, which have wavy edges and a crinkly surface, and mucoid. Rough colonies seem often to be associated with larger cells or even filaments.[4, 6]

A given bacterial strain may give colonies of a single type, smooth (S) or rough (R), or may give a mixture of forms. The S and R forms may be separated and subcultured: they may breed true, S giving S and R giving R, or revert. The trend of the so-called dissociation is influenced by the nature of the medium, by the addition of specific chemical reagents, by age, by irradiation, and by various other factors. Most species of bacteria have been observed to show some manifestation or other of the phenomenon. Sometimes the variant forms revert easily to the parent type: sometimes they are relatively stable. The reversion is sometimes sudden, erratic, and apparently spontaneous. Some variants appear to be quite stable, but can be made to revert when subjected to a special treatment. Hadley[6] suggested that rough colonies only reverted when the variant strain had not been thoroughly isolated and purified. Yet even stable rough strains have been made to revert by drastic means such as passage through an animal. The different colony forms are linked in varying degrees with other bacterial properties such as morphology, pathogenicity, and biochemical reactions.

Some observers have thought that the different forms arising by 'dissociation' were parts of a regular bacterial life cycle—just as one might encounter frog-spawn, tadpoles, and frogs in the course of a series of observations. But there is really no evidence for such an idea, which is not generally believed in.[7, 8]

The general pattern of stability and reversion of rough forms is strongly reminiscent of that of drug-adapted or medium-adapted cells, and it must be borne in mind that the 'dissociation' changes occur in conditions of overcrowding, exhaustion of foodstuffs, and intense accumulation of products which may be toxic.

Sometimes after the colony has reached a relatively large size other striking changes in morphology may appear in that localized patches of renewed growth arise. This growth may sometimes take the form of distinct wedges or sectors but the commonest expression of its occurrence is the formation of *papillae*. When this takes place the overall picture is as if small new colonies have been scattered at random over the surface or round the periphery of the original colony (Plate 1).

The subject of papilla formation will be dealt with in some detail since it not only involves important questions about mutants but throws a good deal of light on colony formation in general.

4. Papilla formation

Papilla formation was first observed long ago, and since Haddow[9] has thoroughly reviewed the literature between 1906 and 1937, most of his

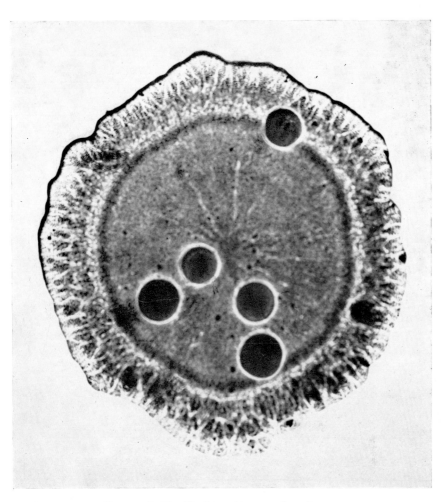

PLATE 1. Papilla formation on phenol-agar

references need not be repeated here. Papillae often appear on colonies growing on an agar medium which contains alternative sources of nutrient, and a well-known example is that of *Escherichia coli mutabile*. When this organism is plated on the surface of an agar medium containing peptone and lactose, primary colonies arise at the expense of the peptone, and during their development papillae appear. If a suitable indicator, such as neutral red, is incorporated in the medium, the cells in the papillae indicate their ability to ferment lactose by becoming red, the primary colony remaining white.[10, 11] Some formulations of peptone–lactose agar contain a mixture of two dyes, such as eosin and methylene blue, to give a sharper differentiation. Lewis[12] showed, however, that papilla formation could also take place on minimal agar containing lactose as the sole source of carbon, and with *Escherichia coli mutabile* the papillae appeared on the primary colonies within five to eight days of incubation.

The assumption is often made that the papillae are formed from spontaneous mutants arising during growth on the first substrate and capable of utilizing the second. As early as 1922 Beijerinck[13] adopted this view since, he claimed, the changes were discrete and intermediate strains did not occur. Later Ryan[14] devised a method for estimating mutation rates based on papilla formation, and it has also been claimed that, since the distribution of the numbers of papillae among colonies is in accord with the Poisson formula,[15, 16] the mutations are spatially or clonally random. Lewis[12] originally favoured the idea of an adaptive response but eventually adopted the spontaneous mutation point of view. The explanation of the behaviour on minimal agar media requires two further assumptions if this latter idea is adopted; either that the primary colony arises at the expense of impurities in the medium, a topic which has already been discussed, or that, although the cells initially plated can utilize lactose slowly, better adapted types emerge while they are doing so.

Haddow[9] showed that papilla formation was essentially a function of the ageing of the primary colony. He looked upon it as an irreversible differentiation resulting from an adaptation to unfavourable or inhibiting conditions. The inhibition, he maintained, may be due (*a*) to gradual depletion of the medium; (*b*) to the action of toxic substances in the environment; and (*c*) possibly to the competitive effect of non-utilizable substances in the substrate.

Papilla formation has also been observed on agar plates containing drugs or other inhibiting substances. For example, Penfold[17] described the occurrence of papillae when *Escherichia coli* is plated on agar media containing sodium monochloracetate, glyceryl-α-chlorhydrin, or sodium phenylacetate. The occurrence of daughter colonies has been stated to be stimulated by sodium fluoride,[18] and Ryan[14] has shown that 5-hydroxy-7-nitro-benzimidazole increased the frequency of h+ papillae (histidine independent) when an h− strain (histidine dependent) of *Escherichia coli* was plated on agar.

Subcultures made from the papillae are often capable of growing freely on the new substrate or in the presence of the toxic agent, and this is often taken to indicate a heritable mutation. This evidence, however, is not unambiguous, since if cells on the periphery, or at other places in the colony, formed in the first stage of growth initiate further growth after a long period of adaptation, then that adaptation may well be carried over in the new subculture. We shall in the following section discuss the results of experiments carried out to determine the conditions under which this change in morphology takes place in various systems. First of all the behaviour in the presence of drugs will be examined. Attention will then be turned to minimal media containing a slowly utilizable substrate as the sole source of carbon, and finally the necessarily more complex systems involving mixed nutrients will be considered.

5. Papilla formation in the presence of phenol[19]

The special interest of the situation found with *Aerobacter aerogenes* and phenol is that the bacteria develop little or no adaptation to this toxic agent. A concentration can be chosen at which growth is still possible at a substantially reduced rate and 50 to 100 subcultures in liquid medium containing phenol lead to no improvement. Indeed, after as many as 200 subcultures any improvement in growth rate is very slight.[20] No phenol-resistant mutants can thus reasonably be assumed to occur during normal conditions of culturing and if, as in fact happens, papillae arise on colonies ageing on agar plates containing phenol, the question of their real nature becomes extremely pertinent.

The results of some experiments with phenol-agar are summarized in Table 18. At low inoculum sizes practically all the cells survived, at the phenol concentration employed, to form colonies which eventually became large. As the inoculum was increased both the colony diameter and the survival dropped progressively, on account of overcrowding and plate exhaustion (see Chapter XI). The papillae first appeared on the seventh day, by which time the colonies had practically reached their maximum size. After 8 days of incubation the largest colonies were found to have most papillae and the number dropped progressively as the colony diameter diminished until at the smallest sizes there were none at all.

The product (number of colonies) × (surface area of colony) remained of the same order of magnitude, a fact indicating that the total amount

TABLE 18

The effect of inoculum size on papilla formation on colonies of Aerobacter aerogenes *plated on phenol-agar* (500 *mg/l.*)

Inoculum	Number of colonies on plate (n)	Mean diameter of colonies (mm)	Mean number of papillae per colony	n × surface area of colony
$2 \cdot 1 \times 10^4$	$1 \cdot 4 \times 10^4$	0·25	0	687
$1 \cdot 0 \times 10^3$	781	1·09	0	727
520	441	1·40	0·0045	690
208	199	1·72	0·14	463
104	90	2·50	1·34	442
52	54	3·00	3·40	382

The plates were measured after eight days of incubation at 37° C.

TABLE 19

Respreading of papillae from phenol plates

	Concentration (mg/l.)	Inoculum	% of colonies with papillae by 8 days	Range of colony diameters (mm)
Primary plating	500	70	100	3·2 to 4·0
Respreading	1 500	10	100	3·0 to 3·8
,,	2 ,,	31	60	3·0 to 4·0
,,	3 ,,	25	100	3·7 to 4·0
,,	4 ,,	14	100	3·4 to 3·7
,,	5 ,,	33	3	3·3 to 4·8
Repeat	5a ,,	30	30	3·0 to 3·5
	5b ,,	30	60	2·9 to 3·0
	6 ,,	30	55	4·3 to 8·2

of growth was much the same on all the plates though the distribution of the population among colonies varied very considerably. There should thus have been about the same probability of spontaneous mutation on all the plates and hence about the same total of papilla formation on each plate as a whole. But in fact there were no papillae at all on the plates containing many very small colonies from large inocula. Thus the formation of papillae in the presence of phenol would seem to be a result of special conditions arising in the larger and more overcrowded colonies. In any case it would be difficult to assume that these centres of new growth originate from drug-resistant mutants in a situation where resistance does not develop at all.

They would, in these circumstances, have to be nutritional mutants of some kind, but this assumption does not help in the interpretation of the experiments. Moreover, when inocula are taken from the papillae, and the cells replated on phenol-agar, in conditions where the maximum number of papillae would be expected, the phenomenon is repeated over and over again (Table 19).

The strains derived from the papillae showed signs of having suffered a slight general damage to their metabolism but otherwise there was little difference between them and the others.

6. Papilla formation with some other drugs[19]

Thymol and crystal violet are two drugs to which, in sharp contrast with its behaviour with phenol, *Aerobacter aerogenes* readily becomes

TABLE 20

The relation between colony diameter and papilla formation by
Aerobacter aerogenes *on thymol-agar (200 mg/l.)*

Inoculum	Number of colonies on plates (n)	Mean diameter (mm)	Mean number of papillae per colony	n × area of colonies
		Series 1		
6·4 × 10³	3·8 × 10³	0·65	0	1262
320	242	1·66	0	524
16	12	3·25	3·0	100
		Series 2		
6·4 × 10³	1·2 × 10³	0·97	0	883
320	141	1·80	0·05	359
16	7	2·65	3·3	39

In series 1 the plates were incubated for 11 days and in series 2 for 7 days at 37° C.

resistant. Here again papillae develop. As with phenol, however, they are not observed when the colony diameter remains below a certain limit (Tables 20 and 21). The actual total area of growth in the small colonies without papillae is here actually greater than in the large ones containing papillae so that the chances of mutation on the plate should be at least as good.

The result emphasizes once more that the formation of papillae is a function of large ageing colonies. In situations where resistance develops it would be expected that inocula taken from colonies which have once grown will on respreading develop more rapidly. This will lead to an earlier exhaustion of the plate, and the opportunity for ageing phenomena to show their effects will be curtailed by the earlier cessation of any kind of growth at all. Thus papilla formation might be expected to disappear with continued respreading. In any event if the papillae

TABLE 21

The relation between colony diameter and papilla formation by Aerobacter aerogenes *on crystal violet-agar* (10 *mg/l.*)

Inoculum	Number of colonies on plates (*n*)	Mean diameter (*mm*)	Mean number of papillae per colony	*n × area of colonies*
1.5×10^4	1.4×10^4	0.75	0	6188
750	636	1.54	0	1185
38	23	2.53	8.0	116

The plates were incubated for 7 days at 37° C.

arise entirely from mutants formed in a colony of normal cells, inocula from them should give no further formation at the first respread. Tests with a number of drugs do not reveal this pattern of behaviour and in fact during repeated respreadings papillae appear and disappear in a rather erratic manner (Table 22).

Not all agents to which resistance develops cause changes in colony morphology. Examples in this category are brilliant green, proflavine, and *m*-cresol. Sometimes an intermediate type of behaviour is observed as the colony ages. Its surface loses its appearance of relatively uniform texture and assumes that of a mosaic with lens-shaped insertions which are not gas inclusions, but could be papilla-like growths following the line of internal cracks or faults in the primary colony. This behaviour is found on occasion with many of the substances listed in Table 22.

7. Papilla formation in the presence of slowly-utilizable carbon sources[3]

Escherichia coli mutabile utilizes lactose slowly and *Aerobacter aerogenes* is reluctant to grow on either D-arabinose or dulcitol. On a minimal agar medium containing one of these substances as the sole source of carbon a slight amount of primary colony formation usually takes place by the utilization of traces of unavoidable impurity (see Chapter VIII, section 5). These primary colonies, however, remain small until utilization of the principal carbon source begins.

When a small number of cells of *Escherichia coli mutabile* is spread on the surface of lactose agar, papillae do not appear until the colonies are of a large size and by this time utilization of the lactose must have occurred (Table 23). Again the correlation between large ageing colonies

TABLE 22

Agents which induce papilla formation[19]

Agent and concentration in mg/l.	Fraction surviving on drug plate	Colony diameter at which papillae appeared (mm)	Behaviour on respreading	Fraction surviving on respreading
Phenol, 500, 600	0·8 to 1·0	2·0 to 3·5	+(6)	0·9 to 1·0
Thymol, 200	4×10^{-4}	4·0	±(3)	(1) $2·6 \times 10^{-6}$
				(2) $1·2 \times 10^{-5}$
				(3) 0·55
Crystal violet, 20	$1·1 \times 10^{-4}$	1·8 to 4·0	+(2)	(1) 0·1
				(2) 0·14
Cadmium chloride, 100	0·78	3·5 to 5·0	±(2)*	(1) 0·29
				(2) 0·41
8-azaguanine, 40	0·84	2·0 to 2·5	−(1)*	1·0
Sodium fluoride, 500	0·44	1·5 to 2·0	+(1)	1·0
Urea, 200	0·52	5·0 to 5·5	−(1)*	0·57
Janus black, 200	10^{-4}	1·8 to 4·5	+(1)	1·0
Chloramphenicol, 21	$1·8 \times 10^{-5}$	—	+(1)	0·64
Phloxine, 100	$2·5 \times 10^{-2}$	4·0 to 6·0	—	—
Acid alizarine, 100	0·36	2·0 to 2·5	—	—
Rhodamine, 100	0·90	3·3 to 4·5	—	—
Sodium monochloracetate,				
100	0·85			
500	0·56	\} Number of colonies with papillae		
1000	3×10^{-6}	increased with concentration		
2000	$1·6 \times 10^{-6}$			

+ signifies papillae persisted on respreading, the number of respreads being shown in brackets.
− signifies that they disappeared.
± signifies that they disappeared gradually.
In experiments marked * a few small lenticular areas appeared.
Aerobacter aerogenes was used in all experiments except those with sodium monochloracetate when *Escherichia coli mutabile* was used.

and the incidence of papillae is observed. Similar results are obtained with *Aerobacter aerogenes* and either D-arabinose or dulcitol. With these sugars the range of times at which the colonies reached the large size was greater than in the corresponding experiment with lactose, and papillae were most in evidence on those colonies which had taken the longest time to develop.

8. Influence of agar concentration on papilla formation[3]

The concentration of the agar in a medium influences the form of the colony and the rate of development, but the diameter–time relation is not a direct function of the growth rate, since the degree of convexity

TABLE 23

Escherichia coli mutabile (*lac⁻*) on lactose-agar

52 cells plated: 49 colonies formed
10 selected at random for measurement

Colony	Time (days) for colony to reach diameter of			% surface area covered by papillae when diameter was		
	0·5 mm	0·75 mm	1·0 mm	0·5 mm	0·75 mm	1·0 mm
1	3·7	6·5	14·0	0	0	24·7
2	3·8	6·7	13·0	0	0	21·0
3	3·9	7·0	12·3	0	0	51·1
4	4·0	7·4	15·4	0	0	33·8
5	4·0	8·0	15·0	0	0	26·2
6	3·7	6·8	13·6	0	0	42·5
7	3·5	6·7	13·0	0	0	31·0
8	4·0	11·9	14·8	0	8·3	44·0
9	3·8	6·8	15·0	0	0	28·6
10	3·4	6·6	13·0	0	0	21·4

TABLE 24

Agar concentration and papilla formation
(Escherichia coli mutabile-*lactose-agar*)

Concentration of agar in medium	Mean value of time (days) for colony diameter of		Mean value of % surface area covered by papilla when diameter was	
%	0·75 mm	1·0 mm	0·75 mm	1·0 mm
1·0	7·3	9·0	36	42
1·5	5·7	8·5	2·3	47
2·0	3·7	5·3	0	0
2·5	1·7	2·9	0	0
3·0	2·6	4·7	0	0·3

of the colonies also changes. Agar concentration has also a marked influence on the appearance of papillae. At the common agar concentration of between 1·0 and 1·5 per cent papillae were found to be abundant whereas at higher levels they seldom appeared at all (Table 24).

9. Comparison of secondary cultures derived from colony and from papilla[3]

When cultures derived from colony and papilla respectively, which have arisen on minimal lactose agar, are retested on the same medium the papilla culture is slightly more lactose-positive than that derived from the colony (Table 25). The difference is not as marked as would have been expected with mutant and non-mutant types of cells, and,

TABLE 25

The behaviour on minimal lactose-agar of cultures derived respectively from papilla and colony of Escherichia coli mutabile

| Expt. | Time (days) for 10 colonies (chosen at random when very small) to reach lac^+ size (1·0 mm diameter) | |
	Colony culture	Papilla culture
1	5·4, 5·5, 5·5, 6·4, 7·0, 8·0, 8·5, 10·2, 10·2, 10·5 mean 7·7	3·7, 4·5, 4·6, 5·0, 5·5, 5·6, 6·0, 6·0, 6·0, 6·2 mean 5·3
2	5·2, 5·8, 6·0, 6·0, 6·0, 6·3, 6·5, 7·0, 7·5, 8·0 mean 6·4	3·7, 4·1, 5·1, 5·1, 5·7, 5·7, 5·8, 5·8, 6·0, 6·0 mean 5·3

The colony was obtained from a minimal lactose-agar plate after 12 days' incubation at 37° C. Cultures were grown overnight in glucose-ammonium sulphate medium before diluting and respreading.

TABLE 26

The behaviour on minimal D-arabinose-agar of cultures derived respectively from papilla and colony of Aerobacter aerogenes

| Expt. | Time (days) for 10 colonies (chosen at random when very small) to reach A^+ size (0·75 mm diameter) | |
	Colony culture	Papilla culture
1	5·2, 5·3, 5·4, 5·5, 5·5, 5·5, 5·5, 5·6, 5·6, 6·0 mean 5·5	5·4, 5·4, 5·5, 5·7, 5·7, 5·8, 5·8, 6·0, 6·0, 6·5 mean 5·8
2	4·2, 4·7, 5·0, 5·0, 5·2, 5·2, 5·2, 5·3, 5·4, 5·4 mean 5·1	5·0, 5·2, 5·2, 5·3, 5·3, 5·4, 5·4, 5·4, 5·7, 6·0 mean 5·4

The colony was obtained from a minimal D-arabinose-agar plate after 14 days' incubation at 37° C. Cultures were grown overnight in glucose-ammonium sulphate medium before diluting and respreading.

indeed, in the corresponding experiment with *Aerobacter aerogenes* and D-arabinose it is not observed at all (Table 26).

On eosin-methylene blue agar, a medium containing peptone and lactose as carbon sources, a lactose-positive strain of *Escherichia coli mutabile* was observed to show a positive reaction within 2 days of incubation. The corresponding negative (unadapted) strain required at least 8 days before most of the colonies had lactose-positive papillae on them. Cultures derived from these papillae, it is true, showed a considerable percentage of positive reactions in 3 to 4 days but cultures taken from the primary colony itself had also advanced to a certain extent towards the lactose-positive state (Table 27). Presumably the

TABLE 27

The behaviour on EMB agar of cultures derived respectively from papilla and colony of Escherichia coli mutabile

		Time (days) for the given percentages of positive reactions						
		Streaked on EMB agar			Spread on EMB agar (%)			
		2 days	3 days	4 days	25	50	75	100
1	Colony culture	−ve	−ve	50% +ve	3	4	4	4
	Papilla culture	−ve	75% +ve	100% +ve	2	2	3	4
2	Colony culture	−ve	10% +ve	30% +ve	4	4	4	4
	Papilla culture	−ve	80% +ve	100% +ve	4	4	4	4

The colony was obtained from an EMB agar plate after 11 days' incubation at 37° C. Part of a colony and part of a papilla on that colony were emulsified with a few ml of phosphate buffer and each culture was (*a*) streaked directly on EMB agar, and (*b*) diluted and spread on EMB and minimal lactose-agars.

Note. A 'positive' reaction refers to that characteristic of the lactose-positive strain.

cells in the primary colony grow rapidly on the peptone and then begin to utilize lactose, though not to the stage at which the production of acid is sufficient to cause the positive colour change. Meanwhile the occurrence of more rapid growth entirely at the expense of the lactose gives rise to the papillae. That the difference between papilla and colony on eosin-methylene blue agar is greater than on minimal lactose or D-arabinose agar is explained by the fact that on minimal agar growth of the primary colony cannot proceed very far without the utilization of the added sugar.

10. General consideration of the factors affecting colony morphology

Taken as a whole the results presented so far show that the appearance of papillae on colonies is very far from unambiguous evidence for the presence of spontaneously arising mutants. Ageing of the primary colony would in fact appear to be the vital factor and this interpretation is substantiated further by the following evidence. After 2 to 3 weeks of ageing a colony of *Aerobacter aerogenes* growing on a glucose-agar plate developed lenticular areas (see section 6). This effect could be produced more rapidly by touching the surface of a colony which had reached one-half of its optimum size with a hot platinum wire or by adding more glucose by means of a gutter cut round a fully developed colony. In both instances lenticular areas appeared in the subsequent growth. Moreover, when plates, on which confluent growth had arisen as a result of a very heavy inoculum, were kept for several weeks they developed a mottled appearance, the growth having become thinner in some places and thicker in others.

There is thus a tendency for densely packed communities of cells to develop heterogeneities on prolonged ageing. This can on occasion be a consequence of lysis and resynthesis which may occur at various points on the colony. The question now arises as to why the new growth does not conform to the pattern of the old. The failure to do so could be the result of differences in the size and the surface characteristics of the cells, and if so it would apply equally to mutants and non-mutants, adapted and unadapted and to young and old cells. On the basis of the considerations advanced in section 3 a plausible picture of the formation of papillae on the surface of a colony can be constructed. The primary colony is usually of a convex form. It is supplied by nutrient from below and the elevation of the central part is a result of the forcing up by new cells of the earlier formed layers. Renewed growth on the surface, as occurs in papilla formation, would then necessitate a diffusion channel for nutrient, and this could be provided by the faults and discontinuities mentioned earlier. These reach the surface at more or less randomly localized points, and the new growth will tend to spread from them. The localization will be greater if the primary colony has aged, since growth will spread from new young cells rather than their aged neighbours.

Ageing of the primary colony usually proceeds to a considerable extent in experiments with media containing alternative sources of carbon. In these conditions renewal of growth will proceed preferentially from any newly formed young cells, even if some excess of nutrient diffuses away from the mouth of the channel.

The conditions for the formation of papillae on the periphery rather than on the surface of a colony are somewhat different. Here a mutant arising by chance on the edge of the primary colony could certainly act as a centre of new growth. If the mutant arose while the primary growth was still under way various types of structure could arise according to the relative growth rates of the original cells and the mutant. This is the explanation usually assumed, and in this way Shinn[21] envisages the formation of wedges, sectors, outbursts, islands, and secondary colonies. It is, however, not the only possible explanation of the various kinds of observation, since if there has been a period of rapid growth on one nutrient and then a long delay before use of the second nutrient begins, the statistical distribution of the lags from place to place may be very wide. Eventually regrowth starts somewhere, and when it has done so may well tend to be localized at that spot if there is stimulation of neighbouring cells by intermediates escaping from those actually dividing. Furthermore, renewed growth may well be favoured at certain points of the periphery rather than at others by the inhomogeneous structure of the agar gel itself.

A quite general cause of discontinuity exists which would apply equally to growth from mutants, newly adapted cells, aged cells, or cells whose metabolism has been modified by conditions of changed aeration, overcrowding, or other biochemical variations. We will draw a distinction simply between 'early' and 'late' cells without specifying where the difference lies. During the early stages of colony formation the first nutrient of a mixed medium (e.g. peptone) is utilized, the concentration of metabolic products is still low, aeration is adequate, no adaptation has occurred, and no mutants are likely to be present. All or any of these factors may change later and cells which differ from the early ones in size and surface character may now be formed predominantly. In isolation these late cells would form a close-packed structure of their own which for physical reasons could be different from that arising in the earlier stages of growth. When, however, they arise in the presence of a mass of early cells they may be constrained to conform as nearly as may be to the already established packing pattern of these. This behaviour would be analogous to that of substances which crystallize from solution and conform to the lattice of an existing nucleus even in conditions where that form is unstable and would not arise by itself. Eventually, however, the unstable morphology gives place to a more stable one, and at the place where the change occurs papillae begin to appear. Adapted forms or indeed forms which have suffered any biochemical change are just as likely as true mutants to have a different colony morphology. Thus although papillae could indeed arise from mutants this is not the only cause. As we have seen they occur in cases where no mutant forms need be suspected: they may not appear until long after adaptation or the growth of mutants without papilla formation has taken place: and finally the difference between cells taken from colony and from papilla is often not very marked. Thus papilla formation in general would appear to be the expression rather of a complex combination of various colloidal phenomena than a simple overgrowing of the primary colony by mutants. Colony structure involves the packing of cells into something like a space lattice, and the form of this will vary with the surface character and geometry of the cells, which in turn varies with the biochemical conditions.

11. General discussion of morphological factors

Morphological considerations enter at every stage of the study of living matter. The individual cell possesses its spatial map which, as we have seen, determines some very general characteristics of its behaviour. When cells group themselves to communities the colonies or aggregates develop their own morphology which may involve marked discontinuities. In the more closely cohering communities of cells which constitute tissues the discontinuities lead to the evolution of separate organs.

Living matter is never a single homogeneous mass. In the genetic material itself the determinants are spread out as a sequence of nucleotide bases in the nucleic acids, and, in the proteins (which, if not genetic information-bearing material themselves are indispensable concomitants) the amino-acid residues form elaborate linear sequences.

Since nucleic acids and enzymes, which condition the whole series of chemical changes, ensure a complex distribution in space of the initiating centres of action, the field of chemical reactivity in a portion of living matter must be highly non-uniform from point to point of a cell. If a nucleic acid sequence determines the properties of an organism, some chemical reaction or other must be conditioned by a limited element of the sequence, and substances formed in its immediate vicinity must diffuse away. They will react eventually with other substances, some of which directly or indirectly are derived from other elements of the information chain. The concentrations of all these substances, which determine the rate and nature of these further chemical reactions, must, from the manner in which they arise, form complex spatial patterns.

The spatial patterns of concentration, different for different substances, determine the places at which functions like products of concentrations governing coagulation or precipitation can attain specified values. A spatial pattern of precipitation or of coagulation represents the appearance of structure and morphology. Many factors complicate the course of events. Suppose, for example, two substances A and B

are diffusing in a given direction and both are subject to reactions on the way, A being more reactive than B. The ratio A/B will gradually drop until B/A may be great enough to allow the reaction of B to supplant that of A. Then a change in the composition of what is formed will occur. Thus events initiated by the elements of a linear genetic map have consequences which may be represented by an elaborate three-dimensional map of chemical reactivity.

The departure from homogeneity enhances itself. As chain molecules grow and extend through space they offer adsorptive sites which may exert a specific directional influence on the chemistry of the regions through which they pass and this influence will be a function of the particular substrates which have found their way to these regions from their respective points of origin. Some of the macromolecules of the cell form sheets extended in two dimensions and these not only form still more elaborately patterned adsorption sites, but, in so far as they constitute walls and membranes, create a spatially non-uniform set of permeability relations channelling the entry of substrates from without.

Some parts of the cell substance are formed by the reaction of intermediates arriving from different origins, and any phenomena akin to the delayed precipitation responsible for Liesegang rings will add further diversity. If substrate diffuses from without and is consumed specially at, for example, two specialized sites in the cell, then in the region between these two sites a zone of impoverishment is created and this too has its effects on the chemical events in the region.

Long-chain molecules form aggregates, sometimes of a more or less crystalline kind, and the variety of bundles, sheets, and other agglomerates may create actual ducts and channels, so that what was an open field of manœuvre becomes, so to say, a town of traffic-congested streets.

What happens in a limited degree in the cell happens over again in a pattern of higher order with agglomerations of cells.

The inevitable development of morphology forces division on the cell in the manner discussed in Chapter XIV. Collections of cells cannot remain in close proximity without profound influences on one another. Once this formation of extended arrays of cells occurs further changes become possible and indeed inevitable. The chemical conditions throughout the mass can remain constant even less than they can throughout the volume of a single cell. The result is a challenge to adaptive changes at different parts of the conglomerate. The challenge can be met by modification of metabolic patterns, conceivably by mutations, or by the stimulation of some genetic elements more than others. The nature of the response raises problems somewhat similar to those about adaptive changes in general, but whatever the nature of the modifications themselves may be the new kind of metabolism can lead to a new kind of communal aggregation of the cells.

If it does, then cell differentiation has occurred. The differentiated regions are now subject to still further geometrical conditions in that the chemical happenings at any point are a function not only of the distance from external sources of substrates but of the distance over which possible metabolites have to travel from the undifferentiated tissue of cells. This increases the possibility of still further modifications in certain regions.

These differentiated cell communities with distinct biochemical patterns of their own may come into a symbiotic relation, in that substances produced by one may now assist, or retard the growth of the other. In the course of evolution mutual assistance of adjacent groups of cells would be favoured by natural selection. The different regions then begin to fulfil the functions of separate organs.

In a cell colony of the kind considered earlier in this chapter the individuals are easily separable, but none the less cell walls contain macromolecular substances of the type well suited to give rise to adhesion. Indeed, various common species of bacteria, even in liquid suspension, form clusters or chains. In differentiated cell communities the nature of the interactions between adjacent members is susceptible of wide variation. Once changes set in they can become cumulative in the sense of an observation of Rosenberg[22] that in tissue cultures the development of the cells is sensitive to changes in the substratum on which they grow.

We have now arrived at a picture of a very crude living system with differentiated organs. In so far as the supply to and the excretion from a complex organism depend upon its geometry the whole scheme of things would be disrupted if cell multiplication continued indefinitely. Just as cultures enter the stationary phase when supply fails or inhibitors accumulate or as colonies reach a limiting size, so the differentiated tissue of an organ must eventually cease to divide, and for essentially similar reasons. The masses of non-dividing cells will then form a section of the whole organism dependent on other regions for the substrates maintaining the reactions of respiration or turnover essential for continued viability. Thus a set of mutual dependences is established of a higher order than that prevailing within a single cell. The close connexion between growth, division, and survival, characteristic of single cells, is now merged in more elaborate dependences.

The suspension of division does not mean lack of metabolic activity, and as S. Cohen points out, complex macromolecules may in organs like the liver be released from the cell or degraded as new ones are synthesized.[23] When there is turnover of this kind the balance of growth and division is no longer of so much importance. (To their lack of such ability to cope with seriously unbalanced growth Cohen attributes phenomena such as the 'thymineless death' of simple bacteria.[24])

The developing potentialities of structural differentiation as organisms become more complex are favoured by the ability of macromolecular substances to form fibres and sheets. Fibres can align themselves into rods, sheets can fold into tubes, the coiling and uncoiling of long-chain molecules gives a basis for elasticity. Thus the molecular structure is translated into the kind of mechanical structure in which surface tension, osmosis due to selective permeability, and flow of liquids in capillaries can all contribute to the distribution of nutrients, metabolites, and waste products. The way is now open for the evolution of circulatory systems and elaborate transfer mechanisms.

We have already seen that bacteria in a liquid culture may influence one another by metabolites in the medium. In organisms where differentiation has occurred substances produced by one part in certain phases of the growth of the whole may be conveyed to others whose development in turn they affect. Thus we have the origin of phenomena like hormone action.

An element of axial symmetry is already inherent in the linear array of information in the nucleic acids (and possibly proteins). If two centres A and B are ultimately responsible for some chemical reaction, then circles about the axis joining A to B represent the loci of points whose distances from A and from B respectively are all the same. Some of these loci may be of significance in the onset of structural changes, those, for example, governed by precipitation. Linear growth of polymers with a tendency to crystallize makes for axial symmetry, while the inflow and outflow of nutrients and waste products would come most simply into equilibrium in a system with spherical symmetry.

In more extended masses of living matter the relation with the environment may impose other kinds of geometrical order. Plants have a strong tendency to develop elements of symmetry about the axis of gravity. Different influences compete, and many living things combine elements of symmetry with enantiomorphism, traceable back ultimately to the asymmetry of optically active molecules.

Molecular asymmetry, as Pasteur showed, may on occasion be

reflected in the macroscopic asymmetry of entire crystals: molecular forms determine the space lattice in which crystals grow. The lines of the space lattice may, under conditions of rapid growth and sparse supply, be traced out in the macroscopic form of simple inorganic substances, as in the fern-like forms of snow crystals with their innumerable branchings. Similar tendencies exist with macromolecules and reveal themselves in more complex ways, since these molecules align themselves imperfectly and may enter into crystalline alignments over part of their length while forming part of an amorphous mass over the rest.

Tendencies to radial and to axial symmetry can give rise to spiral arrangements. At the same time growth depends upon chemical substances whose concentrations vary through space after the manner of a 'field'. The fields of different kinds of chemical activities are separate and a given type of reaction may depend upon the product or some other function of two or more superposed fields. The axial and radial symmetries can characterize these fields themselves, and if periodic precipitations or nucleus formation, after the manner of Liesegang rings, determine new centres of growth, then we have the origin of branchings, and phenomena like phyllotaxis in plants.

It is far beyond the scope of this book to deal with questions of morphology in general, but it is worth pointing out that the vast complexity of natural forms arises from variations on a few themes and that most of these are already discernible in the physical chemistry of a single bacterial cell.

REFERENCES

1. G. A. Morrison and Sir Cyril Hinshelwood, *J. chem. Soc.* p. 380 (1949).
2. B. J. McCarthy and Sir Cyril Hinshelwood, *Proc. R. Soc.* B **150**, 474 (1959).
3. A. C. R. Dean and Sir Cyril Hinshelwood, *Proc. R. Soc.* B **147**, 10 (1957).
4. K. Roelcke and H. Intlekofer, *Zentbl. Bakt.* **142**, 42 (1938).
5. W. Braun, *Bact. Rev.* **11**, 75 (1947); see also W. Burrows, *Textbook of Microbiology*, p. 150, W. B. Saunders & Co., Philadelphia (1963), and C. N. Hinshelwood, *The Chemical Kinetics of the Bacterial Cell*, p. 194, Clarendon Press, Oxford (1946) for general references.
6. P. Hadley, *J. infect. Dis.* **60**, 129 (1937).
7. I. M. Lewis, *J. Bact.* **34**, 191 (1937).
8. L. F. Rettger and Hazel B. Gillespie, *J. Bact.* **26**, 289 (1933); **30**, 213 (1935).
9. A. Haddow, *Acta International Union against Cancer*, **2**, 367 (1937).
10. M. Neisser, *Zentbl. Bakt.* **38B**, 98 (1906).
11. R. Massini, *Arch. Hyg. Bakt.* **61**, 250 (1907).
12. I. M. Lewis, *J. Bact.* **28**, 619 (1934).

13. M. W. Beijerinck, *Verzamelde Geschriften*, Delft (1922).

14. F. J. Ryan, Miriam Schwartz, and Phyllis Fried, *J. Bact.* **69**, 552 (1955).

15. F. J. Ryan, *Nature, Lond.* **169**, 882 (1952).

16. J. Lederberg, *Heredity*, **2**, 177 (1948).

17. W. J. Penfold, *Proc. R. Soc. Med.* **4**, 97 (1910–11); *J. Hyg., Camb.* **13**, 35 (1913).

18. Y. Tomita, *Jap. J. Bact.* **7**, 469 (1952).

19. A. C. R. Dean and Sir Cyril Hinshelwood, *Proc. R. Soc.* B **147**, 1 (1957).

20. L. S. Phillips and Sir Cyril Hinshelwood, *J. chem. Soc.* p. 3679 (1953).

21. L. E. Shinn, *J. Bact.* **38**, 5 (1939).

22. M. D. Rosenberg, *Science*, **139**, 411 (1963).

23. S. S. Cohen and Hazel D. Barner, *Pediatrics*, **16**, 704 (1955).

24. S. S. Cohen, *Texas Rep. Biol. Med.* **15**, 154 (1957); see also *The Chemical Basis of Heredity*, edited by W. D. McElroy and B. Glass, p. 651, Johns Hopkins Press, Baltimore (1957).

XIII

MUTANTS AND SELECTION

1. Introduction

THE capacity of a bacterial culture for developing new properties in a new environment has already been widely illustrated. The growth rate in new kinds of nutrient medium may improve from nearly zero to an optimum, inhibition by drugs may be overcome as resistance develops, and new reaction patterns reflected in an altered balance of enzymes may be established. The discussion in earlier chapters has shown how these adaptive phenomena are to be expected on the basis of almost inescapable assumptions about the general nature of cell organization. Indeed, it is very difficult to see how a cell could possess the integrated properties which it undoubtedly does without being capable of adaptive responses. But the explanatory force of natural selection has been so dominant in biology generally that there has been a widespread reluctance to admit any mechanism save that of population shifts in favour of organisms which have already gained in some way the capacity to thrive better in the new environment.

That direct adaptations do occur and that they can affect the major part of the population is shown by a great deal of varied evidence. Sometimes highly drug-resistant strains of bacteria can be cultivated by a gradual process in which there is almost complete survival at each step and no opportunity for the selection of resistant mutants (p. 169). Sometimes considerable increases in mass occur throughout an adapting culture before there is any detectable increase in numbers of cells (as would be necessary if effective metabolism were confined to a few mutants, p. 221). Often enough imperfect adaptation of a strain is shown not by the refusal of single cells spread on a plate to grow but simply by their taking a longer time over it, a time which shows a progressive reduction as adaptation advances (p. 221). The development of enzymes in adapting cells may occur far more rapidly than, or indeed altogether without, any cell multiplication (p. 223).

A vast mass of evidence confirms the almost inevitable prediction that systems like cells with integrated functions can and must adapt themselves to the conditions of their milieu. One reiterated argument to the contrary has been that properties like drug-resistance can on occasion be very tenaciously held. If the persistence is described as stable heredity then the development of a lasting drug-resistance involves the inheritance of an acquired character which is 'Lamarckian' and therefore unthinkable.

This feeling has sometimes led to a considerable logical confusion. As everyone knows, the rather crude experiments by which new characters imposed on plants or animals in their lifetime have been tested for heritability have almost always, perhaps always, led to negative results. This might conceivably mean only that somatic changes in complex living organisms have very little chance of affecting the highly specialized and segregated germ cells, in which event bacteria, which are soma and germ cell at the same time, might constitute a special case without, one would have thought, causing much scandal. Objection is sometimes excited even by the statement (Chapter X) that persistent drug-resistance or stable enzyme adaptation are not really examples of stable heredity at all. They are, as an experimental fact, purely relative and the adaptive changes show every possible rate of reversion from the extremely rapid to the very slow. Furthermore, it is questionable whether substrate-adaptation and drug-resistance should be described as 'acquired characters'. They represent the quantitative enhancement of capacities already present, and there would seem to be no reason to postulate separate and specific genetic information for each possible quantitative level of every existing property. In cells which multiply by binary fission a greater or lesser degree of reluctance to move back to a former overall organization when the original environment is restored is a manifestation of inertia rather than heredity. And, with every weight given to the ultimate dependence of the properties of living matter on codes of information, it is wholly contrary to principles of physics and chemistry to allow no range of latitude in their expression. When these principles predict that adaptability and stability phenomena for systems such as the cell must be of just the kind observed, one would have supposed the way clear for a balanced assessment of the separate roles of genetic information on the one hand, and cell integration on the other, in determining properties and behaviour.

In this connexion it is unfortunate that confusion has prevailed, and writers who discussed or reported experiments on adaptive responses have frequently been accused, even when they have explicitly stated the contrary, of denying the existence of mutations or of disregarding them, or even of ignoring the essential dependence of living matter on a copying process.

The base sequence in nucleic acid may obviously become changed. If it does, the properties of the organism will change too: so also may its potentiality for adaptive changes within the general latitude of the information supplied. If the modified properties give better growth or survival in a given medium, the mutant cells will gain predominance and replace the others. This much is obvious. Direct adaptive response, on the one hand, and mutation followed by selection on the other, are two quite separate mechanisms. Neither excludes the other. Nor does the study of one imply denial of the other. Hitherto we have been chiefly concerned with the direct adjustments, because the principal theme of this book is the organization of cell reactions considered from the kinetic standpoint. We shall now discuss more fully the question of mutational changes.

We may first consider how far mutations would reveal themselves in the kind of experiments designed for the study of adaptive changes in general. The example of *Aerobacter aerogenes* and streptomycin is a very instructive one.[1] When the bacteria are spread on a nutrient plate containing quite a low concentration of the drug (1 unit/ml) only one cell in about 10^8 multiplies. Substrains derived from those which do survive grow equally well at any concentration of streptomycin from one unit to several hundred per millilitre. They can be termed first-stage mutants (p. 164). This is in the sharpest contrast with what is found for many drugs, for example with chloramphenicol where a moderate concentration allows nearly all the cells plated to form colonies[2] and the resistance is graded as a function of the drug concentration to which the bacteria have become adapted.[3] A sharply contrasted behaviour is also found when the first stage streptomycin-resistant mutants are exposed to concentration of over 1000 units/ml, when the cells are all capable of surviving and show gradual and progressive improvement with continuous ranges of resistance. Selective enrichment of the more resistant from a whole spectrum of types is ruled out by the study of histograms of resistance distribution. Colonies showing the highest and lowest resistance at a given stage are replated and the histograms from each are the same.[1] Thus with *Aerobacter* and streptomycin the same techniques reveal the operation of each kind of mechanism in the appropriate range of drug concentration.†

† Some examples of the development of drug-resistance for which we have quoted evidence of direct adaptation have been interpreted in terms of mutation on the basis of a test called the *fluctuation test*.[4] This test consists in the inoculation of the same number of bacteria from the same parent culture into a number of tubes of medium, incubation for a standard time, and then counting of the numbers of resistant colonies

In this connexion it is very significant that with streptomycin the replica plating technique (p. 164) gives positive results,[1,7] whereas with chloramphenicol the increase of resistance observed in replica plating experiments[8] is no greater than corresponds to relatively minor changes of medium.[9] † If cultures of *Aerobacter* are made in the absence of light and other radiation they contain far fewer first-stage mutants, the proportion of which rises on cultivation in daylight. Thus there is here a certain presumption that they are formed by the action of radiation (see section 3).

The action of radiation is usually destructive, and one way in which it could act would be by damaging the receptors which normally take up the drug. Streptomycin-resistant cells have indeed sometimes been found to be less ready to take up the drug than sensitive cells (see reference 1 for details).

formed when the culture is plated on a drug-agar medium. The variance of the results so found is compared with that found when a corresponding set of samples from any one culture is plated on the drug medium. It is usually found that the variance is greater when the tests are made on samples derived from different cultures than it is when they are made on samples taken from the same culture. The argument then used is that the random occurrence of mutations in the individual cultures, leading to few or many resistant cells according as they have occurred late or early in the period of growth, explains the greater variance. This argument rests upon the assumption that the variance of different samples from cultures will depend, apart from sampling errors, only on this factor. The validity of the method has been strongly challenged.[5,6] In fact, uniformity of conditions, in respect of matters such as aeration, cannot possibly be as closely controlled with samples of different cultures as it can with one single culture. Furthermore, if there is a competition between adaptation and dying off of the cells, the times at which the last surviving cells in a culture can be detected shows very great variation. In short, the fluctuation test ignores causes of variation other than the incidence of mutation, while in fact such causes are quite strongly operative in most biological systems.

† A striking confirmation of the difference between low-grade streptomycin resistance and chloramphenicol resistance is provided by experiments on the behaviour of *Aerobacter aerogenes* in a medium containing both drugs.[10] When 6×10^8 cells were inoculated in parallel into media containing severally streptomycin at 1 unit/ml, chloramphenicol at 30 mg/l., and both drugs at these respective concentrations, the lag in the mixture was slightly longer than the sum of the (similar) lags observed in presence of either drug alone. Plating experiments show that the first stage streptomycin-resistant mutants occur with a frequency of about 10^{-7} to 10^{-8}. No cross resistance is found between the two drugs, and if resistance to chloramphenicol were attributed to resistant mutants as with streptomycin, a similar frequency would have to be assumed to account for the nearly equal lags in the individual media. The frequency of a double mutant would therefore not be expected to exceed about 10^{-14}. Since only 6×10^8 cells were inoculated, and since the first stage streptomycin-resistant mutants have to be selected from these, the probability that any of these are also chloramphenicol-resistant at 30 mg/l. is quite negligible. It would be difficult, on a mutational basis, to explain how any of the cells can begin to multiply in the mixed-drug medium. Any slight growth before the drugs have time to act could only account for a factor of less than 2 in the 10^{-14} ratio referred to.

It was therefore reasonable to envisage the two kinds of drug resistance, one in which the cell is protected by its inability to take up the drug, which might be called the negative kind: the other in which a reaction pattern is established which by-passes or antagonizes the action of the drug, the positive kind. Either kind could conceivably arise in either way, but a destructive mutation would be more likely to favour the negative kind.

The next important questions are how mutations can be brought about and in what they consist chemically or physically. They may arise spontaneously through the direct modification of the nucleic acids by the action of chemical substances, the so-called mutagens (section 2), and by the action of radiation (section 3).

Spontaneous mutants are sometimes spoken of as arising by 'chance' or 'errors in replication' but these forms of statement need closer examination since chance normally refers to the combination of multiple unknown causes, and there is nothing at all in cells (so far as we know) corresponding to the lapses which cause human beings to make errors. In the synthesis of a nucleic acid there are, according to current beliefs, stereospecific reasons why the sequence of bases should follow an existing pattern. The incorporation at a given stage of the poly-condensation reaction of a base not complementary to that in the guiding nucleic acid structure would be energetically much less favoured than that of the base which fitted. But this is a question of activation energy, and other things being equal, two analogous reactions differing in activation energy by ΔE will proceed at rates in the ratio $e^{\Delta E/RT}$ in favour of that with the lower activation energy. Although, if ΔE is reasonably great, this ratio may be very large, there is no question of the absolute exclusion of one reaction by the other. Once in a way, therefore, when a rare distribution of molecular energies happens to prevail near the reaction site, the 'wrong' base could and indeed should find its way into the macromolecule.

This principle, while allowing in a perfectly natural way for the appearance of occasional 'spontaneous' mutants, involves another consequence which some might deem more disturbing. Rates of reaction are dependent not only on activation energies but also on the concentra-tions of the reacting substances. For equal activation energies the relative rates of incorporation of two base types would be proportional to the relative concentrations, and a very large excess concentration of one type could compensate for a less favourable activation energy. Suppose now that as a result of temporary adaptive changes in a new medium a cell acquires a reaction pattern in which the availability of base X in a certain locus is greatly increased. This circumstance will favour the occasional incorporation of X in usurpation of a place normally occupied by another base Y in the nucleic acid. The changed code, for the ordinary steric reasons, once established, will tend to persist for some time even in the original medium. But while it persists it is creating a local demand for X rather than Y. The provision of more X would give better growth and, by the principles explained in Chapter V, enzyme systems capable of supplying this will expand. Once they have done this, the tendency, on mass action grounds, for Y to eject X in the code disappears. Thus we see that, in principle, changed metabolic patterns could favour code changes and that these in their turn could stimulate the kind of metabolism which would preserve them. This would represent induced mutation followed by stabilization. Whether this factor is quantitatively powerful enough to account in any example for the stabilization phenomena discussed in Chapter X is a quite open question and, as we have seen, the facts can be explained without necessarily invoking it. Nevertheless, detailed consideration of what is meant by 'spontaneous' does show that the relation of codes and their expression is a matter of some subtlety. It is very rare indeed in Nature that one thing can affect another while suffering absolutely no reciprocal action. Codes, although very stable and very difficult to influence, cannot in principle be absolutely immune even to directed changes.

The most simple and obvious way of obtaining a mutant is by the direct chemical modification of bases already in the nucleic acids of the cells, as, for example, by the action of nitrous acid. This method, and less direct chemical actions, are considered in the following section.

Radiations of different kinds are a common and powerful cause of mutations, in the great majority of examples leading to deficiencies. This is what would be expected if the radiation brought about a rather general and not very specific damage. It has, however, been pointed out that, from the way in which radiation-induced mutants are usually looked for, loss of characters is more likely to be observed than gain of characters.[11] The mutation is revealed normally by the fact that a strain previously capable of growth in a minimal medium now requires the addition of one or more adjuvants such as amino-acids. Nevertheless, the fact remains that these radiation-induced mutants are formed most abundantly in conditions where the majority of the cells are killed. Some of the most useful mutants so produced require one specific amino-acid to supplement a minimal medium in which the original strain grew readily. They are often quite unstable and undergo reversion or repair with relative ease. This is sometimes a gradual process and not nearly so clear-cut and discontinuous as a simple reversion would suggest (see sections 3 and 4).

The study of mutants plays a considerable part in work on the genetic code, and to make this clearer it will be convenient to recapitulate some of the current hypotheses. Work on the transformation of bacteria focused attention on the DNA as an important seat, and by hypothesis perhaps the sole seat, of genetic information. But proteins are synthesized largely on the particulate ribosomes of the cell. The discovery of certain short-lived forms of RNA with a rapid turnover in the cell is taken to support the hypothesis that unstable messenger RNA somehow carries the imprint of the genetic DNA to the site of protein synthesis. When *Escherichia coli* is infected by T2 phage a new kind of messenger RNA is formed and attaches itself to the ribosomes. Studies of protein synthesis, moreover, show that the amino-acids must first be activated by an enzyme, specific for each one, together with adenosine triphosphate, in a reaction with a transfer RNA, also specific for each amino-acid. These transfer RNA molecules bring the amino-acids to the ribosomes where the messenger RNA, bearing the imprint of the genetic DNA, acts as the template for protein formation. There is a good deal that remains obscure in all this, especially the mode of action of the numerous highly specific enzymes. Nevertheless, the basic mode of operation has been strikingly shown in experiments with special cell-free but enzyme-containing extracts of *Escherichia coli* to which polyuridylic acid was added and caused the synthesis of polyphenyl-alanine. From this it would appear that a sequence of uridylic residues does indeed mediate in some way the insertion of phenyl-alanine into a polypeptide chain. Ochoa and others have shown that mixed polynucleotides can act as artificial messengers bringing about the incorporation of various amino-acids into protein-like products. Ochoa thus refers to the messenger RNA as the template, and the transfer RNA as an adaptor responsible for attachment at the right position on the template.[12]

The question now arises as to what code in the base-sequence of the genetic DNA mediates the incorporation of a given amino-acid. There are four possible bases and twenty-odd amino-acids to be dealt with. The number of possible base pairs is 4×4 which is not quite enough, the number of triplets is $4 \times 4 \times 4$ which is several times too many, unless some combinations are ineffective in causing incorporation of anything into the peptide chain ('nonsense') or several combinations will cause the same amino-acid to go in ('degeneracy').

It is in the attempts to solve these questions that mutants come in. A few examples will illustrate the principle.

Tsugito and Fraenkel-Conrat[13] isolated RNA from tobacco-mosaic virus, treated it with nitrous acid to induce a chemical mutation (section 2), reassembled the virus constituents, infected the host, and allowed multiplication to occur. Extracted protein now proved to have a changed amino-acid composition, with proline, aspartic acid, and threonine replaced by leucine, alanine, and serine.

The bacteriophage T4 grows in some strains of *Escherichia coli*, and is subject to a large range of mutations. Some of the mutants revert easily, others are said not to. Numerous crosses of the latter were studied by Benzer:[14] the choice 'avoided any possible confusion between recombination and reverse mutation' so that a qualitative (yes—or no) test for recombination was claimed to be possible. Statistical analysis of the characters of recombinants was interpreted in terms of a 'genetic map'. Characters are ascribed to special regions of this map, and mutations to alterations at one site in a linear array. Recombination frequencies lead to a hypothetical ordering of this array. Many studies are being made on the production of mutants of different types and the properties of recombinants formed from them, and the frequency distribution of recombinant types. The results are used as a basis for hypotheses about the genetic code itself: whether it is triplet or not, whether overlapping (i.e. ABCDE readable as ABC, BCD, and CDE), degenerate, and so on.[15] We shall not, however, discuss these in detail, for several reasons. In the first place, we feel that the picture is likely to prove a rather unstable one, since, as we have already remarked, some of the criteria used create sharp distinctions artificially by methods more or less equivalent to calling 'over ten, plus' and 'under ten, minus'. More important, the results are not normally associated with kinetic studies and lie therefore outside the scope of this book.

It seems legitimate to wonder whether the true nature of coding and code reading can be understood without much more intensive study of the kinetics of the enzyme processes themselves, and especially of those which operate on Ochoa's amino-acids and artificial messengers. More information about the turnover of the labile RNA is probably capable of being built into a picture of how the stereospecifically guided enzymatic polycondensation reactions work. Modern techniques for the detection of free valencies are urgently called for throughout this kind of study.

Mutations are often assumed to involve the addition or deletion of a base from the nucleic acid sequence (see section 2), but it is difficult to form a clear idea about this without some more precise hypothesis about the mechanism of the all-important enzyme reactions. Enzymes, as has been remarked, are all too often treated as though they were Maxwell demons, and too familiar to be asked about. A more kinetic approach to the whole subject is invited by other kinds of reflection and observation. Are mutations commoner in dividing cells, and do they occur spontaneously during division? The great upheaval and rejoining of macromolecular fragments which is conceivable during this phase could possibly on occasion give some abnormal arrangements. Ryan[16] showed, by using cells capable of two kinds of adaptation (from requirement of histidine to independence and from the lactose-negative to the lactose-positive condition) and working under conditions where one character remained constant and acted as a marker of population turnover, that there was no actual lysis and regrowth of cells during the stationary phase (cryptic growth) of cultures in which he observed adaptation. He recognized that no entirely new mutant cells were appearing. He himself attributed what he still regarded as mutations to turnover of genetic material within the individual cells.

The phenomenon of 'phenotypic delay' focuses attention on the whole reaction pattern and not simply on the code. After irradiation the deleterious effects may not become evident for some generations after growth has gone on.

Some mutants are described as 'leaky' which means that a character has indeed been changed, but not from + to −, or vice versa, but only in a partial way. Another interesting class is discussed by Gorini[17]. Various members of this class require for growth a specific amino-acid, varying from mutant to mutant. All, however, in the absence of the specific addition, will grow as streptomycin-dependent strains, the drug replacing any of the amino-acids. Gorini speaks of a situation such 'that environmental factors can influence the outcome of the process [code reading] and that the ribosomes take an unexpectedly active part in the translation step'. It seems doubtful whether a full understanding of this effect can be reached without consideration of the total reaction pattern of the cell and the various ways in which the presumptive mutation may have affected it.

The action of radiation on cells is often lethal. Sometimes 'lethal mutations' are spoken of, but the only reasonable use of this term would seem to be in relation to a process which so damaged a cell that it could only divide a few times, giving each time something less able to fulfil its original function. But there is also an interesting phenomenon of repair (see section 4). The great resistance of *Micrococcus radiodurans* has been shown not to depend upon any kind of special DNA composition, but upon the capacity for a gradual repair of the initial damage inflicted.[18] The repair is associated with the operation of enzymes and is manifested by renewed growth after a long lag which exposure to the radiation induces.

As so frequently, Nature weaves a pattern of great complexity in the ways by which micro-organisms can show changed properties lasting over several or many generations. There are the changes in reaction pattern and spatial map which flow from the integration of the cell as discussed in Chapters V and X. These may be highly persistent. There are changes in the basic information enshrined in the genetic codes. And yet another is possible. As has been suggested for spore-forming bacilli (p. 408), one can envisage interpenetrating and partially independent codes in the same cell, one or other gaining dominance according to the circumstances of growth.[19] This last view has elements in common with theories about repressors and derepressors. In the last resort, however, it does not differ fundamentally from what is envisaged in the network theorem.

2. Chemical agents causing mutagenesis

A wide variety of chemicals have been reported to be mutagenic agents. They include substances such as the acridines, nitrous acid, alkylating agents (for example, the sulphur and nitrogen mustards, ethylene imine, propiolactone, and many others), and analogues of the naturally occurring bases in DNA, such as bromouracil. Like radiations, chemical mutagens are indiscriminate in their action, and many different effects are observed, as would be expected. The infection of susceptible host cells by bacteriophage, by resistance transfer factors, and by other episomic elements might be considered as an example of chemical mutagenesis, although a clear distinction should be drawn between the integration of a fragment of information-bearing DNA into a cell and the alteration by chemical means of the bases already present.

The action of nitrous acid might have been expected to provide the clearest case of all, since it deaminates in decreasing order of frequency, the bases guanine, cytosine, and adenine in DNA and also acts on bases in RNA. Complications arise, however, since still other reactions occur. Nevertheless, it has been stated that it induces mutations in bacteriophages, tobacco-mosaic virus and bacteria. A proposed mechanism for the mutagenic action of nitrous acid is that adenine is changed into hypoxanthine which now pairs with cytosine instead of thymine, cytosine becomes uracil and pairs with adenine in place of guanine, and guanine becomes xanthine which still pairs with cytosine, but by one hydrogen bond less.[20]

In intact tobacco-mosaic virus, as distinct from the RNA isolated from it, only cytosine and adenine are deaminated.[21] Acridines combine with nucleic acids, and a theory of mutagenesis based on their intercalation between the bases in DNA has already been referred to (p. 152). The base-analogues 5-chlorouracil, 5-bromouracil, and 5-iodouracil, it is claimed, can be incorporated into the DNA of bacteria and bacteriophages in place of thymine.[22] The corresponding fluoro-derivative is said to replace uracil in RNA,[23] while guanine can be replaced by 8-azaguanine.[24]

5-Bromouracil has been used extensively, and its virtually complete replacement of the thymine in bacteriophage T4 has been reported.[25] Its mutagenic action has been interpreted as a result of occasional mis-pairing with guanine. This is thought to be a result of the more electro-negative nature of the bromine atom compared with the methyl group it replaces, and the resulting change in the electron distribution in the pyrimidine ring is said to favour a shift from the normal keto to the enol state.[26, 27] Once bromouracil has been incorporated into the DNA strand, however, its mutagenic effect at any one site would depend not only on which base pair is involved but also on neighbouring base pairs. A range of effects would thus be expected.[27]

Aronson[23] has pointed out that it is difficult to draw conclusions about the exact mode of action of base-analogues in intact cells, and says that this is specially true with 5-fluorouracil which has, besides its possible incorporation into RNA in place of uracil, an action on the synthesis of DNA, cell wall, RNA, and protein. In this connexion Cohen and his associates[28] interpret the action of 5-fluorouracil on *Escherichia coli* in terms of disturbances in uracil and thymine metabolism. This possi-bility of metabolic disturbances has also been recognized with 5-bromo-uracil, but the conclusion has been drawn that its mutagenic action, as distinct from any disturbances in metabolism it may cause, is a result of its incorporation into DNA, since bromouracil-induced mutation has been claimed to occur in cells infected with bacteriophage containing the analogue.[29] Chantrenne,[24] however, also maintains that the action of analogues of purines and pyrimidines is manifold and complex, and remarks that 'it is easy to make *ad hoc* hypotheses which would account for the observations'.

The alkylating agents are very reactive, and among the reactions they cause with isolated DNA are alkylation of the phosphate groups, alkylation of the nitrogen atoms in the bases, the N-7 atom of guanine being particularly reactive, and depurination.[30] Speculations have been made about how these changes could give rise to mutations but the situation is far from clear, and indeed it has been said in connexion with mutagenic agents in general that in no case has a mechanism been verified to such an extent as to allow the identification of a particular type of base change.[31]

Various types of mutation can be envisaged. A large part of the genetic material may be altered or indeed removed altogether. On the other hand, a change in a single base pair would constitute a mutation in terms of the Watson–Crick model for the structure of DNA. Such a small change, often referred to as a point mutation, is difficult if not impossible to prove at the present time, and the existence of such mutations is simply inferred from the results of recombination experiments. In these experiments as many independent mutants as possible are crossed with one another and the frequency of the various types of recombinants is said to give an idea of the distance between the sites at which mutation occurs. Much of this work has been carried out in the so-called 'r II' mutants, in which, it is claimed, the changes occur in a specific region of the hereditary material of bacteriophage T4. Benzer[32] defines the smallest indivisible element that is interchangeable in genetic recombination as a *recon* and the smallest element which on alteration can give rise to a mutation as a *muton*. As he points out, the unit of function presents more difficulties in definition, and in genetic experiments it is inferred from the '*cis-trans* test'. When both mutant genomes are inserted into the same cell, this constitutes the *trans* test and if the resulting phenotype is still defective the mutants are said to be non-complementary, that is, they are defective in the same 'function'. The corresponding control experiment consists in inserting the same genetic material in the *cis*-configuration, by using one double mutant and a non-mutant, which, it is stated, usually produces a non-defective phenotype or a close approximation to it. Benzer[32] writes: 'It turns out that a group of non-complementary mutants falls within a limited segment of the genetic map. Such a map segment, corresponding to a function which is unitary as defined by the *cis-trans* test applied to the heterocaryon will be referred to as a 'cistron'.

Each mutational site is thought to correspond to at most a few nucleotide pairs. This idea is based on the following evidence. The length of the r II region corresponds at most to 10^4 and probably to about 10^3 nucleotide pairs; at least 304 different mutational sites have been found, and a Poisson distribution would predict at least another 120; more sites probably exist, since so far mutagenic agents of a restricted specificity have been used.[22]

The replacement of one base pair by another, the deletion of a base pair, the insertion of a new base pair, and the inversion of the order of a number of base pairs joined together are possible and Freese[22] has further classified base changes as transitions or transversions. In single-stranded DNA the replacement of a purine by another purine or of a pyrimidine by another pyrimidine would be a transition while the replacement of a purine by a pyrimidine or vice versa would be a transversion. With double-stranded DNA the replacement of a guanine-cytosine pair by an adenine-thymine pair or the reverse so that the purine-pyrimidine orientation is preserved would be called a transition. When the orientation is reversed, however, the change would be a transversion, for example the replacement of a guanine-cytosine pair by a cytosine-guanine or a thymine-adenine pair. The postulate was made that 5-bromouracil induces transitions and that proflavine induces transversions,[22] although Brenner et al.[33] have claimed that proflavine induces the deletion of existing base pairs or the insertion of new ones rather than transversions.

3. The effect of radiations

Ultraviolet light and ionizing radiations, such as X-rays or the radiations produced during the decay of radioactive isotopes, are often used to induce mutations in living systems. During irradiation free radicals are produced, and in this connexion we may note that treatment of bacterial cells with manganous salts[34] or with Fenton's reagent[35] sometimes produces effects similar to irradiation. The composition of the medium in which the cells have been grown, the part of the growth cycle at which they have been taken, and the presence or the absence of oxygen during the irradiation all have an influence on the ensuing damage. Recovery can sometimes be hastened by what is called photoreactivation, that is by subsequent treatment with ordinary light.

When isolated DNA is treated with ultraviolet light a complex sequence of events takes place. The pyrimidines are reported to be more susceptible than the purines, and the initial effect following the absorption of a photon of energy is probably a chemical alteration of the pyrimidine residues.[36] The structure is then weakened and cross linking of the complementary strands may occur.[36] Transforming DNA which has been inactivated by the action of ultraviolet light can be reactivated by the photoreactivating enzymes from bakers' yeast in the presence of ordinary light, and in this process disruption of the induced cross links may occur.[36] A large part of the biological action of ultraviolet light has been ascribed by some workers to the formation of intrastrand thymine dimers.[36, 37] The powerful forces set up by the creation of strong bonds between thymine residues would, it is argued, either break the DNA molecule or impair its function.

Although nucleic acids absorb strongly in the ultraviolet region of the spectrum, it would indeed be surprising if the only effect of irradiation occurred in the nucleic acids. Certainly if interest lay in the production of genetic mutants it would be an advantage to arrange conditions so that any other effects would be excluded if possible, but any such procedure would influence the overall picture to a considerable extent. A common result of irradiation of *Aerobacter aerogenes* or *Escherichia coli* is the production of strains which are reluctant to grow in a glucose-ammonium sulphate medium to which they were fully adapted before the treatment. As will be seen in the next section, however, a wide spectrum of behaviour is encountered, and this raises the question of the standards to be adopted for mutants. Are all detectable changes to be ascribed to mutation? If an analysis of the sequence of the bases in the DNA could be carried out the problem would be simpler but at present an inference has to be drawn solely from the properties of the strains, and this applies equally to the effects of chemical mutagens.

4. Repair of radiation damage

According to the conditions a wide range of types of damage might be expected to follow irradiation. At one extreme the destruction may be so widespread that death ensues (and in this connexion the term lethal mutation, as we have said, would seem to be meaningless). When the damage is not too severe, recovery often takes place and the process by which it occurs is complex. For example, in the recovery from ultraviolet irradiation photoreactivation by visible light, heat reactivation, host-cell reactivation, and other enzymatic processes have been described.[36, 38] Much attention has been focused on the removal of thymine dimers from the DNA as part of the recovery process.[37] The irradiation of cells with ultraviolet light results in a cessation of DNA synthesis although if the treatment is not too severe the synthesis of RNA and protein may continue.[37] As mentioned in the previous section thymine dimers may appear in the DNA in these conditions, although this is not the only change that may take place. These dimers can be split, it is said, by short-wave ultraviolet light and by the enzymatic processes occurring during photoreactivation by visible light, and their disappearance is said to be correlated with the increase in the ability of irradiated cells to form colonies and with the restoration of the biological activity of irradiated transforming DNA. In *Escherichia coli*, however, a more important process is stated to be the actual removal of the thymine dimers from the DNA in the form of small oligonucleotides. This has been inferred from experiments in which the migration of dimers formed from tritium-labelled thymine from the acid-insoluble fraction to the acid-soluble fraction of the cells was followed during the lag in the synthesis of DNA. The process is thought to be enzymatic and the further postulate has been made that it may be a general method for correcting errors arising in the DNA codes.[37, 39] It is by no means the only step in the process since the broken strands would have to be joined up again presumably after the replacement of the excised segment, and a mistake here could constitute a mutation. Moreover, in the strains *B* and *B/r* of *Escherichia coli* the dimers disappear at about the same rate, but the ability of the cells to form colonies is very different.[39]

It would appear that a necessary condition for recovery is that the cells should be put into an environment where their synthetic machinery can be induced to function, however imperfectly, and this has been confirmed by direct experiment. For example, when cells of *Aerobacter aerogenes* were irradiated with ultraviolet light until about 10^5 of the original 10^9 cells per ml survived, these survivors had a long lag in a simple medium (containing ammonium sulphate as source of nitrogen) in which they had grown readily before the treatment. They still grew readily when the medium was supplemented with asparagine and glutamic acid, but could be 'retrained' to utilize ammonium sulphate alone by serial subculture in a medium in which it was the sole source of nitrogen.[40] When the irradiation was continued still further and only about 100 out of the original population of 10^9 per ml survived, the survivors exhibited an almost continuous spectrum of growth rates in the minimal medium, and in their ability to ferment sugars. A few would not grow at all in the simple medium, but did so after one subculture in an asparagine-glutamic acid medium. Others grew with varying degrees of efficiency. Sometimes the total population reached was low, sometimes it was more or less normal, but the growth rate was always low and only returned to the normal level after many subcultures.[35]

This recovery was a gradual process without the abrupt appearance at any stage of a normal strain. This is shown in Table 28, where the mean generation times measured at every subculture during the recovery process of one of the strains are recorded.[41] The ability to ferment sugars also reappeared in a gradual manner.[42]

TABLE 28

Mean generation times during serial subculture of a damaged strain in the normal synthetic medium

Sub-culture no.	M.g.t. (min)	Sub-culture no.	M.g.t. (min)	Sub-culture no.	M.g.t. (min)	Sub-culture no.	M.g.t. (min)
1	45	19	41	36	37	53	38
2	45	20	39	37	44/30	54	37
3	44			38	36	55	36
4	49	21	38	39	39	56	32
5	43	22	42	40	37	57	36
6	45	23	38			58	36
7	40/52	24	38	41	35	59	35
8	37/51	25	37	42	35	60	36
9	38/43	26	37	43	39		
10	35/43	27	37	44	33	61	35
		28	35	45	32	62	31
11	38	29	38	46	40	63	37
12	39/46	30	38	47	47	64	39
13	38			48	32	65	34
14	38/46	31	37	49	33	66	33
15	35/45	32	38	50	34	67	36
16	40	33	38			68	32
17	36	34	35	51	43	69	30
18	40	35	33	52	36	70	32

Where two figures are given a composite growth curve is indicated

Mean values of the m.g.t. for the successive ranges of 10 sub-cultures:

No.	1–10	11–20	21–30	31–40	41–50	51–60	61–70
M.g.t. (min)	44	40	38	37	36	37	34

Other workers[43] have claimed that definite strains of *Aerobacter aerogenes* having a specific requirement for one or more amino-acids can be isolated in experiments of this sort. This would represent only one extreme of the spectrum of damage and as the following experiments with *Escherichia coli* show it would be misleading to pretend otherwise.[44]

Of 1092 strains isolated after irradiation with ultraviolet light 78 did not grow in the unsupplemented minimal medium. The addition of asparagine was all that was necessary for 7 of them and the further addition of glutamic acid sufficed for another 47. Of the remaining 24 strains 8 grew when any one of several amino-acids was added, 14 required the addition of one specific amino-acid, and 2 required a mixture of amino-acids. By the standard criteria of isolation all of these 78 strains would have been classified as mutants, and yet only 2 of them proved to be stable. Indeed, with 55 of them one passage through supplemented medium was all that was necessary before growth was possible in unsupplemented medium. The question of the standards to be adopted for mutants arises again. If all these unstable strains are mutants, they have presumably suffered changes in their genetic codes, and if this has taken place, the instability of such changes calls for comment. On the other hand, if the damage suffered by the cells has not involved genetic changes the equations of the network theorem (Chapter V) show how recovery, once it has been initiated at all, will proceed until the optimum rate of growth is reached. When this stage had been reached in the experiments just described the resulting strains were indistinguishable from the unirradiated organism.

Modern genetic theory envisages that 'reversion' need not necessarily lead to the original state. For example, with a triplet code a mutation in which an additional base had been added would affect not only the coding unit (codon) in which it occurs but would change the reading of all the code. If a deletion of a base now occurs somewhere else, the message would only be read incorrectly between the two mutation sites, and if they were not too far apart the function of the gene might not be altered very much. In this way an 'addition' mutation would be reversed not only by the removal of the extra base but also by a deletion close to it. The second mutation would then be referred to as a 'suppressor' of the first.[45]

According to the network theorem an extremely complicated pattern of reversion can easily appear. For example, if a strain of bacteria growing at the optimum rate in a given medium is exposed to a drug, the ensuing resistant strain is often unable to grow at the optimum rate in the absence of the drug. Exposure to a second toxic chemical may now result in the first resistance being lost and still further affect the behaviour in the drug-free medium. At each stage the best overall combination of reactions tends to be established, but, as we have seen in Chapter X, the attainment of the final optimum may be a slow process.

Bacteriophage T4 has been used in many of the experiments with chemical mutagens and it is quite possible that its DNA is more accessible than that in entire cells. Thus the results may be simpler. With entire cells it would be surprising if, in addition to any changes that may arise in the code, the impairment of other cell functions did not also occur. Indeed, evidence of this has already been given for 5-fluorouracil (p. 342), and in experiments in which *Aerobacter aerogenes* was subjected to proflavine or to Fenton's reagent the survivors, besides growing slowly in the absence of the drug, also exhibited abnormal fermentation reactions.[42]

5. Types of selective mechanism

If there are n_A cells of type A and n_B of type B in a growth medium where both types grow equally well, the ratio of n_A to n_B will remain constant. If, however, a sample of the population is transferred to a medium in which the growth-rate constant k_A for type A is greater than that k_B for type B, then the ratio n_B/n_A will diminish progressively towards zero. If n_B happened to be much greater than n_A at the time of transfer, there would clearly be a complete change in the character of the population on continued growth in the new medium. This would constitute a simple example of selection, and one can see quite easily that differential death-rates would lead to the same sort of result. One hypothesis, as we have seen, attributes most, if not all, adaptive phenomena in bacteria to the operation of selection. While rejecting this extreme view, we now need to consider certain aspects of how selection operates. With enough carefully chosen auxiliary assumptions some form of the selection hypothesis can usually be made to account for almost any of the facts about adaptation. These auxiliary assumptions themselves increase in arbitrariness and complexity as one proceeds, and one must conclude by declining the main thesis as improbable. Nevertheless, although selection is probably not usually the primary mechanism of bacterial adaptation, it is one which must be superimposed upon other adaptive processes, and the discussion of it comes appropriately after that of those primary changes which its operation may accelerate or intensify.

Adaptation could not in any event be explained away generally in terms of selection of pre-existing mixed types since it occurs to strains which have been derived from single cells. Steady production of mutants would have to be assumed. When quantitative as well as qualitative characters are taken into account an indefinitely large range of these mutant types has to be postulated. Even then, very special and improbable assumptions have to be made about the mutual influences of one mutant strain on the growth rate of another to correlate rates of training and reversion,[46] and it may also be necessary to assume rather improbable properties for the mutants.[47]

Nevertheless, it will be useful to examine one or two specific phenomena from the point of view of selection and to see what sorts of assumptions are required.

As we have seen in a good many examples, training, whether to drugs or to new substrates, is progressive through a series of subcultures. In general, reversion occurs easily if the cells are returned to the original environment after a short training: after longer training there is delayed reversion; and eventually something like complete stability is reached.

Suppose we have two types of cell A and B present in numbers n_A and n_B. The B type may be thrown off in small proportion as mutants during growth in medium I, but does not itself grow so well as the A type. Let the growth-rate constants be k_A and k_B respectively. In this medium I, the numbers settle down to a definite ratio such that n_B/n_A is small. Now let an inoculum be transferred to medium II in which the growth rate K_B of B is greater than that, K_A, of A. We shall have, after time t,

$$n_A = (n_A)_0 \, e^{K_A t}$$

and

$$n_B = (n_B)_0 \, e^{K_B t},$$

whence

$$n_A/n_B = \frac{(n_A)_0}{(n_B)_0} e^{-(K_B - K_A)t}.$$

Since K_B is greater than K_A, n_B will increase indefinitely at the expense of n_A. As soon as the ratio is preponderatingly in favour of the B type the culture will appear to be adapted. n_A diminishes steadily. Now although the equations written down refer to continuous variables, cells are individual countable entities, and at about the time when n_A corresponds to less than one cell in the inoculum transferred in a serial subculture, there will be none of the A type left at all. If, then, the strain consisting entirely of type B is returned to the original medium I, there will be no cells of type A to increase in number, in spite of the fact that k_A is much greater than k_B. The bacteria remain now a homogeneous population of type B, and at any subsequent retransfer to medium II will show optimum growth. That is to say, the training will appear to be stable. (It is to be noted, however, that we must now ignore the earlier assumption of continuous formation of mutants.) If K_B is considerably greater than K_A, the culture in medium II will appear to be practically fully trained as soon as n_B has increased to be even comparable in magnitude with n_A. For example, if n_B constituted one-half the total number of cells, and if only the B type grew at all, the difference between the mixture and a pure culture of type B would only reveal itself by a lag in medium II corresponding to the time taken for the 50 per cent of B in the inoculum to double itself, that is to say, to one generation time. This would be quite a small apparent lag. But with such a mixture the strain A would be able rapidly to regain the upper hand when returned to medium I, that is to say, there would be rapid reversion. The phenomenon of delayed reversion would be met at the stage where, in medium II, n_A had fallen almost but not quite to zero. We suppose that an inoculum consisting of a very few cells $(n_A)_0$ of type A and a large number $(n_B)_0$ of type B is returned to medium I. After time t, the numbers will be

$$n_A = (n_A)_0 e^{k_A t} \quad \text{and} \quad n_B = (n_B)_0 e^{k_B t}$$

respectively. If $(n_A)_0$ is small enough it will be a very long time before n_A once again outweighs n_B even though k_A is much greater than k_B. During this time n_B will have become very great, that is to say, there will have been a large number of subcultures in medium I. Not until n_B has fallen very considerably behind n_A will any loss of power to grow in medium II become apparent. Hence the delay in the detection of reversion. The delay is, of course, only apparent, since the readjustment is in progress all the time, but the nature of the exponential growth law is such that only when there is a very serious departure from 100 per cent of the strain B is its decline detectable by growth tests in medium II.

If, in the original culture in medium I, there were an extremely minute proportion only of type B, and if, further, type B alone were capable of growth in medium II, then on transfer for the first time, there would be a very long apparent lag. In the ordinary way a lag is calculated on the assumption that all the cells grow. If the inoculum consists of $(n_A)_0 + (n_B)_0$, and if only $(n_B)_0$ actually grow, then, over and above any real lag, there will be an apparent lag equal to the time required for $(n_B)_0$ to increase to $(n_A)_0 + (n_B)_0$. If the former is a minute fraction only of the latter, this lag will be long. Furthermore, if only the B type grow in medium II, the resulting strain will be nearly pure B and reversion will be difficult or impossible.

A serious objection to the form of selection hypothesis just outlined is that, in certain examples at least, the relations which have to be postulated between the values of k_A, k_B, K_A, and K_B do not correspond to reality. Shortly, if a strain is to revert when returned to the original medium, then, according to the pure selection hypothesis, this can only be because the trained cells are at a relative disadvantage in it (that is, k_B is less than k_A). This appears sometimes to be definitely not so.

It might be said that independent tests of the growth rates of the trained and untrained types are not delicate enough to reveal a small differential rate in favour of the untrained type. To test this question, the following experiment was made.[48] Cells were trained in glycerol medium until they became completely stable. They were then mixed with an equal proportion of completely untrained cells, and the composite strain was subcultured many times in the parent glucose medium. If, normally, non-reversion depends upon the absence of any residue of the untrained type, and if reversion is simply due to a more ready growth of the untrained strain, then this composite culture should show a loss of adaptation as rapid as that shown by a partially trained one. No loss in the glycerol adaptation in fact occurred, in spite of the deliberate addition of the considerable proportion of untrained cells. Further assumptions can be introduced which make the growth rates of the two types of cell functions of their relative numbers. They become increasingly improbable as they try to account for all the observations.[47, 48]

For example, *Aerobacter aerogenes* shows adaptation to lactose, accompanied by β-galactosidase formation with very little lag. Thus if lactose-positive mutants are involved they are numerous from the start. After longer periods of culture the unstable initial adaptation gives place to the stabilized type. If then there is selection it must be between type A which loses its lactose adaptation when grown in glucose and type B which forms β-galactosidase in glucose medium and retains its lactose adaptation. A and B must be assumed to grow almost at the same rate in lactose except that there is just enough advantage with B to allow it to outgrow A in the course of very many generations. Intermediate levels of lactose adaptation may persist for very long periods of culture in glucose, so that both types A and B would seem to be equally well fitted for growth in glucose, a conclusion which does not tally with the rapid changes which are observed during the early stages of stabilization.[47]

Assumptions can be made about a strong inhibition of the growth of one mutant by the presence of large numbers of the other. Direct experiments on the plating of mixed populations on solid media have shown, in some typical examples, little evidence for this. The absence of the effect has been verified with lactose or D-arabinose as the sole source of carbon and also in the presence of the drugs proflavine, chloramphenicol, brilliant green, streptomycin, and terramycin.[49] Some typical results are given in Table 29.

According to the selection hypothesis the rate of adaptation depends

upon the ratio of the growth-rate constants of the two strains. This
ratio may have any value, and the most diverse rates of training could
be accounted for. If the 'unadapted' strain does not grow in the new
medium, and if the 'adapted' strain is present initially in very small
amount, there will, as already explained, be a long initial lag, the length
of which will be determined by the proportion of the favoured strain
initially present. The interpretation of the composite growth curves

TABLE 29

*Effect of a large number of 'untrained' cells on the growth
of a few 'trained' cells*

Experiment	Inoculum	Number of colonies at the given time	
		1 d	2 d
1	75 lac$^+$ 2 × 10^8 lac$^-$	10 small	73 lac$^+$, ∞ small
	75 lac$^+$	31 small	75 lac$^+$
2	45 terramycin$^+$ 1·5 × 10^6 terramycin$^-$	0	53 large
	91 terramycin$^+$	0	91 large

In experiment 1 the cells were plated on lactose-agar and in experiment 2
on terramycin-agar (5 mg/l.) in which the survival of the sensitive strain is
about 5×10^{-6}.

$^+$ 'Trained' $^-$ 'Untrained'.

met with in the study of adaptive processes has been discussed from the
point of view of alternative reaction mechanisms in an earlier chapter.
The interpretation in terms of selection would be simpler still, and in
some respects more satisfactory, were it not for the inherent improba-
bilities of, and other objections to, that hypothesis. The two separate
components of the growth curve, as illustrated in Figs. 65 and 69, would,
if there were separate strains in competition, have a quite independent
existence. The greater lag of the faster-growing strain would, however,
on this basis, be an apparent one and due simply to its small initial
numbers. The relations are illustrated diagrammatically in Fig. 107.
According to this interpretation, however, one would expect a culture
which had once grown far enough to pass the transition point to be
stable to reversion, which is not by any means necessarily found.

As we have seen, there are good examples of a precise numerical
correspondence between the properties of an adapted strain and the
concentration of the drug at which training is carried out. This would
certainly not be possible as a result of simple selection from a mixture

of a few non-interconvertible types differing among themselves in their sensitivity to the drug. It would only be possible if there existed a continuous spectrum of such strains, and even then a special assumption would have to be made: namely, one about some particular law for the distribution of natural drug resistance among the members of the population.

If one specifies the degree of resistance by the value of the drug concentration, $\bar{P}$, to which a given type of cell is immune, then the

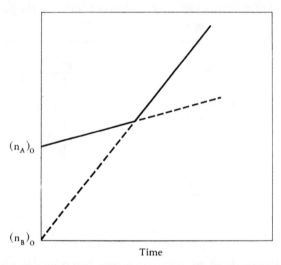

FIG. 107. Composite growth curves on selection hypothesis.

frequency distribution of $\bar{P}$ values among the cells would have to be a remarkably steep one. It would be necessary to suppose that, of all the cells with $\bar{P}$ greater than any assigned value $\bar{P}_1$, the vast majority had values very close to $\bar{P}_1$ itself. This form of distribution would ensure that when cells immune to $\bar{P}_1$ had been selected, there would be among them a residue of still more resistant cells for further selection, but too few to give the culture as a whole an effective resistance greater than that corresponding to $\bar{P}_1$ itself.

The difficulty is that the assumption of this frequency distribution law for the supposed drug resistance is entirely arbitrary.

One respect in which the pure selection hypothesis might appear at first sight to have an advantage is in accounting for the definite 'equilibrium' levels of adaptation at which cultures may settle down. We may recall that cells can be trained to resist very high concentrations of proflavine, that is, $\bar{P}_1$ is very great. On serial subculture in the drug-free medium, there is partial reversion to a stable limit corresponding to $\bar{P}_2$. The value of $\bar{P}_2$ depends upon the length of time for which the training was originally carried on. According to the selection view, one would assume that the cells trained at $\bar{P}_1$ developed a distribution with a sharp maximum in the neighbourhood of $\bar{P}_1$ itself, but including values down to a lower limit $\bar{P}_2$. On subculture in the ordinary drug-free medium the less resistant cells would be assumed to have an advantage which allowed them to increase in relation to the others. Thus $\bar{P}$ for the culture as a whole would move down towards $\bar{P}_2$. This would be the lower limit, since cells with smaller values are assumed to have been eliminated entirely. The longer the original training was continued the more closely would $\bar{P}_2$ approach $\bar{P}_1$ and the higher would be the level of the 'equilibrium' strain.

One difficulty about all this is that, as has been explained, when such shifts of population are tested for in artificially prepared mixtures of strains, they do not happen.

6. Superposition of adaptation and selection

There is no escape from the conclusion that once, by whatever mechanism, certain cells have become better adapted than others to grow and multiply in a given medium, selection must automatically be superimposed on the other adaptive process.

On the one hand, in the course of training, it will accentuate and accelerate the operation of other mechanisms, since the first cells to become adapted, even if they owe their priority only to chance, will have an opportunity to outgrow the rest. In the limit, it is only necessary theoretically for one cell to have become adapted initially. This adaptation will, however, have been conditioned by the drug concentration, or by the nature of the substrates in the medium, so that the degree of immunity will correspond. Thus the rate only, and not the final extent or the character of the adaptation will be modified by selection.

How far the different cells in a medium will vary in the ease with which they acquire adaptive characters is hard to predict. They will have a certain range of ages, and this will cause a slight spread in their responses to the new environment; they will show a certain distribution of sizes, which will be reflected in slight variations in rate of food supply; their division times exhibit some degree of statistical fluctuation. The summation of many small effects gives rise to what will appear as a random variation. With a carefully grown parent culture, and with well-controlled experimental conditions, one would not expect the total range of variation to be great; and it would be surprising if most of the cells did not respond almost at the same time to the simpler and easier forms of adaptation. Where the adaptive process is long and difficult the range of variation might be expected to be much greater.

As selection will accelerate adaptation, so, conversely, it will greatly retard the loss of adaptation. Suppose a population of cells is subjected to conditions in which the adaptation tends to be lost. The algebraic form of the growth law is such that a very small proportion of survivors of the adapted strain will, in any test, still give the culture as a whole the appearance of being largely adapted. For example, if the reverted cells show a lag of 1000 minutes in presence of a drug, then 10 per cent of resistant cells, showing no lag, and having a generation time of 30 minutes, will give the culture as a whole an apparent lag of about 100 minutes only.

An approximate quantitative calculation[50] of the behaviour of a mixed strain containing adapted and reverted cells is of some interest. Suppose there are, for example, 1 per cent of immune cells. Let us consider separately the behaviour of the two parts of the population when inoculated into a medium containing the drug to which the cells were originally adapted. In one case we imagine that we inoculate with 99 sensitive cells, and in the other with 1 resistant cell. But in each we reckon the total inoculum, for the purpose of calculating the lag, as 100. We plot two curves showing the relation between the drug concentration and the apparent lag (that is, the value found by extrapolating the growth curve back to 100).

In Fig. 108 the curve ABC is that for the reverted cells, which constitute the majority. XBY is that for the resistant residue. XBY lies well above the true lag-concentration curve for adapted cells because it is calculated on the assumption that the inoculum is 100, whereas the inoculum is in reality only 1. X in fact lies above the real value by the time taken for the number to increase from 1 to 100, whereas A only lies above it by the time taken for the number to increase from 99 to 100.

Now let us consider the actual behaviour of the mixture of 99 sensitive cells and 1 resistant cell. The two substrains cannot strictly be considered to grow quite independently and in a simple competition, since growth intermediates put into the medium by the one will be available for the other. Nevertheless, we shall obtain a general idea of the lag-concentration curve of the mixture by following the line ABY which represents everywhere the lower of the two values given by ABC or XBY respectively. At the point B the resistant strain, despite its initial paucity of numbers, now reaches the threshold of visible growth before the more numerous, but more sensitive strain.

The type of lag-concentration curve with a shoulder similar to that of *ABY* is not infrequently found with strains of *Aerobacter aerogenes* which have been trained to high concentrations of proflavine, and which do in fact contain cells with varying degrees of adaptation.

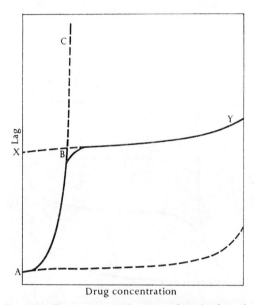

Fig. 108. Lag-concentration curve for mixed strain
of resistant and non-resistant cells.

Figure 109 shows a family of curves corresponding to various propor-tions of resistant and sensitive cells. As the fraction of immune cells drops, the point corresponding to *B* in Fig. 108 rises higher and higher. The family of curves in Fig. 109 is in general character not unlike that found for the lag-concentration curves of the *Aerobacter aerogenes* strains which have suffered varying degrees of reversion by passage through phenol or cresol after having been trained to proflavine.[50] Here, then, we seem to have an example of selection of resistant cells in the test itself, the result being an overall retardation of the loss of immunity.

It should be emphasized that in the immediately foregoing discussion selection is not regarded as the cause of reversion, which is thought to depend upon factors influencing each individual cell. The selection operates merely in the test for residual resistance, and there makes that resistance appear greater than it would otherwise have done.

7. Assumptions about continuous ranges of variation

Arguments in favour of direct adaptation rather than the selection
of pre-existent mutants can, as we have seen in a number of examples,
be based upon experiments which contrast the observed course of the
adaptive process with that which the mutation theory would predict
(see, for example, pp. 222, 230, 335). Such arguments can, as has been observed before, be circumvented by enough special *ad hoc* hypotheses about
the properties of mutants. Suppose, for example, that we study the

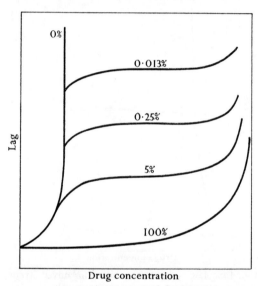

Fig. 109. Lag–concentration curves for various proportions
of resistant cells (indicated by numbers on the curves).

transition between the X^- and the X^+ states of a culture and show that
it is not at all like the selection of a few X^+ from a reconstructed
mixture of the initial and final forms. We can usually postulate a whole
series of mutant steps, some of which are formed during the growth of
the others, and if we do, we can probably explain any course we wish.
But this involves the hypothesis that not merely each character but
each quantitative level of each character is determined by a separate
gene, and since the quantitative levels have to be very numerous and
closely spaced, the value of explanations reached in this way is not high.

(Incidentally, it may be pointed out that this multiplicity of mutations
is not in accord with the theory of repressors and derepressors, which
although more specialized than the views set forth in the theorems of
Chapter V, is not incompatible with them.)

REFERENCES

1. W. T. Drabble and Sir Cyril Hinshelwood, *Proc. R. Soc.* B **154**, 449 (1961); W. T. Drabble, ibid. 571 (1961).
2. A. C. R. Dean, *Proc. R. Soc.* B **153**, 329 (1960).
3. J. B. Woof and Sir Cyril Hinshelwood, *Proc. R. Soc.* B **153**, 321 (1960).
4. S. E. Luria and M. Delbrück, *Genetics*, **28**, 491 (1943).
5. K. R. Eriksen, *Acta path. microbiol. scand.* **26**, 269 (1949).
6. A. C. R. Dean and Sir Cyril Hinshelwood, *Proc. R. Soc.* B **139**, 236 (1952); B **140**, 339 (1952).
7. J. Lederberg and Esther M. Lederberg, *J. Bact.* **63**, 399 (1952); J. Vandermuelen, *Acta path. microbiol. scand.* **41**, 411 (1957); S. Banič, *Schweiz. Z. Path. Bakt.* **19**, 792 (1956); W. J. B. Morgan, *J. gen. Microbiol.* **19**, 517 (1958).
8. L. L. Cavalli-Sforza and J. Lederberg, *Genetics*, **41**, 367 (1956).
9. P. McConnell, unpublished observations.
10. A. C. R. Dean and P. J. Rodgers, unpublished observations.
11. A. W. Ravin, *Symp. Soc. gen. Microbiol.* **3**, 41 (1953).
12. S. Ochoa, *Fed. Proc.* **22**, 62 (1963).
13. A. Tsugita and H. Fraenkel-Conrat, *Proc. natn. Acad. Sci. U.S.A.* **46**, 636 (1960).
14. S. Benzer, *Proc. natn. Acad. Sci. U.S.A.* **47**, 403 (1961).
15. See A. O. W. Stretton, *Br. med. Bull.* **21**, 229 (1965).
16. F. J. Ryan, *J. gen. Microbiol.* **21**, 530 (1959).
17. L. Gorini, *New Scient.* **24**, 776 (1964).
18. B. E. B. Moseley and H. Laser, *Proc. R. Soc.* B **162**, 210 (1965).
19. H. O. Halvorson, *Symp. Soc. gen. Microbiol.* **15**, 343 (1965).
20. See for references, A. Tsugita and H. Fraenkel-Conrat in *Molecular Genetics*, edited by J. H. Taylor, Part I, p. 477, Academic Press, New York (1963).
21. H. Wittmann and B. Wittmann-Liebold, *Cold Spring Harbor Symp. quant. Biol.* **28**, 589 (1963).
22. See for details E. Freese in *Molecular Genetics*, edited by J. H. Taylor, Part I, p. 207, Academic Press, New York (1963).
23. S. P. Champe and S. Benzer, *Proc. natn. Acad. Sci. U.S.A.* **48**, 532 (1962); but see also A. J. Aronsen, *Biochim. Biophys. Acta*, **49**, 98 (1961).
24. R. E. F. Matthews and J. D. Smith, *Nature, Lond.* **177**, 271 (1956); H. G. Mandel and R. Markham, *Biochem. J.* **69**, 297 (1958); D. H. Levin, *J. biol. Chem.* **238**, 1098 (1963); but see also H. Chantrenne, *J. cell. comp. Physiol.* **64** (Suppl. 1), 149 (1964).
25. F. W. Stahl, Jean M. Crasemann, L. Okun, Evelyn Fox, and C. Laird, *Virology*, **13**, 98 (1961); see, however, H. S. Shapiro and E. Chargaff, *Nature, Lond.* **188**, 62 (1960).
26. E. Freese, *Proc. natn. Acad. Sci. U.S.A.* **45**, 622 (1959); see also *The Molecular Mechanisms of Mutations*, Fifth Int. Congr. Biochem., Moscow (1961).
27. E. Strelzoff, *Z. Vererblehre*, **93**, 301 (1962).
28. S. S. Cohen, J. G. Flaks, Hazel D. Barner, Marilyn R. Loeb, and Janet Lichtenstein, *Proc. natn. Acad. Sci. U.S.A.* **44**, 1004 (1958).
29. B. E. Terzaghi, G. Streisinger, and F. W. Stahl, *Proc. natn. Acad. Sci. U.S.A.* **48**, 1519 (1962).

30. P. Brookes and P. D. Lawley, *J. cell. comp. Physiol.* **64** (Suppl. 1), 111 (1964); P. Alexander, Sheila F. Cousens, and K. A. Stacey in Ciba Foundation Symp. on *Drug Resistance in Micro-organisms*, edited by G. E. W. Wolstenholme and Cecilia M. O'Connor, p. 294, Churchill, London (1957).

31. D. A. Kreig in *Progress in Nucleic Acid Research*, edited by J. N. Davidson and W. E. Cohn, Academic Press, New York, **2**, 125 (1963).

32. S. Benzer in *The Chemical Basis of Heredity*, edited by W. D. McElroy and B. Glass, p. 70, The Johns Hopkins Press, Baltimore (1957).

33. S. Brenner, L. Barnett, F. H. C. Crick, and Alice Orgel, *J. molec. Biol.* **3**, 121 (1961).

34. M. Demerec and Jessie Hanson, *Cold Spring Harbor Symp. quant. Biol.* **16**, 215 (1951).

35. A. C. R. Dean and Sir Cyril Hinshelwood, *J. chem. Soc.* p. 1159 (1951).

36. J. Marmur, W. F. Anderson, L. Matthews, K. Berns, E. Gajewska, D. Lane, and P. Doty, *J. cell. comp. Physiol.* **58** (Suppl. 1), 33 (1961).

37. See R. B. Setlow, *J. cell. comp. Physiol.* **64** (Suppl. 1), 51 (1964) and references therein; and D. Shugar and J. Jagger in *Recent Progress in Photobiology*, edited by E. J. Bowen, pp. 37, 59, Blackwell, Oxford (1965).

38. See Symposium on Recovery of Cells from Injury, *J. cell. comp. Physiol.* **58** (Suppl. 1) (1961).

39. R. B. Setlow and W. L. Carrier, *Proc. natn. Acad. Sci. U.S.A.* **51**, 226 (1964).

40. A. R. Peacocke and C. N. Hinshelwood, *Proc. R. Soc.* B **135**, 454 (1948).

41. A. C. R. Dean and Sir Cyril Hinshelwood, *J. chem. Soc.* p. 1169 (1951).

42. A. C. R. Dean and Sir Cyril Hinshelwood, *J. chem. Soc.* p. 1173 (1951).

43. See B. D. Davis in Ciba Foundation Symposium on *Drug Resistance in Micro-organisms*, edited by G. E. W. Wolstenholme and Cecilia M. O'Connor, p. 342, Churchill, London (1957).

44. A. C. R. Dean, *J. chem. Soc.* pp. 2817, 2823 (1952); A. C. R. Dean and Sir Cyril Hinshelwood, ibid. p. 2826 (1952).

45. F. H. C. Crick, L. Barnett, S. Brenner, and R. J. Watts-Tobin, *Nature, Lond.* **192**, 1227 (1961).

46. S. Jackson and Sir Cyril Hinshelwood, *Proc. R. Soc.* B **136**, 562 (1949); Sir Cyril Hinshelwood and S. Jackson, ibid. B **137**, 88 (1950).

47. N. Richards and Sir Cyril Hinshelwood, *Proc. R. Soc.* B **156**, 20 (1962).

48. E. G. Cooke and C. N. Hinshelwood, *Trans. Faraday Soc.* **43**, 733 (1947).

49. A. C. R. Dean and Sir Cyril Hinshelwood, *Proc. R. Soc.* B **142**, 225 (1954); B **144**, 297 (1955).

50. D. S. Davies, C. N. Hinshelwood, and J. M. G. Pryce, *Trans. Faraday Soc.* **41**, 778 (1945).

XIV

CELL DIVISION

1. Introduction

As cells grow they divide periodically. Cultures which are not maintained in active division tend to show losses of enzyme activity and eventually to suffer serious diminution of viability. During the logarithmic phase of growth the size of any cell varies only between limits about an average. To a rough approximation each cell doubles its original mass and then separates into two. But the average size itself changes somewhat with the environmental conditions, and the times between successive divisions show a statistical distribution. Division may be advanced or delayed by growth factors or drugs and occasionally almost completely inhibited.

On the whole, the successive divisions may be said to constitute a rhythm of considerable regularity on which, however, is imposed a sort of '*rubato*', a set of deviations from regularity governed by complex statistical variations.

In the development of the general theorems about growth in the earlier chapters of this book, we have, on the whole, accepted division as something which does occur and which simply allows the rate constants of the different cell processes to remain fairly near to an average value characteristic of the culture as a whole. We must now consider the problem of the nature of the division process in more detail.

2. The general principle underlying cell division

Various analogies with cell division have been cited from time to time, the way in which a liquid column may break up into drops under the influence of surface forces, and the fragmentation of a large crystal into a mosaic of smaller ones. But these leave the essential element of the problem untouched, though they remind us of the importance of potential energy relations.

The cell certainly possesses an internal structure of some kind: it possesses an overall unity of function combined with a spatial heterogeneity. The structure is imposed by strong binding and orienting forces, comprising probably the whole range of chemical and physical interactions. It constitutes in a sense a special kind of phase of matter.

Its structure is determined by a condition of minimum potential energy, mechanical or electrical or both. In solid phases, and indeed in liquid phases too, changes in composition or conditions can lead to instability followed by a transformation to a new structure, as when rhombic sulphur changes to monoclinic, or when a homogeneous liquid mixture separates into two conjugate solutions. These phase transformations are always subject to the conditions that they proceed in the direction of decreasing free energy. A cell which has come into a condition of increased mechanical and electrical potential energy will lower this if a way is open. Something analogous to a phase transformation occurs in the well-known experiment with floating magnets. When the number of these is increased, a single ring of magnets, at a certain stage, breaks up into two concentric rings. In so far as the cell is regarded as a particulate constellation conditions of instability can be imagined to arise as numbers of particles grow. We have no need at this stage to consider the internal structure in detail. All we need to bear in mind is that the spatial map of the cell will seek a minimum potential energy.

Division is necessary for orderly growth. As a cell becomes larger the surface/volume ratio changes, and access of nutrients from the outside becomes more difficult while escape of metabolic products from the interior is impeded. A steady state of autosynthetic growth demands that the consequent changes in reaction rates occur only between moderate limits. Only cells with a division mechanism could behave in this orderly manner, and would be likely to survive evolutionary processes. This fact, with due respect to a familiar type of biological argument, does not explain division in terms of a selective advantage, since natural selection can only operate on something which can arise in the first place. There is, however, a general principle which impels cells to divide periodically.

According to the equations derived from the integration principle (Chapter V), all the various cell constituents are, in the steady state, formed in constant proportions. These constituents are heterogeneously disposed through the volume of the cell, in the form, for example, of nuclear material, membrane, or wall material and so on. When a cell grows a conflict arises between the maintenance of a similar geometrical form, on the one hand, and a constant set of ratios between components, on the other. The incompatibility of constant composition with unchanged geometrical form leads to mechanical stresses which become

progressively more pronounced. The resulting increase of energy ultimately imposes a rearrangement of the matter present. At the point
where the cell has doubled in size a redistribution to give two versions
of the original would entirely run down the accumulated potential
energy. There will, however, be some latitude about the stage at which
the redistribution actually occurs.

The above argument is quite general and independent of any particular
geometry provided only that the cell material does not form one uniform
homogeneous solution, which it certainly does not. To illustrate the
operation of the principle we shall, however, assume the case of a spherical
cell, and we shall idealize the components to 'surface' material and
'average' material. This simplification, we must emphasize, is not
important for the result, and does not affect the principle, though it
shows its working more clearly.

Suppose the surface material occupies a layer of thickness δ over the
surface of the spherical cell, then its amount will be proportional to
$4\pi R^2 \delta$, while 'average material' will be in an amount proportional to
$\frac{4}{3}\pi R^3$, where R is the radius. Suppose the potential energy of the whole
system to be a minimum when $R = R_0$. Now let the cell increase in
size by the normal processes of growth. We will calculate the increase
in potential energy, relative to the minimum at R_0, when the radius is R.
Let us assume that δ is to remain constant, a likely enough assumption
if we are dealing with, for example, a layer of sheet-forming polysaccharide or mucoprotein. According to steady state equations for the
entire mass, the surface material will have increased in the ratio $(R/R_0)^3$.
To cover the new surface with the layer δ in thickness it would only
need to increase in the ratio $(R/R_0)^2$. Thus the surface layer has in fact
suffered an overcrowding in the ratio R/R_0, which is equivalent to a
compression in the ratio R_0/R. If we assume the simplest kind of
elastic behaviour,[1] this compression will lead to a potential energy
increase proportional to the square of the displacement from equilibrium,
namely to

$$\left(\frac{R-R_0}{R_0}\right)^2, \quad \text{or to} \quad \left\{\left(\frac{V}{V_0}\right)^{\frac{1}{3}} - 1\right\}^2.$$

If the cell now divides into two parts, one of the original volume V_0
and one of volume v, and if v is less than V_0, then this smaller part of
the surface material is no longer compressed but stretched. We may
take it that the energy storage on stretching follows a law similar to
that for compression, and the value of $(R-R_0)^2$ is, of course, independent
of the sign.

The excess energy of the V_0 portion is now zero, that of the v portion is

$$\left\{\left(\frac{v}{V_0}\right)^{\frac{1}{3}}-1\right\}^2 \quad \text{or} \quad \left\{\left(\frac{V-V_0}{V_0}\right)^{\frac{1}{3}}-1\right\}^2.$$

When v is quite small the excess energy of this separated portion would be even greater than that of the whole. But as V increases the energy of the separated portion gets smaller and smaller, presently falling below that of the undivided cell, and eventually to zero when $V = 2V_0$.

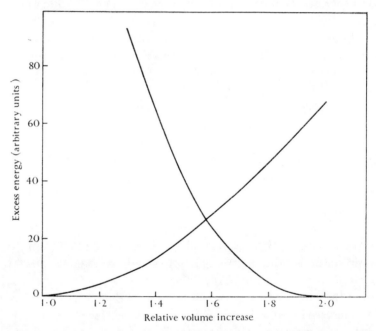

FIG. 110. Energy relations of an undivided and a divided model cell.

As soon as the energy of the two separated portions falls below that of the undivided cell the mechanical urge to rearrange the contents and separate comes into play.

This tendency is shown in Fig. 110 which illustrates the crossing of the two potential energy curves. Where they cross there may still be impediments to division, but until they have crossed there is no mechanical urge to divide.

A similar calculation could be made if we considered the material of some macromolecular chain which, hypothetically, formed n radial spokes from a central nucleus to the circumference. As the total volume increases this would need to increase in the ratio R/R_0. The chemical steady state would make it increase in the ratio $(R/R_0)^3$, causing complex bucklings and associated pressures.

The incompatibilities discussed and others of an analogous kind could all be avoided by a set of extremely *ad hoc* special assumptions: in the surface layer δ would have to increase in proportion to R. The radial spokes just mentioned would have to be assumed to increase in cross-section in proportion to $(R/R_0)^2$ and so on. Such special assumptions would be very difficult to reconcile with a reasonable functional view of the various sheets, chains, and masses which make up the complete cell.

Thus we may conclude that a mechanical urge to periodic division is provided by the essential conflict between conformity, on the one hand, with chemical kinetic mass equations tending to impose a material balance which moves steadily towards increasing mechanical instability and, on the other hand, with the tendency for the matter to rearrange itself into a state of minimum potential energy.

This principle, however, tells us little about the detailed nature and course of the rearrangements.

3. The ordering of the spatial map of the cell

The cell is more than a simple collection of enzymes and information-bearing sites. It has a structure which has been termed a cytoskeleton. Reservations about all the possible implications of that term have been mentioned. The cell is from one point of view a colloidal particle, and from another it has important resemblances to a complex co-polymer.[2, 3] It contains macromolecules of substances of widely variable composition, capable of forming chains, sheets, or quasi-crystalline masses. The chemical types on which these structural parts are based can combine with themselves or with one another and can give compounds of mixed type such as nucleoproteins, mucopeptides, and so on. The chains, sheets, and masses order themselves into a structure, not rigid, not impermeable, and capable indeed of containing pools of metabolites, but showing some measure of relative stability. The whole range of chemical forces will come into play in determining this structure. Thus there would be no great difficulty in conceiving vast co-polymers to constitute, as it were, the girders and partitions used in the building of the cell. In the bolting together of these structural elements every kind of force can play a part but there is an interesting possibility that covalencies may play a somewhat more subtle role than appears at first sight.

The enzyme reactions of a living cell occur with surprising facility. This may possibly be explicable on the basis of a very nicely adjusted correspondence of spacings on enzyme and substrate, a factor which does indeed play a certain, though hardly a major, part in some reactions of inorganic chemistry. But another analogy from chemistry *in vitro* is also very suggestive. Many polymerization reactions are initiated by free radicals which set up a chain reaction of the following type:

$$R \cdot + CH_2{=}CH_2 \to RCH_2 \cdot CH_2 \cdot$$
$$RCH_2CH_2 \cdot + CH_2{=}CH_2 \to RCH_2CH_2CH_2CH_2 \cdot$$

At some stage a process known as chain transfer[4] may give a stable polymer and a small radical which can initiate another chain.

$$R(CH_2CH_2)_n CH_2CH_2CH_2 \cdot \to CH_3 \cdot + R(CH_2CH_2)_n CH{=}CH_2$$

One initial radical thus mediates a large number of polymer chains, so that a few radicals can go a long way in producing a chemical effect. Another phenomenon especially common in gaseous combustion reactions is that known as chain branching.[5] It is illustrated by the following series of steps:

$$R \cdot + O_2 \to ROO$$
$$ROO \cdot + RH \to ROOH + R \cdot$$
$$ROOH \to RO \cdot + HO \cdot$$

Here the number of radicals increases steadily with time until their concentration is such that mutual saturation limits the rise. The actual chain-branching step may be rare and the rate of growth slow. Nevertheless, the steady increase is of the kind which in some systems leads to an eventual explosion. When the rate merely reaches a limit the phenomenon is sometimes referred to as a 'degenerate explosion'.

These analogies suggest some interesting possibilities about occurrences in cells. There is some evidence on physical grounds that cells contain free valencies. These could be thought of as playing a major part in its chemical reactions. A cell which remains alive without growing preserves certain capacities enabling it, when the correct materials are again presented, to synthesize fresh substance by reactions very different from those commonly met in the laboratory. Thus one could conceive of the cell as containing a macromolecular polyfunctional free radical system. Such a system possesses a degree of stability because the free valencies, which in a homogeneous phase would rapidly saturate one another, are held in a relatively rigid spatial separation by the organized cell structure. The protection thus afforded would not be absolute and a slow decay would occur. A steady regeneration of free valencies would be needed. The occurrence of chain reactions in the cell would provide an ideally simple mechanism by which the increase of free energy accompanying the synthesis of substances like protein can be compensated by the decreases accompanying reactions like the oxidation of glucose. With the intervention of chain reactions almost any coupling of reactions becomes simple.

If free valencies do occur in cells and if they play a significant role, then another conclusion follows. When a cell divides, the daughter cells between them must contain roughly twice as many of them as the original cell from which they grew. Thus the free valencies must have been steadily increasing in number during the time between successive divisions. This would mean that the overall reaction scheme would have some of the characteristics of the degenerate explosion referred to above. If so, then the multiplication of free valencies would, as likely as not, exceed the simple doubling necessary to provide the complement of the new cell, and some of those produced would be available for the bolting together of the new long chains and extended sheets, all themselves provided in places with free valencies, to give the new spatial map. The accumulation of prefabricated parts all provided with free valency bolts could in this way play an important part in implementing the division process which more general considerations of potential energy call for.

The general question of the participation of free radicals has been under discussion for some time. Michaelis et al.[6] proposed in 1936 that they might play a part in biological redox reactions, and the wider question of the cell itself as a macromolecular, polyfunctional free radical system was mooted in 1946.[7] More recently with the development of magnetic methods of investigation some experimental evidence has been accumulating.[8] But the view that radicals have a really important role has been contested. Setlow and Pollard,[9] for example, in connexion with the products of irradiation of cells, dismiss chain reactions as unlikely, on the ground that chain propagation demands a wholly homogeneous medium. They say that 'unless such chain reactions can be demonstrated either in polypeptide bonds, or the base-sugar bonds of nucleic acid, or in the carbon–carbon chains of lipids, there are no regions of the cell with the desired homogeneity'. To this several things may be said. First, known chain reactions do occur in media which cannot fairly be described as quite homogeneous. Secondly, it is precisely in connexion with the polymeric structures mentioned that the analogy of radical reactions *in vitro* is most suggestive. Thirdly, radicals

are only removed finally by combining with other radicals. Reaction
of a radical with a solvent liberates another radical, and this process,
while it may divert the course of a chain reaction, does not necessarily
interrupt it altogether. A hydroxyl radical removed by reaction with
an aqueous medium will liberate another,[10] $\cdot OH + H_2O \rightarrow H_2O + H \cdot$
Free valencies could be generated first here and then there over the
whole extent of a macromolecular structure, until, in favourable circumstances, one happened to be formed in a sterically sheltered location
where it could persist for longer than usual. This whole question of free
valencies will be discussed further in Chapter XVI.

4. How centralized is cell organization?

The details of the division process must depend a good deal on the
degree of centralization of the cell system, and on whether the material
basis of the various cell functions occurs once only or is repeated a few
or many times throughout the volume.

Oparin's view[2] about the evolution of cells offers a certain presumption
that an absolutely centralized system is not the most likely. If the cell
arose from earlier and simpler forms of self-reproducing matter, which,
having acquired a boundary wall or membrane, accepted other elements
into their community and gradually increased in complexity, then it
might well retain something of an incompletely centralized character.

Various individual functions of a cell may be damaged or destroyed
by mutagenic agents while the cell itself remains viable and functional
and indeed capable of repairing itself.

Numerous particulate structures are distinguishable in the cell, the
ribosomes, for example,[11] and these form a quite complex constellation
in which repetitions, if not demonstrated, are at least highly possible.

There is much variation in cell size, and in some circumstances cells
may go on dividing so as to become very small.[12, 13] They remain,
however, fully viable and have no obvious defects, so that some appreciable subdivisibility of the function-bearing substance is suggested.

Nuclear structures are much less clearly distinguishable in bacteria
than in some other kinds of cell. Regions of DNA-rich material presumably have some kind of nuclear function, but they can hardly be regarded
as unique centres of control. Moreover, certain masses regarded as of
a nuclear type sometimes divide quite independently of the division
of the whole cell (p. 376).

On the whole, then, the most useful picture of the cell for the purpose
of thinking about division is that of a constellation of many particles

held in a state of maximum stability by a wide range of physical and chemical forces.†

5. Types of division mechanism

The essential driving force in division is the seeking of greater stability, but the paths by which this is reached can be variable just as they can in the phase changes of less elaborately organized matter.

The duplication of some important centre of organization could be the signal for the reorganization of everything round the two new centres. One could call this fancifully the 'bee-swarming' analogy. If the cell is regarded as a constellation of particles, then with increase in their number a tendency to form two independent groups may declare itself, the 'floating magnets' analogy. If free valencies play an important role in the functioning of the cell and the bolting together of the cytoskeleton, then the provision of more and more of them by chain branching could be closely linked with division, the 'degenerate explosion' analogy. If a relative excess of cell-wall-forming material accumulates, it might exert a tendency to wrap up the cell contents into two parcels, the 'packaging' analogy.

None of these mechanisms excludes any of the others. One or other might, in some circumstances, be the limiting factor in causing the onset of division, provided that the general stability relations were already favourable.

The result of a complex interplay of factors, one or other of which might become limiting, suggests that we must expect a good deal of variability in the occurrence of division, and this is precisely what is found, as we shall see in surveying the experimental evidence later in this chapter.

In this connexion a special word should be said about DNA replication since DNA is now generally held to be the major repository of genetic information. It has a tendency to form aggregates of a more or less

---

† This may seem at variance with numerous statements about continuous, linear, or circular chromosomes or DNA strands in bacterial cells.[14, 15] Very long strands or fibres of DNA have indeed been revealed by electron microscopy and autoradiography,[16, 17] but it is open to great question what the necessary processing of the material has done to the original form. One process, for example, involved lysis by Duponol of the cell, removal of protein, and slow 'disentangling' on a dialysis membrane and then overlaying with photographic emulsion for autoradiography. After this, according to the description given, 'the *E. coli* DNA . . . is found mainly in the form of tangled masses. However, a few continuous, unbranched DNA threads of up to 900 μ in length are also found.'[17] Analogies with the drawing and extrusion of plastics and protein threads are hard to escape.

crystalline nature and of variable size.[18] The evidence that certain internal structures in bacterial cells may sometimes divide before the cell itself raises the question whether here the DNA is acting as the key centre of organization which tends to impose a reorganization on the rest when it has multiplied.

It is true that with wide variations of media[46] (DNA/cell) does tend to remain constant, but this is by no means an absolute rule. There is an opposing tendency, as conditions are varied, for (DNA/mass) to stay constant,[12, 13] and, as we have seen, a compromise is reached between the two effects.

Genetic information is supposed to be replicated when a second helix of DNA grows round an original one, guided by the pairing of complementary bases which form hydrogen bonds with one another. If the double helix subsequently unwinds, there are two genetic templates in place of one original one, and this might be taken as the key act leading to cell division. But such a view leaves a great deal unexplained. We have to account for the fact that the free-energy relations favouring double helix formation do not maintain the product in the dimeric state, and what, therefore, the driving force for the unwinding may be. Nor is the DNA the only part of the cell which is replicated. All the other components are reproduced too, and there is no use for a new centre of organization if there is nothing for it to organize.

The replication of the DNA, and possibly the unwinding of helices, form one of the coordinated processes which all occur, more or less, though with some latitude, in step. Any delay in the formation of fresh DNA will, however, delay division, and in these circumstances the formation could become limiting.

6. Kinds of experimental evidence

The preceding discussions will first be summarized. The picture of base-pairing by hydrogen bonds along a DNA helix,[19] while structurally enlightening, leaves too many questions untouched to give a satisfactory picture of cell division. Every component of the cell is potentially concerned in this process which involves a complex interplay of many factors. The multitude of ribosomes in a cell, the scattered distribution of enzymes, the dispersed material of nuclear type suggest that the cell must be regarded as a constellation with no one element in unique control. According to the laws of growth there is a tendency for everything to be formed in balanced proportions, but these proportions, although having optimum values in a given environment, may change.

As a cell grows, the maintenance of constant proportions becomes incompatible with an unchanged geometry, and potential energy changes create a need for the break-up into two smaller versions. The relief of this need is, however, not provided for by the mere fact of its existence, any more than thermodynamic instability of a given phase of matter necessarily and immediately brings about its transformation to a more stable state.

The paths by which instability is relieved are various, and subject to influence by conditions. Different factors may play their parts in proportions which vary with circumstances. Certain internal centres of organization may play a role, the provision of free valencies may be important, the proportions of wall-forming substance to the rest can have a considerable influence.

We shall proceed therefore to discuss the following matters in the light of experiments: the statistical variation of division times, and of the size of cells at division, the influence of drugs and other agents on division, the appearance of dividing cells, the behaviour of individual cells in the period between one division and the next, and related topics in the light of the general ideas which have been developed.

7. Statistical variation of generation times and cell sizes

Bacteria can be kept under continuous observation on a warm stage under the microscope and the successive divisions of individuals and their progeny studied.

Kelly and Rahn[20] made direct measurements upon very large numbers of cells which were kept growing on agar. Under favourable conditions all the cells continued to divide, there being no 'infant mortality', that is, the throwing off of cells which proved themselves unable to produce fresh daughter cells in their turn. The time between successive fissions was found to be extremely variable. But there was no sort of selection of faster-growing or of slower-growing strains. The progeny of a cell which had divided after an unusually short time showed division times which were, on the whole, neither greater nor less than normal, but simply representative themselves of the general average. The range of variation is illustrated by a result which they quote for *Bacillus cereus* of which one cell did not divide for 185 minutes, the next division following in 25 minutes. On one occasion they observed the second and third divisions to follow one another without any interval at all. Kelly and Rahn suggested that mitosis, that is to say, the internal reorganization preceding division, may occur without the actual division of the cell into two. This would explain how two successive fissions could occur in very rapid succession.

The distribution of fission times is shown by the following numbers which refer to *Aerobacter aerogenes* at 30° C, and is taken from among the results in the paper of Kelly and Rahn.[20] The numbers recorded are the numbers of cells out of a total of 323 observed which had fission times within the various 5-minute ranges.

Range (min)	Number	Range (min)	Number
5–10	0	40–45	45
10–15	1	45–50	20
15–20	11	50–55	8
20–25	25	55–60	2
25–30	42	60–65	2
30–35	97	65–70	0
35–40	65	70–75	5

These results have been plotted in the form of a frequency distribution curve in Fig. 111 (with omission of the few examples in the range 70–75 minutes). The numbers have been scaled so that the maximum frequency is represented by the number 100. In the same figure the shaded area is a Gaussian frequency distribution curve so chosen as to have the same maximum and to coincide with the experimental curve at the points where the deviation from the most probable fission time of 35 minutes is equal to ± 5 minutes. The calculated curve is given by

$$y = 100e^{-0 \cdot 0278(x-35)^2}.$$

The experimental curve is evidently not of a strictly Gaussian form, and allows for a considerably greater frequency of large deviations from most probable value than would be predicted, according to the Gauss equation, from the frequency of the smaller deviations.

Nevertheless, the general shape of the curve suggests strongly that there is some standard value for the division time, and that the moment of division is advanced or retarded in each individual case by the operation of a multiplicity of factors of a more or less random nature.

One complication, which may affect the precise form of the frequency distribution of the division times, is that there may be two kinds of delay: one in which some important part of the cell material, constituting a sort of nucleus, itself fails to divide; and the second in which, although the internal processes are completed, the formation of the new dividing walls has not taken place.

Several authors, working with a variety of organisms, have pointed out that division is not simply and solely determined by the size that the cell has attained at the moment when it occurs. If growth rate does

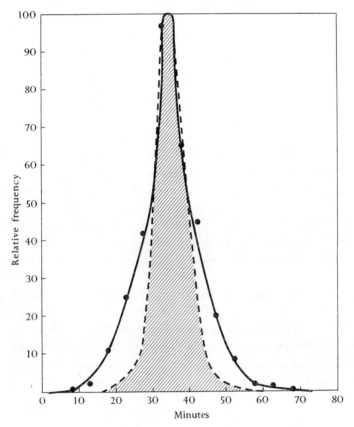

FIG. 111. Distribution of generation times.

not vary much, a statistical spread of division times implies a corresponding spread in the size of the cells formed. The distribution of sizes is considered further in later sections, where normal division and the abnormal division caused by drugs or disturbances in the environment are dealt with together.

8. Observations on individual cells between divisions

Very varied results have been reported on the growth rate of individual cells observed between divisions. Sometimes a linear increase of mass with time is found, sometimes a less than linear one, sometimes a more than linear, and sometimes an exponential increase, as must apply to the culture as a whole in the logarithmic phase.

According to Swann,[21] the rate of increase is not autocatalytic and exponential and according to Prescott[22] there is no observable acceleration in the rate of growth of a cell between divisions, the absolute rate being independent of cell size. The rate of incorporation of ^{14}C into *Tetrahymena* was found not to change, and different quantities which might be taken to measure the extent of growth could vary independently.[22] With yeast also the increase in volume has been stated to occur at a constant rate during most of the cell cycle.[22] More than linear, though less than exponential, increase is reported with *Bacillus megaterium*, and with *Streptococcus faecalis* the rate falls while with *Paramecium* it rises.[22] Collins and Richmond[23] found that with *Bacillus cereus* the rate of increase in length increased as the organism got larger, and there was no interruption at the time of division. In this work entire cultures were studied photographically, a method less likely to give anomalous results than the direct observation of single cells under the possibly abnormal conditions of certain special observation chambers. The distribution of lengths at division showed statistical variations. Schaechter *et al.*[24] found that with *Escherichia coli*, *Proteus vulgaris*, and *Salmonella typhimurium* in steady growth conditions the cells did in fact grow exponentially. They concluded, incidentally, that increase in length did measure increase in mass, since the density as indicated by the refractive index did not vary between individuals at different stages of the division cycle.

The observations of linear increase rates for individual cells has led some authors to question the validity of any kinetic growth equations of an essentially autocatalytic form. This, however, seems to imply a misunderstanding of the whole method of treatment exemplified in Chapter V. The entire bacterial mass in a culture in the steady phase of growth certainly does increase exponentially with time. The substance as a whole is increasing autocatalytically, no matter how or at what intervals it divides itself up into separate cells, and whether these are of uniform or variable size. The constants which enter into the growth equations of Chapter V are average values taken over all the actual cells present, and the average itself does, as a matter of experimental fact, remain constant during the exponential phase of a culture adapted to its environment. But it can only do this in so far as the periodic division allows the average condition of the cells to remain more or less constant. At the most favourable moment of each cell cycle the spatial map is such as to allow those diffusion paths and steric conditions giving an optimum value of the growth constant. As the cell grows the conditions get less favourable, but they are restored again at division, or perhaps soon after. On the whole then, as a given cell grows it has more nucleic acid, so that more protein can potentially be formed, and more enzyme material in the cell, so that more of everything else can potentially be built up in unit time. But this increasing mass of chemically active agents is operating under gradually deteriorating conditions. On balance then the rate of increase in the single cell may rise, fall, or, by compensation, remain more or less constant during parts of its individual cycle. This corresponds precisely with the experimental evidence.

9. Internal changes preceding division

Appropriate staining methods reveal specialized regions of the cell which are of a nuclear character. These may show phenomena of internal division not linked in any rigid way with the division of the cell itself.

Robinow[25] worked with *Escherichia coli* and with *Proteus vulgaris*. He fixed the cells with osmic acid, treated with warm hydrochloric acid, and stained with Giemsa solution. With the correct treatment dumb-bell-shaped bodies could be distinguished lying transversely to the long axis of the cell. A young cell might contain only one such body, which, however, presently increased in size and then divided into two closely contiguous dumb-bells. These in their turn increased in width and finally split longitudinally, that is to say, still transversely to the long axis of the bacterium. After the first division of the original dumb-bell body the whole cell might itself split into two by the development of a constriction, but more usually cells possessing a number of these bodies were formed. These longer bacteria possessed a sort of chambered structure, the division of the cell having awaited two or three divisions of the nuclear material, but light transverse partitions were discernible. Robinow observed that 'mono- and multinucleate elements are single and multiple forms of a basic building unit possessing a single chromatinic body'.

Robinow considered the moment of true cell division to be that when the membranes form between two recently divided chromatinic structures. According to this view many bacteria would really consist of several cells, usually, with young bacteria, two to four.

In certain circumstances (which will be discussed later) bacteria grow to long filaments very many times the normal length. Robinow found that these may sometimes be compartmented, each section being complete in itself, and sometimes without any such orderly arrangement and without internal boundaries. Filaments with the chaotic distribution of chromatinic bodies and without partitions may, according to Robinow, arise spontaneously in cultures of *Escherichia coli* or *Proteus* and can also sometimes be produced by the action of ionizing radiations.

From all this it becomes clear that localized happenings in the cell may precede division and that certain structures may themselves divide after reaching a critical size, an occurrence which may or may not, according to circumstances, be directly linked with the separation of the whole cell into two.

The procedures involved in studying the internal structure of bacteria are often rather drastic and the appearances seen are sometimes criticized as artifacts. Nevertheless, many other authors have reported internal division phenomena of a generally similar kind. Schaechter *et al.*[24] reported the division of various nuclear masses in *Escherichia coli*, *Salmonella typhimurium*, and *Proteus vulgaris*, and this was independent of cell division, the interval between the two processes being as variable as the division time itself. With two strains of *Escherichia coli* the nucleus, they said, commonly divided in the middle third of the cell division cycle, in contrast with many types of plant and animal cell in which karyokinesis is soon followed by division of the whole cell.

According to Powell[26] the separation of daughter cells may be influenced by sets of circumstances which are trivial in relation to the replication processes as a whole. The whole situation is quite complex and many different opinions have been expressed. Some authors stress the importance of the actual formation of new wall, some the nuclear division, some a combination of factors. It seems clear, however, that the internal break-up of nuclear masses is one factor, as we have been led to expect, but that its importance varies with circumstances.

10. Mitotic figures

In many kinds of cell, other than bacteria, the observable phenomena accompanying division are considerably more complex. At the moment it remains an open question whether the more elaborate evolutions sometimes visible constitute merely an embroidery on the simpler theme, and that their understanding will be relatively easy when once the problem of bacterial division has been solved, or whether, on the other hand, there are difficultly observable happenings in the bacterial cell which will only be understood when the fuller and clearer version shown by other cells has been interpreted.

In cells showing the typical mitotic or karyokinetic phenomena a certain part of the substance divides into two granules which move apart and constitute poles between which pass what appear like threads. Other threads radiate in a star-like pattern from the poles, the whole picture being strongly reminiscent of the lines of force around and between two magnetic poles. Other cell material has formed itself into small more or less rod-like structures which are the chromosomes. These, when the bipolar figure just referred to is formed, move and arrange themselves equatorially and transversely to the bipolar axis. They then separate longitudinally into two (or may have done so earlier), and the divided chromosomes move towards the two poles 'for all the world' as D'Arcy Thompson[27] puts it 'as though they were being pulled asunder by actual threads'. Presently two new nuclei are constituted, a partition membrane is formed, and the cell divides by constriction. The precise details and the exact order of events vary from one type of cell to another, and the process as a whole is over in from 30 to 60 minutes.

In view of the existence of crystallizable substances of enormous molecular weight, and of the stretched and unstretched forms of protein chains, one is disposed to believe that the threads and the tensions often referred to in the descriptions of mitotic phenomena may be quite real. Polyfunctional molecules provide a means whereby spatially separated regions of order may be connected mechanically one with the other. Surface tension, osmotic pressure, and electrical effects are all present. D'Arcy Thompson[27] remarks, 'the physical analogies which can be found for various parts of the mitotic process leave me with the impression that when we understand the chemical events in the cell the mechanical evolutions will explain themselves'.

From what has already been said about the energy relations of undivided and divided cells, the obvious way of regarding karyokinetic phenomena is to regard them as the expression of the motion of a collection of particles, moving from a state of higher to one of lower potential energy. Their paths would be dictated by the standard dynamical laws which would impose some kind of streaming figure. Since the various masses comprise complex chains, sheets, and agglomerates of macromolecular substances with every kind of force, including possibly a set of free valencies, the path followed may be quite complicated, and may well vary widely from one type of cell to another. On this view D'Arcy Thompson would be right, but the general picture would not be inconsistent with the findings of authors who suggest that cell-wall formation, or the production of a specific enzyme at some point where a barrier must be broken down, may on occasion limit the rate at which the whole division process can be completed.[28, 29]

11. Separation of division and growth: delayed division

As we have already seen, cells may in some circumstances continue to divide after the exhaustion of nutrients and become smaller without increase in total mass. In this process of division without growth a balance is struck between the two tendencies of maintaining a constant ratio of (DNA/mass) and a constant ratio of (DNA/cell). In the compromise the former rises and the latter falls, some DNA being produced at the expense of RNA.[12, 13]

The counterpart of division without growth is elongation without division. In certain circumstances division may be so much delayed, while elongation proceeds, that filamentous or snake-like cells many times the normal length are formed. In extreme cases the failure of division may even be so complete that the whole bacterial mass develops as a tangled mass of a few threads, each several hundred times the length of a normal cell.

The conditions which favour the formation of these abnormally long cells are (a) the presence of certain drugs which inhibit division without inhibiting growth to the same extent—as when Ainley Walker and Murray[30] obtained filaments by growing *Salmonella typhi* in presence of methyl violet or other dyes—and (b) the transfer of the cells to an unaccustomed medium to which the growth and division functions adapt themselves at different rates.

Under conditions which favour the long filaments, not only does the average cell length increase greatly, but the distribution of sizes becomes very much more scattered. It will be convenient now to consider in turn various detailed investigations which have been made on delayed division. For this purpose it is useful to introduce a quantitative measure of the size abnormality of any given culture. This has been done in the following way.[31] The sizes of cells are measured microscopically by comparison with a suitable ruled grid, the lengths being expressed as a number of arbitrary units. In a sample of a given population the number, ν_l, of cells having lengths in a unit range in the neighbourhood of l is then counted. The dependence of ν_l on l then gives the size distribution, the fact that the lengths are measured in terms of an arbitrary unit being immaterial. Since in a normal culture of the bacteria with which we shall be concerned, none of the cells exceed two units in length, we can measure abnormality by the function

$$\sigma = \sum_{3}^{\infty} \nu_l l.$$

($\sum \nu_l$ can conveniently be scaled to 1 or 100 if required.) For a normal population σ will be zero. (This symbol shonld not to be confused with the independent symbol used for another purpose in Chapter IV.)

12. Filaments formed on transfer to new media

When a strain of *Aerobacter aerogenes* which had been cultured for some time in bouillon was transferred to an artificial medium consisting

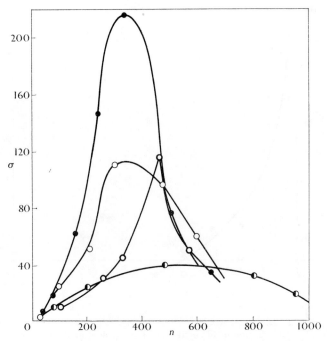

FIG. 112. Variation of size coefficient during growth cycle for various cultures giving filaments.

of ammonium sulphate, glucose, magnesium sulphate, and a phosphate buffer, the size distribution of the population was quite normal provided that the glucose concentration was high (38·5 g/l.). When, however, a small amount of the bouillon culture was transferred to a similar artificial medium containing glucose at one-twentieth the above concentration, cells of all sizes up to twenty or thirty times the normal length appeared. σ increased with n, the count, up to a maximum, after which it fell again, the culture sometimes, though not always, finishing up as a normal population.[31] Some typical variations of σ with n are shown in Fig. 112.

The production of the filaments is very clearly connected with the lack of adaptation to the new medium. When the cells are subcultured serially in the glucose–ammonium sulphate medium (whether the glucose is more or less concentrated) or even in a glucose–asparagine medium,

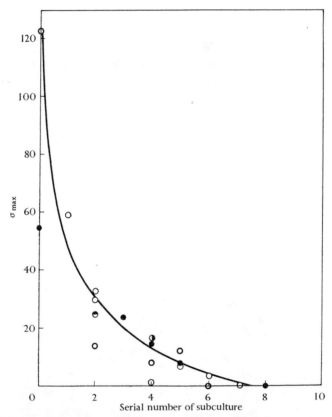

FIG. 113. Elimination of filament formation by adaptation to medium.
The different kinds of point refer to various series of experiments.

the tendency to give long cells on transfer to the dilute glucose medium gradually disappears. The reduction of σ from over 100 (high degree of abnormality) to zero on serial subculture in the artificial medium is shown in Fig. 113.

In the artificial medium growth is slower than in bouillon. In accordance with general principles which have been discussed already, some degree of adaptation is necessary when transfer to this poorer medium occurs. If the division function is to some extent independent of the elongation function, the two may not adapt themselves at the same rate, with the result that a lack of balance leading to filament formation is created.

It has been mentioned that filtrate from grown cultures of *Aerobacter aerogenes* shortens the lag of young inocula, which means that it hastens the onset of growth. If division is not correspondingly hastened, formation of filaments will be favoured, and it is in fact sometimes observed that the addition of the filtrate increases the tendency to give them. Various observations on the influence of inoculum age, inoculum size, and filtrate addition on σ can be correlated in a qualitative way with the help of the hypothesis that two separate factors favour elongation and division respectively, and that the former is diffusible into the medium. When the cells are transferred to a new medium, the rates of formation of the two factors, originally balanced, may no longer be so. Only when adaptation is complete is the balance restored.

The factors respectively favouring division and elongation may be referred to as D and L. They are subject to very specific influences. D appears to be formed much more readily in amino-acid media than in ammonium sulphate media. In a glucose–asparagine medium filaments are never observed.

A certain rather atypical strain of *Aerobacter aerogenes*, characterized by very slow growth in the glucose–ammonium sulphate medium, showed a particularly marked tendency to give long filaments when grown for the first few times in it.[32] If it was first grown in an asparagine–glucose medium, in which the D factor seems to be easily formed and consequently receives little stimulus from training, and then transferred to an ammonium sulphate medium, the lack of balance between the D and L factors became so marked that nothing but a tangled skein of thread of indefinite length appeared. Continued serial subculture eventually gave a normal population.

Filament formation may also be observed when *Aerobacter aerogenes* or *Escherichia coli* is in the early stages of adaptation to other media, for example, when *Escherichia coli* is first transferred to an artificial medium in which ammonium sulphate is replaced by a nitrate as source of nitrogen. The tendency to give abnormally long cells is always lost as the adaptation proceeds. Filaments very similar to those formed by the coliform bacteria are also given under comparable circumstances by *Bacillus subtilis*. There seems to have been no special study of the way in which bacteria such as staphylococci, which are morphologically different from the coliforms or the bacilli, behave in these conditions, though analogous phenomena probably occur. An organism resembling

Staphylococcus aureus was studied by Burke, Swartz, and Klise,[33] who observed on occasion coccus forms, rods, and filaments, which they regarded as parts of a definite 'life cycle'. They remarked that 'unfavourable environment interferes with the regularity of the life cycle, obscuring the stages and resulting in a mixture of morphological forms'. Lack of balance between the functions of size increase and division would very probably explain these observations sufficiently well.

Though it is not referred to as producing specifically filamentous forms, *Corynebacterium diphtheriae* gives cells with abnormal morphology when it is transferred to new media.[34]

A word should be said about the possibility that filaments are merely intruders of a foreign strain in an impure culture, the development of which is favoured by the new medium—a kind of suggestion which at one time was apt to be made in connexion with any manifestation of bacterial variability. Several answers may be made and seem conclusive. In the first place, filaments occur in cultures which have been carefully prepared from isolated single colonies. Secondly, the appearance with special prominence of an intruding strain would only occur in a new medium if this were such as to favour the growth of the filament-forming type at the expense of the normal one. Yet on serial subculture in the new medium this supposedly favoured strain disappears again. To explain this one would have to assume an advantage of the normal form, so that two contradictory assumptions have to be made to account for one set of facts. Thirdly, there is sometimes a definite mathematical relation between the sizes of all the cells in the population. This cannot be easily interpreted by the assumption of a foreign strain. Finally, in many circumstances the filaments may be observed to form and subsequently break up to yield a population of perfectly normal cells.

13. Size distribution in filament-forming cultures[31]

As has been mentioned, in conditions which favour the formation of abnormally long cells the size distribution changes its character and widens very markedly. When *Aerobacter aerogenes* is first transferred to the artificial medium containing dilute glucose, the following law is found to govern the distribution. If n is the total number of cells present, n_l the number with length greater than l, and $\bar{l}$ the average length, then

$$n_l = ne^{-l/l}, \tag{1}$$

whence

$$\frac{d\ln(n_l/n)}{dl} = -\frac{1}{\bar{l}}. \tag{2}$$

Thus if the value of $\log(n_l/n)$ is plotted against l there is a straight line, the slope of which gives $1/2 \cdot 303l$. Some typical results are plotted in Fig. 114, where each line refers to a population sampled at a different stage of the growth cycle, as is indicated by the values of n (in arbitrary units) on the diagram.

Over a considerable range the above exponential distribution law is well obeyed. There is, however, a quite definite departure from it in one respect, namely, that at certain stages of the growth cycle the number of exceptionally long cells is greater than would be expected,

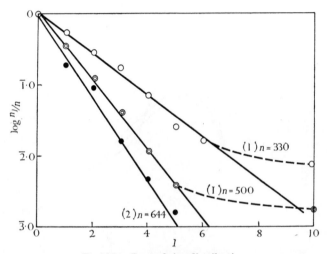

FIG. 114. Law of size distribution.

as is indicated by the course of the dotted lines in the diagram. The number of cells of length up to about five times the average is rather closely given by the law, but the occurrence of those with ten or even twenty times the average length is appreciably more probable than predicted by extrapolation. This appears to be not unrelated to another circumstance. Most of the long cells eventually split, and by the end of the growth cycle have become normal. In a population which has no member greater than about ten times the average, the final distribution when growth is complete is indistinguishable from that of any ordinary culture. But if circumstances have allowed the appearance of cells of even greater length, then these often persist indefinitely and seem to be incapable of subsequent division. This suggests two kinds of influence at work, one which merely delays division and which determines the number of moderately long cells, the other which comes into play when division has been too long delayed and which makes irreversible the initial disturbance of the normal processes. The influence of specific drugs on filament formation will be dealt with later, but in anticipation it may be mentioned that the deviation from the exponential law in populations formed in drug media is very much greater. With *Aerobacter aerogenes* in the dilute glucose medium under the conditions described, the conformity with this law is, however, close enough to be regarded as of some significance.

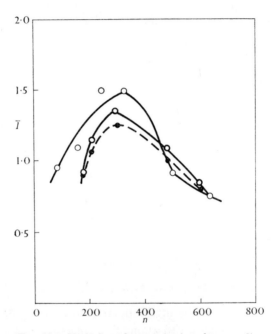

FIG. 115. Variation of mean size in culture media.

  O   inoculum 1, equation (2)
  O   inoculum 2, equation (2)
  ●   inoculum 2, equation (4)

The differing slopes of the lines in Fig. 114 indicate, in accordance with equation (2), that the average length $\bar{l}$ varies through the growth cycle. This variation may be examined in two ways, the comparison of which provides a means of subjecting the equation (1) to a further test. If we introduce the abnormal size coefficient defined in the last section

$$\sigma = \sum_{3}^{\infty} \nu_l l \tag{3}$$

(ν_l being the number of cells in unit range in the neighbourhood of l), ν_l can be related to n_l since the number of cells of length between l and

$l+dl$ is $-dn_l$. Thus, in so far as sums over small finite elements may be replaced by integrals,

$$\sigma = -\int_3^\infty l\, dn_l,$$

and on substitution from (1) for dn_l we obtain

$$\sigma = n(3+\bar{l})e^{-3/\bar{l}},$$

whence
$$\bar{l} = \frac{3}{2 \cdot 303 \log\{(3+\bar{l})n/\sigma\}}. \tag{4}$$

Thus $\bar{l}$ can be found from σ, as well as from the slope of lines such as those in Fig. 114.

Figure 115 shows that the two methods give concordant results, and also illustrates the variation of $\bar{l}$ during the growth cycle—which, in the examples taken, is complete at values of n in the neighbourhood of 1000. $\bar{l}$ first rises and then falls again. The nature of the size distribution is such that relatively small changes in $\bar{l}$ are associated with very large changes in the frequency of the longer cells and in the abnormal appearance of the culture.

The exponential law which, in certain circumstances at least, governs the size distribution, is a common statistical form. A corresponding expression gives the number of gas molecules completing without collision a trajectory which is a particular multiple of the mean free path. The same form represents the probability that a railway which on the average has a disaster for every l miles of running shall achieve l miles without one. The basis of the law is that the events which terminate the undisturbed run, whether of cell elongation, molecular progress through the gas, or immunity of the railway from accident, shall be independent of the process which they interrupt. The chance of a lapse by a signalman (in so far as the law is to be legitimately applicable) is unaffected by the number of miles trains have travelled since the last accident: the arrival of other gas molecules which interfere with the free flight of a given one is not conditioned by the length of path it has already traversed. If, therefore, the exponential law correctly describes the size distribution in the population of cells, it suggests that, under the circumstances prevailing, division is not determined by the size of the cell at the moment when it occurs, but by the probability of certain independent events going on in the cell itself, or in its vicinity. Normally, cell division attains a fairly high degree of probability as soon as enough material has been synthesized: in special circumstances some conjunction of events independent of the actual length of the cell becomes the limiting factor. In any event we see that division depends upon a variety of conditions.

14. Inhibition of division by drugs

The observation by Ainley Walker and Murray[30] that *Salmonella typhi* forms filaments under the influence of dyestuffs has already been mentioned. The phenomenon occurs with other bacteria and with other inhibitors. Most of the references in this section will be to work on a typical strain of *Aerobacter aerogenes* about which more easily comparable observations are available.

The action of the various growth-inhibiting agents is very specific. Proflavine gives fairly long filaments, but sulphanilamide, at least in a wide range of comparable circumstances, gives none.[35] *m*-cresol gives extremely marked long-cell formation, but no trace of a corresponding effect can be induced by phenol.[36] In a medium with dilute glucose ethyl alcohol gives normal forms, but tertiary butyl alcohol will produce very well-defined filaments.[31]

The substances which induce the abnormality are all powerful inhibitors of growth. In terms once more of an elongation factor, L, and a division factor, D, it is a question with a given drug whether L or D is the more adversely affected. If L suffers more serious reduction than D, then there will be no filaments. Since we have to deal with a balance between two influences, it is not surprising that the occurrence of the filaments, even with a particular inhibitor, may depend rather specifically upon the conditions of working. Spray and Lodge[36] found that to obtain the most striking results with *m*-cresol it was necessary to use concentrations approaching those which would inhibit growth completely, and also to transfer the inoculum from a parent culture of such an age that the lag in the new medium would have been almost zero in the absence of the drug.

It is of interest in connexion with ideas on the influence of surface tension on cell division to note that surface active agents such as cetyl trimethylammonium bromide and sodium dodecyl sulphate seem to have little effect in stimulating any abnormal size distribution.[37]

When the cells adapt themselves to resist the action of the drug, the power of the latter to induce filament formation vanishes. If, in untrained cells, a concentration m_1 of proflavine induces it, then after training to $\bar{m}$, there will be none, even under the influence of concentrations much greater than $\bar{m}+m_1$.[38] The mechanism of division is here, apparently, even more easily adapted than that of growth.

Aerobacter aerogenes does not easily adapt itself to resist phenols, and, accordingly, does not lose its susceptibility to the morphological disturbances caused by *m*-cresol. Indeed, so far from this, Spray and Lodge[36] found that after filaments had been produced under the influence of the cresol, these continued to form, even on repeated subculture in a medium free from inhibitor, the power of division having suffered an impairment from which recovery proved to be extremely slow.

In the later stages of growth the filaments formed under the influence of drugs tend to give place to normal forms, as occurs in the absence of drugs but, especially when the distribution has been very abnormal, many of the longest cells may persist. A culture grown under the influence of proflavine, in conditions such that few cells in excess of ten times the normal length appear at any stage, is often normal by the end of the growth cycle, but with one grown under the influence of cresol and showing little but cells twenty to fifty times the usual length, the abnormal size distribution is generally persistent.

If division is unduly delayed it may not occur at all but when a long cell does break up it seems to do so not so much by shedding segments one by one from its end as by a more or less simultaneous series of divisions along its whole length.

15. Influence of osmotic pressure

It has been mentioned that *Aerobacter aerogenes* shows delayed division when first transferred to an artificial medium containing dilute glucose, but that if the glucose concentration is high, the size distribution is normal. The highest value, σ_{max}, to which the size coefficient attains during the growth cycle proves to be a function of the osmotic pressure of the medium. This can be shown by the addition to the dilute glucose medium of various other substances such as sodium chloride, ammonium sulphate, or erythritol (representing a substance chemically similar to glucose but not utilized by the bacteria). These all cause a reduction in σ, and, what amounts to the same thing, of l. The reduction is approximately proportional to the increase in osmotic pressure as shown in Fig. 116. These results suggest that the influence of the glucose concentration itself is primarily an osmotic one. The curves in Fig. 117 show the variation in σ during the growth cycle for various initial concentrations of glucose (expressed as fractions of the highest, 38·5 g/l.). For the concentration 1 (the highest), σ is zero throughout. The marked rise as the glucose concentration drops to 0·1 is very evident. At lower concentrations still, σ_{max} seems to fall again, but this effect is probably illusory. Below 0·1 the total population which the medium will support decreases rapidly. At 0·025, for example, n_{max} is 209 and reference to the figure shows that σ_{max} is only reached at this point. If growth had been able to go on, σ would probably have risen still higher. Indeed, in the figure the maxima from 0·01 to 0·1 appear to have a common envelope, which suggests that if n could increase further σ would do so also.

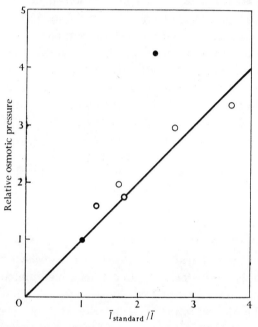

FIG. 116. Influence of osmotic pressure.

When the formation of filaments is caused by proflavine or by m-cresol, addition of enough sodium chloride to the medium completely suppresses them, and the maximum value of σ observed at any stage of the growth cycle is zero. Small additions of sodium chloride, however, actually enhance the filament formation.[39] These effects are shown in Fig. 118, where the abscissae represent the weights of sodium chloride added to each culture tube containing 26 ml of the minimal medium.

16. Influence of temperature on delayed division

Increase of temperature has a pronounced effect in favouring the formation of the filamentous cells. All the results which have been described in the foregoing sections were obtained in experiments at 40°,

at which temperature the growth rate is at its maximum. At 30° the
size distribution becomes much more nearly normal, even when growth
occurs in presence of high concentrations of cresol or proflavine. The
change in the value of σ with the temperature of growth is shown in

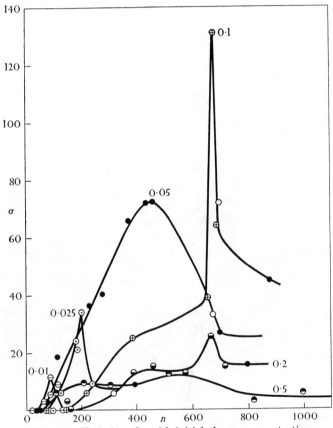

FIG. 117. Variation of σ with initial glucose concentration.

Figs. 119 and 120 in which some results found by A. M. James[39] are
plotted.

In this connexion certain adaptive effects become apparent. Cells
which have been subcultured for some time at 20° show much more
susceptibility to filament formation when grown in presence of drugs
than those which have been acclimatized by serial subculture at 40°
before exposure. This is illustrated by the curves in Fig. 120. No
appreciable adaptive changes in overall growth rate are detectable with
these bacteria in experiments where they are trained by serial subculture at one temperature and then tested in successive growth cycles

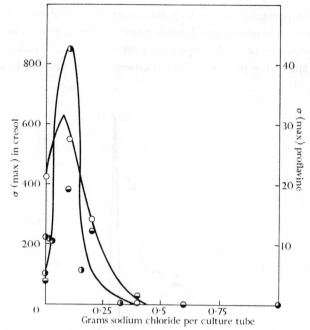

FIG. 118. Influence of salt addition on production of filaments
by cresol or proflavine.

◑, ◐   709 mg/l. *m*-cresol.   ○   43 mg/l. proflavine.

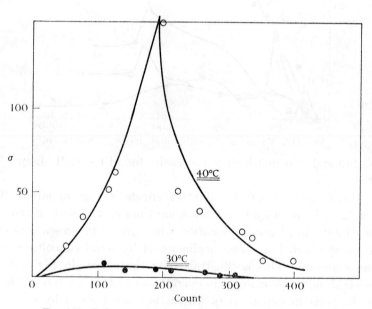

FIG. 119. Influence of temperature on filament formation.

at other temperatures, though such changes should, in principle, occur. But the more delicate balance of what we have called the D and L factors seems to provide a subtler means of revealing such adaptive processes.

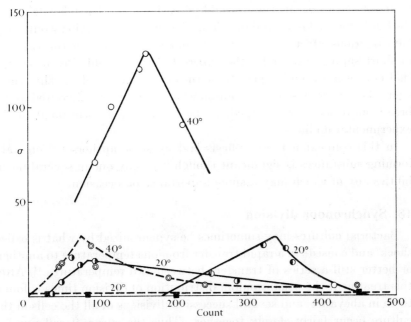

FIG. 120. Influence of temperature and of temperature-adaptation on filament formation.

○	Trained at 20° C, tested at		40° C.
◑, ◐	„	„	„	20° C.
◉	„	40° C,	„	40° C.
■	„	40° C,	„	20° C.

17. Implications of delayed division

The chief conclusion to be drawn from the detailed studies on *Aerobacter aerogenes* is the considerable degree of independence of growth and division. The examples given have referred chiefly to this organism but essentially similar principles have been shown by Nickerson[40] to apply to yeasts, and these same principles are exemplified in the work of numerous authors on size distributions in general.[7, 21, 31, 32, 41, 42, 43]

The working hypothesis that critical concentrations of certain chemical substances have to be built up before the cell divides would account for some of the facts—although, to be sure, it would leave plenty untouched. The attainment of the threshold concentration could obviously be impeded by specific drug actions: it would certainly depend upon the proper adaptation of the manufacturing enzymes. And it would probably be hastened by an increased osmotic pressure in the medium, which would cause withdrawal of water from the cell and so increase the internal concentrations of metabolites. Furthermore, if precipitation of dissolved material had to occur, there would be variable and irregular delays of the kind observed to attend division. The delays in question would only have a serious effect on the cell morphology when the D factor was kept in short supply. Normally the supersaturation would rise so quickly that elongation would appear to be the determining factor. Thus there would be a narrow size distribution when division was favoured and a broad one when it was impeded. This also would correspond to the experimental findings.

In this connexion the emphasis laid by some authors[28, 29] on wall-forming substances is significant though it is only one of several possibilities any of which may assume importance on occasion.

18. Synchronous division

Bacterial cultures may sometimes be synchronized by what is called shock, and consists in a rapid transfer from one temperature to another, or better still a series of transfers between two temperatures.[44] After this treatment the usual random distribution of division times is found to be in abeyance, and several successive divisions of all the cells in the culture occur fairly closely together. Thus the curve of cell number against time assumes a stepped appearance.

The key fact about synchrony is that it is not a stable condition and that after a certain number of divisions, usually relatively few, the randomness reasserts itself. Thus the first question to answer is why cultures once synchronized do not remain so. We have already seen that growth, in the sense of increase of substance, and division are in a considerable measure independent of one another. For constant environmental conditions the chemical steady-state equations for the masses of the various cell components would predict a uniformly balanced formation of them all. But consideration of the conditions for division suggests a much less orderly process.

Since volume, surface, and length are different functions of cell mass, regular increases in the latter, in virtue of the localization of the several kinds of cell component, create mechanical instability which may be of various types. The multiplication of the number of intracellular particles may create yet another kind. The relief of this instability in the course of division will be analogous in many ways to a phase change in a solid or liquid system, a process which is notoriously associated with random delays. The formation of new cell walls and other structures may depend upon coagulation and precipitation, of which the same may be said. If branching chains play a part in the growth of the cell macro-molecules and if free valencies have to appear in the right place at the right time for the bolting together of the complex cytoskeleton of a new cell, then yet another set of probabilities come into play as possible determinants.

Thus it is by no means surprising that cell division is a statistical affair and that asynchrony rather than synchrony is the normal order of things. What then happens when it is temporarily suspended? In the various forms of shock treatment the normal material balance of the cell will be disturbed more or less seriously in all or any of a number of ways. When the temperature is altered, if growth is not arrested, the relative rates of increase of different components will change and so the proportions. There will not be time for the establishment of a new steady state, so some of the material is out of balance. Some parts of the cell substance may not be formed at all. Or all parts may be inhibited. In this last event some enzymes will begin to decay and at differential rates, and diffusible or labile intermediates may be lost. The economy of the cell in one way or another becomes highly unbalanced.

Such a lack of balance could have a multiplicity of effects. Suppose, for example, that division normally depended upon a combination of factors a, b, c,... which must be satisfactorily provided for at the same time. If now as a result of the disturbed material balance a, b,... are easier to provide for than c, then c might become critical and limiting as far as division is concerned. If a metaphor may be conceded to have some descriptive value, in the normal case the unpredictable decision of a committee fixes the moment of action, while in the abnormal one the event awaits the fiat of a single dictator.

If there has been an accumulation of a considerable excess of the materials which make a, b,... easy to provide for, this excess may not be dissipated until after several divisions, and while the store lasts there will be more or less a state of synchrony. There are indeed experimental indications of a connexion between synchronous growth and the accumulation of particular excesses in the cells.[45]

Suppose again that certain cell processes, if too rudely interrupted before a critical stage, leave unstable structures (such as growing chains) which, not being allowed to complete themselves, unravel and return more or less to zero. This effect would gradually reduce the phase differences between cells as more and more are interrupted before the critical point of no return and sent back to base, whence all start again on equal terms when growth is renewed. Such an effect would be reinforced were there any sort of critical limit beyond which completion of the cell cycle up to the point of division would become more or less inevitable even if conditions had become unfavourable. Something of this sort appears to be involved in 'division without growth' (p. 95).

There are many subtleties observed in connexion with synchronous cultures.[44, 45] We shall not enter further into the discussion here, but we believe that they are generally consistent with the picture presented, which treats synchronization not as the removal of an irregularity so much as the creation of an unnatural departure from a normal statistical balance.

REFERENCES

1. See L. R. G. Treloar, *The Physics of Rubber Elasticity*, p. 64, Clarendon Press, Oxford (1949).
2. A. I. Oparin, *The Origin of Life on the Earth*, Rep. Int. Symp. Moscow, p. 221, Acad. Sci. U.S.S.R., Moscow (1957).
3. J. Loeb, *The Dynamics of Living Matter*, Columbia University Press, New York (1906); *Proteins and the Theory of Colloidal Behaviour*, McGraw-Hill, New York (1925).
4. C. J. Danby and C. N. Hinshelwood, *Proc. R. Soc.* A **179**, 169 (1942).
5. C. N. Hinshelwood, *Kinetics of Chemical Change*, Clarendon Press, Oxford (1945); N. Semenoff, *Chemical Kinetics and Chain Reactions*, Clarendon Press, Oxford (1935); V. N. Kondrat'ev, *Chemical Kinetics of Gas Reactions*, Pergamon Press, Oxford (1964); K. J. Laidler, *Chemical Kinetics*, McGraw-Hill, New York (1965).
6. L. Michaelis, M. P. Shubert, and C. V. Smythe, *J. biol. Chem.* **116**, 587 (1936); *Science*, **84**, 139 (1936).
7. C. N. Hinshelwood, *The Chemical Kinetics of the Bacterial Cell*, p. 264, Clarendon Press, Oxford (1946).
8. See, for example, *Formation and Trapping of Free Radicals*, edited by A. M. Bass and H. P. Broida, Academic Press, New York (1960); *Free Radicals in Biological Systems*, edited by M. S. Blois, H. W. Brown, R. M. Lemmon, R. P. Lindblom, and M. Weissbluth, Academic Press, New York (1961); B. Commoner, *Mém. Acad. r. Belg. Cl. Sci.* **33**, 114 (1961); B. Commoner, J. Townsend, and G. E. Pake, *Nature, Lond.* **174**, 689 (1954); R. J. Heckley, R. L. Dimmick, and J. J. Windle, *J. Bact.* **85**, 961 (1963).
9. R. B. Setlow and E. C. Pollard, *Molecular Biophysics*, p. 341, Addison-Wesley, Reading, Mass. (1962).
10. See C. H. Bamford, P. A. Crowe, and R. P. Wayne, *Proc. R. Soc.* A **284**, 455 (1965).

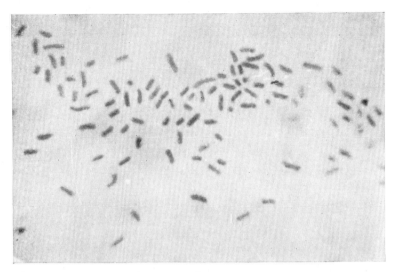

1

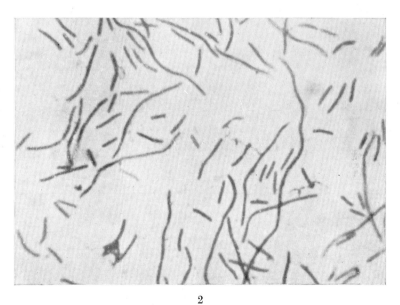

2

PLATE 2. *AEROBACTER AEROGENES*
1. Normal cells; 2. Filaments formed by inhibition of division
(The magnification in 1 and 2 is the same)

11. See Chapter I, sections 11, 12, 14, and 15 for references.

12. A. C. R. Dean and Sir Cyril Hinshelwood, *Proc. R. Soc.* B **151**, 348 (1960).

13. A. C. R. Dean, *Proc. R. Soc.* B **155**, 580 (1962); B **157**, 574 (1963).

14. W. Hayes, *Symp. Soc. gen. Microbiol.* **15**, 294 (1965).

15. C. A. Thomas and L. A. McHattie, *Proc. natn. Acad. Sci. U.S.A.* **52**, 1297 (1964).

16. J. Cairns, *J. molec. Biol.* **3**, 756 (1961); **6**, 208 (1963).

17. J. Cairns, *J. molec. Biol.* **4**, 407 (1962).

18. M. H. F. Wilkins, *Les Prix Nobel en 1962*, p. 126, Imprimerie Royale, P. A. Norstedt und Söner, Stockholm (1963).

19. J. D. Watson and F. H. C. Crick, *Nature, Lond.* **171**, 737 (1953); *Cold Spring Harbor Symp. quant. Biol.* **18**, 123 (1953).

20. G. D. Kelly and O. Rahn, *J. Bact.* **23**, 147 (1932).

21. M. M. Swann, *Cancer Res.* **17**, 727 (1957); **18**, 1118 (1958).

22. D. M. Prescott in *Synchrony in Cell Division and Growth*, edited by E. Zeuthen, p. 71, Interscience, New York (1964).

23. J. F. Collins and M. H. Richmond, *J. gen. Microbiol.* **28**, 15 (1962).

24. M. Schaechter, J. P. Williamson, J. R. Hood, and A. L. Koch, *J. gen. Microbiol.* **29**, 421 (1962).

25. C. F. Robinow, *J. Hyg., Camb.* **43**, 413 (1944); *Symp. Soc. gen. Microbiol.* **6**, 181 (1956).

26. E. O. Powell, *J. gen. Microbiol.* **18**, 382 (1958).

27. W. D'Arcy Thompson, *On Growth and Form*, p. 337, Cambridge University Press (1942).

28. See for details H. J. Rogers, *Symp. Soc. gen. Microbiol.* **15**, 186 (1965).

29. W. J. Nickerson, *Bact. Rev.* **27**, 305 (1963).

30. E. W. Ainley Walker and W. Murray, *Br. med. J.* **2**, 16 (1904).

31. C. N. Hinshelwood and R. M. Lodge, *Proc. R. Soc.* B **132**, 47 (1944).

32. R. M. Lodge and C. N. Hinshelwood, *Trans. Faraday Soc.* **39**, 420 (1943).

33. V. Burke, H. Swartz, and Katherine S. Klise, *J. Bact.* **45**, 415 (1943).

34. Mary E. Maver, *J. infect. Dis.* **49**, 9 (1931).

35. D. S. Davies, C. N. Hinshelwood, and J. M. G. Pryce, *Trans. Faraday Soc.* **40**, 397 (1944).

36. G. H. Spray and R. M. Lodge, *Trans. Faraday Soc.* **39**, 424 (1943).

37. A. R. Peacocke, unpublished observations.

38. A. M. James, unpublished observations.

39. A. M. James and C. N. Hinshelwood, *Trans. Faraday Soc.* **43**, 758 (1947).

40. W. J. Nickerson, *Nature, Lond.* **162**, 241 (1948).

41. W. J. Nickerson and G. Falcone, *Science*, **124**, 722 (1956).

42. W. J. Nickerson and N. J. W. van Rij, *Biochim. Biophys. Acta* **3**, 461 (1949).

43. W. J. Nickerson and F. G. Sherman, *J. Bact.* **64**, 667 (1952).

44. See for details and references O. Maaløe in *The Bacteria*, edited by I. C. Gunsalus and R. Y. Stanier, Academic Press, New York, **4**, 1 (1962).

45. See *Synchrony in Cell Division and Growth*, edited by E. Zeuthen, Interscience, New York, 1964; A. C. R. Dean and Sir Cyril Hinshelwood, *Nature, Lond.* **199**, 7 (1963); *ibid*, **206**, 546 (1965).

46. P. C. Caldwell and Sir Cyril Hinshelwood, *J. Chem. Soc.* p. 1415 (1950).

XV

THE DECLINE OF BACTERIAL POPULATIONS

1. Introduction

A POPULATION of bacteria, or of other unicellular organisms such as yeasts gradually loses viability. That is to say the number of cells capable of growth and division progressively declines. The rate at which this occurs varies both with the nature of the organism and with the conditions under which the population is kept. Bacterial spores may remain capable of germination and growth for years or even centuries. Cultures of bacteria such as *Aerobacter aerogenes*, while in favourable circumstances they suffer few casualties in the course of some days, will usually be decimated before many weeks have passed. The rate of decline is extremely sensitive to the conditions. It is increased above a certain optimum temperature, itself varying widely. The so-called thermophilic bacteria stand temperatures of more than 70° C. *Aerobacter aerogenes* dies rather rapidly above about 45° C. Spores will stand 100° C. Antibiotics and other toxic drugs usually increase the death-rate markedly, and though there is in principle a distinction between inhibition of growth and lethal action, there is often a rough parallelism between the two.

If there is any validity in the view that the great reactivity of living cells depends in some degree on the presence of free valencies, then it is very natural that these should be gradually lost and become saturated unless they are continuously regenerated. In systems involving only small molecules loss of free valencies occurs immeasurably fast. In cells they may be protected by the spatial separation which the macro-molecular framework permits. In spores the degree of protection would have become very high indeed as a result of special structural circumstances. Irradiation is a specially powerful cause of rapid decline.

2. The law of decline

There has been much discussion not only about the interpretation of the law according to which a bacterial population declines with time but about the actual law itself.

It is commonly stated in the form

$$N = N_0 e^{-\lambda t},$$

where N is the number of survivors at time t out of an initial number N_0 and λ is a constant. The meaning of this law, the familiar law of exponential decline followed, for example, in radioactive decay is that in any short interval of time dt the number passing the threshold from

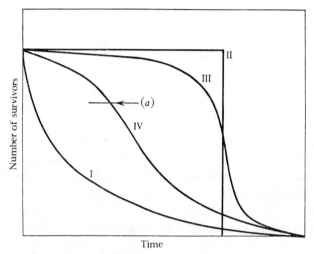

FIG. 121. Death-rate of bacteria according to various hypotheses.

viable to non-viable is a constant fraction of the total still living and is not affected by the history of what has gone before. The implications of this will be considered shortly.

First, however, we must consider how closely this law does justice to the experimental facts. Quite often it does not, and curves are found, not only of type I in Fig. 121 but of types III and IV, which are indicative of a kind of behaviour which might be idealized in curve II. Curve II would indicate that the cell could stand exposure to whatever adverse conditions existed for a certain limited time after which it would no longer be viable. Curves III and IV would indicate also a certain time of tolerance, but one which was greater with some members of the population than with others.

Gradual loss of free valencies, gradual denaturation of proteins, and inactivation of enzymes could all contribute to reduce the cell to a state from which it could recover or not according to the prolongation of the damage. In this sense curves III and IV would seem very probable and such curves are indeed sometimes observed. On the other hand, curves rather closely corresponding to the true exponential form are also observed, so that the question of their meaning still arises. It has been objected that in the conditions of some experiments a considerable proportion of the cells are already dead at the time when the first measurements are made. This means that the observation of a curve such as IV would begin, not at the origin, but at a point like (a), and the result of this would be to make a sigmoid curve rather easily mistakable for an exponential one.

Even when allowance is made for this objection, however, it remains true that in many examples of decline, whether induced by radiation or not, the exponential curve is followed closely enough for an explanation to be required.

Some of the scepticism about the exponential form may have arisen from the fact that the simplest possible interpretation of it gives a naïve picture of the lethal process which it is not very easy to accept.[1, 2, 3] We have to explain why the moment of death is independent of the previous history of the cell. One theory, applied to the example of death brought about by radiation, is that the cell is killed when a single quantum of radiation hits some localized sensitive spot in the bacterium. The corresponding idea applied to drug action involves apparently the idea that a single molecule of the drug can collide with this sensitive spot and bring about a catastrophe. This is a far from satisfactory picture.

A much more sophisticated view of the exponential law can, however, be taken. All that the law demands is that death is determined by some conjunction of probabilities which are as likely to occur at a later moment as at an earlier moment. This demand can be met without the assumption of crude 'missile' theories of external lethal agents. Indeed, a more detailed consideration of what goes on inside the cell shows that progressive damage combined with a suitable conjunction of events which are indeed quite likely to be occurring will account for the whole range of behaviour schematized in Fig. 121, with the exponential law as a limiting case to which the actual behaviour can well approximate.

3. The cell in decline

When cells are not proliferating, the various enzyme activities fairly soon begin to diminish. For this there may be more than one reason, loss of co-enzymes or intermediates, protein denaturation, or actual decomposition of their substance under the influence of proteolytic enzymes. Sometimes, indeed, complete lysis of the whole cell material sets in after a time.

In non-growing bacteria as, for example, in *Aerobacter aerogenes*, quite a lively exchange of material occurs, as has been shown by the use of tracers such as radioactive sulphur, phosphorus, and carbon, and a good deal of this exchange occurs only while the cell is still alive.[4] It would seem that various systems inside the cell can go on building themselves up or repairing their losses even after the complete integration necessary for growth has been destroyed.

Lysis represents the irreversible completion of reactions which at an earlier stage are kept in balance by fresh synthesis, and during the earlier phases of cell decline we must envisage a considerable making and unmaking of cell material.[5, 6] If there is no nutrient supplied from without or if the amount is inadequate, the slow decay of parts of the cell sets in, and the incidence of this will be different in the various areas of enzyme activity. Some regions will experience what amounts to a partial internal lysis. The products of this degradative action are precisely the kind of material themselves to constitute a supply of nutrient, and so long as most of the cell economy remains more or less intact, this reinforcement of growth medium allows new synthesis to occur at appropriate points. Thus matter coming from the degradation of one part of the cell is reprocessed in repairing another. This process of decay and renewal will go on variously and complexly all over the economy, and although the total result is gradual decline and the dissolution of the cell economy, nevertheless salvage and reconstruction keep destruction in check for a considerable time.

During this turbulent phase of its history, the cell is subject to the kinds of demand that it faces during adaptation to new media. The proportions of the enzymes may well change. In the confused struggle to counter lysis by repair, some portions of the economy will fare better than others, but no true steady state is now possible, and the conditions will be slowly changing so that the balance of advantage may shift. During this time, moreover, the different enzymes in the cell are virtually in competition for substance, and since one gains new substance at the expense of others, we are confronted with a situation in which various parts of the cell are in the relation of predator and prey. When this happens we may have a state of affairs in which individual parts of the cell machinery actually wax and wane with time [7–10] in the sort of way that was shown by Volterra[11] to occur among populations of predatory species of animals whose numbers, according to his equations, can show cyclic variations.

4. Cyclic variations in components

We can give only a highly simplified and idealized treatment of this problem, but the added complexities of the real situation can hardly destroy the property which the simple model possesses of cyclic variation.

Consider two cell components such as enzymes. The first, X, gives a product which reaches a concentration c_1 in the internal medium

$$dc_1/dt = k_1 x - k_1' c_1 = 0,$$

where x is the amount of X.

The product causes lysis of a component Y at a rate $k_2 y c_1$ which equals $(k_2 k_1/k_1')xy$, where y is the amount of Y. Y is being rebuilt at a rate $k_0 c_0 y$, being supplied with some material at concentration c_0.

Thus
$$dy/dt = k_0 c_0 y - Kxy, \tag{1}$$
where
$$K = k_2 k_1/k_1'.$$

When Y is lysed, the products are rapidly used by X, and their concentration reaches for a time a nearly steady state given by

$$dc_2/dt = Kxy - k_2' c_2 = 0.$$

The rebuilding of X is proportional to c_2 and thus to $(K/k_2')xy$, so that

$$dx/dt = (k_0' K/k_2')xy - k_0'' x. \tag{2}$$

The equations (1) and (2) may be written

$$dx/dt = axy - bx$$
$$dy/dt = \alpha y - \beta xy$$

which are of the same form as Volterra's equations. Elimination of x and y from these equations gives

$$\beta \frac{dx}{dt} + a \frac{dy}{dt} - \frac{\alpha}{x} \frac{dx}{dt} - \frac{b}{y} \frac{dy}{dt} = 0.$$

According to the solution of this equation x and y are both periodic functions of time.

This simple example shows how, in principle, lysis and repair might lead to fluctuations. But the analogy of predator and prey is not the only possible one, even though the probable release of lytic enzymes makes it a quite plausible one. As the internal economy of the cell gradually shifts and the metabolic pools change, new reaction patterns tend to impose themselves, and various combinations of synthetic processes permitting repair may come into play. But they may be attended by lags, and these may differ from one department of the cell to another. There can be intermissions in the processes of repair which will also contribute to a fluctuating balance.

Since the general trend of events is towards the final dissolution of the cell, there is no question of a permanently maintained periodicity, but over a quite considerable period of time there can well be cyclical rises and falls in the activity of particular enzymes superposed on the general decline. The periodicities can affect a great many different departments of the cell, and there need be no particular relation between them. Some cell functions may be decaying and partially recovering with a high frequency and others with a much lower frequency. The phases of the different fluctuations will vary randomly from cell to cell since all the cells in a culture are of different ages at the moment when growth ceases and decline sets in.

Specific activities of the cell, as a result of the complex pattern of more or less periodic fluctuations, will reach maxima or minima at certain moments. Since there is no simple relation between their frequencies and since the phase varies randomly from cell to cell, there will be an assignable probability that for any given cell a specified number of these functions will pass through their minima simultaneously. This probability will be independent of the previous history of the cell (to the extent that the fluctuations are periodic), so that in these circumstances this conjunction of minima will appear as much an affair of pure chance as the moment when a radioactive atom disintegrates.

If we make the assumption that the cell loses the power to recover its viability from the moment when a certain number of its functions have passed simultaneously through a minimum, then, according to the picture which has been described, the logarithmic law of decline follows. The chance that 'death' should occur during a time interval between t and $t+dt$ is proportional only to $\lambda\, dt$ where λ is a constant: whence follows the result $N = N_0\, e^{-\lambda t}$.

This law follows from assumptions which are only approximately true, but, as we have seen, the law itself is only approximately true. The problem was to see how this approximation could be possible at all.

The criterion adopted in the above discussion for defining the moment of 'death' or loss of viability was itself not quite sharp. If there is a simultaneous passage of various activities through a minimum, then clearly the cell is less likely to be able to recover in a new medium than it would have been had fewer of its functions been at their lowest ebb.

But it might be expected that the chance of recovery would depend upon the vigour of the restorative treatment applied. This is precisely what is observed. The number of 'survivors' in a declining bacterial culture proves to be a function of the medium in which the viability is tested. A poor medium measures fewer survivors than a richer medium, just as might be expected according to what has been said, but as would not be expected according to some 'bullet' theory of lethal action.

The rate of decline even in the absence of obviously lethal agents like drugs varies a great deal with circumstances. It depends upon the previous history of the culture, which naturally affects the initial enzyme balance and the composition of any metabolite pools in the cells. It depends upon the initial population density of the cells themselves, which influences the concentration of escaping products in the medium and also affects the competition for medium components, including oxygen. It depends also to a very considerable extent on the nature of the medium in which the culture is kept. Cohen and his associates[12] have described a phenomenon, for which there are probably numerous analogues, designated by them 'thymineless death'. Certain strains of bacteria which required thymine for growth died much less rapidly in a wholly non-nutrient medium than in one containing all the requisites for growth except the thymine itself. The operation of parts of the cell machinery in conditions where the absence of the thymine prevented the completely integrated functioning caused so much disturbance of the normal cell organization that recovery became impossible, sooner than it would have done during the gradual processes of spontaneous decay.

A complementary phenomenon is observed in what Postgate and Hunter[13] term 'substrate-accelerated death'. Here the rate of decline (observed with *Aerobacter aerogenes* and *Serratia marcescens*) is accelerated by the addition to a non-nutrient buffer of various substrates necessary for normal growth but insufficient to support it by themselves.

5. Deviations from the logarithmic law

The logarithmic law has been seen to be an approximation, and the condition that it should apply is that the random coincidence of events in the cell plays more part than the progressive decline. The principal types of deviation are (1) that initially the death-rate is lower than the law predicts, (2) that the final stages of the decline are more protracted than is expected from the law, and (3) that a combination of (1) and (2) occur together.

In so far as progressive and cumulative actions of an unfavourable environment make themselves felt, (1) is just what would be expected. The second type of deviation, giving a tail of abnormally persistent survivors, might be taken to indicate some specially resistant members of the initial population. It would certainly be observed with strains of sporulating bacteria if at the moment when growth ceased some had turned into spores and others not. There are indications also in non-sporulating bacteria that at certain stages of the individual cell cycle the resistance to influences such as heat or toxic agents is at a maximum. Cells near this maximum when growth of the culture stops could conceivably maintain their greater toughness for long enough to manifest abnormal longevity.

The more resistant survivors could in principle be mutant types which have arisen from any of the causes leading to mutation. While the long-lived tail of the survival curve may on occasion represent mutants, mutation is not an essential condition for it, since after the selection of the most resistant members of a declining population of *Aerobacter aerogenes*, subculture of these and retest shows not 'inherited' resistance but average behaviour.[14]

With this same strain of *Aerobacter* the abnormally long survival of some of the population during exposure to drugs or to acid seemed to be due to an active adjustment of their internal economy to the conditions of the test. This was indicated by the fact that the relative proportion of survivors increased as the rigour of the conditions was lessened, so that the time available for adjustment increased. It was also suggested by the circumstance that the proportion of longer-lived cells was raised when glucose and oxygen were provided in the medium to support internal metabolic changes.[14]

The precise form of the survival curve, then, depends upon the criteria used to assess viability, the previous history of the culture, including any exposure to mutagenic influences, the length and conditions of the survival test itself and the possible incidence of adaptive processes. Furthermore, the role of cyclical processes of lysis and repair, on the one hand, and of irreversible decline, on the other, may be expected to vary. It is not surprising, therefore, that a wide variety of survival curves have been observed.[1, 3, 13–17]

6. Influence of heat on bacterial activity

Bacteria are rapidly killed when the temperature is raised outside a certain range, which, however, varies a good deal from one species to another. *Aerobacter aerogenes* degenerates very rapidly when the temperature rises above about 45° C and few of the common types of bacteria will survive a temperature of more than 50° to 60°. There is, however, a group of organisms known as thermophilic bacteria which grow readily and perform their biochemical functions with complete efficiency at about 70° C. They occur in hot springs, and in the intestinal contents of animals whence they find their way into the soil and into the air. Functioning at a higher temperature than most bacteria while showing biochemical reactions of essentially similar type they tend to have high rates of multiplication.

Below the optimum growth temperature the multiplication rate of bacteria follows approximately the Arrhenius law which applies almost universally to unorganized systems. Since, however, growth depends upon a whole sequence of reactions, all of which have their individual temperature coefficients, some degree of complexity is only to be expected. The lag phase, for instance, need not show the same temperature dependence as the rate of multiplication in the logarithmic phase, and the proportions of the various cell constituents can vary with the temperature of cultivation. In the lower temperature ranges the change in rate may be two or three times for a 10° rise in temperature. Above the optimum temperature the rate falls very rapidly as a result of the inactivation of enzymes and the denaturation of proteins. The law followed is a complex one as is to be expected. We may write approximately:

effective rate of growth = rate of synthesis — rate of degeneration.

Each of the terms on the right may be taken to conform more or less to the Arrhenius law so that the effective growth rate is of the form

$$A_1 e^{-E_1/RT} - A_2 e^{-E_2/RT},$$

where T is the absolute temperature, E_1 and E_2 are activation energies, and A_1 and A_2 are constants.

The value of E_2 is much greater than that of E_1 and at lower temperatures the rate increases roughly in accordance with the left-hand exponential. Over a fairly narrow region the two terms will nearly balance, so that here the rate changes little. The generation time of *Aerobacter aerogenes*, for example, varies little between 35° and 40° C. But just above this region the negative term assumes the greater importance and the growth rate is soon reduced to zero.[18]

The reason why the degeneration of enzymes and the denaturation of proteins have very high temperature coefficients is of some interest.

At low temperatures there is a high degree of specialized order in the configurations of living biological structures. This disappears when the degeneration occurs. The activation energy is made up of very numerous packets distributed among many different bonds, so that the entropy of activation is also high. The transition state which is passed through on the way to denaturation, contains a very high total energy, essentially because so many items contribute to it, but since it is distributed in a highly disordered way, a high entropy compensates for the large energy. The measured activation energy for the denaturation of various proteins and the inactivation of certain enzymes may run up to 100 000 calories and over. A chemical reaction of simple molecules with an activation energy of this magnitude would attain a measurable rate only at a temperature of many hundred degrees, but the biological reactions can go rapidly at rather low temperatures because the great entropy increase attending the disordering of large ordered molecules provides the necessary compensation.[19, 20, 21]

In a good many examples the balance of the energy and the entropy factors leaves the denaturation or inactivation rates not very different one from another. For egg albumin, haemoglobin, pepsin, rennin, and trypsin the measured activation energies range from 40 000 to 132 000 calories, in spite of which the free energies of activation (quantities proportional to the logarithm of the reaction rate) vary from 21 900 to 25 700 only.[20] The biological origins of these substances are similar, so that the data for comparison have in a sense been selected by nature. Other structures are conceivable in which the energy–entropy relations are different enough for degeneration not to set in until much higher temperatures are reached. Such structures may possibly occur in the thermophilic bacteria, and in the heat-resistant bacterial spores.

Some bacteria are abnormally resistant to the destructive action of radiation. The precise cause of their resistance is not known, but it has been suggested that they contain an enzyme (or enzymes) capable of repairing the damage which the radiation has caused (see p. 341). The sensitivity to ionizing and to ultra-violet radiation varies very greatly among bacteria, by a factor of many hundred times. The organism *Micrococcus radiodurans* is especially resistant. Moseley and Laser[22] have shown that when the fraction of survivors is plotted against the dose of radiation which the culture has received, the form of the curve varies, not only from one species of bacteria to another but from one mutant of *Micrococcus radiodurans* to another. The bacterial DNA appears to have no special properties in the resistant varieties. After irradiation the survivors show a lag before growth, during which the resistance recovers, and the suggestion of enzyme repair processes is therefore made.

7. Suspension of biochemical activity. Bacterial spores

Most bacteria are likely to die if they cannot periodically renew their substance. Some types, however, can by special means pass into a state where not only growth and division but respiration and metabolism are almost entirely suspended. In this dormant condition they may remain alive for an almost indefinite time.

Bacteria belonging to the groups *Bacillus* and *Clostridium* are capable of undergoing what amounts to a polymorphic change. As a result of complex internal rearrangements of material, they assume the form of spores which are very much more resistant than the normal forms to heat, to desiccation, to toxic agents, and to adverse conditions generally. It is only relevant to treat this matter in connexion with decline in so far as the spores show an almost negligible degree of chemical activity. They are sometimes referred to as resting forms of the organisms. They possess the capacity of surviving under ordinary temperature conditions for many years and even, it has been reported, for centuries. Bacteria which are normally active biochemically gradually die off unless they can grow and divide. The spores have gained their longevity at the expense of almost complete inertness. It used to be said that spores were formed in response to an unfavourable environment. This is not correct, since spore formation often requires very nicely adjusted biochemical conditions and the presence of special medium constituents.[23, 24] The extensive sporulation of a culture demands that the supply of nutrients should be running out, and this no doubt could be called an unfavourable circumstance, but the absence of nutrient is necessary not so much to allow the spore to form as to prevent its subsequent germination. Some cells in a culture may be forming spores while others are germinating. With one strain of a sporulating bacterium forms having enhanced heat resistance were found to be thrown off in almost constant proportion during most of the logarithmic phase, and there was only a quite narrow range of the growth cycle just at the very start of the logarithmic phase when the culture could be completely sterilized by heating to 90° C.[25]

The great interest of spore formation is that it reveals the normal constituents of the cell to be capable of assuming alternative spatial maps. The rearrangements are accompanied by certain chemical transformations as well. If the reactivity and the mortality of vegetative bacteria is in any way connected with the presence of free valencies, then in the spore these must be hidden away in protected locations where they are out of reach of attacking reagents and prevented from saturating one another mutually.

The drastic rearrangements, and concurrent chemical activity, which occur during sporulation represent an internal upheaval at least as deep-seated as that involved in cell division. Thus sporulation and normal division are processes which must often be in competition. Spore formation entails much biochemical activity. On the other hand, vigorous synthesis leads to germination. Hence the balance between effective sporulation and germination must always be rather delicately held, and this may well be the reason why the yield of spores from any given culture is very erratic, and why attempts to define optimum conditions for the process are difficult.

Quite elaborate morphological changes accompany sporulation. The new structure appears first at one end of the cell, separates off part of the cytoplasm including a good deal of DNA, and then grows into the mature spore. Germination, which occurs when the spore is transferred to an appropriate nutrient medium, also involves a complex sequence of chemical and morphological changes. The water content of spores is low and they are stated all to contain dipicolinic acid, a substance not normally found in vegetative cells, and which during germination is excreted in the form of its calcium salt. They also appear to contain a good deal less DNA than vegetative cells, and the enzyme balance is different. During the actual process of sporulation extensive shifts in the pattern of biochemical reactions take place, and it has been stated that the sporulating cell in some respects resembles a bacterium which has been transferred to a medium in which its carbon source is provided by acetate. The proteins of spores have been reported to be different from those of the bacteria from which they are derived, and a heat-resistant catalase has been described which is immunologically different from that of the bacterium, and other heat-resisting enzymes from spores have been described, as well as certain enzymes apparently more resistant to radiation.[26] It is evident, therefore, that profound changes in the cell economy have occurred. According to Halvorson the protein of spores is synthesized during the actual process of sporulation. He states, however, that there is no evidence that messenger RNA formed before sporulation remains in the spore itself. Another interesting observation is that when spores which have lain dormant for some time are induced to germinate, the growing cells divide synchronously for several generations.[26]

The delicate machinery involved in sporulation is easily thrown out of gear. When sporulating strains of *Saccharomyces cerevisiae* are caused to become drug-resistant they lose the power of forming their characteristic four-spored asci (p. 228). They regain this capacity after prolonged cultivation in a favourable medium, but by then are found to have lost their drug-resistance.

Halvorson[26] envisages the coexistence in sporulating micro-organisms of two separate genetic systems which may be alternatively activated and inhibited, and likens their relation to that of bacterium and bacteriophage. The spore genome is repressed in conditions where rapid growth can occur, while the formation of messenger RNA corresponding to vegetative growth is inhibited by a product resulting from the transcription of the spore genome.

However this may be, it is clear that with some organisms alternative spatial maps are possible and that the morphological change from one to the other involves concomitant chemical activity of no mean order. If there is in fact any substance in the suspicion that free valencies play a significant role in determining the chemical activity of living matter, then it would be tempting to suppose that in the spore state the structure, not only of the girder network of the cell as a whole but also that of individual proteins and other macromolecules, has changed in such a way as to give greatly increased steric protection to the free bonds. These would be further shielded from the attack of diffusible substances by the absence of the aqueous medium within the cell.

REFERENCES

1. A. J. Clark, *The Mode of Action of Drugs*, Arnold, London (1933).
2. J. H. Gaddum, *Proc. R. Soc.* B **121**, 598 (1937); *Nature, Lond.* **156**, 463 (1945).
3. H. Berry and I. Michaels, *Q. J. Pharm. Pharmac.* **20**, 348 (1947).
4. T. C. N. Carroll, C. J. Danby, A. C. R. Dean, and Sir Cyril Hinshelwood, *J. chem. Soc.* p. 893 (1952) and unpublished observations.
5. A. C. R. Dean and Sir Cyril Hinshelwood, *Proc. R. Soc.* B **151**, 580 (1960); A. C. R. Dean, *Proc. R. Soc.* B **155**, 580 (1962); B **157**, 574 (1963).
6. See J. Mandelstam, *Bact. Rev.* **24**, 289 (1960); and J. Mandelstam and H. O. Halvorson, *Biochim. Biophys. Acta*, **40**, 43 (1960).
7. Sir Cyril Hinshelwood, *Nature, Lond.* **167**, 666 (1951); *J. chem. Soc.* p. 1304 (1953).
8. A. C. R. Dean and Sir Cyril Hinshelwood, *Progr. Biophys. biophys. Chem.* **5**, 1 (1955).

9. R. J. Goldacre, *Proc. First Int. Congr. Cybernetics* (Namur), 1956, p. 726 (1956).
10. P. Weiss and J. L. Kavanau, *J. gen. Physiol* **41,** 1 (1957).
11. V. Volterra, *Nature, Lond.* **118,** 558 (1926); *Mem. r. Acad. Lincei* **2,** 31 (1926).
12. S. S. Cohen, *Texas Reports on Biology and Medicine,* 1957, **15,** 154; and in *The Chemical Basis of Heredity,* edited by W. D. McElroy and B. Glass, p. 651, The Johns Hopkins Press, Baltimore (1957).
13. J. R. Postgate and J. R. Hunter, *J. gen. Microbiol.* **29,** 233 (1962); **34,** 459 (1964); *Nature, Lond.* **198,** 273 (1963).
14. See A. A. Eddy and Sir Cyril Hinshelwood, *Proc. R. Soc.* B **141,** 118 (1953); A. A. Eddy, *Proc. R. Soc.* B **141,** 126, 137 (1953), and references therein.
15. J. Henderson Smith, *Ann. appl. Biol.* **8,** 27 (1921).
16. R. C. Jordan and S. E. Jacobs, *J. Hyg., Camb.* **43,** 275 (1944).
17. A. P. Harrison Jr., *Proc. R. Soc.* B **152,** 418 (1960).
18. R. M. Lodge and C. N. Hinshelwood, *J. chem. Soc.* p. 1683 (1939).
19. C. N. Hinshelwood, *Kinetics of Chemical Change,* Clarendon Press, Oxford (1945).
20. S. Glasstone, K. J. Laidler, and H. Eyring, *The Theory of Rate Processes,* p. 442, McGraw-Hill, New York (1941).
21. H. Eyring and A. E. Stearn, *Chem. Rev.* **24,** 253 (1939).
22. B. E. B. Moseley and H. Laser, *Proc. R. Soc.* B **162,** 210 (1965).
23. W. G. Murrell, *Symp. Soc. gen. Microbiol.* **11,** 100 (1961).
24. H. O. Halvorson in *The Bacteria,* edited by I. C. Gunsalus and R. Y. Stanier, Academic Press, New York, **4,** 223 (1962).
25. R. M. Lodge and C. N. Hinshelwood, unpublished observations.
26. H. O. Halvorson, *Symp. Soc. gen. Microbiol.* **15,** 343 (1965).

XVI

CONCLUDING OBSERVATIONS

1. General

THROUGHOUT this book we have been concerned, apart from occasional references to other micro-organisms, with bacteria, which as unicellular organisms are representative of the simplest kinds of relatively independent living things. The aim has been to see in a general way, though in one not too far removed from detailed experimental evidence, how the main characteristics of life, in its physical manifestations, emerge from the interplay of basic laws of nature. This is an aim quite distinct from the solution of problems like the determination of the exact structure of proteins and nucleic acids, or the characterization of individual enzymes or the exact analysis of cell walls. In many respects it is less ambitious than any of these, yet in one way it goes beyond them in that it seeks some understanding of function and of the dependence of the whole on its parts which no structural considerations by themselves can afford.

The complexity and thermodynamic instability of most of the constituents of living matter are such that these substances can be built up only at the expense of free energy supplied by concomitant reactions in which free energy is normally run down. The necessary linking itself implies an interdependence of various functions, and, as we have seen, the dependence of protein on nucleic acid, of nearly all synthetic reactions on enzymes, and the regulation of raw material supplies by the cell wall and membrane makes this closed set of relationships one of the major facts about living cells. The structural and the functional aspects interplay in very powerful ways. The stereospecificity of the macromolecular structures allows highly preferential adsorptions, and permits the occurrence of template action. These giant structures are well adapted for the preservation of free valencies in an active form and so facilitate the chain reactions which not only control macromolecular growth, but are ideally adapted to the free energy couplings without which the unstable macromolecules themselves could not be formed.

Integrated systems of the kind described possess, as has been shown, those fundamental capacities of living matter, plasticity and adaptability, and the tendency to undergo automatic adjustments to achieve optimum growth in new environments to which they may be transferred. The stability of the different states of adjustment can be very varied and sometimes an induced change may be so persistent as to invite the use of the term heritable, to which there is no objection as long as it does not bring misconceptions in its train.

Division of cells as they grow is forced upon them by the interplay of chemical and mechanical factors. A steady state of development is possible with a collection of cells which could not be maintained with one mass of matter alone (Chapter XIV). Thus cells become parts of communities, and other kinds of interaction and mutual dependence arise, in cell colonies, in tissues, and in multicellular organisms. This hierarchical ordering of things is evident throughout nature, subatomic particles organized into atoms, atoms into molecules, molecules into polymeric structures and into cells, and the cells themselves into more elaborate communities. Organized systems involve mutual dependences and these cannot remain the same as the numbers of the members increase and their interactions are thereby modified. Hence the evolution and elaboration into new systems of progressively higher orders.

At the basis of living matter is the stereospecific copying process which tends to maintain, not absolutely, but in a very important degree, constancy of type among cells. The structural sequences, of bases in nucleic acids, and, indirectly if not directly, amino-acid residues in proteins, constitute what is now usually called a code of information or genetic code. Changes in the structure of a nucleic acid can demonstrably cause changes in polypeptides, as in the experiments of Ochoa (pp. 25, 338) and it is reasonable, and indeed inevitable, that every cell property should be ultimately referable to a structural pattern. What, however, is not permissible, save as a very rough approximation, is to regard the cell as a simple sum of genetically determined elements, since before information contained in the various basal structures can become manifest as a cell property a series of highly complex interactions must have occurred. There was an old theory about the structure and colour of organic compounds according to which visible colour depended upon the presence in the molecule of groups called 'chromophores', and could be enhanced by other groups called 'auxochromes'. In fact, we know that the colour depends upon the absorption spectrum, which is a function of the molecular vibration frequencies, and that these are determined by nothing less than the structure of the molecule as a whole. Nevertheless, it remains true that certain groups in the molecule do have a powerful enough influence on some of the normal modes of vibration to make a frequency in the visible region very likely. Thus the old theory has a certain degree of truth in it although based upon a rather dubious principle. In the same way, one can speak of genetic determinants but it would be wrong to suppose a single one-to-one correspondence between some unit of property change and a corresponding change in a genetic unit. There is little doubt that the change of a single nucleotide base could have a whole range of subtle effects, though some, no doubt, would be more important than others. This principle is, of course, illustrated by the acceptance in genetic theory of modifiers, repressors, derepressors, and the like.

Equally mistaken would be the idea that every change, quantitative as well as qualitative, in cell properties must be referred back to the structural change in one of the information-bearing centres. As the earlier chapters have shown, there is a good deal of latitude, within a given genetic framework, for the quantitative expression of these properties.

The finite probability of mutational changes means, of course, that the evolution of a population of living things continues indefinitely. But even without mutation there are factors at work which seldom allow a community such as a bacterial population to be entirely independent of its own past history. Except in a continuous culture apparatus, bacteria have periods of active growth alternating with periods of stagnation and decline. The enzyme balance changes with the state of the medium and the age of the cells, and the condition of the cell at the end of one phase of growth depends, therefore, upon the time at which nutrients run out or toxic products bring things to a halt. The state in which the cells are left at the end of one cycle determines the lag in the next and so on. Thus there are fluctuations in the general physiology of the bacteria. If during any one period of growth an adaptive change has occurred which, according to the principles explained in Chapter X, is only slowly reversible, then more or less aperiodic changes may be superposed on the shorter range fluctuations. For this reason the controls in tests of bacterial properties, and especially in any experiments dealing with genetic recombination, need to be subjected to quite unusually rigorous standards. It is not surprising if living organisms appear sometimes to be wayward and unpredictable. Nevertheless, with well-designed experiments and an appreciation of the conditions under which the best approximation to steady states can be expected, it is quite possible to observe quantitatively reproducible behaviour at least well enough to allow significant laws of growth and regulation to be revealed.

2. Branching chain reactions

The question of the intervention in cell processes of branching chain reactions has been referred to in several places already. Although in a measure speculative, the idea is worthy of further consideration. This has been deferred, since the matters in connexion with which it has previously been mentioned were in fact essentially quite independent of any hypothesis about chains. We will, however, now consider the free radical hypothesis in its own right.

At the outset it may be said that one of the most attractive aspects of the idea is its power of rendering intelligible the quite peculiar facility with which reactions difficult to bring about at all *in vitro* occur in the living world. The common invocation of enzymes may lull curiosity by invoking familiarity, but the fact remains that the enzyme reactions of living cells are phenomena of a quite amazing quality. The enzymes may indeed be isolated from the cell and continue to function, at any rate for a time, but they are never formed except by the action of living matter itself. Some quite special agency seems to be at work.

That free radical signals can be detected in some biological systems and in living cells by physical methods has already been mentioned (Chapter XIV, section 3). Perhaps the most serious doubt is whether they could be maintained over long periods when the cell is not actively functioning. In fact, cells do tend to decline and die when not kept in functional activity (Chapter XV), but the rate at which they do so is not necessarily great. It is, however, by no means true that all free radical systems are highly unstable, since free valencies may on occasion be protected from attack by steric inaccessibility. This protection is not at all unlikely in a cell, which does not consist of a homogeneous phase, but has an elaborate internal structure of macromolecules, bolted together presumably at various points and surrounded by the wall. On this girder-like structure free valencies could exist without much likelihood of rapid destruction by mutual saturation. Reaction with diffusible compounds in the aqueous medium would not cause serious loss. A free valency can only be saturated by another free valency, and if it reacts with a saturated molecule it creates a new free bond in the very act by which it is itself destroyed. If a free bond on a macro-molecular framework is saturated by a hydrogen atom from a molecule of water, it releases a hydroxyl radical which, before it can escape from the cell, is likely to encounter more macromolecular strands or surfaces, in the wall itself in the last resort, and there generate a new free valency which differs from the old one only in its location in the macromolecular skeleton.

Thus for a considerable time there could be maintained a flickering pattern of free bonds, appearing and disappearing at one point after another of the whole polymeric complex.

Storage of reactive centres has been observed in the chemistry of non-living matter. When methyl methacrylate is exposed to light it polymerizes, but, once started, the reaction continues for some considerable time in the dark. If there is no monomer, the polymer may remain active for days and will start growing again as soon as more material is provided. The rate is now proportional to the area of the container which was originally illuminated, so that evidently the reaction takes place in the layer deposited on the wall. It has a negative temperature coefficient, which means that little or no activation energy is needed, and is inhibited by H-atoms or iodine.[1, 2] Other kinetic experiments show that gas-phase polymerization can be terminated by collision of growing radicals.[1, 2] Thus the active form on the surface, requiring no activation energy and destroyed by H-atoms, would seem to consist of free radicals which are shielded from saturation by their adsorption. This affords a rough-and-ready form of steric protection which can be imagined to occur in a more elaborate way in the cytoskeleton.

The phenomena just described may be compared with those occurring in dried barley seeds, which after irradiation show free radical signals, stated to come chiefly from protein and nucleic acid. The radicals persist for hours or days. As the signals decay, the damage, resulting from the original irradiation, to the biological function of the seeds increases progressively, and the effect has been explained by the assumption that large persistent radicals gradually react with other vital parts.[3] This might seem to suggest the precise opposite of a useful function in growth, but then the radicals in question have been randomly generated by radiation instead of being concerned in the orderly sequence of integrated cell processes. The radicals are rapidly removed by water. Kirby-Smith and Randolph[4] report that freeze-dried bacteria kept in a vacuum showed no appreciable electron spin resonance signal until oxygen was admitted. After admission of oxygen a signal appeared and remained stable for some time.

The finite life of radicals raises the question of the maintenance of the supply in living cells. In the chemistry of non-living matter oxidation processes very commonly depend on branching chains,[5] the branching occurring when, for example, an unstable peroxide splits into two free radicals, $ROOH \rightarrow RO\cdot + \cdot OH$. Oxidation processes, or equivalent dismutations play a major role in the functioning of cells, providing the free-energy release by which the formation of thermodynamically unstable constituents can be compensated. As has been pointed out, any mystery about this compensatory coupling disappears as soon as free-radical processes are assumed to be involved. The final free-energy balance is struck only when the active chain-propagating radicals ultimately recombine, and during the intermediate stages they can intervene in the most diverse reactions, thermodynamics demanding only that the ultimate balance is on the right side.

The ready fission of certain peroxides depends upon the weakness of the single O—O bond, which has considerably less than half the strength of the double bond in O_2. If a bond X—Y is abnormally weak, less energy is absorbed in breaking it. Thus in a reaction $XY + A = X + AY$ in which AY is itself normal, more energy than normal would be evolved in the process as a whole. In this sense the bond in the molecule X—Y could be called an energy-rich bond. Throughout biochemistry there is much talk of the energy-rich bonds in certain phosphates such as adenosine triphosphate (ATP) and adenosine diphosphate (ADP).[6, 7] The hydrolysis of one phosphate group from either of these substances involves a much greater free-energy drop (c. 10 kcal) than occurs in the hydrolysis of adenosine monophosphate or the general run of organic phosphates.[7] Thus in adenosine triphosphate the second and third phosphate groups are linked by abnormally weak bonds. ADP and ATP play an extraordinarily important role in biochemistry, a fact which is ascribed to their 'energy-richness'. This same property would also facilitate the disruption of one of the bonds to yield two free radicals, thus initiating a branching chain. It is highly suggestive that oxidation and the reactions of high-energy phosphates are both ubiquitous in cell chemistry, and both of a nature likely to involve the possibility of chain-branching.

Most of the biochemically important reactions of ATP are enzyme-mediated, and there is no doubt that stereospecificity plays a major part in enzyme action. It has been invoked as a reason for the importance of adenosine triphosphate rather than other unstable organic phosphates.[7] But steric effects alone seem quite inadequate to explain why ATP should intervene so often where there is no question of incorporation of adenine into a product. Nor does stereospecific adsorption in itself seem likely to confer great reactivity. The readiness of chemisorbed hydrogen to react depends upon the concomitant formation of free atoms, but there is no obvious reason why adsorption-alignment of molecules should necessarily make them specially ready to enter into polycondensation reactions. If, however, the stereospecifically adsorbed or complexed molecules become active according to the flickering pattern of free valencies referred to above, then effective joining up could well be expected. Thus it is tempting to regard the high-energy phosphates as potential sources of radicals.

The activation energy for the initial free radical formation would not need to be very low. (It is quite considerable for the splitting of ROOH in combustion reactions.) In a branching chain the radical concentration grows very rapidly indeed once initiation is provided for. In combustion reactions the growth may carry the process from an immeasurably slow rate to explosion in almost negligible time. Thus a quite small source of chain branching in the cell will provide all that is needed.

In this way the whole aspect of stereospecificity would be complementary to free radical chemistry conditioned by oxidation reactions with chain-branching intermediates, the dissociation of energy-rich phosphate bonds, and possibly other processes (conceivably some connected with $XS.SY \rightarrow XS\cdot + \cdot SY$). If so, then the ability to provide structures capable of storing the free valencies for some time when they are not being generated would explain the unique position of the living cell as a chemical system.

As we have emphasized, enzyme reactions are not self-evident mechanisms. In some theories amino-acids are conveyed to a site of synthesis by transfer nucleic acids, lined up there and finally joined by what has been described as a sort of 'zipper action'. There is no obvious chemical translation of this mechanical metaphor, but the appearance of free valencies could cause a chain condensation in previously aligned molecules. The free valencies need not be generated in the first instance exactly where required, but could travel by processes of the type:

$$\begin{matrix} H & H & H & & H & H & H & & H & H & H \\ | & | & | & & | & | & | & & | & | & | \\ -C-C-C-H & \rightarrow & H-C-C-C-H & \rightarrow & H-C-C-C- \\ | & | & | & & | & | & & | & | & | \\ H & H & H & & H & H & & H & H & H \end{matrix}$$

and so provide moveable centres of abnormal reactivity. The following scheme shows how molecules might become welded together with a radical acting somewhat in the capacity of a blow-lamp.

$$(1) \quad X-C \overset{\displaystyle O}{\underset{\displaystyle \diagup OH}{\|}} \quad \overset{\displaystyle \diagup H}{NH-Y} + R \cdot$$

$$(2) \quad X-C- \overset{\displaystyle O}{\|} \quad \overset{\displaystyle \diagup H}{NH-Y} + ROH$$

$$(3) \quad X-C-NH-Y+H \cdot \overset{\displaystyle O}{\|}$$

Free radical mechanisms provide extremely adaptable systems in which almost any set of reaction products may be formed. They may, for this very reason, sometimes be deemed too unspecific for ready testing. But this objection can hardly be raised in connexion with cell reactions. We envisage no chaotic set of free-radical reactions in a homogeneous phase but a sterically organized and fully integrated system of related events, as has been illustrated throughout the preceding chapters.

As we have seen, the laws of growth force periodic division on the cell. It is this circumstance which gives the hypothesis of free-radical intervention a new and important turn. If free valencies are involved in the extraordinary chemical reactivity of living matter, then the successive divisions of the cell demand a steady increase in the number of free valencies present in the total mass. In other words, chain branching must be occurring all the time, and since the whole process is restrained and orderly, the branching must be of the so-called degenerate type, that is, occurring relatively slowly.

If this is so, a continuous chain-branching process has been in progress since life began. As we have seen, the oxidation reactions and possible splittings of high-energy phosphates are precisely of the type to give chain branching. They are, moreover, processes which still involve substantial activation energies, so they cannot multiply the radicals in the uncontrollable manner that leads to gaseous explosions. Thus if we are prepared to consider the role of free radicals at all, the necessary branching to allow for cell division can be suggestively coupled with the dominance in cell chemistry of oxidation-reduction processes (or the corresponding dismutation reactions) and the behaviour of unstable polyphosphates. And, we may repeat, chain reactions generally are

E e

ideally adapted for the simple, one-step biochemical processes which seem always to be the preferred ones.

The actual mechanism of cell division involves somehow the construction of two cytoskeletons for each original one. Replication of macromolecular chains, guided stereospecifically, and activated perhaps by free valencies, is not in itself sufficient. The new macromolecules have to be ordered into the spatial map of a new cell. The chain idea helps in several ways to understand aspects of cell division. Chain transfer may occur fairly extensively, a growing polymer radical splitting off a small radical which initiates a fresh chain. In this process certain entities reach a critical size and then initiate the formation of others. If something of the sort happens in the cell, there will, when the moment comes for division, be a supply of components duplicated individually and ready to undergo reorganization.

Transient and labile compounds occur during cell growth. Messenger RNA is a short-lived body with a high rate of turnover.[8] So too is transfer RNA.[8] The comings and goings about the cell which are postulated for these substances are all ultimately leading to the growth of large relatively stable macromolecules, and we cannot help being reminded that growing macroradicals of every size-range would be always present somewhere in the cell in the course of the processes going on there in radical-initiated polycondensation reactions.

The chain branching does not of course need to have produced exactly twice the original number of free valencies by the time the cell has doubled its mass. It can easily have produced a surplus, and these spare valencies are just what is needed to bolt together the parts of the new cytoskeleton when the time comes for the various prefabricated parts to be ordered into the new cell.

Thus the conception of the cell as a macromolecular polyfunctional free radical system illuminates a range of different aspects of its chemistry: why this is completely different from *in vitro* chemistry, how energy-coupling occurs, how single unit processes are combined, how free radicals are preserved from decay by the structure itself. The multiplication of the free valencies in the essential chain-branching process provides, moreover, for the reorganization of the duplicated fragments at the time when potential energy demands force reorganization upon the growing system.

If the picture seems fanciful, we may perhaps reflect that, on the basis of much classical chemistry, vital processes themselves would have appeared fantastic to the point of unbelievability.

Wöhler's synthesis of urea by way of ammonium cyanate, whether or not it was really relevant to the discrediting of vitalism, was, for all its importance, a side issue biologically, since living organisms probably do not make urea by routes much resembling that used by Wöhler.[9] The mystery of cell chemistry lies not so much in what is made or even in the formal chemical equations expressing the production, as in the unique sets of integrated processes involved. In the foregoing speculations we have not in any sense attempted to replace an orthodox view by an unorthodox one, but simply to inquire whether a well-known, powerful, and subtle chemical mechanism may not be here unobtrusively at work.

3. The origin of living matter

The question of origins is not an essential theme of this book, since the organization and function of the cell can be perfectly well considered without reference to the way in which living matter first arose. Nevertheless, certain general comments are pertinent to the main arguments.

At one stage of its history this planet had a reducing atmosphere containing *inter alia* hydrocarbons and ammonia, which were exposed to thermal, electrical, and radiant energy. In these circumstances, as laboratory experiments have shown, amino-acids and other complex compounds can be formed.[10] In the primeval solutions organic substances which would now be rapidly consumed by micro-organisms could survive, and slowly, as conditions became appropriate, give rise to a vast selection of others. If the right conditions of organization could be brought about, then there is little doubt that living matter would be formed.

The great question has been how the kind of organization which can lead to self-reproduction ever came about at all. The possible answers would seem to be a miraculous event, some inherent driving force in nature, or chance. Most people who are prepared to entertain the first idea would in any case regard the miraculous element about existence as long antecedent to the mere appearance of some primitive organized matter on the Earth. An inherent driving force is either miraculous or explicable in scientific terms, and if the latter, it must somehow come within the ambit of the laws of physics and chemistry. Physicochemical interpretations of events in which new forms of matter appear practically always involve the assumption of initial local fluctuation from average behaviour. So we are in any event left with the question of chance.

On the one hand, it has been pointed out that, given long enough, any combination of possible events, however improbable, will occur.[11]

If the result of the combination is to give a self-reproducing system, the question of origins is answered. On the other hand, it has been argued that to give a living cell the improbability of the required combination is so transcendent that origin by chance is inconceivable in the time for which the Earth has existed.[12] Even this argument would lose its force if we envisaged the traversing of space by living cells, somehow contained and borne, since if space and time are infinite, the time limit no longer matters. Discussion on these lines becomes rather like a debate on the product of zero and infinity, even if the philosophers do not intervene to tell us that our words have no meaning.

But the first formation of self-reproducing systems need not be so transcendentally improbable after all, if, instead of considering a cell as we now know it, we think of the most primitive kind of system which does have the power of producing copies of itself. The fact that relatively simple machines can be made with the capacity for assembling others like themselves shows this idea to be quite a reasonable one.[13]

The first self-reproducing systems then might be comparatively simple, and the complications might be added cumulatively during the course of long ages. Imagine a small crystal growing at the expense of a supersaturated solution. A thermodynamic fluctuation has been needed to bring it above the critical size, and thereafter it grows. An ordered structure arises out of a disordered assemblage, but the total free energy decreases, because the running down of potential energy more than compensates the lowered entropy of the spatial distribution. Here is one of the simplest examples of the creation of order from disorder, paid for by concomitant changes. When the crystal exceeds a certain size it may become unstable, because it is no longer capable of standing the internal strains caused by local temperature fluctuations: it breaks up into a number of smaller crystals, each of which can now repeat the process undergone by the parent. Thus the system is in a very rudimentary way organized and self-reproducing, and it depends upon an increase of one term in the total free energy at the expense of another.

Now, imagine a polycondensation reaction in which a solid polymer grows at the expense of simple units. This can give rise to crystalline structures of high molecular weight, and these can be interpolymers of varied texture. They could quite easily possess wholly different chemical characters at two ends. If one growing end of such a structure entered into chemical reactions giving products which could be utilized by the other, there would be a rudimentary organization of another kind.

Once the very simplest kind of self-reproducing, functioning structure develops, it can afford to wait as long as may be necessary for the chance encounter with free radicals or other agents which modify it by the introduction of new side chains or new groups giving yet further possibilities of coordinated chemical activity.

What the chemical nature of the simplest possible kind of structure may be remains unknown, yet the available analogies support the idea that it may not have to be of such complexity as the present highly evolved forms of living matter would suggest. These have been selected through long ages as the most efficient and the best adapted, and the crude early models are now obsolete.

Ideas of this kind have been discussed in some detail by Oparin,[14] who rightly points out how critical a stage was reached when the primitive living matter acquired a cell wall and so could exist as self-contained units capable of incorporating further elements, when advantageous, into themselves (see p. 132).

At first sight, bacteriophages and other virus-like bodies might seem to offer a picture of a specially primitive type of cell. But since they can only really function with the aid of the machinery of other cells, they can hardly be regarded as exemplifying in any sense the precursors of the cells we know today. Rather the viruses themselves constitute a special problem. They possess a replication code and the capacity for becoming integrated, sometimes harmoniously and sometimes with ultimately destructive effect, into the systems of other cells, but not for reproducing themselves autonomously. If there were viruses which could reproduce themselves when in a symbiotic relation with one or more other viruses but not singly, then they might indeed appear to be re-enacting an early stage in the evolution of living things, but this phenomenon is not known, though the synthetic capacities of nucleic acid-primed cell-free enzyme preparations may give a rough idea of what went on at some stage of the story suggested by Oparin.

A more attractive view about phages is that they represent something which has developed subsequently to the kind of cells they can invade.[15] Having regard to the way in which cells can enlarge their systems of integration by the incorporation of elements from without, and in the light of the possibility that sporing bacteria might contain alternative codes,[16] we might perhaps envisage a converse kind of event where part of the cell organization declared a partial independence and became separated. The new structure remains an entity capable of existing and surviving apart from the cell whence it originated, but not capable of reproducing itself except in conjunction with cells, or at any rate enzymes derived directly from them.[17] However this may be, the viruses and phages are probably of more interest in connexion with the general theme of integration than in connexion with the origin of living matter itself.

4. Structure and function

If the structure of a cell is known in all its chemical details, and if vague principles of vitalism are declined, then all the properties and potentialities of that cell follow from the laws of physics and chemistry. One immensely important aspect of the structure is the set of sequences in which various monomer units are arranged in the titanic macro-molecules of nucleic acids, proteins, and polysaccharides. That of the DNA is possibly, though not certainly, the determinant of all the others, but this question is not really essential to what we have to say, since if, for example, some protein sequence were also a determinant, the two specifications taken together would constitute the information necessary for cell replication. The minimum of information about structure which would correctly guide reproduction constitutes the genetic code.

Let us suppose that the genetic code of a cell has been worked out in detail by some sufficiently high-powered analytical and structural chemistry. The major question remains of how the information is read and acted upon, and how the cell properties emerge. Structure and function are closely related matters, but the knowledge of one by no means solves problems presented by the other. We know perfectly well the kind of information which DNA molecules contain, and we can easily think of a hypothetical code, but we could not easily say to what kind of cell it would lead. We should be in no different position with a code known to be authentically contained in a real organism.

A complete understanding of the structure–function relation will demand an amount of detailed knowledge of every step of the cell biochemistry so enormous that partial and approximate solutions of the problem have in the meantime to be sought. To seek them in no way implies a denial of the obvious fact that ultimately the secret of the cell lies in its code and in the laws of physics and chemistry. But to emphasize the former and forget the importance of the latter is to forgo all real understanding of function. Indeed, physicochemical laws can tell us much about cell properties without very specific assumptions of the actual details of the code. To seek enlightenment in this direction is certainly not to ignore the importance of the code itself.

Various lines of approach are possible, in the absence of the very difficultly obtainable radical solution, to the problem of function.

Models likening the cell to a mechanical or electrical system can be constructed. Many suggestive analogies can be seen in this way. Penrose,[13] for example, has devised mechanical models in which the parts when shaken together will form replicas of a pattern offered to them, but will not form this pattern spontaneously. Turing[18] discussed the principles according to which one computing machine could be programmed to imitate any other machine, in which connexion Stahl[19] remarks that presumably, if a cell is governed by a code, it should be possible to find a machine to imitate it. The limitation of such models, informative as they may be on matters of principle, is that they do not really resemble cells, in which chemistry has at least as much to say as electricity and mechanics.

Another approach which has given much stimulus to research has been to specify certain elements in the code as control genes, and to interpret various functional responses of the cell in terms of the activity or non-activity of these. The basic fact which these theories of repressors, derepressors and the like call attention to is that all the potentialities of the cell are not manifest all the time, and that adjustments and regulations of function within the permissiveness of any given code occur and call for explanation. It has been one of the major themes of this book that just such adjustments and regulations are predicted by the laws of chemical kinetics when these are applied to systems of the general type which we know the cell to be.

This kinetic approach has occasionally been represented as something in contrast to or even in conflict with genetics and what is sometimes arbitrarily given the name of molecular biology. This opposition does not exist. In the network theorem of Chapter V, protein formation, for example, is made dependent on something else (which can quite well be nucleic acid) and there is nothing to suggest that what depends upon what is not determined by the information contained in a structural code. But the conditions of total integration do yield, without further *ad hoc* assumptions, explanations for adaptive behaviour, and for functional regulation. There is nothing to forbid the identification of some of the various entities in the equations with bodies like messenger nucleic acids, but certain results are seen to follow without very detailed hypotheses about them.

Thus while the exact structure of a nucleic acid may determine the potentialities which an organism possesses, more general principles can and do govern the extent to which they are exhibited in given circumstances.

It has long been recognized that the reproduction of living matter must depend, at the molecular level, on a copying mechanism analogous to some kind of template action, and the picture of this becomes progressively clearer as the chemistry of nucleic acids and proteins develops. The molecules containing the information codes must be relatively stable, or there would be no heredity at all. They are not, however, unchangeable: hence the possibility of mutations. But to make mutations responsible for all changes is as arbitrary as to ignore them altogether. Cells which had no regulatory and adaptive machinery of their own would appear to be extremely inefficient and handicapped in the evolutionary competition. What is more, if the observations recorded in different sections of this book and the arguments put forward have any validity at all, then cells, with the kind of chemical make-up which they in fact have, would need to ignore some basic principles of science in order to preserve the kind of rigidity which has occasionally been demanded of them.

One of the sources of the richness and subtlety shown by the behaviour of living matter is the way in which, in the individual, physicochemical laws can play variations on the fundamental theme expressed in the genetic code, while populations can also respond in another way to rarer and more catastrophic changes in the code itself.

REFERENCES

1. H. W. Melville, *Proc. R. Soc.* A **163**, 511 (1937).
2. C. H. Bamford and M. J. S. Dewar, *Proc. R. Soc.* A **197**, 356 (1949).
3. A. D. Conger, *J. cell comp. Physiol.* **58** (Suppl. 1), 27 (1961).
4. J. S. Kirby-Smith and M. L. Randolph, *J. cell comp. Physiol.* **58** (Suppl. 1), 1 (1961).
5. C. N. Hinshelwood, *Kinetics of Chemical Change*, Clarendon Press, Oxford (1945); N. Semenoff, *Chemical Kinetics and Chain Reactions*, Clarendon Press, Oxford (1935); V. N. Kondrat'ev, *Chemical Kinetics of Gas Reactions*, Pergamon Press, Oxford (1964).
6. See, for example, F. Lippman in *Adv. Enzymol.* **1**, 9 (1941); and also in *Molecular Biology*, edited by D. Nachmansohn, p. 37, Academic Press, New York (1960).
7. B. Pullman and A. Pullman, *Quantum Biochemistry*, Interscience, New York (1963).
8. See Chapter I, section 15.
9. F. Wöhler, *Pogg. Ann.* **12**, 253 (1828).
10. See for details and references P. H. Abelson, *Carnegie Institution of Washington Year Book*, **55**, 171 (1955–6); **56**, 179 (1956–7); A. I. Oparin, *The Origin of Life on the Earth*, translated by Ann Synge, p. 143, Oliver and Boyd, Edinburgh (1957).

11. P. T. Landsberg, *Nature, Lond.* **203,** 928 (1964).

12. E. P. Wigner, *The Logic of Personal Knowledge,* essays presented to M. Polanyi, Routledge & Kegan Paul, London (1961).

13. L. S. Penrose, *Ann. hum. Genet.* **23,** 59 (1958); L. S. Penrose and R. Penrose, *Nature, Lond.* **179,** 1183 (1957).

14. A. I. Oparin, Rep. Int. Symp. Moscow, *The Origin of Life on the Earth,* Acad. Sci., U.S.S.R., Moscow (1957); *Chemical Origin of Life,* C. C. Thomas, Springfield, Illinois, U.S.A. (1964).

15. K. Yamafuji, *Proc. 4th Int. Congr. Biochem.* **12,** 100 (1958) (Symposium on Biochemistry of Insects).

16. H. O. Halvorson, *Symp. Soc. gen. Microbiol.* **15,** 343 (1965).

17. See N. A. Mitchison and I. B. Holland, *New Scient.* **28,** 12, 13 (1965).

18. A. M. Turing, *Proc. Lond. math. Soc.* Series 2, **42,** 230 (1937); **43,** 544 (1937); see also reference 19 and J. von Neumann, *The Computer and the Brain,* pp. 71, 73, Yale University Press, New Haven (1958).

19. W. R. Stahl, *Perspect. Biol. Med.* **8,** 373 (1965).

AUTHOR INDEX

The roman numerals refer to chapters, the arabic figures refer to the numbered references listed at the end of each chapter.

SUBJECT INDEX

F f

PRINTED IN GREAT BRITAIN
AT THE UNIVERSITY PRESS, OXFORD
BY VIVIAN RIDLER
PRINTER TO THE UNIVERSITY